PENGUIN BOOKS

POETS AT WORK

GEORGE PLIMPTON is perhaps best known for his widely read accounts of his experiences as an amateur playing sport at the professional level: *Out of My League* (baseball); *Paper Lion* (football); *The Bogeyman* (golf); *Shadow Box* (boxing); and *Open Net* (hockey). Editor of the literary quarterly *The Paris Review*, he has also co-edited a number of best-selling books: *American Journey: The Times of Robert F. Kennedy*; *Edie: An American Biography*; and *D.V.* His most recent book is *The Curious Case of Sidd Finch*, a novel.

DONALD HALL was born in Connecticut in 1928 and lives on a family farm in New Hampshire where he freelances, writing magazine articles, juveniles, memoirs, textbooks, plays, criticism, short stories, and biography. He has collected four volumes of essays about poetry, of which the most recent is *Poetry and Ambition* (1988). His nine books of poems include *Kicking the Leaves* (1976), *The Happy Man* (1986), and *The One Day* (1988), which won the National Book Critics Circle Award.

The Paris Review was founded in 1953 by a group of young Americans including Peter Matthiessen, Harold L. Humes, George Plimpton, Thomas Guinzburg, and Donald Hall. While the emphasis of its editors was on publishing creative work rather than nonfiction (among writers who published their first short stories there were Philip Roth, Terry Southern, Evan S. Connell, and Samuel Beckett), part of the magazine's success can be attributed to its continuing series of interviews on the craft of writing.

Previously Published

WRITERS AT WORK
The *Paris Review* Interviews

THIRD SERIES

Edited by GEORGE PLIMPTON and introduced by ALFRED KAZIN

William Carlos Williams	Saul Bellow
Blaise Cendrars	Arthur Miller
Jean Cocteau	James Jones
Louis-Ferdinand Céline	Norman Mailer
Evelyn Waugh	Allen Ginsberg
Lillian Hellman	Edward Albee
William Burroughs	Harold Pinter

FOURTH SERIES

Edited by GEORGE PLIMPTON and introduced by WILFRID SHEED

Isak Dinesen	John Dos Passos
Conrad Aiken	Vladimir Nabokov
Robert Graves	Jorge Luis Borges
George Seferis	John Berryman
John Steinbeck	Anthony Burgess
Christopher Isherwood	Jack Kerouac
W. H. Auden	Anne Sexton
Eudora Welty	John Updike

FIFTH SERIES

Edited by GEORGE PLIMPTON and introduced by
FRANCINE DU PLESSIX GRAY

P. G. Wodehouse	Joyce Carol Oates
Pablo Neruda	Archibald MacLeish
Henry Green	Isaac Bashevis Singer
Irwin Shaw	John Cheever
James Dickey	Kingsley Amis
William Gass	Joseph Heller
Jerzy Kosinski	Gore Vidal
Joan Didion	

SIXTH SERIES

Edited by GEORGE PLIMPTON and introduced by
FRANK KERMODE

Rebecca West	Kurt Vonnegut, Jr.
Stephen Spender	Nadine Gordimer
Tennessee Williams	James Merrill
Elizabeth Bishop	Gabriel García Márquez
Bernard Malamud	Carlos Fuentes
William Goyen	John Gardner

SEVENTH SERIES

Edited by GEORGE PLIMPTON and introduced by
JOHN UPDIKE

Malcolm Cowley	Arthur Koestler
William Maxwell	May Sarton
Philip Larkin	Eugene Ionesco
Elizabeth Hardwick	John Ashbery
Milan Kundera	John Barth
Edna O'Brien	Philip Roth
Raymond Carver	

EIGHTH SERIES

Edited by GEORGE PLIMPTON and introduced by
JOYCE CAROL OATES

Joseph Brodsky	Elie Wiesel
James Laughlin	Robert Fitzgerald
Anita Brookner	Leon Edel
Robert Stone	John Hersey
John Irving	Cynthia Ozick
E. B. White	Derek Walcott
E. L. Doctorow	

Poets at Work

The *Paris Review* Interviews

Edited by George Plimpton

Introduction by Donald Hall

PENGUIN BOOKS

PENGUIN BOOKS
Published by the Penguin Group
Viking Penguin, a division of Penguin Books USA Inc.,
40 West 23rd Street, New York, New York 10010, U.S.A.
Penguin Books Ltd, 27 Wrights Lane,
London W8 5TZ, England
Penguin Books Australia Ltd, Ringwood,
Victoria, Australia
Penguin Books Canada Ltd, 2801 John Street,
Markham, Ontario, Canada L3R 1B4
Penguin Books (N.Z.) Ltd, 182–190 Wairau Road,
Auckland 10, New Zealand

Penguin Books Ltd, Registered Offices:
Harmondsworth, Middlesex, England

First published in simultaneous hardcover and paperback editions by
Viking Penguin, a division of Penguin Books USA Inc., 1989
Published simultaneously in Canada

1 3 5 7 9 10 8 6 4 2

The interviews in this collection are selected from *Writers at Work*,
Series 1–8, published by Viking Penguin Inc.

Grateful acknowledgment is made to the following for permission to
reprint excerpts from copyrighted works:
Macmillan, Inc., and Macmillan Administration (Basingstoke) Ltd.:
"The Dynasts" by Thomas Hardy.
Random House, Inc., and Faber and Faber Ltd.: *Collected Poems* by W. H. Auden.
Houghton Mifflin Company: *New & Collected Poems 1917–1976* by
Archibald MacLeish. Copyright © Archibald MacLeish, 1976.

LIBRARY OF CONGRESS CATALOGING IN PUBLICATION DATA
Poets at work : the Paris Review interviews / edited by George
Plimpton ; introduction by Donald Hall.
p.   cm.
ISBN 0 14 01.1791 1
1. Poets, American—20th century—Interviews.   2. Poets,
Commonwealth of Nations—20th century—Interviews.   3. Poetry—
Authorship.   4. American poetry—20th century—History and
criticism.   5. English poetry—Commonwealth of Nations authors—
History and criticism.   I. Plimpton, George.   II. Paris Review.
PS323.5.P65   1989
811'.5'09—dc19   88-22465
                                                            CIP

Printed in the United States of America
Set in Electra

Contents

Contents

Introduction

The first poets-at-work interview, not included here, took place in 1619 at Hawthornden in Scotland. Ben Jonson walked north from London, pausing to commission a pair of shoes, and spent some weeks with his friend William Drummond. Drummond took note of Johnson's remarks, apparently without letting his subject know that he was being recorded. When his guest departed, Drummond summed him up: "He is a great lover and praiser of himself, a condemner and scorner of others, given rather to lose a friend than a jest, jealous of every word and action of those about him, especially after drink, which is one of the elements in which he lives . . ." (Drummond, it must be conceded, was another of the *genus irritable vatum*.) In Drummond's transcript Jonson speaks of prosody on occasion, but mostly delivers judgment: Samuel Daniel is a good honest man but no poet; John Harington's Ariosto is the worst translation ever made; Shakespeare wants art . . . In a few of his remarks, he grudges favor; he is even generous. Although he avers that John Donne deserves hanging for getting his meter wrong, elsewhere he allows that Donne is "the first poet in the world, in some things . . ."

Poets like to talk about poetry. In this book poets speak in tones that we recognize as characteristic. When her interviewer asked how old she was on some occasion, Marianne Moore supplied two pieces of information and asked, "Can you deduce my probable age?"

Otherwise these interviews differ, often according to the point in the poets' lives at which they occur. Some interviews take place in mid-career: the work and the life examined on one afternoon in a sunny study with the tape recorder turning. Other interviews occur toward the end of the working life, suggesting a possible finality: I remember Ezra Pound's gratitude for the opportunity to set things straight.

All the interviews share the matter of poetry and the manner of a characteristic voice. Here are nine passages from the tabletalk of nine poets:

a) "You've got to *score*. They say not, but you've got to score . . ."

b) "If the stone isn't hard enough to maintain the form, it has to go out."

c) ". . . my slight product . . . conspicuously tentative— . . ."

d) "I wonder what an 'intention' means! One wants to get something off one's chest."

e) "I am an actress in my own autobiographical play."

f) "It's a feeling that begins somewhere in the pit of the stomach and rises up forward in the breast and then comes out through the mouth and ears . . ."

g) "Hughes writes the kind of stuff I throw away."

h) "There's nothing more embarrassing than being a poet."

i) ". . . from the moment life cannot be one continual orgasm, real happiness is impossible . . ."

Match with: (1) Elizabeth Bishop, (2) John Ashbery, (3) Robert Frost, (4) Marianne Moore, (5) Ezra Pound, (6) T. S. Eliot, (7) James Dickey, (8) Anne Sexton, (9) Allen Ginsberg.*

Poets like to tell stories as much as novelists do. This series of interviews was mined for *The Oxford Book of American Literary Anecdotes*. Some dialogue here might be better suited to the stage, possibly in a review called *The Poetry Follies*.

MARIANNE MOORE: The theater is the most pleasant, in fact my favorite, form of recreation.

---

* The answers, for those who are unsure of themselves: a-3; b-5; c-4; d-6; e-8; f-9; g-7; h-1; i-2.

INTERVIEWER: Do you go often?
MARIANNE MOORE: No. Never.

Frost describes his first meeting with Pound ("He was all silent with eagerness") so that we can set it on the stage, although Frost's jiujitsu story ("He grabbed my wrist, tipped over backward, and flipped me over his head") may remain too improbable for theater. Pound himself is never so relaxed as when he eases into anecdote. When the ill William Carlos Williams tires and his wife, Flossie, takes over, she tells how the doctor and his family—the *only* artistic types with a permanent address—give shelter to Bohemian friends over the decades: Marsden Hartley, John Reed . . . Apparently Maxwell Bodenheim faked a broken arm in order to avail himself of the Williams's hospitality. Conrad Aiken tells that story better than Flossie does. One of our pleasures in *Poets at Work* is to watch the same scenes from differing viewpoints. Eliot, Pound, Aiken, and Frost all touch on poetic London before the Great War. Elizabeth Bishop is another who tells a story well, including an account of a poetry reading by the young Robert Lowell; maybe her interview is best of all.

Many of these interviews are the most-quoted sources when critics write about the life and the work together. Writers constantly cite Eliot above (d) without reference to its source. These interviews are literary history as gossip, full of famous revelations which have become commonplace. Reading them is like discovering that Shakespeare and Pope are composed of book titles. We find not only familiar revelations but also the classic texts for poetic *ideas*, like the Ginsberg interview with its doctrines of spontaneity. That interview especially preserves its historical moment intact, detailed and colorful, like Pompeii under the ashes of Vesuvius.

These oral histories were almost always revised by reflection, distance, and the ballpoint pen. I remember Eliot finding that the word "creature," applied to Conrad Aiken in cold print, sounded more condescending than he intended to show himself. If something true is lost by revision, I suspect that far more is gained: The moment is finer for a coat of varnish: Gossip becomes archival.

It is true that the phenomenon of these *Paris Review* interviews, begun in 1952, pointed toward the culture of celebrity. When George Plimpton talked with E. M. Forster at Kings College, he did not know that he surveyed the highway for Andy Warhol and *Interview*. From that beginning the interview printed as dialogue has become a common literary form for better and worse but mostly for worse. The *Paris Review* interviews have been consistently better than others—because they follow the tone established almost forty years ago, in which the interviewer remains almost anonymous. The questioner is a version of ourselves; dressed in the costume of the common reader, the questioner forgoes the egotism of a voice; the interviewer is ourself gifted with a key to the *atelier*, gifted maybe with a greedy ear . . .

A recurrent theme in *Poets at Work* is collaboration. This book displays considerable egotism, yet for the most part these egos accept the help of others and proffer their own help in return. There is the famous case of Pound cutting the manuscript of *The Waste Land*—of which Eliot's account here was for long our most revealing source. "[Pound] didn't try to turn you into an imitation of himself." Later Eliot speaks of his profession as an editor who made suggestions on the manuscripts of younger poets for decades. Pound tells us about working with Yeats and Ford. Elsewhere, we hear of Richard Eberhart counseling the young Robert Lowell, the slightly older Lowell sharing himself between Allen Tate and John Crowe Ransom, the moderately-still-older Lowell going to Randall Jarrell and Stanley Kunitz. Common is the search for help, which is also the search *to* help. We hear of Ginsberg working with William Burroughs and Jack Kerouac, Sexton with Maxine Kumin, Bishop with Frank Bidart, Robert Fitzgerald with Flannery O'Connor.

Of course there is countermotion to community, some of it comic like Ben Jonson's bitchery. When the interviewer asks James Dickey if he corresponds with other poets, Dickey tells us that he is "almost completely out of touch with them. They often write to me, but because of my heavy schedule I almost never have time to answer." Robert Frost tells stories of London in the teens that reveal his contempt for poets who help each other.

When he says of Pound, Flint, Aldington, H.D., and Hulme that "they met every week to rewrite each other's poems," his voice loads itself with deprecation; he told them (as he tells us) that this workshopping "sounded like a parlor game to me," and adds that he was "just kidding." Ho ho. It was life and death to Frost to do his own work, all alone—and to stop there.

Frost was the exception. The history of poetry is a history of rivalries which are also friendships, not only Pound and Williams, Pound and Eliot, Pound and Yeats, not only Dylan Thomas and Vernon Watkins, but Wordsworth, Coleridge, and Southey; Keats and Leigh Hunt, not to mention neoclassicists and Elizabethans in their coffee houses and gin mills. Not to mention the footsore Ben Jonson drinking sack, running down his peers, and distributing pieces of praise.

The community of poets surprises us because we entertain stereotypes associating poets with lonely alienation. Generosity is typically part of the poet's work. This community is not—or it need not be—the sordid business of favor trading; nor is it merely a series of acts of kindness, like Boy Scouts helping old folks across the streets. It resembles more nearly the DNA that uses human bodies to replicate itself. This collaboration supports a mutual and enduring endeavor. Poets do not take turns helping each other over difficulties: They work together to build the house of poetry.

Poets at Work

1. Robert Penn Warren

Robert Penn Warren was born in Guthrie, Kentucky, in 1905. He attended Vanderbilt University, where his early work was published in the literary magazine *Fugitive*. He was associated with the group of Vanderbilt poets and critics known, after the magazine, as the Fugitives, including among others Allen Tate, John Crowe Ransom, Merrill Moore, and Donald Davidson.

After his graduation from Vanderbilt in 1925, Warren won fellowships to the University of California and Yale. In 1930 he attended Oxford on a Rhodes Scholarship. He has taught extensively since then—at Vanderbilt, Southwestern College, Louisiana State, Minnesota, and Yale. In 1934, at Louisiana State, he founded the *Southern Review* with Cleanth Brooks.

Warren's novels are *Night Rider* (1938), awarded the Houghton Mifflin Literary Fellowship; *At Heaven's Gate* (1943); *All the King's Men* (1946), for which he won a Pulitzer Prize; *World Enough and Time* (1950); *Band of Angels* (1955); and *Blackberry Winter*, a novelette he wrote in 1946. A collection of short stories entitled *Circus in the Attic* was published in 1948, and *Brother to Dragons*, a dramatic poem, in 1953.

Collections of his poetry have appeared under the titles *Thirty-Six Poems* (1935), *Eleven Poems on the Same Theme* (1942), *Selected Poems* (1944), and *Promises: Poems 1954–1956* (1957), which was a winner of both the National Book Award and a Pulitzer Prize. His *Selected Poems New and Old* (1967) was awarded the Bollingen Prize, and *Now and Then* (1979) received the Pulitzer Prize. Warren was awarded the Presidential Medal of Freedom in 1980, a MacArthur Foundation fellowship in 1981, and the Commonwealth Award in 1980. He is a poet laureate.

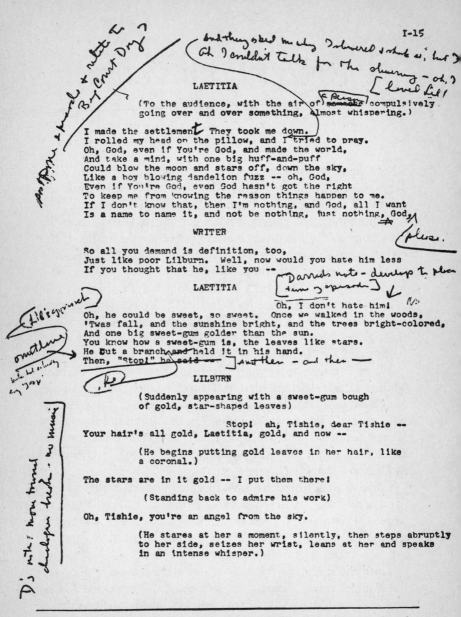

LAETITIA

(To the audience, with the air of compulsively
going over and over something, almost whispering.)

I made the settlement. They took me down.
I rolled my head on the pillow, and I tried to pray.
Oh, God, even if You're God, and made the world,
And take a mind, with one big huff-and-puff
Could blow the moon and stars off, down the sky,
Like a boy blowing dandelion fuzz -- oh, God,
Even if You're God, even God hasn't got the right
To keep me from knowing the reason things happen to me.
If I don't know that, then I'm nothing, and God, all I want
Is a name to name it, and not be nothing, just nothing, God.

WRITER

So all you demand is definition, too,
Just like poor Lilburn. Well, now would you hate him less
If you thought that he, like you --

LAETITIA

Oh, I don't hate him!
Oh, he could be sweet, so sweet. Once we walked in the woods,
'Twas fall, and the sunshine bright, and the trees bright-colored,
And one big sweet-gum golder than the sun.
You know how a sweet-gum is, the leaves like stars.
He cut a branch and held it in his hand.
Then, "Stop!" he said --

LILBURN

(Suddenly appearing with a sweet-gum bough
of gold, star-shaped leaves)

Stop! ah, Tishie, dear Tishie --
Your hair's all gold, Laetitia, gold, and now --

(He begins putting gold leaves in her hair, like
a coronal.)

The stars are in it gold -- I put them there!

(Standing back to admire his work)

Oh, Tishie, you're an angel from the sky.

(He stares at her a moment, silently, then steps abruptly
to her side, seizes her wrist, leans at her and speaks
in an intense whisper.)

A work sheet from a verse play written by Robert Penn Warren, based
on the narrative poem Brother to Dragons.

Bee W. Dabney

Robert Penn Warren

This interview took place in the apartment of Ralph Ellison at the American Academy in Rome: a comfortable room filled with books and pictures. Mr. Warren, who might be described as a sandy man with a twinkle in his eye, was ensconced in an armchair while the Interviewers, manning tape recorder and notebook, were perched on straight-back chairs. Mrs. Ellison, ice-bowl tinkling, came into the room occasionally to replenish the glasses: all drink pastis.

INTERVIEWER: First, if you're agreeable, Mr. Warren, a few biographical details just to get you "placed." I believe you were a Rhodes Scholar—

WARREN: Yes, from Kentucky.

INTERVIEWER: University of Kentucky?

WARREN: No, I attended Vanderbilt. But I was Rhodes Scholar from Kentucky.

3

INTERVIEWER: Were you writing then?

WARREN: As I am now, trying to.

INTERVIEWER: Did you start writing in college?

WARREN: I had no interest in writing when I went to college. I was interested in reading—oh, poetry and standard novels, you know. My ambitions were purely scientific, but I got cured of that fast by bad instruction in freshman chemistry and good instruction in freshman English.

INTERVIEWER: What were the works that were especially meaningful for you? What books were—well, doors opening?

WARREN: Well, several things come right away to mind. First of all, when I was six years old, "Horatius at the Bridge" I thought was pretty grand—when they read it to me, to be more exact.

INTERVIEWER: And others?

WARREN: Yes, "How They Brought the Good News from Ghent to Aix," at about age nine; I thought it was pretty nearly the height of human achievement. I didn't know whether I was impressed by riding a horse that fast or writing the poem. I couldn't distinguish between the two, but I knew there was something pretty fine going on. . . . Then "Lycidas."

INTERVIEWER: At what age were you then?

WARREN: Oh, thirteen, something like that. By that time I knew it wasn't what was happening in the poem that was important— it was the poem. I had crossed the line.

INTERVIEWER: What about prose works?

WARREN: Then I discovered Buckle's *History of Civilization*. Did you ever read Buckle?

INTERVIEWER: Of course, and Motley's *Rise of the Dutch Republic*. Most Southern bookshelves contain that.

WARREN: And Prescott . . . and *The Oregon Trail* is always hovering around there somewhere. The thing that interested me about Buckle was that he had the one big answer to everything: *geography*. History is all explained by geography. I read Buckle and then I could explain everything. It gave me quite a hold over the other kids; they hadn't read Buckle. I had the answer to everything. Buckle was my Marx. That is, he gave you one answer to everything, and the same dead-sure certainty. After I had had my session with Buckle and the one-answer system at the age of thirteen, or whatever it was, I was somewhat inoculated against Marx and his one-answer system when he and the depression hit me and my work when I was about twenty-five. I am not being frivolous about Marx. But when I began to hear some of my friends talk about him in 1930, I thought, "Here we go again, boys." I had previously got hold of one key to the universe: Buckle. And somewhere along the way I had lost the notion that there was ever going to be just one key.

But getting back to that shelf of books, the Motley and Prescott and Parkman, et cetera, isn't it funny how unreadable most history written now is when you compare it with those writers?

INTERVIEWER: Well, there's Samuel Eliot Morison.

WARREN: Yes, a very fine writer. Another is Vann Woodward, he writes very well indeed. And Bruce Catton. But Catton maybe doesn't count, he's not a professional historian. If he wants to write a book on history that happens to be good history and good writing at the same time, there isn't any graduate school to try to stop him.

INTERVIEWER: It's very interesting that you were influenced by historical writing so early in life. It has always caught one's eye how history is used in your work, for instance *Night Rider*.

WARREN: Well, that isn't a historical novel. The events belonged to my early childhood. I remember the troops coming in when martial law was declared in that part of Kentucky. When I wrote the novel I wasn't thinking of it as history. For one thing, the world it treated still, in a way, survived. You could still talk to the old men who had been involved. In the 1930s I remember going to see a judge down in Kentucky—he was an elderly man then, a man of the highest integrity and reputation—who had lived through that period and who by common repute had been mixed up in it—his father had been a tobacco grower. He got to talking about that period in Kentucky. He said, "Well, I won't say who was and who wasn't mixed up in some of those things, but I will make one observation: I have noticed that the sons of those who were opposed to getting a fair price for tobacco ended up as either bootleggers or brokers." But he was an old-fashioned kind of guy, for whom bootlegging and brokerage looked very much alike. Such a man didn't look "historical" thirty years ago. Now he looks like the thigh bone of a mastodon.

INTERVIEWER: It seems clear that you don't write "historical" novels; they are always concerned with urgent problems, but the awareness of history seems to be central.

WARREN: That's so. I don't think I do write historical novels. I try to find stories that catch my eye, stories that seem to have issues in purer form than they come to one ordinarily.

INTERVIEWER: A kind of unblurred topicality?

WARREN: I wrote two unpublished novels in the thirties. *Night Rider* is the world of my childhood. *At Heaven's Gate* was contemporary. My third published, *All the King's Men*, was worlds I had seen. All the stories were contemporary. The novel I'm writing now, and two I plan, are all contemporary.

INTERVIEWER: *Brother to Dragons* was set in the past.

WARREN: It belonged to a historical setting, but it was not a departure: it was a matter of dealing with issues in a more mythical form. I hate costume novels, but maybe I've written some and don't know it. I have a romantic kind of interest in the objects of American history: saddles, shoes, figures of speech, rifles, et cetera. They're worth a lot. Help you focus. There *is* a kind of extraordinary romance about American history. That's the only word for it—a kind of self-sufficiency. You know, the grandpas and the great-grandpas carried the assumption that somehow their lives and their decisions were important; that as they went up, down, here and there, such a life was important and that it was a man's responsibility to live it.

INTERVIEWER: In this connection, do you feel that there are certain times which are basic to the American experience, even though a body of writing in a given period might ignore or evade them?

WARREN: First thing, without being systematic, what comes to mind without running off a week and praying about it, would be that America was based on a big promise—a great big one: the Declaration of Independence. When you have to live with that in the house, that's quite a problem—particularly when you've got to make money and get ahead, open world markets, do all the things you have to, raise your children, and so forth. America is stuck with its self-definition put on paper in 1776, and that was just like putting a burr under the metaphysical saddle of America—you see, that saddle's going to jump now and then, and it pricks. There's another thing in the American experience that makes for a curious kind of abstraction. We suddenly had to define ourselves and what we stood for in one night. No other nation ever had to do that. In fact, one man did it—one man in an upstairs room, Thomas Jefferson. Sure, you might say that he was the amanuensis for a million or so people stranded on the edge of the continent and backed by a wilderness, and there's some sense in that notion. But *somebody* had to formulate it— in fact, just overnight, whatever the complicated background of that formulation—and we've been stuck with it ever since. With the very words it used. Do you know the Polish writer Adam Gurowski?* He was of a highly placed Polish family; he came and worked as a civil servant in Washington, a clerk, a kind of self-appointed spy on democracy. His book *America*—of 1857, I think—begins by saying that America is unique among nations because other nations are accidents of geography or race, but America is based on an idea. Behind the comedy of proclaiming that idea from Fourth of July platforms there is the solemn notion, *Believe and ye shall be saved.* That abstraction sometimes does become concrete, is a part of the American experience, and of the American problem—the lag between idea and fact, between word and flesh.

INTERVIEWER: What about historical time? America has had so much happening in such a short time.

WARREN: Awful lot of foreshortening in it. America lives in two times, chronological time and history. The last widow drawing a pension from the War of 1812 died just a few years ago. My father was old enough to vote when the last full-scale battle against

---

* Adam Gurowski, 1805–1866, author of *America and Europe* (1857) and *My Diary: Notes on the Civil War* (1866) among other works.

Indians was fought—a couple of regiments, I think, of regulars with artillery.

INTERVIEWER: From the first, your work is explicitly concerned with moral judgments, even during a period of history when much American fiction was concerned with moral questions only in the narrow way of the "proletarian" and "social realism" novels of the 1930s.

WARREN: I think I ought to say that behind *Night Rider* and my next novel, *At Heaven's Gate*, there was a good idea of the shadow not only of the events of that period but of the fiction of that period. I am more aware of that fact now than I was then. Of course only an idiot could have not been aware that he was trying to write a novel about, in one sense, "social justice" in *Night Rider* or, for that matter, *At Heaven's Gate*. But in some kind of a fumbling way I was aware, I guess, of trying to find the dramatic rub of the story at some point a little different from and deeper than the point of dramatic rub in some of the then current novels. But what I want to emphasize is the fact that I was fumbling rather than working according to plan and convictions already arrived at. When you start any book you don't know what, ultimately, your issues are. You try to write to find them. You're fiddling with the stuff, hoping to make sense, whatever kind of sense you can make.

INTERVIEWER: At least you could say that as a Southerner you were more conscious of what some of the issues were. You couldn't, I assume, forget the complexity of American social reality, no matter what your aesthetic concerns, or other concerns.

WARREN: It never crossed my mind when I began writing fiction that I could write about anything except life in the South. It never crossed my mind that I knew about anything else; knew, that is, well enough to write about. Nothing else ever nagged you enough to stir the imagination. But I stumbled into fiction rather late. I've got to be autobiographical about this. For years I didn't have much interest in fiction, that is, in college. I was reading my head off in poetry, Elizabethan and the moderns, Yeats, Hardy, Eliot, Hart Crane. I wasn't seeing the world around me—that is, in any way that might be thought of as directly related to fiction.

Be it to my everlasting shame that when the Scopes trial was going on a few miles from me I didn't even bother to go. My head was too full of John Ford and John Webster and William Blake and T. S. Eliot. If I had been thinking about writing novels about the South I would have been camping in Dayton, Tennessee—and would have gone about it like journalism. At least the Elizabethans saved me from that. As for starting fiction, I simply stumbled on it. In the spring of 1930 I was at Oxford, doing graduate work. I guess I was homesick and not knowing it. Paul Rosenfeld, who, with Van Wyck Brooks and Lewis Mumford, was then editing the old *American Caravan*, wrote and asked me why I didn't try a long story for them. He had had the patience one evening to listen to me blowing off about night-rider stories from boyhood. So Oxford and homesickness, or at least back-homeward-looking, and Paul Rosenfeld made me write *Prime Leaf*, a novelette which appeared in the *Caravan*, and was later the germ of *Night Rider*. I remember playing hooky from academic work to write the thing, and the discovery that you could really enjoy trying to write fiction. It was a new way of looking at things, and my head was full of recollections of the way objects looked in Kentucky and Tennessee. It was like going back to the age of twelve, going fishing and all that. It was a sense of freedom and excitement.

INTERVIEWER: When you started writing, what preoccupations, technically and thematically, had you in common with your crowd?

WARREN: I suppose you mean the poets called the Fugitive Group in Nashville—Allen Tate, John Crowe Ransom, Donald Davidson, Merrill Moore, et cetera?

INTERVIEWER: Yes.

WARREN: Well, in one sense, I don't know what the group had in common. I think there is a great fallacy in assuming that there was a systematic program behind the Fugitive Group. There was no such thing, and among the members there were deep differences in temperament and aesthetic theory. They were held together by geography and poetry. They all lived in Nashville, and they were all interested in poetry. Some were professors, some businessmen, one was a banker, several were students. They met informally to argue philosophy and read each other the poems they wrote. For some of them these interests were incidental to their main concerns. For a couple of others, like Tate, it was poetry or death. Their activity wasn't any "school" or "program." Mutual respect and common interests, that was what held them together—that and the provincial isolation, I guess.

INTERVIEWER: But did you share with them any technical or thematic preoccupations?

WARREN: The answer can't, you see, apply to the group. But in a very important way, that group was my education. I knew individual writers, poems, and books through them. I was exposed to the liveliness and range of the talk and the wrangle of argument. I heard the talk about techniques, but techniques regarded as means of expression. But most of all I got the feeling that poetry was a vital activity, that it related to ideas and to life. I came into the group rather late. I was timid and reverential, I guess. And I damned well should have been. Anyway, there was little or no talk in those days about fiction. Some of the same people, a little later, however, did give me in a very concrete way a sense of how literature can be related to place and history.

INTERVIEWER: It's very striking when you consider writing by Southerners before the twenties. Some think that few writers in the South were then as talented or competent, or as confident as today. This strikes me as a very American cultural phenomenon in spite of its specifically regional aspects. Would you say that this was a kind of repetition of what occurred in New England, say, during the 1830s?

WARREN: Yes, I do see some parallel between New England before the Civil War and the South after World War I to the present. The old notion of a shock, a cultural shock, to a more or less closed and static society—you know, what happened on a bigger scale in the Italian Renaissance or Elizabethan England. After 1918 the modern industrial world, with its good and bad, hit the South; all sorts of ferments began. As for individual writers, almost all of them of that period had had some important experience outside the South, then returned there—some strange mixture of continuity and discontinuity in their experience—a jagged quality. But more than mere general cultural or personal shocks, there was a moral shock in the South, a tension that grew out of the race situation. That moral tension had always been there, but it took new and more exacerbated forms after 1920. For one thing, the growing self-consciousness of the Negroes opened up possibilities for expanding economic and cultural horizons. A consequence was that the Southerner's loyalties and pieties—real values, mind you—were sometimes staked against his religious and moral sense, equally real values. There isn't much vital imagination, it seems to me, that doesn't come from this sort of shock, imbalance, need to "relive," redefine life.

INTERVIEWER: There is, for us, an exciting spiral of redefinition in your own work from *I'll Take My Stand* through the novels to *Segregation.* It would seem that these works mark stages in a combat with the past. In the first, the point of view seems orthodox and unreconstructed. How can one say it? In recent years your work has become more intense and has taken on an element of personal confession which is so definite that one tends to look, for example, on *Segregation* and *Brother to Dragons* as two facets of a single attitude.

WARREN: You've thrown several different things at me here. Let me try to sort them out. First you refer to the Southern Agrarian book *I'll Take My Stand,* of 1930, and then to my recent little book on *Segregation.* My essay in *I'll Take My Stand* was about the Negro in the South, and it was a defense of segregation. I haven't read that piece, as far as I can remember, since 1930, and I'm not sure exactly how things are put there. But I do recall very distinctly the circumstances of writing it. I wrote it at Oxford at about the same time I began writing fiction. The two things were tied together—the look back home from a long distance. I remember the jangle and wrangle of writing the essay and some kind of discomfort in it, some sense of evasion, I guess, in writing it, in contrast with the free feeling of writing the novelette *Prime Leaf,* the sense of seeing something fresh, the holiday sense plus some stirring up of something inside yourself. In the essay, I reckon, I was trying to prove something, and in the novelette

trying to find out something, see something, feel something—
exist. Don't misunderstand me. On the objective side of things,
there wasn't a power under heaven that could have changed
segregation in 1929—the South wasn't ready for it, the North
wasn't ready for it, the Negro wasn't. The Court, if I remember
correctly, had just reaffirmed segregation too. No, I'm not talking
about the objective fact, but about the subjective fact, yours truly,
in relation to the objective fact. Well, it wasn't being outside the
South that made me change my mind. It was coming back home.
In a little while I realized I simply couldn't have written that
essay again. I guess trying to write fiction made me realize that.
If you are seriously trying to write fiction you can't allow yourself
as much evasion as in trying to write essays. But some people
can't read fiction. One reviewer—a professional critic—said that
Band of Angels is an apology for the plantation system. Well, the
story of *Band* wasn't an apology *or* an attack. It was simply trying
to say something about something. But God Almighty, you have
to spell it out for some people, especially a certain breed of
professional defender-of-the-good, who makes a career of holding
the right thoughts and admiring his own moral navel. Well, that's
getting off the point. What else was it you threw at me?

INTERVIEWER: Would you say that each book marks a redefinition of reality arrived at through a combat with the past? A
development from the traditional to the highly personal reality?
A confession?

WARREN: I never thought of a combat with the past. I guess I
think more of trying to find what there is valuable to us, the line
of continuity to us, and *through* us. The specific Southern past,
I'm now talking about. As for combat, I guess the real combat is
always with yourself, Southerner or anybody else. You fight your
battles one by one and do the best you can. Whatever patterns
there are develop, aren't planned—the really basic patterns, I
mean, the kind you live into. As for confession, that wouldn't
have occurred to me, but I do know that in the last ten years or
a little more the personal relation to my writing changed. I never
bothered to define the change. I quit writing poems for several
years; that is, I'd start them, get a lot down, then feel that I wasn't

connecting somehow. I didn't finish one for several years, they felt false. Then I got back at it, and that is the bulk of what I've done since *Band of Angels*—a new book of poems which will be out in the summer. When you try to write a book—even objective fiction—you have to write from the inside not the outside—the inside of yourself. You have to find what's there. You can't predict it—just dredge for it and hope you have something worth the dredging. That isn't "confession"—that's just trying to use whatever the Lord lets you lay hand to. And of course you have common sense enough and structural sense enough to know what is relevant. You don't choose a story, it chooses you. You get together with that story somehow; you're stuck with it. There certainly is some reason it attracted you, and you're writing it trying to find out that reason; justify, get at that reason. I can always look back and remember the exact moment when I encountered the germ of any story I wrote—a clear flash.

INTERVIEWER: What is your period of incubation? Months? Years?

WARREN: Something I read or see stays in my head for five or six years. I always remember the date, the place, the room, the road, when I first was struck. For instance, *World Enough and Time*. Katherine Anne Porter and I were both at the Library of Congress as Fellows. We were in the same pew, had offices next to each other. She came in one day with an old pamphlet, the trial of Beauchamp for killing Colonel Sharp. She said, "Well, Red, you better read this." There it was. I read it in five minutes. But I was six years making the book. Any book I write starts with a flash but takes a long time to shape up. All of your first versions are in your head, so by the time you sit down to write you have some line developed in your head.

INTERVIEWER: What is the relation of sociological research and other types of research to the forms of fiction?

WARREN: I think it's purely accidental. For one writer a big dose of such stuff might be fine, for another it might be poison. I've known a good many people, some of them writers who think of literature as *material* that you "work up." You don't "work up" literature. They point at Zola. But Zola didn't do that, nor did

Dreiser. They may have thought they did, but they didn't. They weren't "working up" something—in one sense, something was working them up. You see the world as best you can—with or without the help of somebody's research, as the case may be. You see as much as you can, and the events and books that are interesting to you should be interesting to you because you're a human being, not because you're trying to be a writer. Then those things may be of some use to you as a writer later on. I don't believe in a schematic approach to material. The business of researching for a book strikes me as a sort of obscenity. What I mean is, researching for a book in the sense of trying to find a book to write. Once you are engaged by a subject, are in your book, have your idea, you may or may not want to do some investigating. But you ought to do it in the same spirit in which you'd take a walk in the evening air to think things over. You can't research to get a book. You stumble on it, or hope to. Maybe you will, if you live right.

INTERVIEWER: Speaking of craft, how conscious are you of the dramatic structure of your novels when you begin? I ask because in your work there is quite a variety of sub-forms, folklore, set pieces like "The Ballad of Billy Potts" or the Cass Mastern episode in *All the King's Men.* Are these planned as part of the dramatic structure, or do they arise while you are being carried by the flow of invention?

WARREN: I try to think a lot about the craft of other people— that's a result of my long years of teaching. You've been explaining things like how the first scene of *Hamlet* gets off, thinking of how things have been done . . . I suppose some of this sinks down to your gizzard. When it comes to your own work you have made some objective decisions, such as which character is going to tell the story. That's a prime question, a question of control. You have to make a judgment. You find one character is more insistent, he's more sensitive and more pointed than the others. But as for other aspects of structure and craft, I guess, in the actual process of composition or in preliminary thinking, I try to immerse myself in the motive and *feel* toward meanings, rather than plan a structure or plan effects. At some point, you know, you have to try to get one with God and *then* take a hard cold look at what you're doing and work on it once more, trusting in your viscera and nervous system and your previous efforts as far as they've gone. The hard thing, the objective thing, has to be done before the book is written. And if anybody dreams up "Kubla Khan," it's going to be Coleridge. If the work is done the dream will come to the man who's ready for that particular dream; it's not going to come just from dreaming in general. After a thing is done, then I try to get tough and critical with myself. But damn it, it may sometimes be too late. But that is the fate of man. What I am trying to say is that I try to forget the abstractions when I'm actually composing a thing. I don't understand other approaches that come up when I talk to other writers. For instance, some say their sole interest is experimentation. Well, I think that you learn all you can and try to use it. I don't know what is meant by the word "experiment"; you ought to be playing for keeps.

INTERVIEWER: Yes, but there is still great admiration of the so-called "experimental writing" of the twenties. What of Joyce and Eliot?

WARREN: What is "experimental writing"? James Joyce didn't do "experimental writing"—he wrote *Ulysses*. Eliot didn't do "experimental writing" he wrote *The Waste Land*. When you fail at something you call it an "experiment," an élite word for flop. Just because lines are uneven or capitals missing doesn't mean experiment. Literary magazines devoted to experimental writing are usually filled with works by middle-aged or old people.

INTERVIEWER: Or middle-aged young people.

WARREN: Young fogeys. In one way, of course, all writing that is any good *is* experimental; that is, it's a way of seeing what is possible—what poem, what novel is possible. Experiment—they define it as putting a question to nature, and that is true of writing undertaken with seriousness. You put the question to human nature—and especially your own nature—and see what comes out. It is unpredictable. If it is predictable—not experimental in that sense—then it will be worthless.

INTERVIEWER: The *Southern Review* contained much fine work, but little that was purely "experimental"—isn't that so?

WARREN: Yes, and there were a lot of good young, or younger, writers in it. Not all Southern either—about half, I should say.

INTERVIEWER: I remember that some of Algren's first work appeared there.

WARREN: Oh, yes, two early stories, for example; and a longish poem about baseball.

INTERVIEWER: And the story, "A Bottle of Milk for Mother."

WARREN: And the story "Biceps." And three or four of Eudora's first stories were there—Eudora Welty—and some of Katherine Anne's novelettes—Katherine Anne Porter.

INTERVIEWER: There were a lot of critics in it—young ones too.

WARREN: Oh yes, younger then, anyway. Kenneth Burke, F. O. Matthiessen, Theodore Spencer, R. P. Blackmur, Delmore Schwartz, L. C. Knights . . .

INTERVIEWER: Speaking of critics reminds me that you've written criticism as well as poetry, drama, and fiction. It is sometimes said that the practice of criticism is harmful to the rest; have you found it so?

WARREN: On this matter of criticism, something that appalls me is the idea going around now that the practice of criticism is opposed to the literary impulse—is *necessarily* opposed to it. Sure, it *may* be a trap, it may destroy the creative impulse, but so may drink or money or respectability. But criticism is a perfectly natural human activity, and somehow the dullest, most technical criticism may be associated with full creativity. Elizabethan criticism is all, or nearly all, technical—meter, how to hang a line together—kitchen criticism, how to make the cake. People deeply interested in an art are interested in the "how." Now I don't mean to say that that is the only kind of valuable criticism. Any kind is good that gives a deeper insight into the nature of the thing— a Marxist analysis, a Freudian study, the relation to a literary or social tradition, the history of a theme. But we have to remember that there is no *one, single, correct* kind of criticism, no *complete* criticism. You only have different kinds of perspectives, giving, when successful, different kinds of insights. And at one historical moment one kind of insight may be more needed than another.

INTERVIEWER: But don't you think that in America now a lot of good critical ideas get lost in terminology, in the gobbledygook style of expression?

WARREN: Every age, every group, has its jargon. When the jargon runs away with the insight, that's no good. Sure, a lot of people think they have the key to truth if they have a lingo. And a lot of modern criticism has run off into lingo, into academicism—the wrong kind of academicism, that pretends to be unacademic. The real academic job is to absorb an idea, to put it into perspective along with other ideas, not to dilute it to lingo. As for lingo, it's true that some very good critics got bit by the bug that you could develop a fixed critical vocabulary. Well, you can't, except within narrow limits. That is a trap of scientism.

INTERVIEWER: Do you see some new ideas in criticism now emerging?

WARREN: No, I don't see them now. We've had Mr. Freud and Mr. Marx and—

INTERVIEWER: Mr. Fraser and *The Golden Bough*.

WARREN: Yes, and Mr. Coleridge and Mr. Arnold and Mr. Eliot and Mr. Richards and Mr. Leavis and Mr. Aristotle, et cetera. There have been, or are, many competing kinds of criticism with us—but I don't see a new one, or a new development of one of the old kind. It's an age groping for its issue.

INTERVIEWER: What about the New Criticism?

WARREN: Let's name some of them—Richards, Eliot, Tate, Blackmur, Winters, Brooks, Leavis (I guess). How in God's name can you get that gang into the same bed? There's no bed big enough and no blanket would stay tucked. When Ransom wrote his book called *The New Criticism*, he was pointing out the vindictive variety among the critics and saying that he didn't agree with any of them. The term is, in one sense, a term without any referent—or with too many referents. It is a term that belongs to the conspiracy theory of history. A lot of people—chiefly aging, conservative professors scared of losing prestige, or young instructors afraid of not getting promoted, middle-brow magazine editors, and the flotsam and jetsam of semi-Marxist social-significance criticism left stranded by history—they all had a communal nightmare called the New Criticism to explain their vague discomfort. I think it was something they ate.

INTERVIEWER: What do you mean—conspiracy?

WARREN: Those folks all had the paranoidal nightmare that there was a conspiracy called the New Criticism, just to do them personal wrong. No, it's not quite that simple, but there is some truth in this. One thing that a lot of so-called New Critics had in common was a willingness to look long and hard at the literary object. But the ways of looking might be very different. Eliot is a lot closer to Arnold and the Archbishop of Canterbury than he is to Yvor Winters, and Winters is a lot closer to Irving Babbitt than to Richards, and the exegeses of Brooks are a lot closer to Coleridge than to Ransom, and so on. There has been more nonsense talked about this subject than about any I can think of. And a large part of the nonsense, on any side of the question, derives from the assumption that any one kind of criticism is "correct" criticism. There is no correct or complete criticism.

INTERVIEWER: You had a piece in the *New Republic* once in which you discuss Faulkner's technique. One of the things you emphasize is Faulkner's technique of the "still moment." I've forgotten what you called it exactly—a suspension, in which time seems to hang.

WARREN: That's the frozen moment. Freeze time. Somewhere, almost in a kind of pun, Faulkner himself uses the image of a frieze for such a moment of frozen action. It's an important quality in his work. Some of these moments harden up an event, give it its meaning by holding it fixed. Time fluid versus time fixed. In Faulkner's work that's the drama behind the drama. Take a look at Hemingway; there's no time in Hemingway, there are only moments in themselves, moments of action. There are no parents and no children. If there's a parent he is a grandparent off in America somewhere who signs the check, like the grandfather in *A Farewell to Arms*. You never see a small child in Hemingway. You get death in childbirth but you never see a child. Everything is outside of the time process. But in Faulkner there are always the very old and the very young. Time spreads and is the important thing, the terrible thing. A tremendous flux is there, things flowing away in all directions. Moments not quite ready to be shaped are already there, waiting, and we feel their presence. What you most remember about Jason in *The Sound and the Fury*, say, is the fact that he was the treasurer when the children made and sold kites, and kept the money in his pocket. Or you remember Caddy getting her drawers muddy. Everything is already there, just waiting to happen. You have the sense of the small becoming large in time, the large becoming small, the sweep of time over things—that, and the balance of the frozen, abstracted moment against violent significant action. These frozen moments are Faulkner's game. Hemingway has a different game. In Hemingway there's no time at all. He's out of history entirely. In one sense, he tries to deny history, he says history is bunk, like Henry Ford.

I am in no sense making an invidious comparison between the two writers—or between their special uses of time. They are both powerfully expressive writers. But it's almost too pat, you know, almost too schematic, the polar differences between those two writers in relation to the question of time. Speaking of pairs of writers, take Proust and Faulkner. There may be a lot written on the subject, but I haven't encountered much of it. They'd make a strange but instructive pair to study—in relation to time.

INTERVIEWER: Wouldn't you say that there seems to be in the early Hemingway a conscious effort *not* to have a very high center of consciousness within the form of the novel? His characters may have a highly moral significance, but they seldom discuss issues; they prefer to hint.

WARREN: Sure, Hemingway sneaks it in, but he is an intensely conscious and even philosophical writer. When the snuck-in thing or the gesture works, the effect can be mighty powerful. By contrast, French fiction usually has a hero who deals very consciously with the issues. He is his own chorus to the action, as well as the man who utters the equivalent of the Elizabethan soliloquy. Nineteenth-century fiction also dealt with the issues. Those novels could discuss them in terms of a man's relation to a woman, or in terms of whether you're going to help a slave run away, or in terms of what to do about a man obsessed with fighting evil, nature, what have you, in the form of a white whale.

INTERVIEWER: Your own work seems to have this explicit character. Jack Burden in *All the King's Men* is a conscious center and he is a highly conscious man. He's not there as an omniscient figure, but is urgently trying to discover something. He is involved.

WARREN: Burden got there by accident. He was only a sentence or two in the first version—the verse play from which the novel developed.

INTERVIEWER: Why did you make the change?

WARREN: I don't know. He was an unnamed newspaper man, a childhood friend of the assassin; an excuse for the young doctor, the assassin of the politician Willie Stark, to say something before he performed the deed. When after two years I picked up the verse version and began to fool with a novel, the unnamed newspaper man became the narrator. It turned out, in a way, that what he thought about the story was more important than the story itself. I suppose he became the narrator because he gave me the kind of interest I needed to write the novel. He made it possible for me to control it. He is an observer, but he is involved.

INTERVIEWER: For ten years or more it has been said in the United States that problems of race are an obsession of Negro writers, but that they have no place in literature. But how can a Negro writer avoid the problem of race?

WARREN: How can you expect a Southern Negro not to write about race, directly or indirectly, when you can't find a Southern white man who can avoid it?

INTERVIEWER: I must say that it's usually white Northerners who express a different opinion, though a few Negroes have been seduced by it. And they usually present their argument on aesthetic grounds.

WARREN: I'd like to add here something about the historical element which seems to me important for this general question. The Negro who is now writing protest *qua* protest strikes me as anachronistic. Protest *qua* protest denies the textures of life. The problem is to permit the fullest range of life into racial awareness. I don't mean to imply that there's nothing to protest about, but aside from the appropriate political, sociological, and journalistic concerns, the problem is to see the protest in its relation to other things. Race isn't an isolated thing—I mean as it exists in the U.S.—it becomes a total symbol for every kind of issue. They all flow into it—and out of it. Well, thank God. It gives a little variety to life. At the same time it proclaims the unity of life. You know the kind of person who puts on a certain expression and then talks about "solving" the race problem. Well, it's the same kind of person and the same kind of expression you meet when you hear the phrase "solving the sex problem." This may be a poor parallel, but it's some kind of parallel. Basically the issue isn't to "solve" the "race problem" or the "sex problem." You don't solve it, you just experience it. Appreciate it.

INTERVIEWER: Maybe that's another version of William James's "moral equivalent of war." You argue and try to keep the argument clean, all the human complexities in view.

WARREN: What I'm trying to say is this. A few years ago I sat in a room with some right-thinking friends, the kind of people who think you look in the back of the book for every answer— attitude A for situation A, attitude B for situation B, and so on through the damned alphabet. It developed that they wanted a world where everything is exactly alike and everybody is exactly alike. They wanted a production belt of human faces and human attitudes, and the same books on every parlor table.

INTERVIEWER: Hell, who would want such a world?

WARREN: "Right-thinkers" want it, for one thing. I don't want that kind of world. I want variety and pluralism—and *appreciation*. Appreciation in the context of some sort of justice and decency, and freedom of choice in conduct and personal life. I'd like a country in which there was a maximum of opportunity for any individual to discover his talents and develop his capacities— discover his fullest self and by so doing learn to respect other selves a little. Man is interesting in his differences. It's all a question of what you make of the differences. I'm not for differences *per se*, but you just let the world live the differences, live

them out, live them up, and see how things come out. But I feel
pretty strongly about attempts to legislate *un*difference. That is
just as much tyranny as trying to legislate difference. Apply that
to any differences between healthy and unhealthy, criminal and
noncriminal. Furthermore, you can't legislate the future of anybody, in any direction. It's not laws that are going to determine
what our great-grandchildren feel or do. The tragedy of a big half
of American liberalism is its attempts to legislate virtue. You can't
legislate virtue. You should simply try to establish conditions
favorable for the growth of virtue. But that will never satisfy the
bully-boys of virtue, the plug-uglies of virtue. They are interested
in the production-belt stamp of virtue, attitude A in the back of
the book, and not in establishing conditions of justice and decency
in which human appreciation can find play.

Listen, I'll tell you a story. More than twenty years ago I spent
part of a summer in a little town in Louisiana, and like a good
number of the population whiled away the afternoons by going
to the local murder trials. One case involved an old Negro man
who had shot a young Negro woman for talking meanness against
his baby-girl daughter. He had shot the victim with both barrels
of a twelve-gauge at a range of eight feet, while the victim was
in a crap game. There were a dozen witnesses to the execution.
Besides that he had sat for half an hour on a stump outside the
door of the building where the crap game was going on, before
he got down to business. He was waiting, because a friend had
lost six dollars to the intended victim and had asked the old man
to hold off till he had a chance to win it back. When the friend
got the six dollars back, the old man went to work. He never
denied what he had done. He explained it all very carefully, and
why he had to do it. He loved his baby-girl daughter and there
wasn't anything else he could do. Then he would plead not guilty.
But if he got tried and convicted—and they couldn't fail to con-
vict—he would get death. If, however, he would plead guilty to
manslaughter, he could get off light. But he wouldn't do it. He
said he wasn't guilty of anything. The whole town got involved
in the thing. Well, they finally cracked him. He pleaded guilty

and got off light. Everybody was glad, sure—they weren't stuck with something, they could feel good and pretty virtuous. But they felt bad, too. Something had been lost, something a lot of them could appreciate. I used to think I'd try to make a story of this. But I never did. It was too complete, too self-fulfilling, as fact. But to get back to the old man. It took him three days to crack, and when he cracked he was nothing. Now we don't approve of what he did—a status homicide the sociologists call it, and that is the worst sort of homicide, worse than homicide for gain, because status homicide is irrational, and you can't make sense of it, and it is the mark of a low order of society. But because status homicide is the mark of a low order of society, what are we to think about the old man's three-day struggle to keep his dignity? And are we to deny value to this dignity because of the way "they" live down there?

INTERVIEWER: You feel, then, that one of the great blocks in achieving serious fiction out of sad experience is the assumption that you're on the right side?

WARREN: Once you start illustrating virtue as such you had better stop writing fiction. Do something else, like Y-work. Or join a committee. Your business as a writer is not to illustrate virtue, but to show how a fellow may move toward it—or away from it.

INTERVIEWER: Malraux says that "one cannot reveal the mystery of human beings in the form of a plea for the defense."

WARREN: Or in the form of an indictment, either.

INTERVIEWER: What about the devil's advocate?

WARREN: He can have a role, he can be Jonathan Swift or something.

INTERVIEWER: I wonder what these right-thinkers feel when they confront a Negro, say, the symbol of the underdog, and he turns out to be a son of a bitch. What do they do—hold a conference to decide how to treat him?

WARREN: They must sure have a problem.

INTERVIEWER: The same kind of people, they have to consult with themselves to determine if they can laugh at certain situations in which Negroes are involved—like minstrel shows. A whole world of purely American humor got lost in that shuffle, along with some good songs.

WARREN: It's just goddamned hard, you have to admit, though, to sort out things that are symbolically charged. Sometimes the symbolic charge is so heavy you have a hard time getting at the real value really there. You always can, I guess, if the context is right. But hell, a lot of people can't read a context.

INTERVIEWER: It's like the problem of Shylock in *The Merchant of Venice*.

WARREN: Yes, suppress the play because it might offend a Jew. Or *Oliver Twist*. Well, such symbolic charges just have to be reckoned with and taken on their own terms and in their historical perspective. As a matter of fact, such symbolic charges are present, in one degree or another, in all relationships. They're simply stepped up and specialized in certain historical and social situations. There are mighty few stories you can tell without offending somebody—without some implicit affront. The comic strip of *Li'l Abner*, for instance, must have made certain persons of what is called "Appalachian white" origin feel inferior and humiliated. There are degrees as well as differences in these things. Context is all. And a relatively pure heart. *Relatively* pure—for if you had a pure heart you wouldn't be in the book-writing business in the first place. We're stuck with it in ourselves—what we can write about, if anything; what you can make articulate; what voices you have in your insides and in your ear.

—RALPH ELLISON
EUGENE WALTER
1957

Note: There is an integral relationship between this interview and the interview with Ralph Ellison which appeared in issue no. 8 of *The Paris Review*.

2. T. S. Eliot

Thomas Stearns Eliot was born September 26, 1888, in St. Louis, of a distinguished Boston family, deeply rooted in the New England tradition and in the Unitarian Church. He lived in St. Louis until he was eighteen, and in 1906 entered Harvard, where he received his M.A. in four years. After a year at the Sorbonne, he returned to Harvard and worked for his Ph.D. His dissertation on F. H. Bradley and Meinong's *Gegenstandstheorie* was accepted, he says, "because it was unreadable," and he never took his degree. In 1914 Eliot visited Germany in the summer, and that winter, after the outbreak of the war, read philosophy at Oxford. He settled in England at that time. From 1917 to 1919 he was assistant editor of the *Egoist* and published his first book of poems, *Prufrock and Other Observations*, and many essays including *Ezra Pound, His Metric and Poetry*. It was in 1922, however, with the appearance of *The Waste Land*, that his name came to the forefront of contemporary literature.

Among other titles for which he is famous are the poems *Ash Wednesday* (1930) and *Four Quartets* (1943); the plays *Murder in the Cathedral* (1935), *Family Reunion* (1939), *The Cocktail Party* (1950), and *The Elder Statesman* (1958); and essays, *The Sacred Wood* (1920), *Andrew Marvell* (1922), *Thoughts after Lambeth* (1931), *The Uses of Poetry and the Uses of Criticism* (1933), and *Essays Ancient and Modern* (1936). Eliot's *Collected Poems* and *Collected Plays* were both published in 1962.

The Criterion, Eliot's magazine, in which *The Waste Land* first appeared, existed for seventeen years and was highly regarded in literary and philosophical circles.

Eliot became a British subject in 1927. In 1948 he received the Order of Merit from King George VI and was awarded the Nobel Prize in literature. He died in 1965.

was exploring his own mind also.   The compositions in verse and
in prose fiction ~~to which I have just referred~~ may I think be ignored, except for ~~the~~ information ^such^ they can yield about their author; and his other writings, those concerned directly with theological, social or political matter, should be ~~xxxxixxxxx~~ considered
as by-products of a mind of which the primary activity was literary
criticism.

    I ~~first~~ met Middleton Murry ~~by~~ appointment at some meeting
place whence he was to conduct me to his home for dinner and ^for^ a
discussion of his projects for The Athenaeum, a defunct weekly
which was to be revived under his editorship.   I had heard of
him earlier, in the circle of Lady Ottoline Morrell where I had
already met Katherine Mansfield on one occasion, but we had held
no communication ~~until~~ ^before^ he wrote to ~~invite me to~~ ^propose^ ~~a~~ ^this^ meeting.   I do
not know what he had been told about me; what is important is that
he had read (having had it brought to his attention (no doubt) at
Garsington) my first ~~volume~~ ^book^ of Verse, Prufrock, and that it was
entirely because of ~~him this verse~~ ^the the impression this little book had made upon him^ that he wished to ask me to
become ^his^ Assistant Editor. ~~of The Athenaeum under him.~~ ^write^   Of my cri-
tical writings he knew nothing: I gave him some copies of The
Egoist to enable him to judge of my abilities.   It speaks of the
man, however, that he had made up his mind that he wanted my help
^in his editorial^ ^and^
~~with~~ this venture without having seen any criticism of mine, ~~and~~
wholly on the strength of Prufrock. ^his opinion of^   After a good deal of hesi-
tation I declined; and I think that I was wise to do so, and to
remain for some years at my desk in the City.   I did however
become one of Murry's regular contributors, reviewing some book

Part of a manuscript by T. S. Eliot.

D. CAMMELL

T. S. Eliot

The interview took place in New York, at the apartment of Mrs.
Louis Henry Cohn, of House of Books, Ltd., who is a friend of
Mr. and Mrs. Eliot. The bookcases of the attractive living room
contained a remarkable collection of modern authors. On a wall
near the entrance hung a drawing of Mr. Eliot, done by his sister-
in-law, Mrs. Henry Ware Eliot. An inscribed wedding photograph
of the Eliots stood in a silver frame on a table. Mrs. Cohn and
Mrs. Eliot sat on a sofa at one end of the room, while Mr. Eliot
and the interviewer faced each other in the center. The microphone
of a tape recorder lay on the floor between them.

    Mr. Eliot looked particularly well. He was visiting the United
States briefly on his way back to London from a holiday in Nassau.
He was tanned, and he seemed to have put on weight in the three
years since the interviewer had seen him. Altogether, he looked
younger and seemed jollier. He frequently glanced at Mrs. Eliot

*during the interview, as if he were sharing with her an answer
which he was not making.*

*The interviewer had talked with Mr. Eliot previously in London.
The small office at Faber and Faber, a few flights above Russell
Square, displayed a gallery of photographs on its walls: there was
a large picture of Virginia Woolf, with an inset portrait of Pius
XII; there were I. A. Richards, Paul Valéry, W. B. Yeats, Goethe,
Marianne Moore, Charles Whibley, Djuna Barnes, and others.
Many young poets had stared at the faces there, during a talk
with Mr. Eliot. One of them told a story which illustrated some
of the unsuspected in Mr. Eliot's conversation. After an hour of
serious literary discussion, Mr. Eliot paused to think if he had a
final word of advice; the young poet, an American, was about to
go up to Oxford as Mr. Eliot had done forty years before. Then,
as gravely as if he were recommending salvation, Mr. Eliot advised
the purchase of long woolen underwear because of Oxford's damp
stone. Mr. Eliot was able to be avuncular while he was quite
aware of comic disproportion between manner and message.*

*Similar combinations modified many of the comments which
are reported here, and the ironies of gesture are invisible on the
page. At times, actually, the interview moved from the ironic and
the mildly comic to the hilarious. The tape was punctuated by the
head-back Boom Boom of Mr. Eliot's laughter, particularly in
response to mention of his early derogation of Ezra Pound, and
to a question about the unpublished, and one gathers improper,
King Bolo poems of his Harvard days.*

INTERVIEWER: Perhaps I can begin at the beginning. Do you
remember the circumstances under which you began to write
poetry in St. Louis when you were a boy?

ELIOT: I began I think about the age of fourteen, under the
inspiration of Fitzgerald's *Omar Khayyam*, to write a number of
very gloomy and atheistical and despairing quatrains in the same
style, which fortunately I suppressed completely—so completely
that they don't exist. I never showed them to anybody. The first
poem that shows is one which appeared first in the *Smith Academy
Record*, and later in *The Harvard Advocate*, which was written

as an exercise for my English teacher and was an imitation of Ben Jonson. He thought it very good for a boy of fifteen or sixteen. Then I wrote a few at Harvard, just enough to qualify for election to an editorship on *The Harvard Advocate*, which I enjoyed. Then I had an outburst during my junior and senior years. I became much more prolific, under the influence first of Baudelaire and then of Jules Laforgue, whom I discovered I think in my junior year at Harvard.

INTERVIEWER: Did anyone in particular introduce you to the French poets? Not Irving Babbitt, I suppose.

ELIOT: No, Babbitt would be the last person! The one poem that Babbitt always held up for admiration was Gray's *Elegy*. And that's a fine poem but I think this shows certain limitations on Babbitt's part, God bless him. I have advertised my source, I think; it's Arthur Symons's book on French poetry, * which I came across in the Harvard Union. In those days the Harvard Union was a meeting place for any undergraduate who chose to belong to it. They had a very nice little library, like the libraries in many Harvard houses now. I liked his quotations and I went to a foreign bookshop somewhere in Boston (I've forgotten the name and I don't know whether it still exists) which specialized in French and German and other foreign books and found Laforgue, and other poets. I can't imagine why that bookshop should have had a few poets like Laforgue in stock. Goodness knows how long they'd had them or whether there were any other demands for them.

INTERVIEWER: When you were an undergraduate, were you aware of the dominating presence of any older poets? Today the poet in his youth is writing in the age of Eliot and Pound and Stevens. Can you remember your own sense of the literary times? I wonder if your situation may not have been extremely different.

ELIOT: I think it was rather an advantage not having any living poets in England or America in whom one took any particular interest. I don't know what it would be like but I think it would be a rather troublesome distraction to have such a lot of domi-

* *The Symbolist Movement in Literature.*

nating presences, as you call them, about. Fortunately we weren't bothered by each other.

INTERVIEWER: Were you aware of people like Hardy or Robinson at all?

ELIOT: I was slightly aware of Robinson because I read an article about him in *The Atlantic Monthly* which quoted some of his poems, and that wasn't my cup of tea at all. Hardy was hardly known to be a poet at that time. One read his novels, but his poetry only really became conspicuous to a later generation. Then there was Yeats, but it was the early Yeats. It was too much Celtic twilight for me. There was really nothing except the people of the 90s who had all died of drink or suicide or one thing or another.

INTERVIEWER: Did you and Conrad Aiken help each other with your poems, when you were co-editors on the *Advocate*?

ELIOT: We were friends but I don't think we influenced each other at all. When it came to foreign writers, he was more interested in Italian and Spanish, and I was all for the French.

INTERVIEWER: Were there any other friends who read your poems and helped you?

ELIOT: Well, yes. There was a man who was a friend of my brother's, a man named Thomas H. Thomas who lived in Cambridge and who saw some of my poems in *The Harvard Advocate*. He wrote me a most enthusiastic letter and cheered me up. And I wish I had his letters still. I was very grateful to him for giving me that encouragement.

INTERVIEWER: I understand that it was Conrad Aiken who introduced you and your work to Pound.

ELIOT: Yes it was. Aiken was a very generous friend. He tried to place some of my poems in London, one summer when he was over, with Harold Monro and others. Nobody would think of publishing them. He brought them back to me. Then in 1914, I think, we were both in London in the summer. He said, "You go to Pound. Show him your poems." He thought Pound might like them. Aiken liked them, though they were very different from his.

INTERVIEWER: Do you remember the circumstances of your first meeting with Pound?

ELIOT: I think I went to call on him first. I think I made a good impression, in his little triangular sitting room in Kensington. He said, "Send me your poems." And he wrote back, "This is as good as anything I've seen. Come around and have a talk about them." Then he pushed them on Harriet Monroe, which took a little time.

INTERVIEWER: In an article about your *Advocate* days, for the book in honor of your sixtieth birthday, Aiken quotes an early letter from England in which you refer to Pound's verse as "touchingly incompetent." I wonder when you changed your mind.

ELIOT: Hah! *That* was a bit brash, wasn't it? Pound's verse was first shown me by an editor of *The Harvard Advocate*, W. G. Tinckom-Fernandez, who was a crony of mine and Conrad Aiken's and the other Signet* poets of the period. He showed me those little things of Elkin Mathews, *Exultations* and *Personae.*† He said, "This is up your street; you ought to like this." Well, I didn't, really. It seemed to me rather fancy old-fashioned romantic stuff, cloak-and-dagger kind of stuff. I wasn't very much impressed by it. When I went to see Pound, I was not particularly an admirer of his work, and though I now regard the work I saw then as very accomplished, I am certain that in his later work is to be found the grand stuff.

INTERVIEWER: You have mentioned in print that Pound cut *The Waste Land* from a much larger poem into its present form. Were you benefited by his criticism of your poems in general? Did he cut other poems?

ELIOT: Yes. At that period, yes. He was a marvelous critic because he didn't try to turn you into an imitation of yourself. He tried to see what you were trying to do.

INTERVIEWER: Have you helped to rewrite any of your friends' poems? Ezra Pound's, for instance?

---

* Harvard's literary club.
† Early books of Pound, published by Elkin Mathews in 1909.

ELIOT: I can't think of any instances. Of course I have made innumerable suggestions on manuscripts of young poets in the last twenty-five years or so.

INTERVIEWER: Does the manuscript of the original, uncut *Waste Land* exist?

ELIOT: Don't ask me. That's one of the things I don't know. It's an unsolved mystery. I sold it to John Quinn. I also gave him a notebook of unpublished poems, because he had been kind to me in various affairs. That's the last I heard of them. Then he died and they didn't turn up at the sale.

INTERVIEWER: What sort of thing did Pound cut from *The Waste Land*? Did he cut whole sections?

ELIOT: Whole sections, yes. There was a long section about a shipwreck. I don't know what that had to do with anything else, but it was rather inspired by the Ulysses Canto in *The Inferno*, I think. Then there was another section which was an imitation *Rape of the Lock*. Pound said, "It's no use trying to do something that somebody else has done as well as it can be done. Do something different."

INTERVIEWER: Did the excisions change the intellectual structure of the poem?

ELIOT: No. I think it was just as structureless, only in a more futile way, in the longer version.

INTERVIEWER: I have a question about the poem which is related to its composition. In *Thoughts after Lambeth* you denied the allegation of critics who said that you expressed "the disillusionment of a generation" in *The Waste Land*, or you denied that it was your intention. Now F. R. Leavis, I believe, has said that the poem exhibits no progression; yet on the other hand, more recent critics, writing after your later poetry, found *The Waste Land* Christian. I wonder if this was part of your intention.

ELIOT: No, it wasn't part of my conscious intention. I think that in *Thoughts after Lambeth*, I was speaking of intentions more in a negative than in a positive sense, to say what was not my intention. I wonder what an "intention" means! One wants to get something off one's chest. One doesn't know quite what it is that one wants to get off the chest until one's got it off. But I

couldn't apply the word "intention" positively to any of my poems.
Or to any poem.

INTERVIEWER: I have another question about you and Pound
and your earlier career. I have read somewhere that you and
Pound decided to write quatrains, in the late teens, because *vers
libre* had gone far enough.

ELIOT: I think that's something Pound said. And the suggestion
of writing quatrains was his. He put me onto *Emaux et Camées*.*

INTERVIEWER: I wonder about your ideas about the relation of
form to subject. Would you then have chosen the form before
you knew quite what you were going to write in it?

ELIOT: Yes, in a way. One studied originals. We studied Gautier's poems and then we thought, "Have I anything to say in
which this form will be useful?" And we experimented. The form
gave the impetus to the content.

INTERVIEWER: Why was *vers libre* the form you chose to use in
your early poems?

ELIOT: My early *vers libre*, of course, was started under the
endeavor to practice the same form as Laforgue. This meant
merely rhyming lines of irregular length, with the rhymes coming
in irregular places. It wasn't quite so *libre* as much *vers*, especially
the sort which Ezra called "Amygism."† Then, of course, there
were things in the next phase which were freer, like "Rhapsody
on a Windy Night." I don't know whether I had any sort of model
or practice in mind when I did that. It just came that way.

INTERVIEWER: Did you feel, possibly, that you were writing
against something, more than from any model? Against the poet
laureate perhaps?

ELIOT: No, no, no. I don't think one was constantly trying to
reject things, but just trying to find out what was right for oneself.
One really ignored poet laureates as such, the Robert Bridges. I
don't think good poetry can be produced in a kind of political
attempt to overthrow some existing form. I think it just supersedes.

* Poems by Théophile Gautier.
† A reference to Amy Lowell, who captured and transformed imagism.

People find a way in which they can say something. "I can't say it that way, what way can I find that will do?" One didn't really *bother* about the existing modes.

INTERVIEWER: I think it was after "Prufrock" and before "Gerontion" that you wrote the poems in French which appear in your *Collected Poems*. I wonder how you happened to write them. Have you written any since?

ELIOT: No, and I never shall. That was a very curious thing which I can't altogether explain. At that period I thought I'd dried up completely. I hadn't written anything for some time and was rather desperate. I started writing a few things in French and found I *could*, at that period. I think it was that when I was writing in French I didn't take the poems so seriously, and that, not taking them seriously, I wasn't so worried about not being able to write. I did these things as a sort of *tour de force* to see what I could do. That went on for some months. The best of them have been printed. I must say that Ezra Pound went through them, and Edmond Dulac, a Frenchman we knew in London, helped with them a bit. We left out some, and I suppose they disappeared completely. Then I suddenly began writing in English again and lost all desire to go on with French. I think it was just something that helped me get started again.

INTERVIEWER: Did you think at all about becoming a French symbolist poet like the two Americans of the last century?

ELIOT: Stuart Merrill and Viélé-Griffin. I only did that during the romantic year I spent in Paris after Harvard. I had at that time the idea of giving up English and trying to settle down and scrape along in Paris and gradually write French. But it would have been a foolish idea even if I'd been much more bilingual than I ever was, because, for one thing, I don't think that one can be a bilingual poet. I don't know of any case in which a man wrote great or even fine poems equally well in two languages. I think one language must be the one you express yourself in in poetry, and you've got to give up the other for that purpose. And I think that the English language really has more resources in some respects than the French. I think, in other words, I've probably done better in English than I ever would have in French even if I'd become as proficient in French as the poets you mentioned.

INTERVIEWER: Can I ask you if you have any plans for poems now?

ELIOT: No, I haven't any plans for anything at the moment, except that I think I would like, having just got rid of *The Elder Statesman* (I only passed the final proofs just before we left London), to do a little prose writing of a critical sort. I never think more than one step ahead. Do I want to do another play or do I want to do more poems? I don't know until I find I want to do it.

INTERVIEWER: Do you have any unfinished poems that you look at occasionally?

ELIOT: I haven't much in that way, no. As a rule, with me an unfinished thing is a thing that might as well be rubbed out. It's better, if there's something good in it that I might make use of elsewhere, to leave it at the back of my mind than on paper in a drawer. If I leave it in a drawer it remains the same thing but if it's in the memory it becomes transformed into something else. As I have said before, *Burnt Norton* began with bits that had to be cut out of *Murder in the Cathedral*. I learned in *Murder in the Cathedral* that it's no use putting in nice lines that you think are good poetry if they don't get the action on at all. That was when Martin Browne was useful. He would say, "There are very nice lines here, but they've nothing to do with what's going on on stage."

INTERVIEWER: Are any of your minor poems actually sections cut out of longer works? There are two that sound like "The Hollow Men."

ELIOT: Oh, those were the preliminary sketches. Those things were earlier. Others I published in periodicals but not in my collected poems. You don't want to say the same thing twice in one book.

INTERVIEWER: You seem often to have written poems in sections. Did they begin as separate poems? I am thinking of "Ash Wednesday," in particular.

ELIOT: Yes, like "The Hollow Men," it originated out of separate poems. As I recall, one or two early drafts of parts of "Ash Wednesday" appeared in *Commerce* and elsewhere. Then gradually I came to see it as a sequence. That's one way in which my mind does seem to have worked throughout the years poetically—doing things separately and then seeing the possibility of fusing them together, altering them, and making a kind of whole of them.

INTERVIEWER: Do you write anything now in the vein of *Old Possum's Book of Practical Cats* or *King Bolo*?

ELIOT: Those things do come from time to time! I keep a few notes of such verse, and there are one or two incomplete cats that probably will never be written. There's one about a glamour cat. It turned out too sad. This would never do. I can't make my children weep over a cat who's gone wrong. She had a very questionable career, did this cat. It wouldn't do for the audience of my previous volume of cats. I've never done any dogs. Of course dogs don't seem to lend themselves to verse quite so well, collectively, as cats. I may eventually do an enlarged edition of my cats. That's more likely than another volume. I did add one poem, which was originally done as an advertisement for Faber and Faber. It seemed to be fairly successful. Oh, yes, one wants to keep one's hand in, you know, in every type of poem, serious and frivolous and proper and improper. One doesn't want to lose one's skill.

INTERVIEWER: There's a good deal of interest now in the process of writing. I wonder if you could talk more about your actual habits in writing verse. I've heard you composed on the typewriter.

ELIOT: Partly on the typewriter. A great deal of my new play, *The Elder Statesman*, was produced in pencil and paper, very roughly. Then I typed it myself first before my wife got to work on it. In typing myself I make alterations, very considerable ones. But whether I write or type, composition of any length, a play for example, means for me regular hours, say ten to one. I found that three hours a day is about all I can do of actual composing. I could do polishing perhaps later. I sometimes found at first that I wanted to go on longer, but when I looked at the stuff the next day, what I'd done after the three hours were up was never satisfactory. It's much better to stop and think about something else quite different.

INTERVIEWER: Did you ever write any of your non-dramatic poems on schedule? Perhaps the *Four Quartets*?

ELIOT: Only "occasional" verse. The *Quartets* were not on schedule. Of course the first one was written in '35, but the three which were written during the war were more in fits and starts. In 1939 if there hadn't been a war I would probably have tried to write another play. And I think it's a very good thing I didn't have the opportunity. From my personal point of view, the one good thing the war did was to prevent me from writing another play too soon. I saw some of the things that were wrong with *Family Reunion*, but I think it was much better that any possible play was blocked for five years or so to get up a head of steam. The form of the *Quartets* fitted in very nicely to the conditions under which I was writing, or could write at all. I could write them in sections and I didn't have to have quite the same continuity; it didn't matter if a day or two elapsed when I did not write, as they frequently did, while I did war jobs.

INTERVIEWER: We have been mentioning your plays without talking about them. In *Poetry and Drama* you talked about your first plays. I wonder if you could tell us something about your intentions in *The Elder Statesman*.

ELIOT: I said something, I think, in *Poetry and Drama* about my ideal aims, which I never expect fully to realize. I started, really, from *The Family Reunion*, because *Murder in the Cathedral* is a period piece and something out of the ordinary. It is written in rather a special language, as you do when you're dealing with another period. It didn't solve any of the problems I was interested in. Later I thought that in *The Family Reunion* I was giving so much attention to the versification that I neglected the structure of the play. I think *The Family Reunion* is still the best of my plays in the way of poetry, although it's not very well constructed.

In *The Cocktail Party* and again in *The Confidential Clerk*, I went further in the way of structure. *The Cocktail Party* wasn't altogether satisfactory in that respect. It sometimes happens, disconcertingly, at any rate with a practitioner like myself, that it isn't always the things constructed most according to plan that are the most successful. People criticized the third act of *The Cocktail Party* as being rather an epilogue, so in *The Confidential Clerk* I wanted things to turn up in the third act which were fresh events. Of course, *The Confidential Clerk* was so well constructed in some ways that people thought it was just meant to be farce.

I wanted to get to learn the technique of the theater so well that I could then forget about it. I always feel it's not wise to violate rules until you know how to observe them.

I hope that *The Elder Statesman* goes further in getting more poetry in, at any rate, than *The Confidential Clerk* did. I don't feel that I've got to the point I aim at and I don't think I ever will, but I would like to feel I was getting a little nearer to it each time.

INTERVIEWER: Do you have a Greek model behind *The Elder Statesman*?

ELIOT: The play in the background is the *Oedipus at Colonus*. But I wouldn't like to refer to my Greek originals as models. I have always regarded them more as points of departure. That was one of the weaknesses of *The Family Reunion*; it was rather too close to the *Eumenides*. I tried to follow my original too literally and in that way led to confusion by mixing pre-Christian and post-Christian attitudes about matters of conscience and sin and guilt.

So in the subsequent three I have tried to take the Greek myth as a sort of springboard, you see. After all, what one gets essential and permanent, I think, in the old plays, is a situation. You can take the situation, rethink it in modern terms, develop your own characters from it, and let another plot develop out of that. Actually you get further and further away from the original. *The Cocktail Party* had to do with Alcestis simply because the question arose in my mind, what would the life of Admetus and Alcestis be, after she'd come back from the dead; I mean if there'd been a break like that, it couldn't go on just as before. Those two people were the center of the thing when I started and the other characters only developed out of it. The character of Celia, who came to be really the most important character in the play, was originally an appendage to a domestic situation.

INTERVIEWER: Do you still hold to the theory of levels in poetic drama (plot, character, diction, rhythm, meaning) which you put forward in 1932?

ELIOT: I am no longer very much interested in my own theories about poetic drama, especially those put forward before 1934. I have thought less about theories since I have given more time to writing for the theater.

INTERVIEWER: How does the writing of a play differ from the writing of poems?

ELIOT: I feel that they take quite different approaches. There is all the difference in the world between writing a play for an audience and writing a poem, in which you're writing primarily for yourself—although obviously you wouldn't be satisfied if the poem didn't mean something to other people afterward. With a poem you can say, "I got my feeling into words for myself. I now have the equivalent in words for that much of what I have felt." Also in a poem you're writing for your own voice, which is very important. You're thinking in terms of your own voice, whereas in a play from the beginning you have to realize that you're preparing something which is going into the hands of other people, unknown at the time you're writing it. Of course I won't say there aren't moments in a play when the two approaches may not converge, when I think ideally they *should*. Very often in Shakespeare they do, when he is writing a poem and thinking in terms of the theater and the actors and the audience all at once. And the two things are one. That's wonderful when you can get that. With me it only happens at odd moments.

INTERVIEWER: Have you tried at all to control the speaking of your verse by the actors? To make it seem more like verse?

ELIOT: I leave that primarily to the producer. The important thing is to have a producer who has the feeling of verse and who can guide them in just how emphatic to make the verse, just how far to depart from prose or how far to approach it. I only guide the actors if they ask me questions directly. Otherwise I think that they should get their advice through the producer. The important thing is to arrive at an agreement with him first, and then leave it to him.

INTERVIEWER: Do you feel that there's been a general tendency in your work, even in your poems, to move from a narrower to a larger audience?

ELIOT: I think that there are two elements in this. One is that I think that writing plays (that is *Murder in the Cathedral* and *The Family Reunion*) made a difference to the writing of the *Four Quartets*. I think that it led to a greater simplification of language and to speaking in a way which is more like conversing with your reader. I see the later *Quartets* as being much simpler and easier to understand than *The Waste Land* and "Ash Wednesday." Sometimes the thing I'm trying to say, the subject matter, may be difficult, but it seems to me that I'm saying it in a simpler way.

The other element that enters into it, I think, is just experience and maturity. I think that in the early poems it was a question of not being able to—of having more to say than one knew how to say, and having something one wanted to put into words and rhythm which one didn't have the command of words and rhythm to put in a way immediately apprehensible.

That type of obscurity comes when the poet is still at the stage of learning how to use language. You have to say the thing the difficult way. The only alternative is not saying it at all, at that stage. By the time of the *Four Quartets*, I couldn't have written in the style of *The Waste Land*. In *The Waste Land*, I wasn't even bothering whether I understood what I was saying. These things, however, become easier to people with time. You get used to having *The Waste Land*, or *Ulysses*, about.

INTERVIEWER: Do you feel that the *Four Quartets* are your best work?

ELIOT: Yes, and I'd like to feel that they get better as they go on. The second is better than the first, the third is better than the second, and the fourth is the best of all. At any rate, that's the way I flatter myself.

INTERVIEWER: This is a very general question, but I wonder if you could give advice to a young poet about what disciplines or attitudes he might cultivate to improve his art.

ELIOT: I think it's awfully dangerous to give general advice. I think the best one can do for a young poet is to criticize in detail a particular poem of his. Argue it with him if necessary; give him your opinion, and if there are any generalizations to be made, let him do them himself. I've found that different people have different ways of working and things come to them in different ways. You're never sure when you're uttering a statement that's generally valid for all poets or when it's something that only applies to yourself. I think nothing is worse than to try to form people in your own image.

INTERVIEWER: Do you think there's any possible generalization to be made about the fact that all the better poets now, younger than you, seem to be teachers?

ELIOT: I don't know. I think the only generalization that can be made of any value will be one which will be made a generation later. All you can say at this point is that at different times there are different possibilities of making a living, or different limitations on making a living. Obviously a poet has got to find a way of making a living apart from his poetry. After all, artists do a great deal of teaching, and musicians too.

INTERVIEWER: Do you think that the optimal career for a poet would involve no work at all but writing and reading?

ELIOT: No, I think that would be—but there again one can only talk about oneself. It is very dangerous to give an optimal career for everybody, but I feel quite sure that if I'd started by having independent means, if I hadn't had to bother about earning a living and could have given all my time to poetry, it would have had a deadening influence on me.

INTERVIEWER: Why?

ELIOT: I think that for me it's been very useful to exercise other activities, such as working in a bank, or publishing even. And I think also that the difficulty of not having as much time as I would like has given me a greater pressure of concentration. I mean it has prevented me from writing too much. The danger, as a rule, of having nothing else to do is that one might write too much rather than concentrating and perfecting smaller amounts. That would be *my* danger.

INTERVIEWER: Do you consciously attempt, now, to keep up with the poetry that is being written by young men in England and America?

ELIOT: I don't now, not with any conscientiousness. I did at one time when I was reading little reviews and looking out for new talent as a publisher. But as one gets older, one is not quite confident in one's own ability to distinguish new genius among younger men. You're always afraid that you are going as you have seen your elders go. At Faber and Faber now I have a younger colleague who reads poetry manuscripts. But even before that, when I came across new stuff that I thought had real merit, I would show it to younger friends whose critical judgment I trusted and get their opinion. But of course there is always the danger that there is merit where you don't see it. So I'd rather have younger people to look at things first. If they like it, they will show it to me, and see whether I like it too. When you get something that knocks over young people of taste and judgment and older people as well, then that's likely to be something important. Sometimes there's a lot of resistance. I shouldn't like to feel that I was resisting, as my work was resisted when it was new, by people who thought that it was imposture of some kind or other.

INTERVIEWER: Do you feel that younger poets in general have repudiated the experimentalism of the early poetry of this century? Few poets now seem to be resisted the way you were resisted, but some older critics like Herbert Read believe that poetry after you has been a regression to out-dated modes. When you talked about Milton the second time, you spoke of the function of poetry as a retarder of change, as well as a maker of change, in language.

ELIOT: Yes, I don't think you want a revolution every ten years.

INTERVIEWER: But is it possible to think that there has been a counterrevolution rather than an exploration of new possibilities?

ELIOT: No, I don't see anything that looks to me like a counterrevolution. After a period of getting away from the traditional forms, comes a period of curiosity in making new experiments with traditional forms. This can produce very good work if what has happened in between has made a difference: when it's not merely going back, but taking up an old form, which has been out of use for a time, and making something new with it. That is not counterrevolution. Nor does mere regression deserve the name. There is a tendency in some quarters to revert to Georgian scenery and sentiments: and among the public there are always people who prefer mediocrity, and when they get it, say, "What a relief! Here's some real poetry again." And there are also people who like poetry to be modern but for whom the really creative stuff is too strong—they need something diluted.

What seems to me the best of what I've seen in young poets is not reaction at all. I'm not going to mention any names, for I don't like to make public judgments about younger poets. The best stuff is a further development of a less revolutionary character than what appeared in earlier years of the century.

INTERVIEWER: I have some unrelated questions that I'd like to end with. In 1945 you wrote, "A poet must take as his material his own language as it is actually spoken around him." And later you wrote, "The music of poetry, then, will be a music latent in the common speech of his time." After the second remark, you disparaged "standardized BBC English." Now isn't one of the changes of the last fifty years, and perhaps even more of the last five years, the growing dominance of commercial speech through the means of communication? What you referred to as "BBC English" has become immensely more powerful through the ITA and BBC television, not to speak of CBS, NBC, and ABC. Does this development make the problem of the poet and his relationship to common speech more difficult?

ELIOT: You've raised a very good point there. I think you're right, it does make it more difficult.

INTERVIEWER: I wanted you to make the point.

ELIOT: Yes, but you wanted the point to be made. So I'll take the responsibility of making it: I do think that where you have these modern means of communication and means of imposing the speech and idioms of a small number on the mass of people at large, it does complicate the problem very much. I don't know to what extent that goes for film speech, but obviously radio speech has done much more.

INTERVIEWER: I wonder if there's a possibility that what you mean by common speech will disappear.

ELIOT: That is a very gloomy prospect. But very likely indeed.

INTERVIEWER: Are there other problems for a writer in our time which are unique? Does the prospect of human annihilation have any particular effect on the poet?

ELIOT: I don't see why the prospect of human annihilation should affect the poet differently from men of other vocations. It will affect him as a human being, no doubt in proportion to his sensitiveness.

INTERVIEWER: Another unrelated question: I can see why a man's criticism is better for his being a practicing poet, better although subject to his own prejudices. But do you feel that writing criticism has helped you as a poet?

ELIOT: In an indirect way it has helped me somehow as a poet—to put down in writing my critical valuation of the poets who have influenced me and whom I admire. It is merely making an influence more conscious and more articulate. It's been a rather natural impulse. I think probably my best critical essays are essays on the poets who had influenced me, so to speak, long before I thought of writing essays about them. They're of more value, probably, than any of my more generalized remarks.

INTERVIEWER: G. S. Fraser wonders, in an essay about the two of you, whether you ever met Yeats. From remarks in your talk about him, it would seem that you did. Could you tell us the circumstances?

ELIOT: Of course I had met Yeats many times. Yeats was always very gracious when one met him and had the art of treating younger writers as if they were his equals and contemporaries. I can't remember any one particular occasion.

INTERVIEWER: I have heard that you consider that your poetry belongs in the tradition of American literature. Could you tell us why?

ELIOT: I'd say that my poetry has obviously more in common

with my distinguished contemporaries in America than with anything written in my generation in England. That I'm sure of.

INTERVIEWER: Do you think there's a connection with the American past?

ELIOT: Yes, but I couldn't put it any more definitely than that, you see. It wouldn't be what it is, and I imagine it wouldn't be so good; putting it as modestly as I can, it wouldn't be what it is if I'd been born in England, and it wouldn't be what it is if I'd stayed in America. It's a combination of things. But in its sources, in its emotional springs, it comes from America.

INTERVIEWER: One last thing. Seventeen years ago you said, "No honest poet can ever feel quite sure of the permanent value of what he has written. He may have wasted his time and messed up his life for nothing." Do you feel the same now, at seventy?

ELIOT: There may be honest poets who do feel sure. I don't.

—DONALD HALL
1959

3. Robert Frost

Robert Frost was born in San Francisco on March 26, 1874. His father, an editor, politician, and Democrat, had gone there to escape the Republican atmosphere of New England. Sympathizing with the Southern cause, he christened his son Robert Lee Frost. When the senior Frost died, young Robert returned with his mother to New England to live with his paternal grandfather in Lawrence, Massachusetts. Here he soon began, but with little encouragement, his life-long commitment to poetry. He attended Dartmouth but could not abide the academic routine. At twenty-two he entered Harvard, specializing in Latin and Greek during his two years there. He then went to live on a farm in Derry, New Hampshire, teaching, doing occasional work for a local newspaper, and continuing to write his poems. It was a trip to England, however, in 1912, which gave his literary career its decisive push forward. There his first two books were published— A Boy's Will and North of Boston. When he returned to America in 1915, he was already well known, and his future as a poet and teacher was secure.

Mr. Frost received the Pulitzer Prize for poetry four times— in 1924, for New Hampshire; in 1931, for Collected Poems; in 1937, for A Further Range; and in 1943, for A Witness Tree. His last collection, In the Clearing, was published in 1962.

More than any other quality in Frost, his individualism stood out. He spurned what he called "the necessary group." As in other areas of life, he believed "there are too many gangs, cliques, or coteries in poetry. Maybe that's one of the ways they have to manage it. But I'm a lone wolf."

Robert Frost died on January 29, 1963.

I only say it as worth the thinking of
Best loyalty in friendship and in love
In lives like these me ought be a different thing
From what they say any used to be O King.

I do not like the way you shut / your eyes
when you say that," the King replies.
"Stand up and say it." The Vizier stood up
So suddenly he overset his cup.

"Never more dangerous than when affable
The King enjoys the moment to the full
He looks from face to face all down the board
To see with whom he has or hasn't scored.

The statesman stumbled: I don't know who started
this argument. But would you call false-hearted
The one who from devils dreads faction
Gave an attachment up for an attraction?

"you stand yourself of extrication.
you went bog got down in a situation. But
just what are you preparing to forsake
If you can tell us so we stay awake."

The men quivered wide awake with fear
Of what was happening to the Vizier.
Their only comfort in the thought
that they were not the traitors being caught

that shock

Manuscript page from an unpublished poem by Robert Frost.

HANS BECK

Robert Frost

Mr. Frost came into the front room of his house in Cambridge, Massachusetts, casually dressed, wearing high plaid slippers, offering greetings with a quiet, even diffident friendliness. But there was no mistaking the evidence of the enormous power of his personality. It made you at once aware of the thick, compacted strength of his body, even then at eighty-six; it was apparent in his face, actually too alive and spontaneously expressive to be as ruggedly heroic as in his photographs.

The impression of massiveness, far exceeding his physical size, wasn't separable from the public image he created and preserved. That this image was invariably associated with popular conceptions of New England was no simple matter of his own geographical preferences. New England is of course evoked in the scenes and titles of many of his poems and, more importantly, in his Emersonian tendencies, including his habit of contradicting himself, his capacity to "unsay" through the sound of his voice what his *words seem to assert. His special resemblance to New England, however, was that he, like it, had managed to impose upon the world a wholly self-created image. It was not the critics who defined him, it was Frost himself. He stood talking for a few minutes in the middle of the room, his remarkably ample, tousled white hair catching the late afternoon sun reflected off the snow in the road outside, and one wondered for a moment how he had managed over so long a life never to let his self-portrait be altered despite countless exposures to light less familiar and unintimidating. In the public world he resisted countless chances to lose himself in some particular fashion, some movement, like the Georgians, or even in an area of his own work which, to certain critics or readers, happened for the moment to appear more exotically colorful than the whole. In one of the most revealing parts of this interview, he said of certain of his poems that he didn't "want them out," the phrase itself, since all the poems involved have been published, offering an astonishing, even peculiar, evidence of the degree to which he felt in control of his poetic character. It indicated, too, his awareness that attempts to define him as a tragic philosophical poet of man and nature could be more constricting, because more painfully meaningful to him, than the simpler definitions they were designed to correct.*

More specifically, he seemed at various points to find the most immediate threat to his freedom in the tape recorder. Naturally, for a man both voluble and often mischievous in his recollections, Frost did not like the idea of being stuck, as he necessarily would be, with attitudes expressed in two hours of conversation. As an aggravation of this, he knew that no transcript taken from the tape could catch the subtleties of voice which give life and point to many of his statements. At a pause in the interview, Mr. Robert O'Clair, a friend and colleague at Harvard who had agreed to sit in as a sort of witness, admitted that we knew very little about running a tape recorder. Frost, who'd moved from his chair to see its workings, readily agreed. "Yes, I noticed that," he laughed, "and I respect you for it," adding at once—and this is the point of the story—that "they," presumably the people "outside," "like to hear me say nasty things about machines." A thoroughly supple knowledge of the ways in which the world tried to take him and a confidence that his own ways were more just and liberating was apparent here and everywhere in the conversation.

Frost was seated most of the time in a blue overstuffed chair which he had bought to write in. It had no arms, he began, and this left him the room he needed.

FROST: I never write except with a writing board. I've never had a table in my life. And I use all sorts of things. Write on the sole of my shoe.

INTERVIEWER: Why have you never liked a desk? Is it because you've moved around so much and lived in so many places?

FROST: Even when I was younger I never had a desk. I've never had a writing room.

INTERVIEWER: Is Cambridge your home base now pretty much?

FROST: In the winter. But I'm nearly five months in Ripton, Vermont. I make a long summer up there. But this is my office and business place.

INTERVIEWER: Your place in Vermont is near the Bread Loaf School of Writing, isn't it?

FROST: Three miles away. Not so near I know it's there. I'm a way off from it, down the mountain and up a side road. They connect me with it a good deal more than I'm there. I give a lecture at the school and a lecture at the conference. That's about all.

INTERVIEWER: You were a co-founder of the school, weren't you?

FROST: They say that. I think I had more to do with the starting of the conference. In a very casual way, I said to the president [of Middlebury], "Why don't you use the place for a little sociability after the school is over?" I thought of no regular business— no pay, no nothing, just inviting literary people, a few, for a week or two. The kitchen staff was still there. But then they started a regular business of it.

INTERVIEWER: When you were in England from 1912 to 1915, did you ever think you might possibly stay there?

FROST: No. No, I went over there to be poor for a while, nothing else. I didn't think of printing a book over there. I'd never offered a book to anyone here. I was thirty-eight years old, wasn't I? Something like that. And I thought the way to a book was the magazines. I hadn't too much luck with them, and nobody ever noticed me except to send me a check now and then. So I didn't think I was ready for a book. But I had written three books when I went over, the amount of three books—*A Boy's Will*, *North of Boston*, and part of the next [*Mountain Interval*] in a loose-leaf heap.

INTERVIEWER: What were the circumstances of your meeting Pound when you were in England?

FROST: That was through Frank Flint. The early imagist and translator. He was a friend of Pound and belonged in that little group there. He met me in a bookstore, said, "American?" And I said, "Yes. How'd you know?" He said, "Shoes." It was the Poetry Book Shop, Harold Monro's, just being organized. He said, "Poetry?" And I said, "I accept the omen." Then he said, "You should know your fellow countryman, Ezra Pound." And I said, "I've never heard of him." And I hadn't. I'd been skipping literary magazines—I don't ever read them very much—and the gossip, you know, I never paid much attention to. So he said, "I'm going to tell him you're here." And I had a card from Pound afterwards. I didn't use it for two or three months after that.

INTERVIEWER: He saw your book—*A Boy's Will*—just before publication, didn't he? How did that come about?

FROST: The book was already in the publishers' hands, but it hadn't come out when I met Pound, three or four months after he sent me his card. I didn't like the card very well.

INTERVIEWER: What did he say on it?

FROST: Just said, "At home, sometimes." Just like Pound. So I didn't feel that was a very warm invitation. Then one day walking past Church Walk in Kensington, I took his card out and went in to look for him. And I found him there, a little put out that I hadn't come sooner, in his Poundian way. And then he said, "Flint tells me you have a book." And I said, "Well, I ought to have." He said, "You haven't seen it?" And I said, "No." He said, "What do you say we go and get a copy?" He was eager about being the first one to talk. That's one of the best things you can say about Pound: he wanted to be the first to jump. Didn't call people up on the telephone to see how they were going to jump. He was all silent with eagerness. We walked over to my publisher; he got the book. Didn't show it to me—put it in his pocket. We went back to his room. He said, "You don't mind our liking this?" in his British accent, slightly. And I said, "Oh, go ahead and like it." Pretty soon he laughed at something, and I said I knew where that was in the book, what Pound would laugh at. And then pretty soon he said, "You better run along home, I'm going to review it." And I never touched it. I went home without my book and he kept it. I'd barely seen it in his hands.

INTERVIEWER: He wrote perhaps the first important favorable review, didn't he?

FROST: Yes. It was printed in the States, in Chicago, but it didn't help me much in England. The reviewing of the book there began right away, as soon as it was out. I guess most of those who reviewed it in England didn't know it had already been reviewed in Chicago. It didn't sound as though they did. But his review had something to do with the beginning of my reputation. I've always felt a little romantic about all that—that queer adventure he gave me. You know he had a mixed, a really curious position over there. He was friends with Yeats, Hueffer, and a very few others.

INTERVIEWER: Did you know Hueffer?

FROST: Yes, through him. And Yeats, through him.

INTERVIEWER: How much did you see of Yeats when you were in England?

FROST: Oh, quite a little, with Pound nearly always—I guess always.

INTERVIEWER: Did you feel when you left London to go live on a farm in Gloucestershire that you were making a choice against the kind of literary society you'd found in the city?

FROST: No, my choices had been not connected with my going to England even. My choice was almost unconscious in those days. I didn't know whether I had any position in the world at all, and I wasn't choosing positions. You see, my instinct was not to belong to any gang, and my instinct was against being confused with the—what do you call them?—they called themselves Georgians, Edwardians, something like that, the people Edward Marsh was interested in. I understand that he speaks of me in his book, but I never saw him.

INTERVIEWER: Was there much of a gang feeling among the literary people you knew in London?

FROST: Yes. Oh, yes. Funny over there. I suppose it's the same over here. I don't know. I don't "belong" here. But they'd say, "Oh, he's that fellow that writes about homely things for that crowd, for those people. Have you anybody like that in America?" As if it were set, you know. Like Masefield—they didn't know Masefield in this gang, but, "Oh, he's that fellow that does this thing, I believe, for that crowd."

INTERVIEWER: Your best friend in those years was Edward Thomas?

FROST: Yes—quite separate again from everybody his age. He was as isolated as I was. Nobody knew he wrote poetry. He didn't write poetry until he started to war, and that had something to do with my life with him. We got to be great friends. No, I had an instinct against belonging to any of those crowds. I've had friends, but very scattering, a scattering over there. You know, I could have . . . Pound had an afternoon meeting once a week with Flint and Aldington and H. D. and at one time Hulme, I think. Hulme started with them. They met every week to rewrite each other's poems.

INTERVIEWER: You saw Hulme occasionally? Was it at these rewriting sessions, or didn't you bother with them?

FROST: Yes, I knew Hulme, knew him quite well. But I never went to one of those meetings. I said to Pound, "What do you do?" He said, "Rewrite each other's poems." And I said, "Why?" He said, "To squeeze the water out of them." "That sounds like a parlor game to me," I said, "and I'm a serious artist"—kidding, you know. And he laughed and he didn't invite me any more.

INTERVIEWER: These personal associations that you had in England with Pound and Edward Thomas and what you call the

Georgians—these had nothing to do with your establishing a sense of your own style, did they? You'd already written what were to be nearly the first three volumes of your poetry.

FROST: Two and a half books, you might say. There are some poems out in Huntington Library that I must have written in the nineties. The first one of mine that's still in print was in '90. It's in print still, kicking round.

INTERVIEWER: Not in *A Boy's Will*—the earliest poem published in there was written in '94, I think.

FROST: No, it's not in there. First one I ever *sold* is in there. The first one I ever had printed was the first one I wrote. I never wrote prose or verse till 1890. Before that I wrote Latin and Greek sentences.

INTERVIEWER: Some of the early critics like Garnett and Pound talk a lot about Latin and Greek poetry with reference to yours. You'd read a lot in the classics?

FROST: Probably more Latin and Greek than Pound ever did.

INTERVIEWER: Didn't you teach Latin at one time?

FROST: Yes. When I came back to college after running away, I thought I could stand it if I stuck to Greek and Latin and philosophy. That's all I did those years.

INTERVIEWER: Did you read much in the Romantic poets? Wordsworth, in particular?

FROST: No, you couldn't pin me there. Oh, I read all sorts of things. I said to some Catholic priests the other day when they asked me about reading, I said, "If you understand the word 'catholic,' I was very catholic in my taste."

INTERVIEWER: What sort of things did your mother read to you?

FROST: That I wouldn't be able to tell you. All sorts of things, not too much, but some. She was a very hard-worked person— she supported us. Born in Scotland, but grew up in Columbus, Ohio. She was a teacher in Columbus for seven years—in mathematics. She taught with my father one year after he left Harvard and before he went to California. You know they began to teach in high schools in those days right after coming out of high school themselves. I had teachers like that who didn't go to college. I had two noted teachers in Latin and Greek who weren't college women at all. They taught Fred Robinson.* I had the same teachers he had. Fritz Robinson, the old scholar. My mother was just like that. Began teaching at eighteen in the high school, then married along about twenty-five. I'm putting all this together rather lately, finding out strolling round like I do. Just dug up in Pennsylvania the date of her marriage and all that, in Lewistown, Pennsylvania.

INTERVIEWER: Your mother ran a private school in Lawrence, Massachusetts, didn't she?

FROST: Yes, she did, round Lawrence. She had a private school. And I taught in that some, as well as taking some other schools. I'd go out and teach in district schools whenever I felt like springtime.

INTERVIEWER: How old were you then?

FROST: Oh, just after I'd run away from Dartmouth, along there in '93, '4, twenty years old. Every time I'd get sick of the city I'd go out for the springtime and take school for one term. I did that I think two or three times, that same school. Little school with twelve children, about a dozen children, all barefooted. I did newspaper work in Lawrence, too. I followed my father and mother in that, you know. I didn't know what I wanted to do with myself to earn a living. Taught a little, worked on a paper a little, worked on farms a little, that was my own departure. But I just followed my parents in newspaper work. I edited a paper a while—a weekly paper—and then I was on a regular paper. I see its name still up there in Lawrence.

INTERVIEWER: When you started to write poetry, was there any poet that you admired very much?

FROST: I was the enemy of that theory, that idea of Stevenson's that you should play the sedulous ape to anybody. That did more harm to American education than anything ever got out.

INTERVIEWER: Did you ever feel any affinity between your work and any other poet's?

* Editor of *Chaucer*, and formerly a professor of English at Harvard.

FROST: I'll leave that for somebody else to tell me. I wouldn't know.

INTERVIEWER: But when you read Robinson or Stevens, for example, do you find anything that is familiar to you from your own poetry?

FROST: Wallace Stevens? He was years after me.

INTERVIEWER: I mean in your reading of him, whether or not you felt any—

FROST: Any affinity, you mean? Oh, you couldn't say that. No. Once he said to me, "You write on subjects." And I said, "You write on bric-a-brac." And when he sent me his next book he'd written "S'more bric-a-brac" in it. Just took it good-naturedly. No, I had no affinity with him. We were friends. Oh, gee, miles away. I don't know who you'd connect me with.

INTERVIEWER: Well, you once said in my hearing that Robert Lowell had tried to connect you with Faulkner, told you you were a lot like Faulkner.

FROST: Did I say that?

INTERVIEWER: No, you said that Robert Lowell told you that you were a lot like Faulkner.

FROST: Well, you know what Robert Lowell said once? He said, "My uncle's dialect—the New England dialect, *The Bigelow Papers*—was just the same as Burns's, wasn't it?" I said, "Robert! Burns's was not a dialect, Scotch is not a dialect. It's a language." But he'd say anything, Robert, for the hell of it.

INTERVIEWER: You've never, I take it then, been aware of any particular line of preference in your reading?

FROST: Oh, I read 'em all. One of my points of departure is an anthology. I find a poet I admire, and I think, well, there must be a lot to that. Some old one—Shirley, for instance, "The glories of our blood and state"—that sort of splendid poem. I go looking for more. Nothing. Just a couple like that and that's all. I remember certain boys took an interest in certain poems with me in old times. I remember Brower one day in somebody else's class when he was a student at Amherst—Reuben Brower, afterwards the Master of Adams House at Harvard. I remember I said, "Anyone want to read that poem to me?" It was "In going to my naked bed as one that would have slept," Edwards's old poem. He read it so well I said, "I give you A for life." And that's the way we joke with each other. I never had him regularly in a class of mine. I visited other classes up at Amherst and noticed him very early. Goodness sake, the way his voice fell into those lines, the natural way he did that very difficult poem with that old quotation—"The falling out of faithful friends is the renewing of love." I'm very catholic, that's about all you can say. I've hunted. I'm not thorough like the people educated in Germany in the old days. I've none of that. I hate the idea that you ought to read the whole of anybody. But I've done a lot of looking sometimes, read quite a lot.

INTERVIEWER: When you were in England did you find yourself reading the kind of poetry Pound was reading?

FROST: No. Pound was reading the troubadours.

INTERVIEWER: Did you talk to one another about any particular poets?

FROST: He admired at that time, when I first met him, Robinson and de la Mare. He got over admiring de la Mare anyway, and I think he threw out Robinson too. We'd just bring up a couple of little poems. I was around with him quite a little for a few weeks. I was charmed with his ways. He cultivated a certain rudeness to people that he didn't like, just like Willy Whistler. I thought he'd come under the influence of Whistler. They cultivated the French style of boxing. They used to kick you in the teeth.

INTERVIEWER: With grace.

FROST: Yes. You know the song, the nasty song: "They fight with their feet—" Among other things, what Pound did was show me Bohemia.

INTERVIEWER: Was there much Bohemia to see at that time?

FROST: More than I had ever seen. I'd never had any. He'd take me to restaurants and things. Showed me jiu jitsu in a restaurant. Threw me over his head.

INTERVIEWER: Did he do that?

FROST: Wasn't ready for him at all. I was just as strong as he was. He said, "I'll show you, I'll show you. Stand up." So I stood up, gave him my hand. He grabbed my wrist, tipped over backwards and threw me over his head.

INTERVIEWER: How did you like that?

FROST: Oh, it was all right. Everybody in the restaurant stood up. He used to talk about himself as a tennis player. I never played tennis with him. And then he'd show you all these places with these people that specialized in poets that dropped their aitches and things like that. Not like the "beatniks," quite. I remember one occasion they had a poet in who had a poem in the *English Review* on Aphrodite, how he met Aphrodite at Leatherhead.* He was coming in and he was a navvy. I don't remember his name, never heard of him again—may have gone on and had books. But he was a real navvy. Came in with his bicycle clips on. Tea party. Everybody horrified in a delighted way, you know. Horror, social horror. Red-necked, thick, heavy-built fellow, strong fellow, you know, like John L. Lewis or somebody. But he was a poet. And then I saw poets made out of whole cloth by Ezra. Ezra thought he did that. Take a fellow that had never written anything and think he could make a poet out of him. We won't go into that.

INTERVIEWER: I wonder about your reaction to such articles as the recent lead article by Karl Shapiro in the *New York Times Book Review* which praised you because presumably you're not guilty of "Modernism" as Pound and Eliot are. [*Telephone rings.*]

FROST: Is that my telephone? Just wait a second. Halt! [*Interruption. Frost leaves for phone call.*]

FROST: Where were we? Oh yes, you were trying to trace me.

---

* Frost is thinking of a poet named John Helston, author of "Aphrodite at Leatherhead," which took up fourteen pages of the *English Review* for March 1913. Frost's recollection gives a special flavor, if one is needed, to the note appended to the poem by the editors of the magazine: "Without presuming to 'present' Mr. Helston after the manner of fashionable actors, we think it will interest the public to know that he was for years a working mechanic— turner, fitter, etc.—in electrical, locomotive, motor-car, and other workshops."

INTERVIEWER: I wasn't trying to trace you. I was—

FROST: Oh, this thing about Karl Shapiro. Yeah, isn't it funny? So often they ask me—I just been all around, you know, been out West, been all around—and so often they ask me, "What is a modern poet?" I dodge it often, but I said the other night, "A modern poet must be one that speaks to modern people no matter when he lived in the world. That would be one way of describing it. And it would make him more modern, perhaps, if he were *alive* and speaking to modern people."

INTERVIEWER: Yes, but in their way of speaking, Eliot and Pound seem to many people to be writing in a tradition that is very different from yours.

FROST: Yes. I suppose Eliot's isn't as far away as Pound's. Pound seemed to me very like a troubadour, more like the troubadours or a blend of several of them, Bertrand de Born and Arnault Daniel. I never touched that. I don't know Old French. I don't like foreign languages that I haven't had. I don't read translations of things. I like to say dreadful, unpleasant things about Dante. Pound, though, he's supposed to know Old French.

INTERVIEWER: Pound was a good linguist, wasn't he?

FROST: I don't know that. There's a teacher of his down in Florida that taught him at the University of Pennsylvania. He once said to me, "Pound? I had him in Latin, and Pound never knew the difference between a declension and a conjugation." He's death on him. Old man, still death on Ezra. [*Breaks into laughter.*] Pound's gentle art of making enemies.

INTERVIEWER: Do you ever hear from Pound? Do you correspond with him now?

FROST: No. He wrote me a couple of letters when I got him out of jail last year. Very funny little letters, but they were all right.

INTERVIEWER: Whom did you speak to in Washington about that?

FROST: Just the Attorney General. Just settled it with him. I went down twice with Archie [MacLeish] and we didn't get anything done because they were of opposite parties, I think. And I don't belong to any party.

INTERVIEWER: Yes, but weren't you named Robert Lee because your father was a stanch Democrat around the time of the Civil War? That makes you a Democrat of sorts, doesn't it?

FROST: Yeah, I'm a Democrat. I was born a Democrat—and been unhappy ever since 1896. Somebody said to me, "What's the difference between that and being a Republican?" Well, I went down after we'd failed, and after Archie thought we'd failed, I just went down alone, walked into the Attorney General's office and said, "I come down here to see what your mood is about Ezra Pound." And two of them spoke up at once. "Our mood's your mood; let's get him out." Just like that, that's all. And I said, "This week?" They said, "This week if you say so. You go get a lawyer, and we'll raise no objection." So, since they were Republicans, I went over and made friends with Thurman Arnold, that good leftish person, for my lawyer. I sat up that night and wrote an appeal to the court that I threw away, and, in the morning, just before I left town, I wrote another one, a shorter one. And that's all there was to it. Ezra thanked me in a very short note that read: "Thanks for what you're doing. A little conversation would be in order." Then signed, in large letters. And then he wrote me another one, a nicer one.

INTERVIEWER: Did you see him before he left for Italy?

FROST: No, no, I didn't want to high-hat him. I wanted him to feel kind of free from me. Bet he feels, evidently, a little gratitude of some kind. He's not very well, you know. Some of them didn't want . . . [*What Frost was about to say here, it turned out later in the interview, not recorded, was that some friends of Pound—he mentioned Merrill Moore—felt Pound would be better off staying in St. Elizabeths Hospital. Moore said that Pound had a room to himself and a cabana!*] Well, it's a sad business. And he's a poet. I never, I never questioned that. We've been friends all the way along, but I didn't like what he did in wartime. I only heard it second-hand, so I didn't judge it too closely. But it sounded pretty bad. He was very foolish in what he bet on and whenever anybody really loses that way, I don't want to rub it into him.

INTERVIEWER: I've been asking a lot of questions about the relationship of your poetry to other poetry, but of course there are many other non-literary things that have been equally important. You've been very much interested in science, for example.

FROST: Yes, you're influenced by the science of your time, aren't you? Somebody noticed that all through my book there's astronomy.

INTERVIEWER: Like "The Literate Farmer and the Planet Venus"?

FROST: Yes, but it's all through the book, all through the book. Many poems—I can name twenty that have astronomy in them. Somebody noticed that the other day: "Why has nobody ever seen how much you're interested in astronomy?" That's a bias, you could say. One of the earliest books I hovered over, hung around, was called *Our Place Among the Infinities*, by an astronomer in England named Proctor, noted astronomer. It's a noted old book. I mention that in one of the poems: I use that expression "our place among the infinities" from that book that I must have read as soon as I read any book, thirteen or fourteen, right in there I began to read. That along with *Scottish Chiefs*. I remember that year when I first began to read a book through. I had a little sister who read everything through, lots of books, everybody's books— very young, precocious. Me, I was—they turned me out of doors for my health.

INTERVIEWER: While we're thinking about science and literature, I wonder if you have any reaction to the fact that Massachusetts Institute of Technology is beginning to offer a number of courses in literature?

FROST: I think they'd better tend to their higher mathematics and higher science. Pure science. They know I think that. I don't mean to criticize them too much. But you see it's like this: the greatest adventure of man is science, the adventure of penetrating into matter, into the material universe. But the adventure is our property, a human property, and the best description of us is the humanities. Maybe the scientists wanted to remind their students that the humanities describe you who are adventuring into science, and science adds very little to that description of you, a little tiny bit. Maybe in psychology, or in something like that, but it's awful little. And so, the scientists to remind their students of all this give them half their time over there in the humanities now. And that seems a little unnecessary. They're worried about us and the pure sciences all the time. They'd better get as far as they can into their own subject. I was over there at the beginning of this and expressed my little doubts about it. I was there with Compton one night—he was sitting on the platform beside me. "We've been short"—I turned to him before the audience— "we've been a little short in pure science, haven't we?" He said, "Perhaps—I'm afraid we may have been." I said, "I think that better be tended to." That's years ago.

INTERVIEWER: You just mentioned psychology. You once taught psychology, didn't you?

FROST: That was entirely a joke. I could teach psychology. I've been asked to join a firm of psychiatrists, you know [by Merrill Moore], and that's more serious. But I went up there to disabuse the Teacher's College of the idea that there is any immediate connection between any psychology and their classroom work, disabuse them of the notion that they could mesmerize a class if they knew enough psychology. That's what they all thought.

INTERVIEWER: Weren't you interested at one time in William James?

FROST: Yes, that was partly what drew me back to Harvard. But he was away all the time I was around here. I had Santayana, Royce, and all the philosophy crowd, Munsterberg, George Herbert Palmer, the old poetical one. I had 'em all. But I was there waiting for James, and I lost interest.

INTERVIEWER: Did Santayana interest you very much at the time?

FROST: No, not particularly. Well, yes. I always wondered what he really meant, where he was headed, what it all came to. Followed that for years. I never knew him personally. I never knew anybody personally in college. I was a kind of—went my own way. But I admired him. It was golden utterance—he was something to listen to, just like his written style. But I wondered what he really meant. I found years afterward somewhere in his words that all was illusion, of two kinds, true and false. And I decided false illusion would be the truth: two negatives make an affirmative.

INTERVIEWER: While we're on things other than poetry that you were and are interested in, we might get onto politics for a moment. I remember one evening your mentioning that Henry Wallace became somehow associated with your poem, "Provide, Provide."

FROST: People exaggerate such things. Henry Wallace was in Washington when I read the poem. Sat right down there in the first row. And when I got to the end of it where it says, "Better to go down dignified—With boughten friendship at your side— Than none at all. Provide, Provide!" I added, "Or somebody else will provide for ya." He smiled; his wife smiled. They were right down there where I could see them.

INTERVIEWER: Well, you don't have a reputation for being a New Dealer.

FROST: They think I'm no New Dealer. But really and truly I'm not, you know, all that clear on it. In "The Death of the Hired Man" that I wrote long, long ago, long before the New Deal, I put it two ways about home. One would be the manly way: "Home is the place where, when you have to go there, They have to take you in." That's the man's feeling about it. And then the wife says, "I should have called it/Something you somehow hadn't to deserve." That's the New Deal, the feminine way of it, the mother way. You don't have to deserve your mother's love. You have to deserve your father's. He's more particular. One's a Republican, one's a Democrat. The father is always a Republican toward his son, and his mother's always a Democrat. Very few have noticed that second thing; they've always noticed the sarcasm, the hardness of the male one.

INTERVIEWER: That poem is often anthologized, and I wonder if you feel that the poems of yours that appear most often in the ˈ˞ˈ⁓˞es represent you very well.

I'm always pleased when somebody digs up a new one. how. I leave that in the lap of the gods, as they say.

INTERVIEWER: There are some I seldom see; for example, "A Servant to Servants" or "The Most of It" or "The Subverted Flower." All of these I noticed the other day are omitted, for instance, from Untermeyer's anthology of your poems. Strange, isn't it?

FROST: Well, he was making his own choice. I never said a word to him, never urged him. I remember he said [Edward Arlington] Robinson only did once. Robinson told him, "If you want to please an old man you won't overlook my 'Mr. Flood's Party.' " That is a beautiful poem.

INTERVIEWER: Do you feel that any particular area of your work hasn't been anthologized?

FROST: I wouldn't know that. "The Subverted Flower," for instance, nobody's ever touched. No—I guess it is; it's in Matty's [F. O. Matthiessen's] anthology. That's the one he made for the Oxford people.

INTERVIEWER: Yes, but its appearance is extremely rare in any selection of your work. It doesn't seem to fit some people's preconceptions about you. Another neglected poem, and an especially good one, is "Putting In the Seed."

FROST: That's—sure. They leave that sort of thing out; they overlook that sort of thing with me. The only person ever noticed that was a hearty old friend of mine down at the University of Pennsylvania, Cornelius Weygandt.* He said, "I know what *that's* about."

INTERVIEWER: Do you ever read that poem in public?

FROST: No, I don't bother with those. No, there are certain ones. I wouldn't read "The Subverted Flower" to anybody outside. It isn't that I'm afraid of them, but I don't want them out. I'm shy about certain things in my books, they're more— I'd rather they'd be read. A woman asked me, "What do you mean by that 'subverted flower'?" I said, "Frigidity in women." She left.

INTERVIEWER: Do you think that it was to correct the public assumption that your poetry is represented by the most anthologized pieces such as "Birches" that Lionel Trilling in his speech

* Author of historical and descriptive studies of New Hampshire.

at your eighty-fifth birthday emphasized poems of a darker mood?

FROST: I don't know—I might run my eye over my book after Trilling, and wonder why he hadn't seen it sooner: that there's plenty to be dark about, you know. It's full of darkness.

INTERVIEWER: Do you suppose he imagined he was correcting some sort of public ignorance—some general mistake about your work?

FROST: He made the mistake himself. He was admitting he made it himself, wasn't he? He was telling what trouble he'd had to get at me. Sort of a confession, but very pleasant.

INTERVIEWER: That's true, but many admirers of yours did object to his emphasis on the "darkness" or "terror" in your poems.

FROST: Yes, well, he took me a little by surprise that night. He was standing right beside me and I had to get up right after him. Birthday party. And it took me—it didn't hurt me, but I thought at first he was attacking me. Then when he began comparing me to Sophocles and D. H. Lawrence I was completely at sea. What the two of them had to do with me, you know. Might be I might like it about Sophocles, but I'd be puzzled, oh, utterly at sea about D. H. Lawrence. It's all right, though. I had to get up and recite soon after that, and so I was a little puzzled what to recite to illustrate what he was talking about. And right there—new to me: I hadn't read his paper. I'd never read him much. I don't read criticism. You see no magazines in the house.

INTERVIEWER: Did you feel better about his talk when you read his substantiation of it in the *Partisan Review*?

FROST: I read his defense of it. Very clever, very—very interesting. Admired him. He's a very—intellectual man. But I read very little, generally, in the magazines. Hadn't read that Shapiro thing you mentioned. That's news to me what he said. Is he a friend of mine?

INTERVIEWER: Oh, yes. He's a friend of yours, but he's like many friends of yours: he chooses to see in you something more simple than your best friends see. It's a bit like J. Donald Adams, also in the *Times*, angrily defending you against Trilling, only J. Donald Adams doesn't understand you very well either.

FROST: What was Shapiro saying?

INTERVIEWER: He was saying that most modern poetry is o.
and overdifficult, that this is particularly true of Pound and Ei.
but that it isn't true of you.

FROST: Well, I don't want to be difficult. I like to fool—
oh, you know, you like to be mischievous. But not in that dull
way of just being dogged and doggedly obscure.

INTERVIEWER: The difficulty of your poetry is perhaps in
your emphasis on variety in tones of voice. You once said
that consciously or unconsciously it was tones of voice that
you counted on to double the meaning of every one of your
statements.

FROST: Yes, you could do that. Could unsay everything I said,
nearly. Talking contraries—it's in one of the poems. Talk by
contraries with people you're very close to. They know what you're
talking about. This whole thing of suggestiveness and *double
entendre* and hinting—comes down to the word "hinting." With
people you can trust you can talk in hints and suggestiveness.
Families break up when people take hints you don't intend and
miss hints you do intend. You can watch that going on, as a
psychologist. I don't know. No, don't . . . no don't you . . . don't
think of me . . . See, I haven't led a literary life. These fellows,
they *really* work away with their prose trying to describe themselves
and understand themselves, and so on. I don't do that. I don't
want to know too much about myself. It interests me to know
that Shapiro thinks I'm not difficult. That's all right. I never wrote
a review in my life, never wrote articles. I'm constantly refusing
to write articles. These fellows are all literary men. I don't have
hours; I don't work at it, you know. I'm not a farmer, that's no
pose of mine. But I have farmed some, and I putter around. And
I walk and I live with other people. Like to talk a lot. But I haven't
had a very literary life, and I'm never very much with the gang.
I'm vice-president, no, I'm Honorary President of the Poetry
Society of America. Once in a great while I go. And I wish them
well. I wish the foundations would take them all, take care of
them all.

INTERVIEWER: Speaking of foundations, why do you think big

business, so long the object of literary ridicule for being philistine, should now be supporting so much literary effort?

FROST: It's funny they haven't sooner, because most of them have been to college and had poetry pushed into them. About half the reading they do in all languages will be in verse. Just think of it. And so they have a kind of respect for it all and they probably don't mind the abuse they've had from our quarter. They're people who're worried that we just don't have enough imagination—it's the lack of imagination they're afraid of in our system. If we had enough imagination we could lick the Russians. I feel like saying, "Probably we won the Civil War with Emily Dickinson." We didn't even know she was there. Poor little thing.

INTERVIEWER: Would you agree that there are probably more good prizes for poetry today than there are good poets?

FROST: I don't know. I hate to judge that. It's nice for them—it's so nice for them to be interested in us, with their foundations. You don't know what'll come of it. You know the real thing is that the sense of sacrifice and risk is one of the greatest stimuli in the world. And you take that all out of it—take that away from it so that there's no risk in being a poet, I bet you'd lose a lot of the pious spirits. They're in it for the—hell of it. Just the same as these fellows breaking through the sound barrier up there, just the same. I was once asked in public, in front of four or five hundred women, just how I found leisure to write. I said, "Confidentially—since there's only five hundred of you here, and all women—like a sneak I stole some of it, like a man I seized some of it—and I had a little in my tin cup." Sounds as if I'd been a beggar, but I've never been consciously a beggar. I've been at the mercy of . . . I've been a beneficiary around colleges and all. And this is one of the advantages to the American way: I've never had to write a word of thanks to anybody I had a cent from. The colleges came between. Poetry has always been a beggar. Scholars have also been beggars, but they delegate their begging to the president of the college to do for them.

INTERVIEWER: I was suggesting just now that perhaps the number of emoluments for poets greatly exceeds the number of people whose work deserves to be honored. Isn't this a situation in which mediocrity will necessarily be exalted? And won't this make it more rather than less difficult for people to recognize really good achievement when it does occur?

FROST: You know, I was once asked that, and I said I never knew how many disadvantages anyone needed to get anywhere in the world. And you don't know how to measure that. No psychology will ever tell you who needs a whip and who needs a spur to win races. I think the greatest thing about it with me has been this, and I wonder if others think it. I look at a poem as a performance. I look on the poet as a man of prowess, just like an athlete. He's a performer. And the things you can do in a poem are very various. You speak of figures, tones of voice varying all the time. I'm always interested, you know, when I have three or four stanzas, in the way I *lay* the sentences in them. I'd hate to have the sentences all lie the same in the stanzas. Every poem is like that: some sort of achievement in performance. Somebody has said that poetry among other things is the marrow of wit. That's probably way back somewhere—marrow of wit. There's got to be wit. And that's very, very much left out of a lot of this labored stuff. It doesn't sparkle at all. Another thing to say is that every thought, poetical or otherwise, every thought is a feat of association. They tell of old Gibbon—as he was dying he was the same Gibbon at his historical parallels. All thought is a feat of association: having what's in front of you bring up something in your mind that you almost didn't know you knew. Putting this and that together. That click.

INTERVIEWER: Can you give an example of how this feat of association—as you call it—works?

FROST: Well, one of my masques turns on one association like that. God says, "I was just showing off to the Devil, Job." Job looks puzzled about it, distressed a little. God says, "Do you mind?" And, "No, no," he says, "No," in that tone, you know, "No," and so on. That tone is everything, the way you say that "no." I noticed that—that's what made me write that. Just that one thing made that.

INTERVIEWER: Did your other masque—*Masque of Mercy*—have a similar impetus?

FROST: I noticed that the first time in the world's history when mercy is entirely the subject is in Jonah. It does say somewhere earlier in the Bible, "If ten can be found in the city, will you spare it? Ten good people?" But in Jonah there is something worse than that. Jonah is told to go and prophesy against the city—and he *knows* God will let him down. He can't trust God to be unmerciful. You can trust God to be anything but unmerciful. So he ran away and—and got into a whale. That's the point of that and nobody notices it. They miss it.

INTERVIEWER: Why do you suppose, Mr. Frost, that among religious groups the masques had their best reception among Jesuits and rabbis?

FROST: Amusing you say that—that's true. The other, the lesser sects without the law, you see, they don't get it. They're too apt to think there's rebellion in them—what they go through with their parents when they're growing up. But that isn't in them at all, you know. They're not rebellious. They're very doctrinal, very orthodox, both of them. But how'd you notice that? It's amusing to me too. You see, the rabbis have been fine to me and so have the SJ's particularly, all over the country. I've just been in Kansas City staying with them. See, the masques are full of good orthodox doctrine. One of them turns on the thought that evil shows off to good and good shows off to evil. I made a couplet out of that for them in Kansas City, just the way I often do, offhand: "It's from their having stood contrasted/That good and bad so long have lasted."

INTERVIEWER: Making couplets "offhand" is something like writing on schedule, isn't it? I know a young poet who claims he can write every morning from six to nine, presumably before class.

FROST: Well, there's more than one way to skin a cat. I don't know what that would be like, myself. When I get going on something, I don't want to just—you know . . . Very first one I wrote I was walking home from school and I began to make it— a March day—and I was making it all afternoon and making it so I was late at my grandmother's for dinner. I finished it, but it burned right up, just burned right up, you know. And what started that? What burned it? So many talk, I wonder how falsely, about what it costs them, what agony it is to write. I've often been quoted: "No tears in the writer, no tears in the reader. No surprise for the writer, no surprise for the reader." But another distinction I made is: however sad, no grievance, grief without grievance. How could I, how could anyone have a good time with what cost me too much agony, how could they? What do I want to communicate but what a *hell* of a good time I had writing it? The whole thing is performance and prowess and feats of association. Why don't critics talk about those things—what a feat it was to turn that that way, and what a feat it was to remember that, to be reminded of that by this? Why don't they talk about that? Scoring. You've got to *score*. They say not, but you've got to score, in all the realms—theology, politics, astronomy, history, and the country life around you.

INTERVIEWER: What do you think of the performances of the poets who have made your birthplace, San Francisco, into their headquarters?

FROST: Have they? Somebody said I saw a lot of them in Kansas City at the end of my audience. They said, "See that blur over there? That's whiskers." No, I don't know much about that. I'm waiting for them to say something that I can get hold of. The worse the better. I like it anyway, you know. Like you say to somebody, "Say something. Say something." And he says, "I burn."

INTERVIEWER: Do young poets send you things?

FROST: Yes, some—not much, because I don't respond. I don't write letters and all that. But I get a little, and I meet them, talk with them. I get some books. I wonder what they're at. There's one book that sounded as if it might be good, "Aw, hell." The book was called "Aw, hell." Because "aw," the way you say "aw," you know, "Aw, hell!" That might be something.

INTERVIEWER: Most of the titles are funny. One is called *Howl* and another *Gasoline*.

FROST: *Gasoline*, eh? I've seen a little of it, kicking round. I saw a bunch of nine of them in a magazine in Chicago when I was through there. They were all San Franciscans. Nothing I could talk about afterwards, though, either way. I'm always glad of anybody that says anything awful. I can use it. We're all like that. You've got to learn to enjoy a lot of things you don't like. And I'm always ready for somebody to say some outrageous thing. I feel like saying, "Hold that now, long enough for me to go away and tell on you, won't you? Don't go back on it tomorrow." Funny world.

INTERVIEWER: When you look at a new poem that might be sent to you, what is it usually that makes you want to read it all or not want to read it?

FROST: This thing of performance and prowess and feats of association—that's where it all lies. One of my ways of looking at a poem right away it's sent to me, right off, is to see if it's rhymed. Then I know just when to look at it. The rhymes come in pairs, don't they? And nine times out of ten with an ordinary writer, one of two of the terms is better than the other. One makeshift will do, and then they get another that's good, and then another makeshift, and then another one that's good. That is in the realm of performance, that's the deadly test with me. I want to be unable to tell which of those he thought of first. If there's any trick about it, putting the better one first so as to deceive me, I can tell pretty soon. That's all in the performance realm. They can belong to any school of thought they want to, Spinoza or Schopenhauer, it doesn't matter to me. A Cartesian I heard Poe called, a Cartesian philosopher, the other day . . . tsssssss . . .

INTERVIEWER: You once saw a manuscript of Dylan Thomas's where he'd put all the rhymes down first and then backed into them. That's clearly not what you mean by performance, is it?

FROST: See, that's very dreadful. It ought to be that you're thinking forward, with the feeling of strength that you're getting them good all the way, carrying out some intention more felt than thought. It begins. And what it is that guides us—what is it? Young people wonder about that, don't they? But I tell them it's just the same as when you feel a joke coming. You see somebody coming down the street that you're accustomed to abuse, ¹ you feel it rising in you, something to say as you pass each other. Coming over him the same way. And where do these thoughts come from? Where does a thought? Something does it to you. It's him coming toward you that gives you the animus, you know. When they want to know about inspiration, I tell them it's mostly animus.

—RICHARD POIRIER
1961

4. Marianne Moore

Marianne Craig Moore was born in St. Louis, Missouri, on November 15, 1887. She attended Metzger Institute in Carlisle, Pennsylvania, then Bryn Mawr, from which she was graduated in 1909. The following year she was graduated from Carlisle Commercial College. From 1911 to 1915 she taught stenography and other commercial subjects at the United States Industrial Indian School, Carlisle, and from 1921 to 1925 was an assistant in the New York Public Library.

Miss Moore's first poems appeared in Bryn Mawr College publications; in 1917 some of her work was published in *The Egoist*, London, and later in Harriet Monroe's *Poetry*. In 1921 Winifred Ellerman (Bryher) and the poet Hilda Doolittle (H.D.), without the knowledge of Miss Moore, brought out *Poems* (The Egoist Press). In 1925, Miss Moore joined the editorial staff of *The Dial* and continued work with that magazine until its demise.

In her lifetime, Marianne Moore won nearly all the prizes for poetry which are presented in this country, and in 1947 she was elected a member of the National Institute of Arts and Letters. Her published work includes *Observations* (1924), *Selected Poems* (1935), *The Pangolin and Other Verse* (1936), *What Are Years* (1941), *Nevertheless* (1944), *Collected Poems* (1951), which was awarded the Bollingen and Pulitzer prizes, *The Fables of La Fontaine* (translation, 1954), *Predilections* (essays, 1955), *Like a Bulwark* (1956), *O to Be a Dragon* (1959), *A Marianne Moore Reader* (1961), and *The Complete Poems of Marianne Moore* (1967).

T. S. Eliot wrote in 1935: "My conviction has remained unchanged for the last fourteen years—that Miss Moore's poems form part of the small body of durable poetry written in our time . . . in which an original sensibility and alert intelligence and deep feeling have been engaged in maintaining the life of the English language."

Marianne Moore died in 1972.

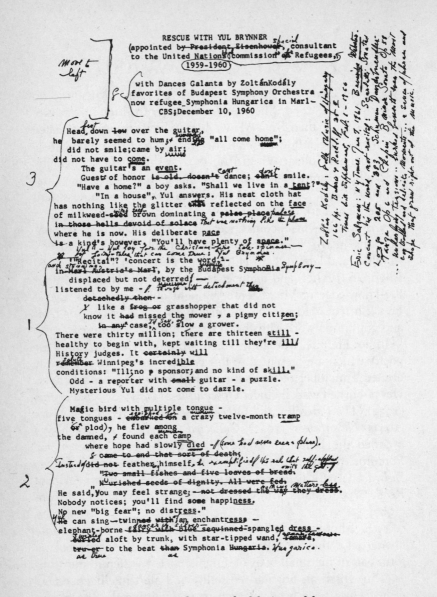

Manuscript of a poem by Marianne Moore.

<figure>HILDEGARDE WATSON</figure>

Marianne Moore

American poetry is a great literature, and it has come to its maturity only in the last sixty years; Walt Whitman and Emily Dickinson in the last century were rare examples of genius in a hostile environment. One decade gave America the major figures of our modern poetry: Wallace Stevens was born in 1879, and T.S. Eliot in 1888. To the ten years which these dates enclose belong H.D., Robinson Jeffers, John Crowe Ransom, William Carlos Williams, Ezra Pound, and Marianne Moore.

Marianne Moore began to publish during the First World War. She was printed and praised in Europe by the expatriates T.S. Eliot and Ezra Pound. In Chicago Harriet Monroe's magazine Poetry, *which provided the enduring showcase for the new poetry, published her too. But she was mainly a poet of New York, of the Greenwich Village group which created magazines called* Others *and* Broom. *The poets with whom she was mostly associated were Alfred Kreymborg, William Carlos Williams, and Wallace*

Stevens—stateside representatives of the miraculous generation.

Marianne Moore settled not in Bloomsbury or Rapallo but in Brooklyn, having moved there from the Village in 1929. To visit her you crossed Brooklyn Bridge, turned left at Myrtle Avenue, followed the elevated for a mile or two, and then turned right onto her street. It was pleasantly lined with a few trees, and Miss Moore's apartment was conveniently near a grocery store and the Presbyterian church which she attended.

The interview took place in November 1960, the day before the election. The front door of Miss Moore's apartment opened onto a long narrow corridor. Rooms led off to the right, and at the end of the corridor was a large sitting room which overlooked the street. On top of a bookcase which ran the length of the corridor was a Nixon button.

Miss Moore and the interviewer sat in her sitting room, a microphone between them. Piles of books stood everywhere. On the walls hung a variety of paintings. One came from Mexico, a gift of Mabel Dodge; others were examples of the heavy, tea-colored oils which Americans hung in the years before 1914. The furniture was old-fashioned and dark.

Miss Moore spoke with an accustomed scrupulosity, and with a humor which her readers will recognize. When she ended a sentence with a phrase which was particularly telling, or even tart, she glanced quickly at the interviewer to see if he was amused, and then snickered gently. Later Miss Moore took the interviewer to an admirable lunch at a nearby restaurant. She decided not to wear her Nixon button because it clashed with her coat and hat.

INTERVIEWER: Miss Moore, I understand that you were born in St. Louis only about ten months before T.S. Eliot. Did your families know each other?

MOORE: No, we did not know the Eliots. We lived in Kirkwood, Missouri, where my grandfather was pastor of the First Presbyterian Church. T.S. Eliot's grandfather—Dr. William Eliot— was a Unitarian. We left when I was about seven, my grandfather having died in 1894, February 20th. My grandfather like Dr.

Eliot had attended ministerial meetings in St. Louis. Also, at stated intervals, various ministers met for luncheon. After one of these luncheons my grandfather said, "When Dr. William Eliot asks the blessing and says 'and this we ask in the name of our Lord Jesus Christ,' he is Trinitarian enough for me." The Mary Institute, for girls, was endowed by him as a memorial to his daughter Mary, who had died.

INTERVIEWER: How old were you when you started to write poems?

MOORE: Well, let me see, in Bryn Mawr. I think I was eighteen when I entered Bryn Mawr. I was born in 1887, I entered college in 1906. Now how old would I have been? Can you deduce my probable age?

INTERVIEWER: Eighteen or nineteen.

MOORE: I had no literary plans, but I was interested in the undergraduate monthly magazine, and to my surprise (I wrote one or two little things for it) the editors elected me to the board. It was my sophomore year—I am sure it was—and I stayed on, I believe. And then when I had left college I offered contributions (we weren't paid) to the *Lantern*, the alumnae magazine. But I didn't feel that my product was anything to shake the world.

INTERVIEWER: At what point did poetry become world-shaking for you?

MOORE: Never! I believe I was interested in painting then. At least I said so. I remember Mrs. Otis Skinner asking at commencement time, the year I was graduated, "What would you like to be?"

"A painter," I said.

"Well, I'm not surprised," Mrs. Skinner answered. I had something on that she liked, some kind of summer dress. She commended it—said, "I'm not at all surprised."

I like stories. I like fiction. And—this sounds rather pathetic, bizarre as well—I think verse perhaps was for me the next best thing to it. Didn't I write something one time, "Part of a Poem, Part of a Novel, Part of a Play?" I think I was all too truthful. I could visualize scenes, and deplored the fact that Henry James had to do it unchallenged. Now, if I couldn't write fiction, I'd like to write plays. To me the theater is the most pleasant, in fact my favorite, form of recreation.

INTERVIEWER: Do you go often?

MOORE: No. Never. Unless someone invites me. Lillian Hellman invited me to *Toys in the Attic*, and I am very happy that she did. I would have had no notion of the vitality of the thing, have lost sight of her skill as a writer if I hadn't seen the play; would like to go again. The accuracy of the vernacular! That's the kind of thing I am interested in, am always taking down little local expressions and accents. I think I should be in some philological operation or enterprise, am really much interested in dialect and intonations. I scarcely think of any that comes into my so-called poems at all.

INTERVIEWER: I wonder what Bryn Mawr meant for you as a poet. You write that most of your time there was spent in the biological laboratory. Did you like biology better than literature as a subject for study? Did the training possibly affect your poetry?

MOORE: I had hoped to make French and English my major studies, and took the required two-year English course—five hours a week—but was not able to elect a course until my junior year. I did not attain the requisite academic stand of eighty until that year. I then elected seventeenth-century imitative writing—Fuller, Hooker, Bacon, Bishop Andrewes, and others. Lectures in French were in French, and I had had no spoken French.

Did laboratory studies affect my poetry? I am sure they did. I found the biology courses—minor, major, and histology—exhilarating. I thought, in fact, of studying medicine. Precision, economy of statement, logic employed to ends that are disinterested, drawing and identifying, liberate—at least have some bearing on—the imagination, it seems to me.

INTERVIEWER: Whom did you know in the literary world, before you came to New York? Did you know Bryher and H.D.?

MOORE: It's very hard to get these things seriatim. I met Bryher in 1921 in New York. H.D. was my classmate at Bryn Mawr. She was there, I think, only two years. She was a non-resident and I did not realize that she was interested in writing.

INTERVIEWER: Did you know Ezra Pound and William Carlos

Williams through her? Didn't she know them at the University of Pennsylvania?

MOORE: Yes. She did. I didn't meet them. I had met no writers until 1916 when I visited New York, when a friend in Carlisle wanted me to accompany her.

INTERVIEWER: So you were isolated really from modern poetry until 1916?

MOORE: Yes.

INTERVIEWER: Was that your first trip to New York, when you went there for six days and decided that you wanted to live there?

MOORE: Oh, no. Several times my mother had taken my brother and me sightseeing and to shop; on the way to Boston, or Maine, and to Washington and Florida. My senior year in college in 1909, I visited Dr. Charles Spraguesmith's daughter, Hilda, at Christmas time in New York. And Louis Anspacher lectured in a very ornamental way at Cooper Union. There was plenty of music at Carnegie Hall, and I got a sense of what was going on in New York.

INTERVIEWER: And what was going on made you want to come back?

MOORE: It probably did, when Miss Cowdrey in Carlisle invited me to come with her for a week. It was the visit in 1916 that made me want to live there. I don't know what put it into her head to do it, or why she wasn't likely to have a better time without me. She was most skeptical of my venturing forth to bohemian parties. But I was fearless about that. In the first place, I didn't think anyone would try to harm me, but if they did I felt impervious. It never occurred to me that chaperones were important.

INTERVIEWER: Do you suppose that moving to New York, and the stimulation of the writers whom you found there, led you to write more poems than you would otherwise have written?

MOORE: I'm sure it did—seeing what others wrote, liking this or that. With me it's always some fortuity that traps me. I certainly never intended to write poetry. That never came into my head. And now, too, I think each time I write that it may be the last time; then I'm charmed by something and seem to have to say something. Everything I have written is the result of reading or of interest in people, I'm sure of that. I had no ambition to be a writer.

INTERVIEWER: Let me see. You taught at the Carlisle Indian School, after Bryn Mawr. Then after you moved to New York in 1918 you taught at a private school and worked in a library. Did these occupations have anything to do with you as a writer?

MOORE: I think they hardened my muscles considerably, my mental approach to things. Working as a librarian was a big help, a tremendous help. Miss Leonard of the Hudson Park branch of the New York Public Library opposite our house came to see me one day. I wasn't in, and she asked my mother did she think I would care to be on the staff, work in the library, because I was so fond of books and liked to talk about them to people. My mother said no, she thought not; the shoemaker's children never have shoes, I probably would feel if I joined the staff that I'd have no time to read. When I came home she told me, and I said, "Why, certainly. Ideal. I'll tell her. Only I couldn't work more than half a day." If I had worked all day and maybe evenings or overtime, like the mechanics, why, it would *not* have been ideal.

As a free service we were assigned books to review and I did like that. We didn't get paid but we had the chance to diagnose. I reveled in it. Somewhere I believe I have carbon copies of those "P-slip" summaries. They were the kind of things that brought the worst-best out. I was always wondering why they didn't honor me with an art book or medical book or even a history, or criticism. But no, it was fiction, silent-movie fiction.

INTERVIEWER: Did you travel at this time? Did you go to Europe at all?

MOORE: In 1911. My mother and I went to England for about two months, July and August probably. We went to Paris and we stayed on the left bank, in a pension in the rue Valette, where Calvin wrote his *Institutes*, I believe. Not far from the Panthéon and the Luxembourg Gardens. I have been much interested in Sylvia Beach's book—reading about Ezra Pound and his Paris days. Where was I and what was I doing? I think, with the objective, an evening stroll—it was one of the hottest summers the world has ever known, 1911—we walked along to 12, rue de l'Odéon, to see Sylvia Beach's shop. It wouldn't occur to me to say, "Here am I, I'm a writer, would you talk to me a while?" I had no feeling at all like that. I wanted to observe things. And we went to every museum in Paris, I think, except two.

INTERVIEWER: Have you been back since?

MOORE: Not to Paris. Only to England in 1935 or 1936. I like England.

INTERVIEWER: You have mostly stayed put in Brooklyn, then, since you moved here in 1929?

MOORE: Except for four trips to the West: Los Angeles, San Francisco, Puget Sound, and British Columbia. My mother and I went through the canal previously, to San Francisco, and by rail to Seattle.

INTERVIEWER: Have you missed the Dodgers here, since *they* went West?

MOORE: Very much, and I am told that they miss us.

INTERVIEWER: I am still interested in those early years in New York. William Carlos Williams, in his *Autobiography*, says that you were "a rafter holding up the superstructure of our uncompleted building," when he talks about the Greenwich Village group of writers. I guess these were people who contributed to *Others*.

MOORE: I never was a rafter holding up anyone! I have his *Autobiography* and took him to task for his misinformed statements about Robert McAlmon and Bryher. In my indignation I missed some things I ought to have seen.

INTERVIEWER: To what extent did the *Others* contributors form a group?

MOORE: We did foregather a little. Alfred Kreymborg was editor, and was married to Gertrude Lord at the time, one of the loveliest persons you could ever meet. And they had a little apartment somewhere in the Village. There was considerable unanimity about the group.

INTERVIEWER: Someone called Alfred Kreymborg your American discoverer. Do you suppose this is true?

MOORE: It could be said, perhaps; he did all he could to promote

me. Miss Monroe and the Aldingtons had asked me simultaneously to contribute to *Poetry* and the *Egoist* in 1917 at the same
time. Alfred Kreymborg was not inhibited. I was a little different
from the others. He thought I might pass as a novelty, I guess.

INTERVIEWER: What was your reaction when H.D. and Bryher
brought out your first collection, which they called *Poems*, in
1921 without your knowledge? Why had you delayed to do it
yourself?

MOORE: To issue my slight product—conspicuously tentative—
seemed to me premature. I disliked the term "poetry" for any but
Chaucer's or Shakespeare's or Dante's. I do not now feel quite
my original hostility to the word, since it is a convenient almost
unavoidable term for the thing (although hardly for me—my
observations, experiments in rhythm, or exercises in composition). What I write, as I have said before, could only be called
poetry because there is no other category in which to put it. For
the chivalry of the undertaking—issuing my verse for me in 1921,
certainly in format choicer than the content—I am intensely
grateful. Again, in 1925, it seemed to me not very self-interested
of Faber and Faber, and simultaneously of the Macmillan Company, to propose a *Selected Poems* for me. Desultory occasional
magazine publications seemed to me sufficient, conspicuous
enough.

INTERVIEWER: Had you been sending poems to magazines before the *Egoist* printed your first poem?

MOORE: I must have. I have a little curio, a little wee book
about two by three inches, or two and a half by three inches, in
which I systematically entered everything sent out, when I got it
back, if they took it, and how much I got for it. That lasted about
a year, I think. I can't care as much as all that. I don't know that
I submitted anything that wasn't extorted from me.

I have at present three onerous tasks, and each interferes with
the others, and I don't know how I am going to write anything.
If I get a promising idea I set it down, and it stays there. I don't
make myself do anything with it. I've had several things in the
New Yorker. And I said to them, "I might never write again,"
and not to expect me to. I never knew anyone who had a passion

for words who had as much difficulty in saying things as I do and I very seldom say them in a manner I like. If I do it's because I don't know I'm trying. I've written several things for the *New Yorker*—and I did want to write *them*.

INTERVIEWER: When did you last write a poem?

MOORE: It appeared in August. What was it about? Oh . . . Carnegie Hall. You see, anything that really rouses me . . .

INTERVIEWER: How does a poem start for you?

MOORE: A felicitous phrase springs to mind—a word or two, say—simultaneous usually with some thought or object of equal attraction: "Its leaps should be *set*/to the flageo*let*"; "Katydid-wing subdivided by *sun*/till the nettings are *legion*." I like light rhymes and un-pompous conspicuous rhymes: Gilbert and Sullivan:

> Yet, *when the danger's near,*
> We *manage to appear*
> As *insensible to fear*
> As *anybody here.*

I have a passion for rhythm and accent, so blundered into versifying. Considering the stanza the unit, I came to hazard hyphens at the end of the line, but found that readers are distracted from the content by hyphens, so I try not to use them. My interest in La Fontaine originated entirely independent of content. I then fell a prey to that surgical kind of courtesy of his.

> I fear that appearances are worshiped throughout France
> Whereas pre-eminence perchance
> Merely means a pushing person.

I like the unaccented syllable and accented near-rhyme:

> By love and his blindness
> Possibly a service was done,
> Let lovers say. A lonely man has no criterion.

INTERVIEWER: What in your reading or your background led you to write the way you do write? Was imagism a help to you?

MOORE: No. I wondered why anyone would adopt the term.

INTERVIEWER: The descriptiveness of your poems has nothing to do with them, you think?

MOORE: No; I really don't. I was rather sorry to be a pariah, or at least that I had no connection with anything. But I *did* feel gratitude to *Others*.

INTERVIEWER: Where do you think your style of writing came from? Was it a gradual accumulation, out of your character? Or does it have literary antecedents?

MOORE: Not so far as I know. Ezra Pound said, "Someone has been reading Laforgue, and French authors." Well, sad to say, I had not read any of them until fairly recently. Retroactively I see that Francis Jammes' titles and treatment are a good deal like my own. I seem almost a plagiarist.

INTERVIEWER: And the extensive use of quotations?

MOORE: I was just trying to be honorable and not to steal things. I've always felt that if a thing had been said in the *best* way, how can you say it better? If I wanted to say something and somebody had said it ideally, then I'd take it but give the person credit for it. That's all there is to it. If you are charmed by an author, I think it's a very strange and invalid imagination that doesn't long to share it. Somebody else should read it, don't you think?

INTERVIEWER: Did any prose stylists help you in finding your poetic style? Elizabeth Bishop mentions Poe's prose in connection with your writing, and you have always made people think of Henry James.

MOORE: Prose stylists, very much. Doctor Johnson on Richard Savage: "He was in two months illegitimated by the Parliament, and disowned by his mother, doomed to poverty and obscurity, and launched upon the ocean of life only that he might be swallowed by its quicksands, or dashed upon its rocks. . . . It was his peculiar happiness that he scarcely ever found a stranger whom he did not leave a friend; but it must likewise be added, that he had not often a friend long without obliging him to become a stranger." Or Edmund Burke on the colonies: "You can shear a wolf; but will he comply?" Or Sir Thomas Browne: "States are not governed by Ergotisms." He calls a bee "that industrious flie," and his home his "hive." His manner is a kind of erudition-proof sweetness. Or Sir Francis Bacon: "Civil War is like the heat of fever; a foreign war is like the heat of exercise." Or Cellini: "I had by me a dog black as a mulberry. . . . I swelled up in my rage like an asp." Or Caesar's *Commentaries,* and Xenophon's *Cynegeticus*: the gusto and interest in every detail! In Henry James it is the essays and letters especially that affect me. In Ezra Pound, *The Spirit of Romance*: his definiteness, his indigenously unmistakable accent. Charles Norman says in his biography of Ezra Pound that he said to a poet, "Nothing, *nothing,* that you couldn't in some circumstance, under stress of some emotion, *actually say.*" And Ezra said of Shakespeare and Dante, "Here we are with the masters; of neither can we say, 'He is the greater'; of each we must say, 'He is unexcelled.' "

INTERVIEWER: Do you have in your own work any favorites and unfavorites?

MOORE: Indeed, I do. I think the most difficult thing for me is to be satisfactorily lucid, yet have enough implication in it to suit myself. That's a problem. And I don't approve of my "enigmas," or as somebody said, "the not ungreen grass." I said to my mother one time, "How did you ever permit me to let this be printed?" And she said, "You didn't ask my advice."

INTERVIEWER: One time I heard you give a reading, and I think you said that you didn't like "In Distrust of Merits," which is one of your most popular poems.

MOORE: I do like it; it is sincere but I wouldn't call it a poem. It's truthful; it is testimony—to the fact that war is intolerable, and unjust.

INTERVIEWER: How can you call it not a poem, on what basis?

MOORE: Haphazard; as form, what has it? It is just a protest—disjointed, exclamatory. Emotion overpowered me. First this thought and then that.

INTERVIEWER: Your mother said that you hadn't asked her advice. Did you ever? Do you go for criticism to your family or friends?

MOORE: Well, not friends, but my brother if I get a chance. When my mother said "You didn't ask my advice" must have been years ago, because when I wrote "A Face," I had written something first about "the adder and the child with a bowl of porridge," and she said "It won't do." "All right," I said, "but I have to produce something." Cyril Connolly had asked me for something for *Horizon*. So I wrote "A Face." That is one of the few things I ever set down that didn't give me any trouble. She said, "I like it." I remember that.

Then, much before that, I wrote "The Buffalo." I thought it would probably outrage a number of persons because it had to me a kind of pleasing jerky progress. I thought, "Well, if it seems bad my brother will tell me, and if it has a point he'll detect it." And he said, with considerable gusto, "It takes my fancy." I was happy as could be.

INTERVIEWER: Did you ever suppress anything because of family objections?

MOORE: Yes, "the adder and the child with a bowl of porridge." I never even wanted to improve it. You know, Mr. Saintsbury said that Andrew Lang wanted him to contribute something on Poe, and he did, and Lang returned it. Mr. Saintsbury said, "Once a thing has been rejected, I would not offer it to the most different of editors." That shocked me. I have offered a thing, submitted it thirty-five times. Not simultaneously, of course.

INTERVIEWER: A poem?

MOORE: Yes. I am very tenacious.

INTERVIEWER: Do people ever ask you to write poems for them?

MOORE: Continually. Everything from on the death of a dog to a little item for an album.

INTERVIEWER: Do you ever write them?

MOORE: Oh, perhaps; usually quote something. Once when I was in the library we gave a party for Miss Leonard, and I wrote a line or two of doggerel about a bouquet of violets we gave her. It has no life or point. It was meant well but didn't amount to anything. Then in college, I had a sonnet as an assignment. The epitome of weakness.

INTERVIEWER: I'm interested in asking about the principles, and the methods, of your way of writing. What is the rationale behind syllabic verse? How does it differ from free verse in which the line length is controlled visually but not arithmetically?

MOORE: It never occurred to me that what I wrote was something to define. I am governed by the pull of the sentence as the pull of a fabric is governed by gravity. I like the end-stopped line and dislike the reversed order of words; like symmetry.

INTERVIEWER: How do you plan the shape of your stanzas? I am thinking of the poems, usually syllabic, which employ a repeated stanza form. Do you ever experiment with shapes before you write, by drawing lines on a page?

MOORE: Never, I never "plan" a stanza. Words cluster like chromosomes, determining the procedure. I may influence an arrangement or thin it, then try to have successive stanzas identical with the first. Spontaneous initial originality—say, impetus—seems difficult to reproduce consciously later. As Stravinsky said about pitch, "If I transpose it for some reason, I am in danger of losing the freshness of first contact and will have difficulty in recapturing its attractiveness."

No, I never "draw lines." I make a rhyme conspicuous, to me at a glance, by underlining with red, blue, or other pencil—as many colors as I have rhymes to differentiate. However, if the phrases recur in too incoherent an architecture—as print—I notice that the words as a tune do not sound right. I may start a piece, find it obstructive, lack a way out, and not complete the thing for a year, or years, am thrifty. I salvage anything promising and set it down in a small notebook.

INTERVIEWER: I wonder if the act of translating La Fontaine's *Fables* helped you as a writer.

MOORE: Indeed it did. It was the best help I've ever had. I suffered frustration. I'm so naïve, so docile, I *tend* to take anybody's word for anything the person says, even in matters of art. The publisher who had commissioned the *Fables* died. I had no publisher. Well, I struggled on for a time and it didn't go very well. I thought, I'd better ask if they don't want to terminate the contract; then I could offer it elsewhere. I thought Macmillan, who took an interest in me, might like it. *Might.* The editor in charge of translations said, "Well, I studied French at Cornell, took a degree in French, I love French, and . . . well, I think you'd better put it away for a while." "How long?" I said. "About ten years; besides, it will hurt your own work. You won't write so well afterward."

"Oh," I said, "that's one reason I was undertaking it; I thought it would train me and give me momentum." Much dejected, I asked, "What is wrong? Have I not a good ear? Are the meanings not sound?"

"Well, there are conflicts," the editor reiterated, as it seemed to me, countless times. I don't know yet what they are or were. (A little "editorial.")

I said, "Don't write me an extenuating letter, please. Just send back the material in the envelope I put with it." I had submitted it in January and this was May. I had had a kind of uneasy hope that all would be well; meanwhile had volumes, hours, and years of work yet to do and might as well go on and do it, I had thought. The ultimatum was devastating.

At the same time Monroe Engel of the Viking Press wrote to me and said that he had supposed I had a commitment for my *Fables*, but if I hadn't would I let the Viking Press see them? I feel an everlasting gratitude to him.

However, I said, "I can't offer you something which somebody else thinks isn't fit to print. I would have to have someone to stabilize it and guarantee that the meanings are sound."

Mr. Engel said, "Who do you think could do that? Whom would you like?"

I said, "Harry Levin," because he had written a cogent, very shrewd review of Edna St. Vincent Millay's and George Dillon's translation of Baudelaire. I admired its finesse.

Mr. Engel said, "I'll ask him. But you won't hear for a long time. He's very busy. And how much do you think we ought to offer him?"

"Well," I said, "not less than ten dollars a book; there would be no incentive in undertaking the bother of it, if it weren't twenty."

He said, "That would reduce your royalties too much on an advance."

I said, "I don't want an advance, wouldn't even consider one."

And then Harry Levin said, quite soon, that he would be glad to do it as a "refreshment against the chores of the term," but of course he would accept no remuneration. It was a very dubious refreshment, let me tell you. (He is precise, and not abusive, and did not "resign.")

INTERVIEWER: I've been asking you about your poems, which is of course what interests me most. But you were editor of *The Dial*, too, and I want to ask you a few things about that. You were editor from 1925 until it ended in 1929, I think. How did you first come to be associated with it?

MOORE: Let me see. I think I took the initiative. I sent the editors a couple of things and they sent them back. And Lola Ridge had a party—she had a large apartment on a ground floor somewhere—and John Reed and Marsden Hartley, who was very confident with the brush, and Scofield Thayer, editor of *The Dial*, were there. And much to my disgust, we were induced each to read something we had written. And Scofield Thayer said of my piece, "Would you send that to us at *The Dial?*"

"I did send it," I said.

And he said, "Well, send it again." That is how it began, I think. Then he said, one time, "I'd like you to meet my partner, Sibley Watson," and invited me to tea at 152 W. 13th St. I was impressed. Doctor Watson is rare. He said nothing, but what he did say was striking and the significance would creep over you because unanticipated. And they asked me to join the staff, at *The Dial*.

INTERVIEWER: I have just been looking at that magazine, the years when you edited it. It's an incredible magazine.

MOORE: *The Dial?* There *were* good things in it, weren't there?

INTERVIEWER: Yes. It combined George Saintsbury and Ezra Pound in the same issue. How do you account for it? What made it so good?

MOORE: Lack of fear, for one thing. We didn't care what other people said. I never knew a magazine which was so self-propulsive. Everybody liked what he was doing, and when we made grievous mistakes we were sorry but we laughed over them.

INTERVIEWER: Louise Bogan said that *The Dial* made clear "the

obvious division between American *avant-garde* and American
conventional writing." Do you think this kind of division continues or has continued? Was this in any way a deliberate policy?

MOORE: I think that individuality was the great thing. We were
not conforming to anything. We certainly didn't have a policy,
except I remember hearing the word "intensity" very often. A
thing must have "intensity." That seemed to be the criterion.

The thing applied to it, I think, that should apply to your own
writing. As George Grosz said, at that last meeting he attended
at the National Institute, "How did I come to be an artist? Endless
curiosity, observation, research—and a great amount of joy in
the thing." It was a matter of taking a liking to things. Things
that were in accordance with your taste. I think that was it. And
we didn't care how unhomogeneous they might seem. Didn't
Aristotle say that it is the mark of a poet to see resemblances
between apparently incongruous things? There was any amount
of attraction about it.

INTERVIEWER: Do you think there is anything in the change of
literary life in America that would make *The Dial* different if it
existed today under the same editors? Were there any special
conditions in the twenties that made the literary life of America
different?

MOORE: I think it is always about the same.

INTERVIEWER: I wonder, if it had survived into the thirties, if
it might have made that rather dry literary decade a little better.

MOORE: I think so. Because we weren't in captivity to anything.

INTERVIEWER: Was it just finances that made it stop?

MOORE: No, it wasn't the depression. Conditions changed. Scofield Thayer had a nervous breakdown, and he didn't come to
meetings. Doctor Watson was interested in photography—was
studying medicine; is a doctor of medicine, and lived in Rochester. I was alone. I didn't know that Rochester was about a night's
journey away, and I would say to Doctor Watson, "Couldn't you
come in for a make-up meeting, or send us these manuscripts
and say what you think of them?" I may, as usual, have exaggerated my enslavement and my preoccupation with tasks—writing letters and reading manuscripts. Originally I had said I would

come if I didn't have to write letters and didn't have to see contributors. And presently I was doing both. I think it was largely
chivalry—the decision to discontinue the magazine—because I
didn't have time for work of my own.

INTERVIEWER: I wonder how you worked as an editor. Hart
Crane complains, in one of his letters, that you rearranged "The
Wine Menagerie" and changed the title. Do you feel that you
were justified? Did you ask for revisions from many poets?

MOORE: No. We had an inflexible rule: do not ask changes of
so much as a comma. Accept it or reject it. But in that instance
I felt that in compassion I should disregard the rule. Hart Crane
complains of me? Well, I complain of *him*. He liked *The Dial*
and we liked him—friends, and with certain tastes in common.
He was in dire need of money. It seemed careless not to so much
as ask if he might like to make some changes ("like" in quotations).
His gratitude was ardent and later his repudiation of it commen-
surate—he perhaps being in both instances under a disability with
which I was not familiar. (Penalizing us for compassion?) I say
"us," and should say "me." Really I am not used to having people
in that bemused state. He was so *anxious* to have us take that
thing, and so *delighted*. "Well, if you would modify it a little,"
I said, "we would like it better." I never attended "their" wild
parties, as Lachaise once said. It was lawless of me to suggest
changes; I disobeyed.

INTERVIEWER: Have you had editors suggest changes to you?
Changes in your own poems, I mean?

MOORE: No, but my ardor to be helped being sincere, I some-
times *induce* assistance: the *Times*, the *Herald Tribune*, the *New
Yorker*, have a number of times had to patch and piece me out.
If you have a genius of an editor, you are blessed: e.g., T. S.
Eliot and Ezra Pound, Harry Levin, and others; Irita Van Doren
and Miss Belle Rosenbaum.

Have I found "help" helpful? I certainly have; and in three
instances, when I was at *The Dial*, I hazarded suggestions the
results of which were to me drama. Excoriated by Herman George
Scheffauer for offering to suggest a verbal change or two in his
translation of Thomas Mann's *Disorder and Early Sorrow*, I must

have posted the suggestions before I was able to withdraw them. In any case, his joyous subsequent retraction of abuse, and his pleasure in the narrative, were not unwelcome. Gilbert Seldes strongly commended me for excisions proposed by me in his "Jonathan Edwards" (for *The Dial*); and I have not ceased to marvel at the overrating by Mark Van Doren of editorial conscience on my reverting (after an interval) to keeping some final lines I had wished he would omit. (Verse! but not a sonnet.)

We should try to judge the work of others by the most that it is, and our own, if not by the least that it is, take the least into consideration. I feel that I would not be worth a button if not grateful to be preserved from myself, and informed if what I have written is not to the point. I think we should feel free, like La Fontaine's captious critic, to say, if asked, "Your phrases are too long, and the content is not good. Break up the type and put it in the font." As Kenneth Burke says in *Counter-Statement*: "[Great] artists feel as opportunity what others feel as a menace. This ability does not, I believe, derive from exceptional strength, it probably arises purely from professional interest the artist may take in his difficulties."

Lew Sarett says, in the *Poetry Society Bulletin*, we ask of a poet: Does this mean something? Does the poet say what he has to say and in his own manner? Does it stir the reader?

Shouldn't we replace vanity with honesty, as Robert Frost recommends? Annoyances abound. We should not find them lethal—a baffled printer's emendations for instance (my "elephant with frog-colored skin" instead of "fog-colored skin," and "the power of the invisible is the invisible," instead of "the power of the visible is the invisible") sounding like a parody on my meticulousness, a "glasshopper" instead of a "grasshopper."

INTERVIEWER: Editing *The Dial* must have acquainted you with the writers of the day whom you did not know already. Had you known Hart Crane earlier?

MOORE: Yes, I did. You remember *Broom*? Toward the beginning of that magazine, in 1921, Lola Ridge was very hospitable, and she invited to a party—previous to my work on *The Dial*—Kay Boyle and her husband, a French soldier, and Hart Crane,

Elinor Wylie, and some others. I took a great liking to Hart Crane. We talked about French bindings, and he was diffident and modest and seemed to have so much intuition, such a feel for things, for books—really a bibliophile—that I took special interest in him. And Doctor Watson and Scofield Thayer liked him—felt that he was one of our talents, that he couldn't fit himself into an IBM position to find a livelihood; that we ought to, whenever we could, take anything he sent us.

I know a cousin of his, Joe Nowak, who is rather proud of him. He lives here in Brooklyn, and is * at the Dry Dock Savings Bank and used to work in antiques. Joe was very convinced of Hart's sincerity and his innate love of all that I have specified. Anyhow, *The Bridge* is a grand theme. Here and there I think he could have firmed it up. A writer is unfair to himself when he is unable to be hard on himself.

INTERVIEWER: Did Crane have anything to do with *Others*?

MOORE: *Others* antedated *Broom*. *Others* was Alfred Kreymborg and Skipwith Cannéll, Wallace Stevens, William Carlos Williams. Wallace Stevens—odd; I nearly met him a dozen times before I did meet him in 1941 at Mount Holyoke, at the college's *Entretiens de Pontigny* of which Professor Gustav Cohen was chairman. Wallace Stevens was Henry Church's favorite American poet. Mr. Church had published him and some others, and me, in *Mésure*, in Paris. Raymond Queneau translated us.

During the French program at Mount Holyoke one afternoon Wallace Stevens had a discourse, the one about Goethe dancing, on a packet-boat in black wool stockings. My mother and I were there; and I gave a reading with commentary. Henry Church had an astoundingly beautiful Panama hat—a sort of pork-pie with a wide brim, a little like Bernard Berenson's hats. I have never seen as fine a weave, and he had a pepper-and-salt shawl which he draped about himself. This lecture was on the lawn.

Wallace Stevens was extremely friendly. We should have had a tape recorder on that occasion, for at lunch they seated us all

---

* *Was*; killed; his car run into by a reckless driver in April 1961.—M.M.

at a kind of refectory table and a girl kept asking him questions such as, "Mr. Stevens have you read the—*Four*—*Quartets?*"

"Of course, but I can't read much of Eliot or I wouldn't have any individuality of my own."

INTERVIEWER: Do you read new poetry now? Do you try to keep up?

MOORE: I am always seeing it—am sent some every day. Some, good. But it does interfere with my work. I can't get much done. Yet I would be a monster if I tossed everything away without looking at it; I write more notes, letters, cards in an hour than is sane.

Although everyone is penalized by being quoted inexactly, I wonder if there is anybody alive whose remarks are so often paraphrased as mine—printed as verbatim. It is really martyrdom. In his book *Ezra Pound*, Charles Norman was very scrupulous. He got several things exactly right. The first time I met Ezra Pound, when he came here to see my mother and me, I said that Henry Eliot seemed to me more nearly the artist than anyone I had ever met. "Now, now," said Ezra. "Be careful." Maybe that isn't exact, but he quotes it just the way I said it.

INTERVIEWER: Do you mean Henry Ware Eliot, T. S. Eliot's brother?

MOORE: Yes. After the Henry Eliots moved from Chicago to New York to—is it 68th Street? It's the street on which Hunter College is—to an apartment there, they invited me to dinner, I should think at T. S. Eliot's suggestion, and I took to them immediately. I felt as if I'd known them a great while. It was some time before I felt that way about T. S. Eliot.

About inaccuracies—when I went to see Ezra Pound at St. Elizabeth's, about the third time I went, the official who escorted me to the grounds said, "Good of you to come to see him," and I said, "Good? You have no idea how much he has done for me, and others." This pertains to an early rather than final visit.

I was not in the habit of asking experts or anybody else to help me with things that I was doing, unless it was a librarian or someone whose business it was to help applicants; or a teacher. But I was desperate when Macmillan declined my *Fables*. I had worked about four years on them and sent Ezra Pound several—although I hesitated. I didn't like to bother him. He had enough trouble without that; but finally I said, "Would you have time to tell me if the rhythms grate on you? Is my ear not good?"

INTERVIEWER: He replied?

MOORE: Yes, said, "The least touch of merit upsets these blighters."

INTERVIEWER: When you first read Pound in 1916, did you recognize him as one of the great ones?

MOORE: Surely did. *The Spirit of Romance.* I don't think anybody could read that book and feel that a flounderer was writing.

INTERVIEWER: What about the early poems?

MOORE: Yes. They seemed a little didactic, but I liked them.

INTERVIEWER: I wanted to ask you a few questions about poetry in general. Somewhere you have said that originality is a by-product of sincerity. You often use moral terms in your criticism. Is the necessary morality specifically literary, a moral use of words, or is it larger? In what way must a man be good if he is to write good poems?

MOORE: If emotion is strong enough, the words are unambiguous. Someone asked Robert Frost (is this right?) if he was selective. He said, "Call it passionate preference." Must a man be good to write good poems? The villains in Shakespeare are not illiterate, are they? But rectitude *has* a ring that is implicative, I would say. And with *no* integrity, a man is not likely to write the kind of book I read.

INTERVIEWER: Eliot, in his introduction to your *Selected Poems*, talks about your function as poet relative to the living language, as he calls it. Do you agree that this is a function of a poet? How does the poetry have the effect on the living language? What's the mechanics of it?

MOORE: You accept certain modes of saying a thing. Or strongly repudiate things. You do something of your own, you modify, invent a variant or revive a root meaning. Any doubt about that?

INTERVIEWER: I want to ask you a question about your correspondence wtih the Ford Motor Company, those letteis which were printed in the *New Yorker*. They were looking for a name

for the car they eventually called the Edsel, and they asked you
to think of a name that would make people admire the car—

MOORE: Elegance and grace, they said it would have—

INTERVIEWER: ". . . some visceral feeling of elegance, fleetness,
advanced features and design. A name, in short, which flashes a
dramatically desirable picture in people's minds."

MOORE: Really?

INTERVIEWER: That's what they said, in their first letter to you.
I was thinking about this in connection with my question about
language. Do you remember Pound's talk about expression and
meaning? He says that when expression and meaning are far apart,
the culture is in a bad way. I was wondering if this request doesn't
ask you to remove expression a bit further from meaning.

MOORE: No, I don't think so. At least, to exposit the irresisti-
bleness of the car. I got deep in motors and turbines and recessed
wheels. No. That seemed to me a very worthy pursuit. I was
more interested in the mechanics. I am interested in mechanisms,
mechanics in general. And I enjoyed the assignment, for all that
it was abortive. Dr. Pick at Marquette University procured a young
demonstrator of the Edsel to call for me in a black one, to convey
me to the auditorium. Nothing was wrong with that Edsel! I
thought it was a very handsome car. It came out the wrong year.

INTERVIEWER: Another thing: in your criticism you make frequent analogies between the poet and the scientist. Do you think
this analogy is helpful to the modern poet? Most people would
consider the comparison a paradox, and assume that the poet and
the scientist are opposed.

MOORE: Do the poet and scientist not work analogously? Both
are willing to waste effort. To be hard on himself is one of the
main strengths of each. Each is attentive to clues, each must
narrow the choice, must strive for precision. As George Grosz
says, "In art there is no place for gossip and but a small place for
the satirist." The objective is fertile procedure. Is it not? Jacob
Bronowski says in the *Saturday Evening Post* that science is not
a mere collection of discoveries, but that science is the process
of discovering. In any case it's not established once and for all;
it's evolving.

INTERVIEWER: One last question. I was intrigued when you wrote that "America has in Wallace Stevens at least one artist whom professionalism will not demolish." What sort of literary professionalism did you have in mind? And do you find this a feature of America still?

MOORE: Yes. I think that writers sometimes lose verve and pugnacity, and he never would say "frame of reference" or "I wouldn't know." A question I am often asked is: "What work can I find that will enable me to spend my whole time writing?" Charles Ives, the composer, says, "You cannot set art off in a corner and hope for it to have vitality, reality, and substance. The fabric weaves itself whole. My work in music helped my business and my work in business helped my music." I am like Charles Ives. I guess Lawrence Durrell and Henry Miller would not agree with me.

INTERVIEWER: But how does professionalism make a writer lose his verve and pugnacity?

MOORE: Money may have something to do with it, and being regarded as a pundit; Wallace Stevens was really very much annoyed at being catalogued, categorized, and compelled to be scientific about what he was doing—to give satisfaction, to answer the teachers. He wouldn't do that. I think the same of William Carlos Williams. I think he wouldn't make so much of the great American language if he were plausible; and tractable. That's the beauty of it; he is willing to be reckless; if you can't be that, what's the point of the whole thing?

—DONALD HALL
1961

5. Robert Lowell

Robert Lowell was born in Boston on March 1, 1917, great-grandnephew of James Russell Lowell. He first attended St. Mark's School, and then Harvard, which he left after two years for Kenyon in order to study poetry, criticism, and the classics under John Crowe Ransom. He then attended Louisiana State University and afterward worked for a short while with a New York publisher. During World War II he was a conscientious objector and served a prison sentence.

In 1947 and 1948 Mr. Lowell was Consultant in Poetry at the Library of Congress. He held a Guggenheim fellowship and an Institute of Arts and Letters grant. He lectured in poetry and creative writing at the State University of Iowa, the Kenyon School of English, and the Salzburg Seminar in American Studies in Austria; he also taught at Boston University. In 1959 he was awarded a fellowship by the Ford Foundation to work as a poet-librettist in association with the Metropolitan Opera and the New York City Opera companies.

His first book of poems was *Land of Unlikeness*, published in 1944. Most of these poems were included in his second volume, *Lord Weary's Castle* (1946). In 1951 he published a third volume of poetry, *The Mills of the Kavanaughs*, and in 1959 *Life Studies*, consisting of new poems and an autobiographical fragment. He first received the Pulitzer Prize for poetry in 1947 for *Lord Weary's Castle* and again in 1973 for *The Dolphins*. Lowell's *Selected Poems* appeared in 1976, and *Day by Day*, a volume of poetry, was published a month before his death in 1977.

Mr. Lowell was married for a short time to Jean Stafford and then to writer Elizabeth Hardwick.

THE VOYAGE

I

For the child playing with its globe and stamps,
the planet equals its rapacity--
how grand the world in the light of the lamps,
how small in the blue day of maturity!

One morning we set sail, giddy with brave
predjudices, judgements, ingenuity--
we swing with the velvet swell of the wave,
our infinite is rocked by the fixed sea.

Some wish to fly a cheapness they detest,
others their crades' terror--others stand
sky-watching the great arc of a woman's breast,
reptilian Circe with her junk and wand.

Not to be changed to reptiles, such men craze
themselves with spaces, light, the burning sky;
cold toughens them, they bronze in the sun's blaze,
and dry the sores of their debauchery.

But the true voyagers are those who move
simply to move--balloons; their heart
is a sick motor thumping in one groove,
their irrational scream is, "Let's depart!"

Oh conscripts lusting for the first fire of the guns,
our sciences have never learned to tag
your dreams--unfathomable, enormous, vague
hopes grease the gears of these automatons!

HANS BECK

Robert Lowell

On one wall of Mr. Lowell's study was a large portrait of Ezra Pound, the tired, haughty outlines of the face concentrated as in the raised outlines of a ring seal in an enlargement. Also bearded, but on another wall, over the desk, James Russell Lowell looked down from a gray old-fashioned photograph on the apex of the triangle thus formed, where his great-grandnephew sat and answered questions.

Mr. Lowell had been talking about the classes he teaches at Boston University.

Four floors below the study window, cars whined through the early spring rain on Marlborough Street toward the Boston Public Garden.

INTERVIEWER: What are you teaching now?

LOWELL: I'm teaching one of these poetry-writing classes and a course in the novel. The course in the novel is called Practical

Criticism. It's a course I teach every year, but the material changes. It could be anything from Russian short stories to Baudelaire, a study of the New Critics, or just fiction. I do whatever I happen to be working on myself.

INTERVIEWER: Has your teaching over the last few years meant anything to you as a writer?

LOWELL: It's meant a lot to me as a human being, I think. But my teaching is part time and has neither the merits nor the burdens of real teaching. Teaching is entirely different from writing. You're always up to it, or more or less up to it; there's no question of its clogging, of its not coming. It's much less subjective, and it's a very pleasant pursuit in itself. In the kind of teaching I do, conversational classes, seminars, if the students are good, which they've been most of the time, it's extremely entertaining. Now, I don't know what it has to do with writing. You review a lot of things that you like, and you read things that you haven't read or haven't read closely, and read them aloud, go into them much more carefully than you would otherwise; and that must teach you a good deal. But there's such a jump from teaching to writing.

INTERVIEWER: Well, do you think the academic life is liable to block up the writer-professor's sensitivity to his own intuitions?

LOWELL: I think it's impossible to give a general answer. Almost all the poets of my generation, all the best ones, teach. I only know one, Elizabeth Bishop, who doesn't. They do it for a livelihood, but they also do it because you can't write poetry all the time. They do it to extend themselves, and I think it's undoubtedly been a gain to them. Now the question is whether something else might be more of a gain. Certainly the danger of teaching is that it's much too close to what you're doing—close and not close. You can get expert at teaching and be crude in practice. The revision, the consciousness that tinkers with the poem—that has something to do with teaching and criticism. But the impulse that starts a poem and makes it of any importance is distinct from teaching.

INTERVIEWER: And protected, you think, from whatever

you bring to in the scrutiny of parts of poems and aspects of novels, etc.?

LOWELL: I think you have to tear it apart from that. Teaching may make the poetry even more different, less academic than it would be otherwise. I'm sure that writing isn't a craft, that is, something for which you learn the skills and go on turning out. It must come from some deep impulse, deep inspiration. That can't be taught, it can't be what you use in teaching. And you may go further afield looking for that than you would if you didn't teach. I don't know, really; the teaching probably makes you more cautious, more self-conscious, makes you write less. It may make you bolder when you do write.

INTERVIEWER: You think the last may be so?

. LOWELL: The boldness is ambiguous. It's not only teaching, it's growing up in this age of criticism which we're all so conscious of, whether we like it or don't like it, or practice it or don't practice it. You think three times before you put a word down, and ten times about taking it out. And that's related to boldness; if you put words down they must do something, you're not going to put clichés. But then it's related to caution; you write much less.

INTERVIEWER: You yourself have written very little criticism, haven't you? You did once contribute to a study of Hopkins.

LOWELL: Yes, and I've done a few omnibus reviews. I do a review or two a year.

INTERVIEWER: You did a wonderful one of Richards' poems.

LOWELL: I felt there was an occasion for that, and I had something to say about it. Sometimes I wish I did more, but I'm very anxious in criticism not to do the standard analytical essay. I'd like my essay to be much sloppier and more intuitive. But my friends are critics, and most of them poet-critics. When I was twenty and learning to write, Allen Tate, Eliot, Blackmur, and Winters, and all those people were very much news. You waited for their essays, and when a good critical essay came out it had the excitement of a new imaginative work.

INTERVIEWER: Which is really not the case with any of the critics writing today, do you think?

LOWELL: The good critics are almost all the old ones. The most brilliant critic of my generation, I think, was Jarrell, and he in a way connects with that older generation. But he's writing less criticism now than he used to.

INTERVIEWER: In your schooling at St. Mark's and Harvard— we can talk about Kenyon in a minute—were there teachers or friends who had an influence on your writing, not so much by the example of their own writing as by personal supervision or direction—by suggesting certain reading, for instance?

LOWELL: Well, my school had been given a Carnegie set of art books, and I had a friend, Frank Parker, who had great talent as a painter but who'd never done it systematically. We began reading the books and histories of art, looking at reproductions, tracing the Last Supper on tracing paper, studying dynamic symmetry, learning about Cézanne, and so on. I had no practical interest in painting, but that study seemed rather close to poetry. And from there I began. I think I read Elizabeth Drew or some such book on modern poetry. It had free verse in it, and that seemed very simple to do.

INTERVIEWER: What class were you in then?

LOWELL: It was my last year. I'd wanted to be a football player very much, and got my letter but didn't make the team. Well, that was satisfying but crushing too. I read a good deal, but had never written. So this was a recoil from that. Then I had some luck in that Richard Eberhart was teaching there.

INTERVIEWER: I'd thought he'd been a student there with you.

LOWELL: No, he was a young man about thirty. I never had him in class, but I used to go to him. He'd read aloud and we'd talk, he was very pleasant that way. He'd smoke honey-scented tobacco, and read Baudelaire and Shakespeare and Hopkins—it made the thing living—and he'd read his own poems. I wrote very badly at first, but he was encouraging and enthusiastic. That probably was decisive, that there was someone there whom I admired who was engaged in writing poetry.

INTERVIEWER: I heard that a very early draft of "The Drunken Fisherman" appeared in the St. Mark's magazine.

LOWELL: No, it was the Kenyon college magazine that published it. The poem was very different then. I'd been reading Winters, whose model was Robert Bridges, and what I wanted was a rather distant, quiet, classical poem without any symbolism. It was in four-foot couplets as smooth as I could write them. The *Kenyon Review* had published a poem of mine and then they'd stopped. This was the one time they said, if you'd submitted this we'd have taken it.

INTERVIEWER: Then you were submitting other poems to the Review?

LOWELL: Yes, and that poem was rather different from anything else I did. I was also reading Hart Crane and Thomas and Tate and Empson's *Seven Types of Ambiguity*; and each poem was more difficult than the one before, and had more ambiguities. Ransom, editing the *Kenyon Review*, was impressed, but didn't want to publish them. He felt they were forbidding and clotted.

INTERVIEWER: But finally he did come through.

LOWELL: Well, after I'd graduated. I published when I was a junior, then for about three years no magazine would take anything I did. I'd get sort of pleasant letters—"One poem in this group interests us, if you can get seven more." At that time it took me about a year to do two or three poems. Gradually I just stopped, and really sort of gave it up. I seemed to have reached a great impasse. The kind of poem I thought was interesting and would work on became so cluttered and overdone that it wasn't really poetry.

INTERVIEWER: I was struck on reading *Land of Unlikeness* by the difference between the poems you rejected for *Lord Weary's Castle* and the few poems and passages that you took over into the new book.

LOWELL: I think I took almost a third, but almost all of what I took was rewritten. But I wonder what struck you?

INTERVIEWER: One thing was that almost all the rejected poems seemed to me to be those that Tate, who in his introduction spoke about two kinds of poetry in the book, said were the more strictly religious and strictly symbolic poems, as against the poems he said were perhaps more powerful because more experienced or relying more on your sense of history. What you took seemed really superior to what you left behind.

LOWELL: Yes, I took out several that were paraphrases of early Christian poems, and I rejected one rather dry abstraction, then whatever seemed to me to have a messy violence. All the poems have religious imagery, I think, but the ones I took were more concrete. That's what the book was moving toward: less symbolic imagery. And as I say, I tried to take some of the less fierce poems. There seemed to be too much twisting and disgust in the first book.

INTERVIEWER: I wondered how wide your reading had been at the time. I wondered, when I read in Tate's introduction that the stanza in one of your poems was based on the stanza in "The Virginian Voyages," whether someone had pointed out Drayton's poem to you.

LOWELL: Tate and I started to make an anthology together. It was a very interesting year I spent with Tate and his wife. He's a poet who writes in spurts, and he had about a third of a book. I was going to do a biography of Jonathan Edwards and he was going to write a novel, and our wives were going to write novels. Well, the wives just went humming away. "I've just finished three pages," they'd say at the end of the day; and their books mounted up. But ours never did, though one morning Allen wrote four pages to his novel, very brilliant. We were in a little study together separated by a screen. I was heaping up books on Jonathan Edwards and taking notes, and getting more and more numb on the subject, looking at old leather-bound volumes on freedom of the will and so on, and feeling less and less a calling. And there we stuck. And then we decided to make an anthology together. We both liked rather formal, difficult poems, and we were reading particularly the Sixteenth and Seventeenth centuries. In the evening we'd read aloud, and we started a card catalogue of what we'd make for the anthology. And then we started writing. It seems to me we took old models like Drayton's Ode— Tate wrote a poem called "The Young Proconsuls of the Air" in that stanza. I think there's a trick to formal poetry. Most poetry is very formal, but when a modern poet is formal he gets more attention for it than old poets did. Somehow we've tried to make it look difficult. For example, Shelley can just rattle off terza rima by the page, and it's very smooth, doesn't seem an obstruction to him—you sometimes wish it were more difficult. Well, someone does that today and in modern style it looks as though he's wrestling with every line and may be pushed into confusion, as though he's having a real struggle with form and content. Marks of that are in the finished poem. And I think both Tate and I felt that we wanted our formal patterns to seem a hardship and something that we couldn't rattle off easily.

INTERVIEWER: But in *Lord Weary's Castle* there were poems moving toward a sort of narrative calm, almost a prose calm— "Katherine's Dream," for example, or the two poems on texts by Edwards, or "The Ghost"—and then, on the other hand, poems in which the form was insisted upon and maybe shown off, and where the things that were characteristic of your poetry at that time—the kind of enjambments, the rhyming, the meters, of course—seem willed and forced, so that you have a terrific logjam of stresses, meanings, strains.

LOWELL: I know one contrast I've felt, and it takes different forms at different times. The ideal modern form seems to be the novel and certain short stories. Maybe Tolstoi would be the perfect example—his work is imagistic, it deals with all experience, and there seems to be no conflict of the form and content. So one thing is to get into poetry that kind of human richness in rather simple descriptive language. Then there's another side of poetry: compression, something highly rhythmical and perhaps wrenched into a small space. I've always been fascinated by both these things. But getting it all on one page in a few stanzas, getting it all done in as little space as possible, revising and revising so that each word and rhythm though not perfect is pondered and wrestled with—you can't do that in prose very well, you'd never get your book written. "Katherine's Dream" was a real dream. I found that I shaped it a bit, and cut it, and allegorized it, but still it was a dream someone had had. It was material that ordinarily, I think, would go into prose, yet it would have had to be much longer or part of something much longer.

INTERVIEWER: I think you can either look for forms, you can do specific reading for them, or the forms can be demanded by what you want to say. And when the material in poetry seems under almost unbearable pressure you wonder whether the form hasn't cookie-cut what the poet wanted to say. But you chose the couplet, didn't you, and some of your freest passages are in couplets.

LOWELL: The couplet I've used is very much like the couplet Browning uses in "My Last Duchess," in *Sordello*, run-on with its rhymes buried. I've always, when I've used it, tried to give the impression that I had as much freedom in choosing the rhyme word as I had in any of the other words. Yet they were almost all true rhymes, and maybe half the time there'd be a pause after the rhyme. I wanted something as fluid as prose; you wouldn't notice the form, yet looking back you'd find that great obstacles had been climbed. And the couplet is pleasant in this way—once you've got your two lines to rhyme, then that's done and you can go on to the next. You're not stuck with the whole stanza to round out and build to a climax. A couplet can be a couplet or can be split and left as one line, or it can go on for a hundred lines; any sort of compression or expansion is possible. And that's not so in a stanza. I think a couplet's much less lyrical than a stanza, closer to prose. Yet it's an honest form, its difficulties are in the open. It really is pretty hard to rhyme each line with the one that follows it.

INTERVIEWER: Did the change of style in *Life Studies* have something to do with working away from that compression and pressure by way of, say, the kind of prose clarity of "Katherine's Dream"?

LOWELL: Yes. By the time I came to *Life Studies* I'd been writing my autobiography and also writing poems that broke meter. I'd been doing a lot of reading aloud. I went on a trip to the West Coast and read at least once a day and sometimes twice for fourteen days, and more and more I found that I was simplifying my poems. If I had a Latin quotation I'd translate it into English. If adding a couple of syllables in a line made it clearer I'd add them, and I'd make little changes just impromptu as I read. That seemed to improve the reading.

INTERVIEWER: Can you think of a place where you added a syllable or two to an otherwise regular line?

LOWELL: It was usually articles and prepositions that I added, very slight little changes, and I didn't change the printed text. It was just done for the moment.

INTERVIEWER: Why did you do this? Just because you thought the most important thing was to get the poem over?

LOWELL: To get it over, yes. And I began to have a certain disrespect for the tight forms. If you could make it easier by adding syllables, why not? And then when I was writing *Life Studies*, a good number of the poems were started in very strict meter, and I found that, more than the rhymes, the regular beat was what I didn't want. I have a long poem in there about my father, called "Commander Lowell," which actually is largely in couplets, but I originally wrote perfectly strict four-foot couplets. Well, with that form it's hard not to have echoes of Marvell. That regularity just seemed to ruin the honesty of sentiment, and became rhetorical; it said, "I'm a poem"—though it was a great help when I was revising having this original skeleton. I could keep the couplets where I wanted them and drop them where I didn't; there'd be a form to come back to.

INTERVIEWER: Had you originally intended to handle all that material in prose?

LOWELL: Yes. I found it got awfully tedious working out transitions and putting in things that didn't seem very important but were necessary to the prose continuity. Also, I found it hard to revise. Cutting it down into small bits, I could work on it much more carefully and make fast transitions. But there's another point about this mysterious business of prose and poetry, form and content, and the reasons for breaking forms. I don't think there's any very satisfactory answer. I seesaw back and forth between something highly metrical and something highly free; there isn't any one way to write. But it seems to me we've gotten into a sort of Alexandrian age. Poets of my generation and particularly younger ones have gotten terribly proficient at these forms. They write a very musical, difficult poem with tremendous skill, perhaps there's never been such skill. Yet the writing seems divorced from culture somehow. It's become too much something specialized that can't handle much experience. It's become a craft, purely a craft, and there must be some breakthrough back into life. Prose is in many ways better off than poetry. It's quite hard to think of a young poet who has the vitality, say, of Salinger or Saul Bellow. Yet prose tends to be very diffuse. The novel is really a much more difficult form than it seems; few people have the wind to write anything that long. Even a short story demands almost poetic perfection. Yet on the whole prose is less cut off from life than poetry is. Now, some of this Alexandrian poetry is very brilliant, you would not have it changed at all. But I thought it was getting increasingly stifling. I couldn't get my experience into tight metrical forms.

INTERVIEWER: So you felt this about your own poetry, your own technique, not just about the general condition of poetry?

LOWELL: Yes, I felt that the meter plastered difficulties and mannerisms on what I was trying to say to such an extent that it terribly hampered me.

INTERVIEWER: This then explains, in part anyway, your admiration for Elizabeth Bishop's poetry. I know that you've said the qualities and the abundance of its descriptive language reminded you of the Russian novel more than anything else.

LOWELL: Any number of people are guilty of writing a complicated poem that has a certain amount of symbolism in it and really difficult meaning, a wonderful poem to teach. Then you unwind it and you feel that the intelligence, the experience, whatever goes into it, is skin-deep. In Elizabeth Bishop's "Man-Moth" a whole new world is gotten out and you don't know what will come after any one line. It's exploring. And it's as original as Kafka. She's gotten a world, not just a way of writing. She seldom writes a poem that doesn't have that exploratory quality; yet it's very firm, it's not like beat poetry, it's all controlled.

INTERVIEWER: What about Snodgrass? What you were trying

to do in *Life Studies* must have something to do with your admiration for his work.

LOWELL: He did these things before I did, though he's younger than I am and had been my student. He may have influenced me, though people have suggested the opposite. He spent ten years at the University of Iowa, going to writing classes, being an instructor; rather unworldly, making little money, and specializing in talking to other people writing poetry, obsessed you might say with minute technical problems and rather provincial experience—and then he wrote about just that. I mean, the poems are about his child, his divorce, and Iowa City, and his child is a Dr. Spock child—all handled in expert little stanzas. I believe that's a new kind of poetry. Other poems that are direct that way are slack and have no vibrance. His experience wouldn't be so interesting and valid if it weren't for the whimsy, the music, the balance, everything revised and placed and pondered. All that gives light to those poems on agonizing subjects comes from the craft.

INTERVIEWER: And yet his best poems are all on the verge of being slight and even sentimental.

LOWELL: I think a lot of the best poetry is. Laforgue—it's hard to think of a more delightful poet, and his prose is wonderful too. Well, it's on the verge of being sentimental, and if he hadn't dared to be sentimental he wouldn't have been a poet. I mean, his inspiration was that. There's some way of distinguishing between false sentimentality, which is blowing up a subject and giving emotions that you don't feel, and using whimsical, minute, tender, small emotions that most people don't feel but which Laforgue and Snodgrass do. So that I'd say he had pathos and fragility—but then that's a large subject too. He has fragility along the edges and a main artery of power going through the center.

INTERVIEWER: Some people were disappointed with *Life Studies* just because earlier you had written a kind of heroic poetry, an American version of heroic poetry, of which there had been none recently except your own. Is there any chance that you will go back to that?

LOWELL: I don't think that a personal history can go on forever, unless you're Walt Whitman and have a way with you. I feel I've done enough personal poetry. That doesn't mean I won't do more of it, but I don't want to do more now. I feel I haven't gotten down all my experience, or perhaps even the most important part, but I've said all I really have much inspiration to say, and more would just dilute. So that you need something more impersonal, and other things being equal it's better to get your emotions out in a Macbeth than in a confession. Macbeth must have tons of Shakespeare in him. We don't know where, nothing in Shakespeare's life was remotely like Macbeth, yet he somehow gives the feeling of going to the core of Shakespeare. You have much more freedom that way than you do when you write an autobiographical poem.

INTERVIEWER: These poems, I gather from what you said earlier, did take as much working over as the earlier ones.

LOWELL: They were just as hard to write. They're not always factually true. There's a good deal of tinkering with fact. You leave out a lot, and emphasize this and not that. Your actual experience is a complete flux. I've invented facts and changed things, and the whole balance of the poem was something invented. So there's a lot of artistry, I hope, in the poems. Yet there's this thing: if a poem is autobiographical—and this is true of any kind of autobiographical writing and of historical writing—you want the reader to say, this is true. In something like Macaulay's *History of England* you think you're really getting William III. That's as good as a good plot in a novel. And so there was always that standard of truth which you wouldn't ordinarily have in poetry—the reader was to believe he was getting the *real* Robert Lowell.

INTERVIEWER: I wanted to ask you about this business of taking over passages from earlier poems and rewriting them and putting them in new contexts. I'm thinking of the passage at the end of the "Cistercians in Germany," in *Land of Unlikeness*, which you rewrote into those wonderful lines that end "At the Indian Killer's Grave." I know that Hart Crane rewrote early scraps a great deal and used most of the rewrites. But doesn't doing this imply a theory of poetry that would talk much more about craft than about experience?

LOWELL: I don't know, it's such a miracle if you get lines that are halfway right; it's not just a technical problem. The lines must mean a good deal to you. All your poems are in a sense one poem, and there's always the struggle of getting something that balances and comes out right, in which all parts are good, and that has experience that you value. And so if you have a few lines that shine in a poem or are beginning to shine, and they fail and get covered over and drowned, maybe their real form is in another poem. Maybe you've mistaken the real inspiration in the original poem and they belong in something else entirely. I don't think that violates experience. The "Cistercians" wasn't very close to me, but the last lines seemed felt; I dropped the Cistercians and put a Boston graveyard in.

INTERVIEWER: But in Crane's "Ode to an Urn," a poem about a personal friend, there are lines which originally applied to something very different, and therefore, in one version or the other, at least can't be called personal.

LOWELL: I think we always bring over some unexplained obscurities by shifting lines. Something that was clear in the original just seems odd and unexplained in the final poem. That can be quite bad, of course; but you always want—and I think Chekhov talks about this—the detail that you can't explain. It's just there. It seems right to you, but you don't have to have it; you could have something else entirely. Now if everything's like that you'd just have chaos, but a few unexplained difficult things—they seem to be the life-blood of variety—they may work. What may have seemed a little odd, a little difficult in the original poem, gets a little more difficult in a new way in the new poem. And that's purely accidental, yet you may gain more than you lose—a new suggestiveness and magic.

INTERVIEWER: Do you revise a very great deal?

LOWELL: Endlessly.

INTERVIEWER: You often use an idiom or a very common phrase

either for the sake of irony or to bear more meaning than it's customarily asked to bear—do these come late in the game, do you have to look around for them?

LOWELL: They come later because they don't prove much in themselves, and they often replace something that's much more formal and worked-up. Some of my later poetry does have this quality that the earlier doesn't: several lines can be almost what you'd say in conversation. And maybe talking with a friend or with my wife I'd say, "This doesn't sound quite right," and sort of reach in the air as I talked and change a few words. In that way the new style is easier to write; I sometimes fumble out a natural sequence of lines that will work. But a whole poem won't come that way; my seemingly relaxed poems are just about as hard as the very worked-up ones.

INTERVIEWER: That rightness and familiarity, though, is in "Between the Porch and the Altar" in several passages which are in couplets.

LOWELL: When I am writing in meter I find the simple lines never come right away. Nothing does. I don't believe I've ever written a poem in meter where I've kept a single one of the original lines. Usually when I was writing my old poems I'd write them out in blank verse and then put in the rhymes. And of course I'd change the rhymes a lot. The most I could hope for at first was that the rhymed version wouldn't be much inferior to the blank verse. Then the real work would begin, to make it something much better than the original out of the difficulties of the meter.

INTERVIEWER: Have you ever gone as far as Yeats and written out a prose argument and then set down the rhymes?

LOWELL: With some of the later poems I've written out prose versions, then cut the prose down and abbreviated it. A rapidly written prose draft of the poem doesn't seem to do much good, too little pain has gone into it; but one really worked on is bound to have phrases that are invaluable. And it's a nice technical problem: how can you keep phrases and get them into meter?

INTERVIEWER: Do you usually send off your work to friends before publishing it?

LOWELL: I do it less now. I always used to do it, to Jarrell and one or two other people. Last year I did a lot of reading with Stanley Kunitz.

INTERVIEWER: At the time you were writing the poems for *Lord Weary's Castle*, did it make a difference to you whether the poet to whom you were sending your work was Catholic?

LOWELL: I don't think I ever sent any poems to a Catholic. The person I was closest to then was Allen Tate, who wasn't a Catholic at the time; and then later it became Jarrell, who wasn't at all Catholic. My two close Catholic writer friends are prose writers, J. F. Powers and Flannery O'Connor, and they weren't interested in the technical problems of poems.

INTERVIEWER: So you feel that the religion is the business of the poem that it's in and not at all the business of the Church or the religious person.

LOWELL: It shouldn't be. I mean, a religion ought to have objective validity. But by the time it gets into a poem it's so mixed up with technical and imaginative problems that the theologian, the priest, the serious religious person isn't of too much use. The poem is too strange for him to feel at home and make any suggestions.

INTERVIEWER: What does this make of the religious poem as a religious exercise?

LOWELL: Well, it at least makes this: that the poem tries to be a poem and not a piece of artless religious testimony. There is a drawback. It seems to me that with any poem, but maybe particularly a religious one where there are common interests, the opinion of intelligent people who are not poets ought to be useful. There's an independence to this not getting advice from religious people and outsiders, but also there's a narrowness. Then there is a question whether my poems are religious, or whether they just use religious imagery. I haven't really any idea. My last poems don't use religious imagery, they don't use symbolism. In many ways they seem to me more religious than the early ones, which are full of symbols and references to Christ and God. I'm sure the symbols and the Catholic framework didn't make the poems religious experiences. Yet I don't feel my experience changed very much. It seems to me it's clearer to me now than it was then, but it's very much the same sort of thing that went into the religious poems—the same sort of struggle, light and darkness, the flux of experience. The morality seems much the same. But the symbolism is gone; you couldn't possibly say what creed I believed in. I've wondered myself often. Yet what made the earlier poems valuable seems to be some recording of experience, and that seems to be what makes the later ones.

INTERVIEWER: So you end up saying that the poem does have some integrity and can have some beauty apart from the beliefs expressed in the poem.

LOWELL: I think it can only have integrity apart from the beliefs; that no political position, religious position, position of generosity, or what have you, can make a poem good. It's all to the good if a poem *can* use politics, or theology, or gardening, or anything that has its own validity aside from poetry. But these things will never *per se* make a poem.

INTERVIEWER: The difficult question is whether when the beliefs expressed in a poem are obnoxious the poem as a whole can be considered to be beautiful—the problem of the *Pisan Cantos*.

LOWELL: The *Pisan Cantos* are very uneven, aren't they? If you took what most people would agree are maybe the best hundred passages, would the beliefs in those passages be obnoxious? I think you'd get a very mixed answer. You could make quite a good case for Pound's good humor about his imprisonment, his absence of self-pity, his observant eye, his memories of literary friends, for all kinds of generous qualities and open qualities and lyrical qualities that anyone would think were good. And even when he does something like the death of Mussolini, in the passage that opens the *Pisan Cantos*, people debate about it. I've talked to Italians who were partisans, and who said that this is the only poem on Mussolini that's any good. Pound's quite wily often: Mussolini hung up like an ox—his brutal appearance. I don't know whether you could say the beliefs there are wrong or not. And there are other poems that come to mind: in Eliot, the Jew spelled with a small j in "Gerontion," is that anti-Semitism or not? Eliot's not anti-Semitic in any sense, but there's certainly a dislike of Jews in those early poems. Does he gain in the fierceness of writing his Jew with a small j? He says you write what you have to write and in criticism you can say what you think you should believe in. Very ugly emotions perhaps make a poem.

INTERVIEWER: You were on the Bollingen Committee at the time the award was made to Pound. What did you think of the great ruckus?

LOWELL: I thought it was a very simple problem of voting for the best book of the year; and it seemed to me Pound's was. I thought the *Pisan Cantos* was the best writing Pound had ever done, though it included some of his worst. It is a very mixed book: that was the question. But the consequences of not giving the best book of the year a prize for extraneous reasons, even terrible ones in a sense—I think that's the death of art. Then you have Pasternak suppressed and everything becomes stifling. Particularly in a strong country like ours you've got to award things objectively and not let the beliefs you'd like a man to have govern your choice. It was very close after the war, and anyone must feel that the poetry award was a trifling thing compared with the concentration camps. I actually think they were very distant from Pound. He had no political effect whatsoever and was quite eccentric and impractical. Pound's social credit, his Fascism, all these various things, were a tremendous gain to him; he'd be a very Parnassan poet without them. Even if they're bad beliefs— and some were bad, some weren't, and some were just terrible, of course—they made him more human and more to do with life, more to do with the times. They served him. Taking what interested him in these things gave a kind of realism and life to his poetry that it wouldn't have had otherwise.

INTERVIEWER: Did you become a translator to suit your own needs or because you wanted to get certain poems, most of them not before translated, into English? Or was it a matter of both, as I suppose it usually is, and as it was for Pound?

LOWELL: I think both. It always seemed to me that nothing very close to the poems I've translated existed in English; and on the other hand, there was some kind of closeness, I felt a kinship. I felt some sort of closeness to the Rilke and Rimbaud poems I've translated, yet they were doing things I couldn't do. They were both a continuation of my own bias and a release from myself.

INTERVIEWER: How did you come to translate Propertius—in fact, how did you come to have such a great interest in Roman history and Latin literature?

LOWELL: At Harvard my second year I took almost entirely English courses—the easiest sort of path. I think that would have been a disaster. But before going to Kenyon I talked to Ford Madox Ford and Ransom, and Ransom said you've just got to take philosophy and logic, which I did. The other thing he suggested was classics. Ford was rather flippant about it, said of course you've got to learn classics, you'll just cut yourself off from humanity if you don't. I think it's always given me some sort of yardstick for English. And then the literature was amazing, particularly the Greek; there's nothing like Greek in English at all. Our plays aren't formally at all like Aeschylus and Sophocles. Their whole inspiration was unbelievably different, and so different that you could hardly think of even the attempt to imitate them, great as their prestige was. That something like *Antigone* or *Oedipus* or the great Achilles moments in the *Iliad* would be at the core of a literature is incredible for anyone brought up in an English culture—Greek wildness and sophistication all different, the women different, everything. Latin's of course much closer. English is a half-Latin language, and we've done our best to absorb the Latin literature. But a Roman poet is much less intellectual than the Englishman, much less abstract. He's nearer nature somehow—somewhat what we feel about a Frenchman but more so still. And yet he's very sophisticated. He has his way of doing things, though the number of forms he explored is quite limited. The amount he could take from the Greeks and yet change is an extraordinary piece of firm discipline. Also, you take almost any really good Roman poet—Juvenal, or Vergil, or Propertius, Catullus—he's much more raw and direct than anything in English, and yet he has this blocklike formality. The Roman frankness interests me. Until recently our literature hasn't been as raw as the Roman, translations had to have stars. And their history has a terrible human frankness that isn't customary with us—corrosive attacks on the establishment, comments on politics and the decay of morals, all felt terribly strongly, by poets as well as historians. The English writer who reads the classics is working at one thing, and his eye is on something else that can't be done. We will always have the Latin and Greek classics, and they'll never be absorbed. There's something very restful about that.

INTERVIEWER: But, more specifically, how did Latin poetry—your study of it, your translations—affect your measure of English poetry?

LOWELL: My favorite English poetry was the difficult Elizabethan plays and the Metaphysicals, then the nineteenth century, which I was aquiver about and disliked but which was closer to my writing than anything else. The Latin seemed very different from either of these. I immediately saw how Shelley wasn't like Horace and Vergil or Aeschylus—and the Latin was a mature poetry, a realistic poetry, which didn't have the contortions of the Metaphysicals. What a frail, bony, electric person Marvell is compared with Horace!

INTERVIEWER: What about your adaptation of Propertius?

LOWELL: I got him through Pound. When I read him in Latin I found a kind of Propertius you don't get in Pound at all. Pound's Propertius is a rather Ovidian figure with a great deal of Pound's fluency and humor and irony. The actual Propertius is a very excited, tense poet, rather desperate; his line is much more like parts of Marlowe's *Faustus*. And he's of all the Roman poets the most like a desperate Christian. His experiences, his love affair with Cynthia, are absolutely rending, destroying. He's like a fallen Christian.

INTERVIEWER: Have you done any other translations of Latin poems?

LOWELL: I did a monologue that started as a translation of Vergil and then was completely rewritten, and there are buried translations in several other poems. There's a poem called "To Speak of Woe That Is in Marriage" in my last book that started as a translation of Catullus. I don't know what traces are left, but it couldn't have been written without the Catullus.

INTERVIEWER: You've translated Pasternak. Do you know Russian?

LOWELL: No, I have rewritten other English translations, and seldom even checked with Russian experts. I want to get a book of translations together. I read in the originals, except for Russian, but I have felt quite free to alter things, and I don't know that Pasternak would look less close than the Italian, which I have studied closely. Before I publish, I want to check with a Russian expert.

INTERVIEWER: Can I get you back to Harvard for a minute? Is it true you tried out for the Harvard *Advocate*, did all the dirty work for your candidacy, and then were turned down?

LOWELL: I nailed a carpet down. I forget who the editor was then, but he was a man who wrote on Frost. At that time people who wrote on Frost were quite different from the ones who write on him now; they tended to be conservative, out of touch. I wasn't a very good writer then, perhaps I should have been turned down. I was trying to write like William Carlos Williams, very simple, free verse, imagistic poems. I had a little group I was very proud of which was set up in galleys; when I left Harvard it was turned down.

INTERVIEWER: Did you know any poets at the time?

LOWELL: I had a friend, Harry Brown, who writes dialogue for movies and has been in Hollywood for years. He was a terribly promising poet. He came to Harvard with a long correspondence with Harriet Monroe and was much more advanced than anyone else. He could write in the style of Auden or Webster or Eliot or Crane. He'd never graduated from high school, and wasn't a student, but he was the person I felt closest to. My other friends weren't writers.

INTERVIEWER: Had you met any older poets—Frost, for instance, who must have been around?

LOWELL: I'd gone to call on Frost with a huge epic on the First Crusade, all written out in clumsy longhand on lined paper. He read a page of that and said, "You have no compression." Then he read me a very short poem of Collins, "How Sleep the Brave," and said, "That's not a great poem, but it's not too long." He was very kindly about it. You know his point about the voice coming into poetry: he took a very unusual example of that, the opening of *Hyperion*; the line about the Naiad, something about her pressing a cold finger to her cold lips, which wouldn't seem like a voice passage at all. And he said, "Now Keats comes alive here." That was a revelation to me; what had impressed me was the big Miltonic imitation in *Hyperion*. I don't know what I did with that, but I recoiled and realized that I was diffuse and monotonous.

INTERVIEWER: What decided you to leave Harvard and go to Kenyon?

LOWELL: I'd make the acquaintance of Merrill Moore, who'd been at Vanderbilt and a Fugitive. He said that I ought to study with a man who was a poet. He was very close to Ransom, and the plan was that I'd go to Vanderbilt; and I would have, but Ransom changed to Kenyon.

INTERVIEWER: I understand you left much against the wishes of your family.

LOWELL: Well, I was getting quite morose and solitary, and they sort of settled for this move. They'd rather have had me a genial social Harvard student, but at least I'd be working hard this way. It seemed to them a queer but orderly step.

INTERVIEWER: Did it help you that you had had intellectual and literary figures in your family?

LOWELL: I really didn't know I'd had them till I went to the South. To my family, James Russell Lowell was the ambassador to England, not a writer. Amy seemed a bit peculiar to them. When I began writing I think it would have been unimaginable to take either Amy or James Russell Lowell as models.

INTERVIEWER: Was it through Ransom that you met Tate?

LOWELL: I met them at more or less the same time, but actually stayed with Tate before I knew Ransom very well.

INTERVIEWER: And Ford Madox Ford was there at some time, wasn't he?

LOWELL: I met Ford at a cocktail party in Boston and went to dinner with him at the Athens Olympia. He was going to visit the Tates, and said, "Come and see me down there, we're all going to Tennessee." So I drove down. He hadn't arrived, so I got to know the Tates quite well before his appearance.

INTERVIEWER: Staying in a pup-tent.

LOWELL: It's a terrible piece of youthful callousness. They had one Negro woman who came in and helped, but Mrs. Tate was doing all the housekeeping. She had three guests and her own family, and was doing the cooking and writing a novel. And this young man arrived, quite ardent and eccentric. I think I suggested that maybe I'd stay with them. And they said, "We really haven't any room, you'd have to pitch a tent on the lawn." So I went to Sears, Roebuck and got a tent and rigged it on their lawn. The Tates were too polite to tell me that what they'd said had been just a figure of speech. I stayed two months in my tent and ate with the Tates.

INTERVIEWER: And you were showing him your work all the while.

LOWELL: Oh, I became converted to formalism and changed my style from brilliant free verse, all in two months. And everything was in rhyme, and it still wasn't any good. But that was a great incentive. I poured out poems and went to writers' conferences.

INTERVIEWER: What about Ford?

LOWELL: I saw him out there and took dictation from him for a while. That was hell, because I didn't know how to type. I'd take the dictation down in longhand, and he rather mumbled. I'd ask him what he'd said, and he'd say, "Oh, you have no sense of prose rhythm," and mumble some more. I'd get most of his words, then I'd have to improvise on the typewriter.

INTERVIEWER: So for part of Ford's opus we're indebted to you.

LOWELL: A handful of phrases in *The March of Literature*, on the Provençal poets.

INTERVIEWER: That was the summer before you entered Kenyon; but most of the poems in *Land of Unlikeness* were written after you'd graduated, weren't they?

LOWELL: Yes, they were almost all written in a year I spent with the Tates, though some of them were earlier poems rewritten. I think becoming a Catholic convert had a good deal to do with writing again. I was much more interested in being a Catholic than in being a writer. I read Catholic writers but had no intention of writing myself. But somehow, when I started again, I won't say the Catholicism gave me subject matter, but it gave me some kind of form, and I could begin a poem and build it to a climax. It was quite different from what I'd been doing earlier.

INTERVIEWER: Why, then, did you choose to print your work in the small liberal magazines whose religious and political positions were very different from yours? Have you ever submitted to the *New Yorker* or the *Atlantic Monthly*?

LOWELL: I think I may have given something to the *Atlantic* on Santayana; the *New Yorker* I haven't given anything. I think the *New Yorker* does some of the best prose in the country, in many ways much more interesting than the quarterlies and little magazines. But poems are lost in it; there's no table of contents, and some of their poetry is light verse. There's no particular continuity of excellence. There just seems no point in printing there. For a while the little magazines, whose religious-political positions *were* very different from mine, were the only magazines that would publish me, and I feel like staying with them. I like magazines like the *New Statesman*, the *Nation*, the *New Republic*—something a little bit off the track.

INTERVIEWER: Just because they are off the track?

LOWELL: I think so. A political position I don't necessarily agree with which is a little bit adverse seems to me just more attractive than a time-serving, conventional position. And they tend to have good reviews, those magazines. I think you write for a small audience, an ardent critical audience. And you know Graves says that poets ought to take in each other's washing because they're the only responsible audience. There's a danger to that—you get too specialized—but I pretty much agree that's the audience you do write for. If it gets further, that's all fine.

INTERVIEWER: There is, though, a certain inbred, in-group anemia to those magazines, at least to the literary quarterlies. For instance, it would have been almost inconceivable for *Partisan Review*, which is the best of them, I think, to give your last book a bad review or even a sharp review.

LOWELL: I think no magazine likes to slam one of its old contributors. *Partisan* has sometimes just not reviewed a book by someone they liked very much and their reviewer didn't. I know Shapiro has been attacked in *Partisan* and then published there, and other people have been unfavorably reviewed and made rather a point of sending them something afterwards. You want to feel there's a certain degree of poorer writing that wouldn't get published in the magazine your work appears in. The good small magazine may publish a lot of rather dry stuff, but at least it's serious, and if it's bad it's not bad by trying to be popular and put something over on the public. It's a wrenched personal ineptitude that will get published rather than a public slickness. I think that has something to do with good reviews coming out in the magazine. We were talking about *Partisan*'s not slamming one of its contributors, but *Partisan* has a pretty harsh, hard standard of reviewing, and they certainly wouldn't praise one of their contributors who'd gone to pot.

INTERVIEWER: What poets among your contemporaries do you most admire?

LOWELL: The two I've been closest to are Elizabeth Bishop— I spoke about her earlier—and Jarrell, and they're different. Jarrell's a great man of letters, a very informed man, and the best critic of my generation, the best professional poet. He's written the best war poems, and those poems are a tremendous product of our culture, I feel. Elizabeth Bishop's poems, as I said, are more personal, more something she did herself, and she's not a critic but has her own tastes, which may be very idiosyncratic. I enjoy her poems more than anybody else's. I like some of Shapiro very much, some of Roethke and Stanley Kunitz.

INTERVIEWER: What about Roethke, who tries to do just about everything you don't try to do?

LOWELL: We've read to each other and argued, and may be rather alike in temperament actually, but he wants a very musical poem and always would quarrel with my ear as I'd quarrel with his eye. He has love poems and childhood poems and startling surrealistic poems, rather simple experience done with a blaze of power. He rejoices in the rhetoric and the metrics, but there's something very disorderly working there. Sometimes it will smash a poem and sometimes it will make it. The things he knows about I feel I know nothing about, flowers and so on. What we share, I think, is the exultant moment, the blazing out. Whenever I've tried to do anything like his poems, I've felt helpless and realized his mastery.

INTERVIEWER: You were apparently a very close friend of Delmore Schwartz's.

LOWELL: Yes, and I think that I've never met anyone who has somehow as much seeped into me. It's a complicated personal thing to talk about. His reading was very varied, Marx and Freud and Russell, very catholic and not from a conservative position at all. He sort of grew up knowing those things and has a wonderful penetrating humorous way of talking about them. If he met T. S. Eliot his impressions of Eliot would be mixed up with his impressions of Freud and what he'd read about Eliot; all these things flowed back and forth in him. Most of my writer friends were more specialized and limited than Schwartz, most of them took against-the-grain positions which were also narrow. Schwartz was a revelation. He felt the poet who had experience was very much better than the poet with polish. Wordsworth would interest him much more than Keats—he wanted openness to direct experience. He said that if you got people talking in a poem you could do anything. And his own writing, *Coriolanus* and *Shenandoah*, is interesting for that.

INTERVIEWER: Isn't this much what you were saying about your own hopes for *Life Studies*?

LOWELL: Yes, but technically I think that Delmore and I are quite different. There have been very few poets I've been able to get very much from technically. Tate has been one of the closest to me. My early poems I think grew out of my admiration for his poems.

INTERVIEWER: What about poets in the past?

LOWELL: It's hard for me to imitate someone; I'm very self-conscious about it. That's an advantage perhaps—you don't become too imitative—but it's also a limitation. I tremble when I feel I'm being like someone else. If it's Rilke or Rimbaud or Propertius, you know the language is a big bar and that if you imitate you're doing something else. I've felt greater freedom that way. I think I've tried to write like some of the Elizabethans.

INTERVIEWER: And Crane? You said you had read a good deal of Crane.

LOWELL: Yes, but his difficult style is one I've never been able to do much with. He can be very obscure and yet write a much more inspired poem than I could by being obscure. There's a relationship between Crane and Tate, and for some reason Tate was much easier for me. I could see how Tate was done, though Tate has a rhythm that I've never been able to imitate. He's much more irregular than I am, and I don't know where the rhythm comes from, but I admire it very much. Crane said somewhere that he could write five or six good lines but Tate could write twelve that would hang together, and you'd see how the twelve were built. Tate was somehow more of a model: he had a lot of wildness and he had a lot of construction. And of course I knew him and never knew Crane. I think Crane is the great poet of that generation. He got out more than anybody else. Not only is it the tremendous power there, but he somehow got New York City; he was at the center of things in the way that no other poet was. All the chaos of his life missed getting sidetracked the way other poets' did, and he was less limited than any other poet of his generation. There was a fullness of experience; and without that, if you just had his mannerisms, and not his rather simple writing—which if done badly would be sentimental merely—or just his obscure writing, the whole thing would be merely verbal. It isn't with Crane. The push of the whole man is there. But his style never worked for me.

INTERVIEWER: But something of Crane does seem to have gotten into your work—or maybe it's just that sense of power thrashing about. I thought it had come from a close admiring reading of Crane.

LOWELL: Yes, some kind of wildness and power that appeals to me, I guess. But when I wrote difficult poems they weren't meant to be difficult, though I don't know that Crane meant his to be. I wanted to be loaded and rich, but I thought the poems were all perfectly logical. You can have a wonderful time explaining a great poem like "Voyages II," and it all can be explained, but in the end it's just a love poem with a great confusion of images that are emotionally clear; a prose paraphrase wouldn't give you any impression whatever of the poem. I couldn't do that kind of poem, I don't think; at least I've never been able to.

INTERVIEWER: You said that most of the writers you've known have been against the grain. What did you mean?

LOWELL: When I began writing most of the great writers were quite unpopular. They hadn't reached the universities yet, and their circulation was small. Even Eliot wasn't very popular then. But life seemed to be there. It seemed to be one of those periods when the lid was still being blown. The great period of blowing the lid was the time of Schönberg and Picasso and Joyce and the early Eliot, where a power came into the arts which we perhaps haven't had since. These people were all rather traditional, yet they were stifled by what was being done, and they almost wrecked things to do their great works—even rather minor but very good writers such as Williams or Marianne Moore. Their kind of protest and queerness has hardly been repeated. They're wonderful writers. You wouldn't see anyone as strange as Marianne Moore again, not for a long while. Conservative and Jamesian as she is, it was a terrible, private, and strange revolutionary poetry. There isn't the motive to do that now. Yet those were the classics, and it seems to me they were all against the grain, Marianne Moore as much as Crane. That's where life was for the small audience. It would be a tremendous subject to say whether the feelings were against the grain too, and whether they were purifying, nihilistic, or both.

INTERVIEWER: Have you had much contact with Eliot?

LOWELL: I may have seen him a score of times in my life, and he's always been very kind. Long before he published me he had some of my poems in his files. There's some kind of New England connection.

INTERVIEWER: Has he helpfully criticized your work?

LOWELL: Just very general criticism. With the first book of mine Faber did he had a lot of little questions about punctuation, but he never said he liked this or disliked that. Then he said something about the last book—"These are first-rate, I mean it"—something like that that was very understated and gratifying. I feel Eliot's less tied to form than a lot of people he's influenced, and there's a freedom of the twenties in his work that I find very sympathetic. Certainly he and Frost are the great New England poets. You hardly think of Stevens as New England, but you have to think of Eliot and Frost as deeply New England and puritanical. They're a continuation and a criticism of the tradition, and they're probably equally great poets. Frost somehow put life into a dead tradition. His kind of poetry must have seemed almost unpublishable, it was so strange and fresh when it was first written. But still it was old-fashioned poetry and really had nothing to do with modern writing—except that he is one of the greatest modern writers. Eliot was violently modern and unacceptable to the traditionalist. Now he's spoken of as a literary dictator, but he's handled his position with wonderful sharpness and grace, it seems to me. It's a narrow position and it's not one I hold particularly, but I think it's been held with extraordinary honesty and finish and development. Eliot has done what he said Shakespeare had done: all his poems are one poem, a form of continuity that has grown and snowballed.

INTERVIEWER: I remember Jarrell in reviewing *Mills of the Kavanaughs* said that Frost had been doing narrative poems with ease for years, and that nobody else had been able to catch up.

LOWELL: And what Jarrell said is true: nobody except Frost can do a sort of Chaucerian narrative poem that's organized and clear. Well, a lot of people do them, but the texture of their verse is so limp and uninspired. Frost does them with great power. Most of them were done early, in that *North of Boston* period. That was a miracle, because except for Robinson—and I think Frost is a very much greater poet than Robinson—no one was doing that in England or America.

INTERVIEWER: But you hadn't simply wanted to tell a story in *Mills of the Kavanaughs*.

LOWELL: No, I was writing an obscure, rather Elizabethan, dramatic and melodramic poem. I don't know quite how to describe this business of direct experience. With Browning, for instance, for all his gifts—and there is almost nothing Browning couldn't use—you feel there's a glaze between what he writes and what really happened, you feel the people are made up. In Frost you feel that's just what the farmers and so on were like. It has the virtue of a photograph but all the finish of art. That's an extraordinary thing; almost no other poet can do that now.

INTERVIEWER: What do you suppose are the qualities that go into that ability?

LOWELL: I don't know. Prose writers have it much more, and quite a few prose writers have it. It's some kind of sympathy and observation of people. It's the deep, rather tragic poems that I value most. Perhaps it's been overdone with Frost, but there's an abundance and geniality about those poems that isn't tragic. With this sense of rhythm and words and composition, and getting into his lines language that is very much like the language he speaks— which is also a work of art, much better than other people's ordinary speech and yet natural to him; he has that continuity with his ordinary self and his poetic self—he's made what with anyone else would be just flat. A very good prose writer can do this and make something of it. You get it quite often in Faulkner. Though he's an Elizabethan sort of character, rather unlike Frost, he can get this amazing immediacy and simplicity. When it comes to verse the form is so hard that all of that gets drained out. In a very conventional old-fashioned writer, or someone who's trying to be realistic but also dramatic and inspired, though he may remain a good poet, most of that directness and realism goes. It's hard for Eliot to be direct that way, though you get it in bits of *The Waste Land*, that marvelous Cockney section. And he can be himself; I feel Eliot's real all through the *Quartets*. He can be very intelligent or very simple there, and *he's* there, but there are no other people in the *Quartets*.

INTERVIEWER: Have many of your poems been taken from real people and real events?

LOWELL: I think, except when I've used myself or occasionally named actual people in poems, the characters are purely imaginary. I've tried to buttress them by putting images I've actually seen and in indirect ways getting things I've actually experienced into the poem. If I'm writing about a Canadian nun the poem may have a hundred little bits of things I've looked at, but she's not remotely anyone I've ever known. And I don't believe anybody would think my nun was quite a real person. She has a heart and she's alive, I hope, and she has a lot of color to her and drama, and has some things that Frost's characters don't, but she doesn't have their wonderful quality of life. His Witch of Coös is absolutely there. I've gathered from talking to him that most of the *North of Boston* poems came from actual people he knew shuffled and put together. But then it's all-important that Frost's plots are so extraordinary, so carefully worked out though it almost seems that they're not there. Like some things in Chekhov, the art is very well hidden.

INTERVIEWER: Don't you think a large part of it is getting the right details, symbolic or not, around which to wind the poem tight and tighter?

LOWELL: Some bit of scenery or something you've felt. Almost the whole problem of writing poetry is to bring it back to what you really feel, and that takes an awful lot of maneuvering. You may feel the doorknob more strongly than some big personal event, and the doorknob will open into something that you can use as your own. A lot of poetry seems to me very good in the tradition but just doesn't move me very much because it doesn't have personal vibrance to it. I probably exaggerate the value of it, but it's precious to me. Some little image, some detail you've noticed—you're writing about a little country shop, just describing it, and your poem ends up with an existentialist account of your experience. But it's the shop that started it off. You didn't know why it meant a lot to you. Often images and often the sense of the beginning and end of a poem are all you have—some journey to be gone through between those things; you know that, but you don't know the details. And that's marvelous; then you feel the poem will come out. It's a terrible struggle, because what you really feel hasn't got the form, it's not what you can put down in a poem. And the poem you're equipped to write concerns nothing that you care very much about or have much to say on. Then the great moment comes when there's enough resolution of your technical equipment, your way of constructing things, and what you can make a poem out of, to hit something you really want to say. You may not know you have it to say.

—FREDERICK SEIDEL
1961

6. Ezra Pound

Ezra Pound was born in a frontier community of Idaho on October 30, 1885, and was educated at the University of Pennsylvania and at Hamilton College. His first book of poems was published in Venice in 1908, and in his lifetime he published over ninety volumes of poetry, criticism, and translation.

As a young poet, Mr. Pound lived in London, and then in Paris during the early 1920s. Later he moved to Rapallo in Italy, where he remained until the war dislodged him. He was foreign editor for *Poetry* for several years as a young man.

Pound was intensely preoccupied with national monetary systems, which he felt to be the cornerstone of all social order. During World War II he lived in Italy and delivered radio broadcasts denouncing American participation in the war against the Axis. One of the darker footnotes in American history is the treatment Pound received when made prisoner in the spring of 1945. At the American "Disciplinary Training Center" at Pisa he was confined in a cage made of metal airstrip mats, with a concrete floor, having only blankets for a bed, a can for a toilet, and an ever-burning light. After three weeks he collapsed with partial amnesia and claustrophobia. In all he was kept in strict solitary confinement for more than six months, during which time he repeatedly suffered attacks of hysteria and terror. Afterward he was taken to Washington, tried for treason, and judged insane. Following fourteen years in Saint Elizabeths Hospital, he returned in 1958 to Italy, where he lived with his daughter.

Pound's major poetic work, *The Cantos*, began appearing in 1917, and the collected poems were printed in one volume in 1970. His shorter poems were collected in *Personae* (1926, enlarged edition 1950). *Love Poems of Ancient Egypt*, a translation, was published in 1962, and *From Confucius to Cummings*, an anthology of poetry edited by Pound and Marcella Spann, in 1963. Pound died in 1972.

E. Pound

NOTE TO BASE CENSOR

The Cantos contain nothing in the nature of cypher or

intended obscurity . The present Cantos do , naturally ,contain
a number of allusions and " recalls " to matter in the
earlier 71 cantos Already published , and many of these
cannot be made clear to readers unacquainted with the
earlier parts of the poem.

There is also an extreme condensation in the quotations , for
example
        " Mine eyes have " (given as mi-hine eyes hev
refers to the Battle Hymn of the Republic as heard from the
loud speaker . There is not time or place in the narrative to
give the further remarks on X seeing the glory of the lord.

In like manner citations from Homer or MUMMXXXX Sophokles
or Confucius are brief ,and serve to remind the ready reader
that we were not born yesterday.
                        The Chinese ideograms are mainly
translated , or commented in the english text. At any rate
they contain nothing seditious .

The form of the poem and main progress is conditioned by
its own inner shape , but the life of the D.T.C. passing
OUTSIDE the scheme cannot but impinge ,or break into the
main flow. The proper names given are mostly those of men
on sick call seen passing my tent. A very brief allusion to
further study in names ,that is , I am interested to note that
the prevalence of early american names ,either of whites
of the old tradition (most of the early presidents for example)
or of descendents of slaves who took the names of their
masters . Interesting in contrast to the relative scarcity of
melting-pot names.

*Typescript of an explanatory note from Ezra Pound to the censor at
the Pisa Detention Camp, where Pound was held after the war. The
officer, in censoring Pound's correspondence (which included the manuscripts of verse on its way to the publisher), apparently suspected that
the Pisan Cantos were in fact coded messages. Pound is writing to explain this is not the case.* (Courtesy: James Laughlin)

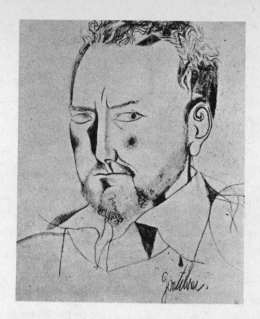

FRANCO GENTILINI

Ezra Pound

After his return to Italy, Ezra Pound spent most of his time in the Tirol, staying at Castle Brunnenberg with his wife, his daughter Mary, his son-in-law Prince Boris de Rachewiltz, and his grandchildren. However, the mountains in this resort country near Merano were cold in the winter, and Mr. Pound liked the sun. The interviewer was about to leave England for Merano, at the end of February, when a telegram stopped him at the door: "Merano ice-bound. Come to Rome."

Pound was alone in Rome, occupying a room in the apartment of an old friend named Ugo Dadone. It was the beginning of March and exceptionally warm. The windows and shutters of Pound's corner room swung open to the noises of the Via Angelo Poliziano. The interviewer sat in a large chair while Pound shifted restlessly from another chair to a sofa and back to the chair. Pound's impression on the room consisted of two suitcases and three books:

the Faber Cantos, *a* Confucius, *and Robinson's edition of Chaucer which he was reading again.*

In the social hours of the evening—dinner at Crispi's, a tour among the scenes of his past, ice cream at a café—Pound walked with the swaggering vigor of a young man. With his great hat, his sturdy stick, his tossed yellow scarf, and his coat, which he trailed like a cape, he was the lion of the Latin Quarter again. Then his talent for mimicry came forward, and laughter shook his gray beard.

During the daytime hours of the interview, which took three days, he spoke carefully and the questions sometimes tired him out. In the morning when the interviewer returned, Mr. Pound was eager to revise the failures of the day before.

INTERVIEWER: You are nearly through the *Cantos* now, and this sets me to wondering about their beginning. In 1916 you wrote a letter in which you talked about trying to write a version of Andreas Divus in Seafarer rhythms. This sounds like a reference to *Canto 1*. Did you begin the *Cantos* in 1916?

POUND: I began the *Cantos* about 1904, I suppose. I had various schemes, starting in 1904 or 1905. The problem was to get a form—something elastic enough to take the necessary material. It had to be a form that wouldn't exclude something merely because it didn't fit. In the first sketches, a draft of the present first *Canto* was the third.

Obviously you haven't got a nice little road map such as the middle ages possessed of Heaven. Only a musical form would take the material, and the Confucian universe as I see it is a universe of interacting strains and tensions.

INTERVIEWER: Had your interest in Confucius begun in 1904?

POUND: No, the first thing was this: you had six centuries that hadn't been packaged. It was a question of dealing with material that wasn't in the *Divina Commedia*. Hugo did a *Légende des Siècles* that wasn't an evaluative affair but just bits of history strung together. The problem was to build up a circle of reference—taking the modern mind to be the mediaeval mind with wash after wash of classical culture poured over it since the Renaissance.

That was the psyche, if you like. One had to deal with one's own subject.

INTERVIEWER: It must be thirty or thirty-five years since you have written any poetry outside the *Cantos*, except for the Alfred Venison poems. Why is this?

POUND: I got to the point where, apart from an occasional lighter impulse, what I had to say fitted the general scheme. There has been a good deal of work thrown away because one is attracted to an historic character and then finds that he doesn't function within my form, doesn't embody a value needed. I have tried to make the *Cantos* historic (Vid. G. Giovannini, *re* relation history to tragedy. Two articles ten years apart in some philological periodical, not source material but relevant) but not fiction. The material one wants to fit in doesn't always work. If the stone isn't hard enough to maintain the form, it has to go out.

INTERVIEWER: When you write a *Canto* now, how do you plan it? Do you follow a special course of reading for each one?

POUND: One isn't necessarily reading. One is working on the life vouchsafed, I should think. I don't know about method. The *what* is so much more important than how.

INTERVIEWER: Yet when you were a young man, your interest in poetry concentrated on form. Your professionalism, and your devotion to technique, became proverbial. In the last thirty years, you have traded your interest in form for an interest in content. Was the change on principle?

POUND: I think I've covered that. Technique is the test of sincerity. If a thing isn't worth getting the technique to say, it is of inferior value. All that must be regarded as exercise. Richter in his *Treatise on Harmony*, you see, says, "These are the principles of harmony and counterpoint; they have nothing whatever to do with composition, which is quite a separate activity." The statement, which somebody made, that you couldn't write Provençal canzoni forms in English, is false. The question of whether it was advisable or not was another matter. When there wasn't the criterion of natural language without inversion, those forms were natural, and they realized them with music. In English the music is of a limited nature. You've got Chaucer's French perfection,

INTERVIEWER: What was your family doing there when you were born?

POUND: Dad opened the Government Land Office out there. I grew up near Philadelphia. The suburbs of Philadelphia.

INTERVIEWER: The wild Indian from the West then was not . . . ?

POUND: The wild Indian from the West is apocryphal, and the assistant assayer of the mint was not one of the most noted bandits of the frontier.

INTERVIEWER: I believe it's *true* that your grandfather built a railroad. What was the story of that?

POUND: Well, he got the railroad into Chippewa Falls, and they ganged up on him and would not let him buy any rails. That's in the *Cantos*. He went up to the north of New York State and found some rails on an abandoned road up there, bought them and had them shipped out, and then used his credit with the lumberjacks to get the road going to Chippewa Falls. What one learns in the home one learns in a way one doesn't learn in school.

INTERVIEWER: Does your particular interest in coinage start from your father's work at the mint?

POUND: You can go on for a long time on that. The government offices were more informal then, though I don't know that any other kids got in and visited. Now the visitors are taken through glass tunnels and see things from a distance, but you could then be taken around in the smelting room and see the gold piled up in the safe. You were offered a large bag of gold and told you could have it if you could take it away with you. You couldn't lift it.

When the Democrats finally came back in, they recounted all the silver dollars, four million dollars in silver. All the bags had rotted in these enormous vaults, and they were heaving it into the counting machines with shovels bigger than coal shovels. This spectacle of coin being shoveled around like it was litter— these fellows naked to the waist shoveling it around in the gas flares—things like that strike your imagination.

Then there's the whole technique of making metallic money.

First, the testing of the silver is much more tricky than testing gold. Gold is simple. It is weighed, then refined and weighed again. You can tell the grade of the ore by the relative weights. But the test for silver is a cloudy solution; the accuracy of the eye in measuring the thickness of the cloud is an aesthetic perception, like the critical sense. I like the idea of the *fineness* of the metal, and it moves by analogy to the habit of testing verbal manifestations. At that time, you see, gold bricks, and specimens of iron pyrites mistaken for gold, were brought up to Dad's office. You heard the talk about the last guy who brought a gold brick and it turned out to be fool's gold.

INTERVIEWER: I know you consider monetary reform the key to good government. I wonder by what process you moved from aesthetic problems toward governmental ones. Did the great war, which slaughtered so many of your friends, do the moving?

POUND: The great war came as a surprise, and certainly to see the English—these people who had never done anything—get hold of themselves, fight it, was immensely impressive. But as soon as it was over they went dead, and then one spent the next twenty years trying to prevent the second war. I can't say exactly where my study of government started. I think the *New Age* office helped me to see the war not as a separate event but as part of a system, one war after another.

INTERVIEWER: One point of connection between literature and politics which you make in your writing interests me particularly. In the *A.B.C. of Reading* you say that good writers are those who keep the language efficient, and that this is their function. You disassociate this function from party. Can a man of the wrong party use language efficiently?

POUND: Yes. That's the whole trouble! A gun is just as good, no matter who shoots it.

INTERVIEWER: Can an instrument which is orderly be used to create disorder? Suppose good language is used to forward bad government? Doesn't bad government make bad language?

POUND: Yes, but bad language is *bound* to make in addition bad government, whereas good language is *not* bound to make bad government. That again is clear Confucius: if the orders aren't clear they can't be carried out. Lloyd George's laws were such a mess, the lawyers never knew what they meant. And Talleyrand proclaimed that they changed the meaning of words between one conference and another. The means of communication breaks down, and that of course is what we are suffering now. We are enduring the drive to work on the subconscious without appealing to the reason. They repeat a trade name with the music a few times, and then repeat the music without it so that the music will give you the name. I think of the *assault*. We suffer from the use of language to conceal thought and to withhold all vital and direct answers. There is the definite use of propaganda, forensic language, merely to conceal and mislead.

INTERVIEWER: Where do ignorance and innocence end and the chicanery begin?

POUND: There is natural ignorance and there is artificial ignorance. I should say at the present moment the artificial ignorance is about eighty-five per cent.

INTERVIEWER: What kind of action can you hope to take?

POUND: The only chance for victory over the brainwash is the right of every man to have his ideas judged one at a time. You never get clarity as long as you have these package words, as long as a word is used by twenty-five people in twenty-five different ways. That seems to me to be the first fight, if there is going to be any intellect left.

It is doubtful whether the individual soul is going to be allowed to survive at all. Now you get a Buddhist movement with everything *except* Confucius taken into it. An Indian Circe of negation and dissolution.

We are up against so many mysteries. There is the problem of benevolence, the point at which benevolence has ceased to be operative. Eliot says that they spend their time trying to imagine systems so perfect that nobody will have to be good. A lot of questions asked in that essay of Eliot's cannot be dodged, like the question of whether there need be any change from the Dantesquan scale of values or the Chaucerian scale of values. If so, how much? People who have lost reverence have lost a great deal. That was where I split with Tiffany Thayer. All these large words fall into clichés.

There is the mystery of the scattering, the fact that the people who presumably understand each other are geographically scattered. A man who fits in his milieu as Frost does, is to be considered a happy man.

Oh, the luck of a man like Mavrocordato, who is in touch with other scholars, so that there is somewhere where he can verify a point! Now for certain points where I want verification there is a fellow named Dazzi in Venice that I write to and he comes up with an answer, as it might be about the forged Donation of Constantine. But the advantages which were supposed to inhere in the university—where there are other people to *contrôl** opinion or to *contrôl* the data—were very great. It is crippling not to have had them. Of course I have been trying over a ten-year period to get any member of an American faculty to mention any other member of his same faculty, in his own department or outside it, whose intelligence he respects or with whom he will discuss serious matters. In one case the gentleman regretted that someone else had *left* the faculty.

I have been unable to get straight answers out of people on what appeared to me to be vital questions. That may have been due to my violence or obscurity with which I framed the questions. Often, I think, so-called obscurity is not obscurity in the language but in the other person's not being able to make out *why* you are saying a thing. For instance the attack on *Endymion* was complicated because Gifford and company couldn't see why the deuce Keats was doing it.

Another struggle has been the struggle to keep the value of a local and particular character, of a particular culture in this awful maelstrom, this awful avalanche toward uniformity. The whole fight is for the conservation of the individual soul. The enemy is the suppression of history; against us is the bewildering prop-

---

* Pound indicates that he is using the French *contrôler*: "to verify, check information, a fact."

aganda and brainwash, luxury and violence. Sixty years ago, poetry was the poor man's art: a man off on the edge of the wilderness, or Frémont, going off with a Greek text in his pocket. A man who wanted the best could have it on a lonely farm. Then there was the cinema, and now television.

INTERVIEWER: The political action of yours that everybody remembers is your broadcasts from Italy during the war. When you gave these talks, were you conscious of breaking the American law?

POUND: No, I was completely surprised. You see I had that promise. I was given the freedom of the microphone twice a week. "He will not be asked to say anything contrary to his conscience or contrary to his duty as an American citizen." I thought that covered it.

INTERVIEWER: Doesn't the law of treason talk about "giving aid and comfort to the enemy," and isn't the enemy the country with whom we are at war?

POUND: I thought I was fighting for a constitutional point. I mean to say, I may have been completely nuts, but I certainly *felt* that it wasn't committing treason.

Wodehouse went on the air and the British asked him not to. Nobody asked me not to. There was no announcement until the collapse that the people who had spoken on the radio would be prosecuted.

Having worked for years to prevent war, and seeing the folly of Italy and America being at war—! I certainly wasn't telling the troops to revolt. I thought I was fighting an internal question of constitutional government. And if any man, any individual man, can say he has had a bad deal from me because of race, creed, or color, let him come out and state it with particulars. The *Guide to Kulchur* was dedicated to Basil Bunting and Louis Zukovsky, a Quaker and a Jew.

I don't know whether you think the Russians ought to be in Berlin or not. I don't know whether I was doing any good or not, whether I was doing any harm. Oh, I was probably offside. But the ruling in Boston was that there is no treason without treasonable intention.

What I was right about was the conservation of individual rights. If, when the executive or any other branch exceeds its legitimate powers, no one protests, you will lose all your liberties. My method of opposing tyranny was wrong over a thirty-year period; it had nothing to do with the Second World War in particular. If the individual, or heretic, gets hold of some essential truth, or sees some error in the system being practiced, he commits so many marginal errors himself that he is worn out before he can establish his point.

The world in twenty years has piled up hysteria—anxiety over a third war, bureaucratic tyranny, and hysteria from paper forms. The immense and undeniable loss of freedoms, as they were in 1900, is undeniable. We have seen the acceleration in efficiency of the tyrannizing factors. It's enough to keep a man worried. Wars are made to make debt. I suppose there's a possible out in space satellites and other ways of making debt.

INTERVIEWER: When you were arrested by the Americans, did you then expect to be convicted? To be hanged?

POUND: At first I puzzled over having missed a cog somewhere. I expected to turn myself in and to be asked about what I learned. I did and I wasn't. I know that I checked myself, on several occasions during the broadcasts, on reflecting that it was not up to me to do certain things, or to take service with a foreign country. Oh, it was paranoia to think one could argue against the usurpations, against the folks who got the war started to get America into it. Yet I hate the idea of obedience to something which is wrong.

Then later I was driven into the courtyard at Chiavari. They had been shooting them, and I thought I was finished then and there. Then finally a guy came in and said he was damned if he would hand me over to the Americans unless I wanted to be handed over to them.

INTERVIEWER: In 1942, when the war started for America, I understand you tried to leave Italy and come back to the United States. What were the circumstances of the refusal?

POUND: Those circumstances were by hearsay. I am a bit hazy in my head about a considerable period, and I think that . . . I know that I had a chance to get as far as Lisbon, and be cooped up there for the rest of the war.

INTERVIEWER: Why did you want to get back to the States at that time?

POUND: I wanted to get back during the election, before the election.

INTERVIEWER: The election was in 1940, wasn't it?

POUND: That would be 1940. I don't honestly remember what happened. My parents were too old to travel. They would have had to stay there in Rapallo. Dad retired there on his pension.

INTERVIEWER: During those years in the war in Italy did you write poetry? The *Pisan Cantos* were written when you were interned. What did you write during those years?

POUND: Arguments, arguments and arguments. Oh, I did some of the Confucius translation.

INTERVIEWER: How was it that you began to write poetry again only after you were interned? You didn't write any cantos at all during the war, did you?

POUND: Let's see—the Adams stuff came out just before the war shut off. No. There was *Oro e Lavoro*. I was writing economic stuff in Italian.

INTERVIEWER: Since your internment, you've published three collections of *Cantos*, *Thrones* just recently. You must be near the end. Can you say what you are going to do in the remaining *Cantos*?

POUND: It is difficult to write a paradiso when all the superficial indications are that you ought to write an apocalypse. It is obviously much easier to find inhabitants for an inferno or even a purgatorio. I am trying to collect the record of the top flights of the mind. I might have done better to put Agassiz on top instead of Confucius.

INTERVIEWER: Are you more or less stuck?

POUND: Okay, I am stuck. The question is, am I dead, as Messrs. A.B.C. might wish? In case I conk out, this is provisionally what I have to do: I must clarify obscurities; I must make clearer definite ideas or dissociations. I must find a verbal formula to combat the rise of brutality—the principle of order versus the split atom.

There was a man in the bughouse, by the way, who insisted that the atom had never been split.

An epic is a poem containing history. The modern mind contains heteroclite elements. The past epos has succeeded when all or a great many of the answers were assumed, at least between author and audience, or a great mass of audience. The attempt in an experimental age is therefore rash. Do you know the story: "What are you drawing, Johnny?"

"God."

"But nobody knows what He looks like."

"They will when I get through!"

That confidence is no longer obtainable.

There *are* epic subjects. The struggle for individual rights is an epic subject, consecutive from jury trial in Athens to Anselm versus William Rufus, to the murder of Becket and to Coke and through John Adams.

Then the struggle appears to come up against a block. The nature of sovereignty is epic matter, though it may be a bit obscured by circumstance. Some of this *can* be traced, pointed; obviously it has to be condensed to get into the form. The nature of the individual, the heteroclite contents of contemporary consciousness. It's the fight for light versus subconsciousness; it demands obscurities and penumbras. A lot of contemporary writing avoids inconvenient areas of the subject.

I am writing to resist the view that Europe and civilization are going to Hell. If I am being "crucified for an idea"—that is, the coherent idea around which my muddles accumulated—it is probably the idea that European culture ought to survive, that the best qualities of it ought to survive along with whatever other cultures, in whatever universality. Against the propaganda of terror and the propaganda of luxury, have you a nice simple answer? One has worked on certain materials trying to establish bases and axes of reference. In writing so as to be understood, there is always the problem of rectification without giving up what is correct. There is the struggle not to sign on the dotted line for the opposition.

INTERVIEWER: Do the separate sections of the *Cantos*, now—

the last three sections have appeared under separate names—
mean that you are attacking particular problems in particular
sections?

POUND: No. *Rock Drill* was intended to imply the necessary
resistance in getting a certain main thesis across—hammering. I
was not following the three divisions of the *Divine Comedy* exactly. One can't follow the Dantesquan cosmos in an age of
experiment. But I have made the division between people dominated by emotion, people struggling upwards, and those who
have some part of the divine vision. The thrones in Dante's
Paradiso are for the spirits of the people who have been responsible
for good government. The thrones in the *Cantos* are an attempt
to move out from egoism and to establish some definition of an
order possible or at any rate conceivable on earth. One is held
up by the low percentage of reason which seems to operate in
human affairs. *Thrones* concerns the states of mind of people
responsible for something more than their personal conduct.

INTERVIEWER: Now that you come near the end, have you made
any plans for revising the *Cantos*, after you've finished?

POUND: I don't know. There's need of elaboration, of clarifi-
cation, but I don't know that a comprehensive revision is in order.
There is no doubt that the writing is too obscure as it stands, but
I hope that the order of ascension in the Paradiso will be toward
a greater limpidity. Of course there ought to be a corrected edition
because of errors that have crept in.

INTERVIEWER: Let me change the subject again, if I may. In
all those years in St. Elizabeth's, did you get a sense of contemporary America from your visitors?

POUND: The trouble with visitors is that you don't get enough
of the opposition. I suffer from the cumulative isolation of not
having had enough contact—fifteen years living more with ideas
than with persons.

INTERVIEWER: Do you have any plans for going back to the
States? Do you want to?

POUND: I undoubtedly want to. But whether it is nostalgia for
America that isn't there any more or not I don't know. This is a
difference between an abstract Adams–Jefferson–Adams–Jackson

America, and whatever is really going on. I undoubtedly have moments when I should like very much to live in America. There are these concrete difficulties against the general desire. Richmond is a beautiful city, but you can't live in it unless you drive an automobile. I'd like at least to spend a month or two a year in the U.S.

INTERVIEWER: You said the other day that as you grew older you felt more American all the time. How does this work?

POUND: It works. Exotics were necessary as an attempt at a foundation. One is transplanted and grows, and one is pulled up and taken back to what one has been transplanted from and it is no longer there. The contacts aren't there and I suppose one reverts to one's organic nature and finds it merciful. Have you ever read Andy White's memoirs? He's the fellow who founded Cornell University. That was the period of euphoria, when everybody thought that all the good things in America were going to function, before the decline, about 1900. White covers a period of history that goes back to Buchanan on one side. He alternated between being Ambassador to Russia and head of Cornell.

INTERVIEWER: Your return to Italy has been a disappointment, then?

POUND: Undoubtedly. Europe was a shock. The shock of no longer feeling oneself in the center of something is probably part of it. Then there is the incomprehension, Europe's incomprehension, of organic America. There are so many things which I, as an American, cannot say to a European with any hope of being understood. Somebody said that I am the last American living the tragedy of Europe.

—DONALD HALL
1962

Note: Mr. Pound's health made it impossible for him to finish proofreading this interview. The text is complete, but may contain details which Mr. Pound would have changed under happier circumstances.

7. William Carlos Williams

William Carlos Williams was born in Rutherford, New Jersey, on September 17, 1883. After schooling in Geneva, Paris, and New York, he was graduated from the University of Pennsylvania Medical School in 1906. He then did graduate work in pediatrics at the University of Leipzig. In 1910 he returned to Rutherford, where he practiced medicine until his retirement in 1951.

His first collection, *Poems* (1909), and those immediately following were strongly influenced by Ezra Pound (whom he had known in Pennsylvania and later in Europe). It was several years later that Williams developed his own style.

Among his many published volumes are *Collected Poems 1921–1931* (1934), *An Early Martyr and Other Poems* (1935), *The Complete Collected Poems of William Carlos Williams 1909–1938* (1938), *Collected Later Poems* (1950), *Collected Earlier Poems* (1951), *The Desert Music* (1954), and *Pictures from Brueghel* (1962). Most important, perhaps, is his "personal epic" poem, *Paterson*, which appeared in five stages (1946–1958). He wrote four novels: *A Voyage to Pagany* (1928), *White Mule* (1937), *In the Money* (1940), and *The Build-Up* (1952); and numerous books of nonfiction, most notably *In the American Grain* (1925), *The Autobiography of William Carlos Williams* (1951), and *Selected Essays of William Carlos Williams* (1954). *Many Loves, and Other Plays: The Collected Plays of William Carlos Williams* and *The Farmers' Daughters*, a collection of short stories appeared in 1961. *The Selected Letters of William Carlos Williams* was published in 1957. In 1950 he was elected to the National Institute of Arts and Letters, and the same year won the National Book Award for poetry. He and Archibald MacLeish shared the Bollingen Prize for Poetry in 1952. Williams died in Rutherford in March 1963.

As Weehawken ▓▓▓ to Hamilton
▓▓▓ to Provence we'll say, he hated it
of which he knew nothing and cared less
and used it inhis scheems - so
founding the counding which was to
increase to be the wonder of the world
in its day

which was to exceed his london on which he patterened it

(A key figure in the development)

                        If any one is important more important
than the edge of a knife or a poem is: or an irrelevance ▓
        - point of a dagger -
in the life of a people: see Da Da or the murders of a
Staline

                or a Li Po

                        or an obscre Montegsmma

or a forgotten Socrates or Aristotle before the destruction
of the library of Alexandria (as note derisively by Berad Shaw)
by fire in which the poes of Sappho were lost

        and brings us (Alex was born out of wedlock)

        illegitimately perversion ▓▓▓▓▓ righed though that alone
does not a make a poet or a statesman

- Wahington was a six foot four man with a wakk voice and a slow
mind which made it inconvenient for him to move fast - and so he
stayed. He had a will bred in the slow woods so that when he
moved the world moved out of has way.

Fragment of the continuation of Paterson.

William Carlos Williams

RUTHERFORD, NEW JERSEY: *Number Nine stood on a terrace at the foot of Ridge Road, just where the road angled into Park Avenue and the stores along the main street. For fifty years the sign beside the walk read* WILLIAM C. WILLIAMS, M.D. *Now it carried the name of his son, with an arrow pointing to the side entrance, and the new office wing. In his last years, Dr. Williams's health suffered from a series of strokes that made it difficult for him to speak, and impaired his physical vigor, so that there would often be a delay before he appeared, pushing out the aluminum storm door and retreating a step or two, extending welcome with a kind of hesitant warmth. On the occasion of the interview, he moved more deliberately than ever, but his greeting was still at pains to be personal. A leisurely progress brought us upstairs past a huge, two-story painting of the Williamsburg Bridge filling the stair well, to the study, a room at the back of the house, overlooking the yard. An electric typewriter, which Dr. Williams could no* longer use, was at the desk, and, though he could scarcely read, a copy of The Desert Music and Other Poems, opened to "The Descent," was propped up in the open drawer. In a corner of the room, over a metal filing cabinet, was an oil painting hung against a wallpaper of geometric simplicity. We sat a little away from the desk, toward the window, with the microphone lying on a stack of small magazines between us.

At the time of these talks, in April 1962, William Carlos Williams was in his seventy-ninth year, author of forty volumes from Poems, 1909, a collection so rare that Mrs. Williams had had trouble holding on to a copy, down through various collected editions and the successive books of Paterson to The Desert Music and Journey to Love. Both of these last volumes were written in an unusual recovery of creative power after Dr. Williams's first serious illness in 1952. Now, with customary impatience, he was fretting to see his latest collection, Pictures from Brueghel, scheduled for publication in June. The doorbell never rang but he expected some word from New Directions, though it was still early in spring.

Because it was so hard for Dr. Williams to talk, there was no question of discoursing on topics suggested in advance, and the conversation went on informally, for an hour or two at a time, over several days. The effort it took the poet to find and pronounce words can hardly be indicated here. Many of the sentences ended in no more than a wave of the hand when Mrs. Williams was not present to finish them. But whatever the topic, the poet's mind kept coming back to the technical matters that interested him in his later years. One of these was his concern was "idiom," the movements of speech that he felt to be especially American, as opposed to English. A rival interest was the "variable foot," a metrical device that was used to resolve the conflict between form and freedom in verse. The question whether one had not to assume a fixed element in the foot as the basis for meter drew only a typical Williams negative, slightly profane, and no effort was made to pursue this much further. As a result, the notion of some mysterious "measure" runs through the interview like an unlaid ghost, prom-

ising enough pattern for shapeliness, enough flexibility for all the subtleties of idiom. No wonder a copy of "The Descent" was in evidence as we began; for however much one may argue over the theory of this verse, it is hard to resist the performance.

On March 4, 1963, William Carlos Williams died in his sleep, at home, of a cerebral hemorrhage that was not unexpected. Two months later Pictures from Brueghel *was awarded the Pulitzer Prize for poetry, and Mrs. Williams accepted, in his name, the Gold Medal for Poetry from the National Institute of Arts and Letters. Though he did not see this interview in print, he approved it in its final stages. Mrs. Williams reports him as having been much entertained by her part in the second half of it.*

WILLIAMS: Well, what's to be done?

INTERVIEWER: I would like to ask you about this new measure that I see here—

WILLIAMS: If I could only talk.

INTERVIEWER: Perhaps we might begin with Rutherford, whether you thought it was a good environment for you.

WILLIAMS: A very—bad environment—for poets. We didn't take anything seriously—in Ruth—in Rutherford. We didn't take poetry very seriously. As far as recording my voice in Rutherford— I read before the ladies, mostly.

INTERVIEWER: You mean the Women's Club? How did they like it?

WILLIAMS: Very much: they applauded. I was quite a hero. [*Picking up a volume*] I remember "By the Road to the Contagious Hospital" was one of the ones I read. The hospital was up in Clifton. I was always intent on saying what I had to say in the accents that were native to me. But I didn't know what I was doing. I knew that the measure was intended to record—something. But I didn't know what the measure was. I stumbled all over the place in these earlier poems. For instance, in this one here [*"Queen-Ann's Lace"*]. I would divide those lines differently now. It's just like the later line, only not opened up in the same way.

INTERVIEWER: You were saying that Rutherford was a bad environment for poets.

WILLIAMS: Yes. But except for my casual conversations about the town, I didn't think anything of it at all. I had a great amount of patience with artisans.

INTERVIEWER: Did you mean it when you said medicine was an interference which you resented?

WILLIAMS: I didn't resent it at all. I just wanted to go straight ahead.

INTERVIEWER: And medicine was not on the way?

WILLIAMS: I don't know whether it would be. I used to give readings at the high school and Fairleigh Dickinson. I was sympathetic with these audiences. I was talking about the same people that I had to do with as patients, and trying to interest them. I was not pretending: I was speaking to them as if they were interested in the same sort of thing.

INTERVIEWER: But were they? Perhaps they felt the double nature of your role, as both poet and doctor, was something of a barrier.

WILLIAMS: No, no. The language itself was what intrigued me. I thought that we were on common territory there.

INTERVIEWER: Did you write the short stories on a different "level" than the poems—as a kind of interlude to them?

WILLIAMS: No, as an alternative. They were written in the form of a conversation which I was partaking in. We were in it together.

INTERVIEWER: Then the composition of them was just as casual and spontaneous as you have suggested. You would come home in the evening and write twelve pages or so without revising?

WILLIAMS: I think so. I was coming *home*. I was placing myself in continuation of a common conversation.

INTERVIEWER: You have insisted that there cannot be a seeking for words in literature. Were you speaking of prose as well as poetry?

WILLIAMS: I think so. Not to choose between words.

INTERVIEWER: Certainly the word does matter though.

WILLIAMS: It does matter, very definitely. Strange that I could say that.

INTERVIEWER: But when you had come home, and were continuing the experience of reality—

WILLIAMS: Reality. Reality. My vocabulary was chosen out of the intensity of my concern. When I was talking in front of a group, I wasn't interested in impressing them with my power of speech, but only with the seriousness of my intentions toward them. I had to make them come alive.

INTERVIEWER: You have said you felt trapped in Rutherford, that you couldn't get out, never had any contact with anyone here. Do you still feel that Rutherford hasn't provided enough of the contact you managed to find during the twenties, in New York, with the Others group? Was that a genuine contribution to your development?

WILLIAMS: That was not a literary thing exactly. But it was about writing—intensely so. We were speaking straight ahead about what concerned us, and if I could have overheard what I was saying then, that would have given me a hint of how to phrase myself, to say what I had to say. Not after the establishment, but speaking straight ahead. I would gladly have traded what I have tried to say, for what came off my tongue, naturally.

INTERVIEWER: Which was not the same?

WILLIAMS: Not free enough. What came off in this writing, finally—this writing [pointing to "The Descent"]—that was pretty much what I wanted to say, in the way I wanted to say it, then. I was searching in this congeries. I wanted to say something in a certain tone of my voice which would be exactly how I wanted to say it, to measure it in a certain way.

INTERVIEWER: Was this in line with what the others in the group were trying to do?

WILLIAMS: I don't think they knew what they were trying to do; but in effect it was. I couldn't speak like the academy. It had to be modified by the conversation about me. As Marianne Moore used to say, a language dogs and cats could understand. So I think she agrees with me fundamentally. Not the speech of English country people, which would have something artificial about it; not that, but language modified by *our* environment; the American environment.

INTERVIEWER: Your own background is pretty much a mixture of English and Spanish, isn't it? Do you think the Spanish has had any influence on your work?

WILLIAMS: There might have been a permanent impression on my mind. It was certainly different from the French. French is too formal; the Spanish language isn't. They were broad men, as in *El Cid*, very much broader than the French. My relation to language was a curious thing. My father was English, but Spanish was spoken in my home. I didn't speak it, but I was read to in Spanish. My mother's relatives used to come up and stay two or three months.

INTERVIEWER: You have said you equated Spanish with the "romantic." Is that a designation you would shrink from?

WILLIAMS: No, not shrink from.

INTERVIEWER: What I was getting at is that you have kept the name "Carlos."

WILLIAMS: I had no choice but to keep the "Carlos."

INTERVIEWER: I understand Solomon Hoheb, your mother's father, was Dutch.

WILLIAMS: Maybe. The Spanish came from the Sephardic Jews. Though the English was strong indeed, through my grandfather.

INTERVIEWER: You've been more conscious of the Spanish, then, than of the other.

WILLIAMS: Yes! I've insisted on breaking with my brother's memory of the Williamses as English. All one needs to do is look at my nose. Flossie says, "I love your nose." And the hell with my nose, after all. The thing that concerns me is the theory of what I was determined to do with measure, what you encounter on the page. It must be transcribed to the page from the lips of the poet, as it was with such a master as Sappho. "The Descent" was very important to me in that way.

INTERVIEWER: You mean that is where it finally happened?

WILLIAMS: Yes, there it happened; and before that it didn't. I remember writing this (*trying to read*):

> *The descent beckons*
> *   as the ascent beckoned.*
> *   Memory is a kind . . .*

INTERVIEWER: . . . *of accomplishment.*
WILLIAMS: *A sort of renewal*
                               even
an initiation, since the spaces it opens are new places.

You see how I run that line? I was very much excited when I
wrote this. I had to do something. I was sitting there with the
typewriter in front of me. I was attempting to imitate myself (I
think I can't even see it at all) but it didn't come alive to me.

INTERVIEWER: It seems to me you were reading it just now.

WILLIAMS: More or less. But something went wrong with me.
I can't make it out any more. I can't type.

INTERVIEWER: Would a tape recorder or a dictaphone be
uncongenial?

WILLIAMS: No, anything that would serve me I'd gladly adopt.

INTERVIEWER: The appearance of this poem on the page suggests
you were conscious of it as a thing—something for the eye.

WILLIAMS: Yes, very good. I was conscious of making it even.
I wanted it to read regularly.

INTERVIEWER: Not just to please the eye?

WILLIAMS: The total effect is very important.

INTERVIEWER: But the care in placing the words—did you ever
feel you would be as happy painting?

WILLIAMS: I'd like to have been a painter, and it would have
given me at least as great a satisfaction as being a poet.

INTERVIEWER: But you say you are a "word man."

WILLIAMS: Yes, that took place early in my development. I was
early inducted into my father's habit of reading—that made me
a poet, not a painter. My mother was a painter. Her brother
Carlos won the Grand Prix—the Gros Lot it was called—then
he financed her to go to Paris, to study painting. Then the money
ran out.

INTERVIEWER: And she met your father through Carlos, whom
he knew in—

WILLIAMS: —Puerto Plata. My father was a businessman, interested in South America. But he always loved books. He used
to read poetry to me. Shakespeare. He had a group who used to

come to our house, a Shakespeare club. They did dramatic readings. So I was always interested in Shakespeare, and Grandmother
was interested in the stage—my father's mother. Emily Dickinson, her name was. Isn't that amazing?

INTERVIEWER: Quite a coincidence: I notice a picture of her
namesake over the desk.

WILLIAMS: Emily was my patron saint. She was also an American, seeking to divide the line in some respectable way. We were
all of us Americans.

INTERVIEWER: Then you did read a good bit of her at some
stage, with your father?

WILLIAMS: My father didn't know anything about Emily Dickinson. He was sold on Shakespeare. [*Doorbell rings. WCW makes
his way downstairs to answer it.*]

INTERVIEWER: [*As he returns*]: You say you were hoping it might
be the new volume?

WILLIAMS: Yes. I am keenly disappointed. But that's always the
way it is with me—my life's blood dripping away. Laughlin has
been a wonderful friend, but it's always so goddam *slow!* I have
still the illusion that I will be able to talk when I make these
connections. It's possible, because I am an emotional creature,
and if I could only talk, to you for instance. Here is a person
well-intentioned toward me, meaning yourself, and I can't talk
to him. It makes me furious.

INTERVIEWER: It's good of you to put up with this business at
all. We were talking about painting and the theater and poetry.
Was that a natural progression for you?

WILLIAMS: More or less; stemming from frustration. I was wondering—I was seeking to be articulate.

INTERVIEWER: At one point you wanted to be an actor.

WILLIAMS: I had no skill as an actor. But through Dad's reading,
the plays of Shakespeare made an impression on me. He didn't
want them to necessarily, just to read them—as words, that came
off as speech.

INTERVIEWER: How did this interest in words make you interested in poetry as opposed, say, to writing novels?

WILLIAMS: That didn't have any connection.

INTERVIEWER: The words weren't sufficiently important in prose?

WILLIAMS: No. I never thought I was a very good prose writer anyway. But when I speak of Emily Dickinson—she was an independent spirit. She did her best to get away from too strict an interpretation. And she didn't want to be confined to rhyme or reason. (Even in Shakespeare, the speech of the players: it was annoying to him to have to rhyme, for Godsake.) And she followed the American idiom. She didn't know it, but she followed it nonetheless. I was a better poet.

INTERVIEWER: You are speaking about language now, not form.

WILLIAMS: Yes; her native speech. She was a wild girl. She chafed against restraint. But she speaks the spoken language, the idiom, which would be deformed by Oxford English.

INTERVIEWER: This new measure of yours, in the later poems, is meant then to accommodate the American speech rhythms.

WILLIAMS: Yes. It's a strange phenomenon, my writing. I think what I have been searching for—

INTERVIEWER: You were suggesting that Emily Dickinson had something to do with it; and her objection to rhyme. But that you were a better poet.

WILLIAMS: Oh, yes [*laughing*]. She was a real good guy. I thought I was a better poet because the American idiom was so close to me, and she didn't get what the poets were doing at that time—writing according to a new method, not the English method, which wouldn't have made much sense to an American. Whitman was on the right track, but when he switched to the English intonation, and followed the English method of recording the feet, he didn't realize it was a different method, which was not satisfactory to an American. Everything started with Shakespeare.

INTERVIEWER: Because it was meant to be spoken?

WILLIAMS: Yes. But when the Shakespearean line was recorded, it was meant to be a formal thing, divided in the English method according to what was written on the page. The Americans shouldn't tolerate that. An Englishman—an English rhetorician, an actor—will speak like Shakespeare, but it's only rhetorical. He can't be true to his own speech. He has to change it in order to conform.

INTERVIEWER: You think it is easier for the English to conform, in poetry, to their kind of speech pattern than it is for an American? You don't think for example that Frost is as true to the American idiom as you are trying to be?

WILLIAMS: No, I don't think so. Eliot, on the other hand, was trying to find a way to record the speech and he didn't find it. He wanted to be regular, to be true to the American idiom, but he didn't find a way to do it. One has to bow down finally, either to the English or to the American.

INTERVIEWER: Eliot went to England; you stayed here.

WILLIAMS: To my sorrow.

INTERVIEWER: To your sorrow? What do you mean by that?

WILLIAMS [*yielding, perhaps*]: It is always better to stick to something.

INTERVIEWER: It's rare to find someone who has. Eliot says he would not be the same if he had stayed. You have said there was a great virtue in the kind of isolation you experienced here.

WILLIAMS: A key question.

INTERVIEWER: And you have been called our most valuable homespun sensitivity.

WILLIAMS: "Homespun sensitivity." Very good.

INTERVIEWER: But you still feel it was a bad environment.

WILLIAMS: It was native, but I doubt that it was very satisfactory to me personally. Though it did provide the accent which satisfied me.

INTERVIEWER: Do you think you could have picked a better one? Do you think you would have been happier in Boston, or Hartford, or New York, or Paris?

WILLIAMS: I might have picked a better one, if I had wanted to—which I did. But if I lived there—if its language was familiar to me, if that was the kind of conversation which I heard, which I grew up with—I could tolerate the vulgarity because it forced me to speak in a particular manner. Not the English intonation.

INTERVIEWER: Do you still feel that the English influence on Eliot set us back twenty years?

WILLIAMS: Very definitely. He was a conformist. He wanted to go back to the iambic pentameter; and he did go back to it, very well; but he didn't acknowledge it.

INTERVIEWER: You say that you could never be a calm speaker, so that this unit you use, which isn't either a foot or a line necessarily, and which works by speech impulses, this is meant to reflect also your own nervous habit of speech—in which things come more or less in a rush.

WILLIAMS: Common sense would force me to work out some such method.

INTERVIEWER: You do pause, though, in the midst of these lines.

WILLIAMS: Very definitely.

INTERVIEWER: Then what is the integrity of the line?

WILLIAMS: If I was consistent in myself it would be very much more effective than it is now. I would have followed much closer to the indicated divisions of the line than I did. It's too haphazard.

INTERVIEWER: The poetry? You admit that in prose, but—

WILLIAMS: —in poetry also. I think I was too haphazard.

INTERVIEWER: In the later poems—like "The Orchestra" here —you think there is still some work to do?

WILLIAMS: It's not successful. It would be classical if it had the proper division of lines. "Reluctant mood," "stretches and yawns." What the devil is that? It isn't firmly enough stated. It's all very complicated—but I can't go on.

INTERVIEWER: You mean you can't find a theory to explain what you do naturally.

WILLIAMS: Yes. It's all in the ear. I wanted to be regular. To continue that—

INTERVIEWER [*picking up a copy of* Paterson V, *from which some clippings fall to the floor*]: These opening lines—they make an image on the page.

WILLIAMS: Yes, I was imitating the flight of the bird.

INTERVIEWER: Then it's directed—

WILLIAMS: —to the eyes. Read it.

INTERVIEWER: "In old age the mind casts off . . ."

WILLIAMS: *In old age*

> *the mind*
>   *casts off*
>   *rebelliously*
>   *an eagle*
>   *from its crag*

INTERVIEWER: Did you ever think of using any other city as subject for a poem?

WILLIAMS: I didn't dare any mention of it in *Paterson,* but I thought strongly of Manhattan when I was looking about for a city to celebrate. I thought it was not particularized enough for me, not American in the sense I wanted. It was near enough, God knows, and I was familiar enough with it for all my purposes—but so was Leipzig, where I lived for a year when I was young, or Paris. Or even Vienna or even Frascati. But Manhattan escaped me.

INTERVIEWER: Someone remarks in one of these clippings that there is no reason the poem should ever end. Part Four completes the cycle, Five renews it. Then what?

WILLIAMS [*laughing*]: Go on repeating it. At the end—the last part, the dance—

INTERVIEWER: "We can know nothing but the dance . . ."

WILLIAMS: *The dance.*

> *To dance to a measure*
>   *contrapuntally,*
>   *Satyrically, the tragic foot.*

That has to be interpreted; but how are you going to interpret it?

INTERVIEWER: I don't presume to interpret it; but perhaps the satyrs represent the element of freedom, of energy within the form.

WILLIAMS: Yes. The satyrs are understood as action, a dance. I always think of the Indians there.

INTERVIEWER: Is anything implied, in "contrapuntally," about the nature of the foot?

WILLIAMS: It means "musically"—it's a musical image. The Indians had a beat in their own music, which they beat with their feet. It isn't an image exactly, a poetic image. Or perhaps it is. The beat goes according to the image. It should all be so simple; but with my damaged brain—

INTERVIEWER: We probably shouldn't be trying to reduce a poetic statement to prose, when we have *The Desert Music* here: "Only the poem . . ."

WILLIAMS: "The counted poem, to an exact measure."

INTERVIEWER: You think it should be more exact then, than you have yet made it.

WILLIAMS: Yes, it should be more exact, in Milton's sense. Milton counted the syllables.

INTERVIEWER: "And I could not help thinking of the wonders of the brain that hears that music."

WILLIAMS: Yes.

INTERVIEWER: "And of our skill *sometimes* to record it." Do you still feel that such modesty is in order?

WILLIAMS: Modesty is in order, God knows—facing the universe of sound.

INTERVIEWER: At least you are not talking about painting now.

WILLIAMS: No. I'm more or less committed to poetry.

[*Talking with Mrs. Williams—the Flossie of* White Mule—*is like going on with a conversation with Dr. Williams: the same honesty, the same warmth, mixed perhaps with briskness and reserve. The living room of their house reflects the interests they have had in common—the paintings, the flowers, the poetry. For fifty years the daily mail brought letters, books, journals, to accumulate in corners and cupboards and on tables around the edges of the room: books from authors and publishers, books with dedications to WCW, or titles borrowed from his poems; and the whole lot of those almost anonymous little magazines that he encouraged with contributions: poems, articles, the inevitable "visit with WCW." On the first day of these particular interviews, a new hi-fi set still in its crate stood in the middle of the room, a gift from the second son, Paul. Now, while waiting for Dr. Williams to come in, Mrs. Williams put on a record, and we listened to the poet's voice for a while, recorded in this same room with occasional sounds of local traffic coming through. It was an aging voice, unmodulated and didactic, but curiously effective in reading the late poems. Mrs. Williams talked about the town of Rutherford, and the poet's brother Edgar, an architect with plans for improving life along the Passaic. She talked of the house when they first moved into it, and of her early impressions of Bill Williams as a young man, at a stage of their life when he was generally off in New York at the clinics, or at various literary gatherings.*]

INTERVIEWER: Did you have to be converted to poetry, in those early days?

MRS. WILLIAMS: No, I was sympathetic. Of course, Bill never paid much attention to me. He used to come to see my sister, who was quite a bit older. She played the piano, and Bill played the violin—not very well. And Edgar sang. Bill didn't read his poetry to me then. He read some to my sister, but she didn't think much of it. Bill's early verse was pretty bad.

INTERVIEWER: I understand Dr. Williams wrote a sonnet a day for a year, when he was at Pennsylvania. Edgar says he called it brainwash, or something worse.

MRS. WILLIAMS: Meeting Ezra Pound seemed to make a difference. It was not really a literary relationship at first. They were too wholly different, but I think that was the turning point. From that time Bill began seriously to want to write poetry. But he realized he couldn't make a living at it.

INTERVIEWER: How did he happen to become a doctor?

MRS. WILLIAMS: His father wanted him to be a dentist. Bill was willing to try. But he hated it. Bill was just too nervous to stand in one spot. But he loved being a doctor, making house calls, and talking to people.

INTERVIEWER: He didn't care to be a surgeon?

MRS. WILLIAMS: He didn't have the long fingers he thought a surgeon should have. That's why he was never a good violinist. But he and Edgar both had ability with their hands. Edgar was a master at drawing, and Bill used to paint. And of course he loves to garden. Two years ago he turned over that whole garden for me when he could scarcely use his right arm. Things would really grow for him.

INTERVIEWER: Was there much literary life in Rutherford?

MRS. WILLIAMS: Not until much later. We had no literary contacts in Rutherford at all: except for Miss Owen, who taught the sixth grade. She knew what Bill was trying to do.

INTERVIEWER: I had the feeling Dr. Williams felt there was no real response to his poetry, even when he read to local groups.

MRS. WILLIAMS: They took what they could get, and ignored the rest—it just wasn't for them. I think to this day very few people in Rutherford know anything about Bill's writing.

INTERVIEWER: Is that a comment on the town or the writing?

MRS. WILLIAMS: I think both. It's a lower-middle-class type of mind, and Bill has never attracted a general audience. My mother used to try to get me to influence him.

INTERVIEWER: To write more conventionally?

MRS. WILLIAMS: Yes. Some of it I didn't like myself, but I never interfered. And I was never blamed for not liking it. [*Telephone rings.*] I'll get it, Bill. [*Answering*] Is it an emergency? No, there are no office hours on Friday. [*Returning from phone*] A patient for young Bill. He left the answering service off. That's what happens.

INTERVIEWER: I suppose you are used to that by now.

MRS. WILLIAMS [*groaning*]: Yes, by now, I'm afraid I am.

INTERVIEWER: Is Dr. Williams not writing now?

MRS. WILLIAMS: No, not for over a year; he can't. He just can't find the words.

INTERVIEWER: Was he writing very much when you were first engaged?

MRS. WILLIAMS: No; once in a while he would send me a poem. But he was busy building up his practice. After we were married he wrote more. I saw to it that he had time, and I made it pleasant for people who came here—because I liked them myself. They were much more interesting than most of the local people. Everyone you can think of used to be in and out. We were the only ones who had a permanent address in all that time. For fifty years, this was headquarters for them all. There was Marsden Hartley—that was his only pastel, over the divan there. He was broke and wanted to go to Germany, so he had an auction at Steiglitz's gallery. An American Place. Bill bought another one at the same time, an unfinished oil up in the study. Maxwell Bodenheim came and stayed a couple of weeks once. He almost drove us crazy. (He was supposed to have a broken arm but Bill was never convinced of it.) He was quite dirty and disagreeable. He couldn't eat carrots, though we had to have them, for the children's sake. And he stuttered terribly. One day we received a telegram from him saying: SEND $200 AT ONCE AM GOING TO MARRY A VERY BEAUTIFUL GIRL. MAXWELL. He was later found murdered in his apartment in New York, with his wife, if she was his wife; probably not the one in the telegram. Then there was Wallace Gould, whom you may not know, a friend of Hartley's from Maine. His mother was an American Indian. And Marianne Moore used to come out with her mother. Bill's writing developed tremendously in that period. There was a group up at Grantwood, near Fort Lee. Malcolm Cowley was in it; and Marcel Duchamp, Man Ray, Alfred Kreymbourg. Robert Brown had the one solid house; the others all lived around in their little shacks. Later on they used to meet in New York, at Lola Ridge's place. She had a big, barnlike studio. I suppose today you would call her a communist, though I never heard any talk of that kind. She was older than most of the young writers. Then there was John Reed, who wrote *Ten Days That Shook the World*; and Louise Bryant—they were all in that group. And there we were. There were arguments; they were all very serious about their writing. They used to get up and read—they would always read. It used to be deadly sometimes. But then I wasn't *too* interested in the group, and after all I had two small children. And then in the thirties, there were the Friends of William Carlos Williams—Ford Madox Ford's group. Toward the end we had a big party for them out here. But that was rather ridiculous. Bill says it was poor old Ford's last gasp for—you know, a group around him. He was dying on his feet. And he did die a couple of years later.

INTERVIEWER: How did you get along with Ezra Pound?

MRS. WILLIAMS: Pound was never around. Pound came over in . . . I think, 1938 to get an honorary degree at Hamilton. And he spent two days with us when he was released from Saint Elizabeth's in 1958, before he sailed for Italy. I wouldn't know what to say of this last impression. He was self-centered, as always. You couldn't talk to him; it was impossible. The only one he ever talked to nicely was Win Scott. It just happened that Win came out to see us, and they got along beautifully. Ezra always tried to tell Bill off, but they got along as friends over the years. Bill wasn't afraid of him; their letters used to be rather acrimonious, back and forth.

INTERVIEWER [*to WCW looking in*]: Apparently those letters don't represent your final attitude?

WILLIAMS: No; the only thing that I remember was the attitude of Flossie's father—

MRS. WILLIAMS: But that has nothing to do with Ezra's last visit here, dear.

WILLIAMS: Just a passing comment. [*Withdraws.*]

MRS. WILLIAMS: Bill and Ezra wrote quite a number of letters to each other when the war started; they were on such opposite sides. Ezra was definitely pro-Fascist, much as he may deny it, and Bill was just the opposite. Not pro-Semitic but not anti-Semitic either, by any means.

INTERVIEWER: After the war, wasn't there some local concern about Dr. Williams's so-called communism?

MRS. WILLIAMS: That was in 1952, when Bill was going down to take the chair of poetry. Senator McCarthy was in the news then, and they were frightened to death in Washington. There was a woman who was lobbying for a reform in poetry, who had no use for free verse. She had a little periodical, I've forgotten the name of it, and she wrote a letter saying what an outrage it was that a man like that—

INTERVIEWER: Of course, this was all in the aftermath of the Bollingen award to Pound.

MRS. WILLIAMS: Bill had nothing to do with that. But if he had been a member of the Fellows then, he would certainly have voted for him.

INTERVIEWER: Was Dr. Williams ever asked to testify against Pound?

MRS. WILLIAMS: They questioned him two or three times. They wanted him to listen to some records, and swear it was Pound. Bill couldn't do that, but he said he would tell them frankly what he knew. And that was all. Every time we went down to Washington, Bill went to see him.

INTERVIEWER: Going back to the First World War: perhaps this isn't something you want to go into, but there were some local reactions then, weren't there?

MRS. WILLIAMS: Against Germans. Yes; that would involve Bill because he was married to me. Bill's mother made my life one hell because I was partly German. Though she wasn't living with us then.

INTERVIEWER: So with one thing and another—Greenwich Village, communism, and the Germans—

MRS. WILLIAMS: Bill was always in a controversy. But I think he stood his ground very well through it all.

WILLIAMS [*coming in, and with his hands on Mrs. Williams' shoulders*]: Maybe you've had enough.

MRS. WILLIAMS: Oh, Bill, it's all right. Don't worry about me. Go out and take a walk.

INTERVIEWER [*to WCW*]: Do you have any recollection of writing a play for the P.T.A. years ago? It was on some local issue, like putting in a school nurse, on which you took a liberal view.

WILLIAMS: I can't think. I was certainly interested in plays. But the only person I ever worked with was Kitty Hoagland.

MRS. WILLIAMS: That was *Many Loves*, much later. Kitty didn't come until the thirties. But Bill wrote four or five small plays during those early years. One about the Dutch around this area; and a very nice little play called *The Apple Tree* that was going to be done at the Provincetown, but Alfred Kreymbourg lost it. And a Puritan play, *Betty Putnam*, that was acted over at the Tennis Club. Do you remember the old tennis courts over on Montross Avenue? There was a very active young group connected with it.

INTERVIEWER: But the town itself didn't quite get all this, I suppose. [*To WCW*] Your brother Edgar says it's a narrow town, and what you have done is in spite of it.

WILLIAMS: Yes. There were some aristocrats back there who would have nothing to do with budding genius.

INTERVIEWER: Not to mention political matters. Edgar says that in the political club which your father started, you were always the liberal.

WILLIAMS: Yes, to my sorrow.

INTERVIEWER: To your sorrow?

MRS. WILLIAMS: He doesn't mean it! I don't see why—

WILLIAMS: Do I mean it? For Godsake, my friends have all been pretty disillusioned friends.

INTERVIEWER: Marianne Moore, who knows you pretty well, says you were always a bit "reckless."

WILLIAMS: I guess she's right. I was a Unitarian. And Unitarians are liberals.

MRS. WILLIAMS: I think Bill has always been willing to be reckless. There was the social credit business for instance, that Bill got involved in in the thirties. They wanted to give a kind of dividend to the people to increase purchasing power. There were large meetings in New York and down at the University of Virginia. But that was about the end of it. In fact many of those involved withdrew from it when they saw how things were going, with the war coming on and all. Some of them were so nervous about that whole episode they wouldn't even speak to Bill. That's the difference. I don't say Bill was naïve; perhaps it was honesty. Bill isn't a radical or a communist or anything else. He's an honest man. And if he gets into it with both feet, it's just too bad. That's the way it's been.

INTERVIEWER: [*to WCW*]: Right?

WILLIAMS: [*Agrees, laughing.*]

INTERVIEWER: If we could talk a few more minutes about personal matters—how did you enjoy Saint Thomas? I understand you have just come back from there.

WILLIAMS: I could stay there forever, with reservations, of

course. Saint Thomas is the place where my father grew up. I remember a photograph of the blizzard area—oh, for Godsake, I mean the hurricane, in eighty-eight.

MRS. WILLIAMS: Bill, dear, I'm sorry, but it must have been in the seventies. It was when your father was a boy.

WILLIAMS: [*with a sigh*]: Yes, yes, yes. [*Laughs.*] I remember a story of the hurricane. Thoroughly documented. How first the water went out of the harbor and left it dry, the ships lying on their beams' ends, and then another shudder and an earthquake worse than they ever had in the area. And I have a distinct memory of some photographs of my father, taken at perhaps twenty-one years of age. I was very much interested in making contact with his memory.

MRS. WILLIAMS: It was a good trip, but Bill gets restless. And it's too difficult at our age.

WILLIAMS: I think we'll not go again.

INTERVIEWER: To get back for a minute to the troubles of 1952—do you think you were working too hard at that time?

WILLIAMS: I was interested in the process of composition—in the theory of it. And I *was* working pretty hard at it. But I couldn't make much of it.

MRS. WILLIAMS: Bill had a contract with Random House for three books. There was no hurry; but that's the only way Bill can work. And he doesn't want to look things over, which is his worst fault. *The Build-Up* was written then. I'm afraid Bill garbled that one. It was just impatience. And he didn't want me to read the things either. I wish I had, there were so many errors in the *Autobiography*. That was inexcusable. Then, one night in the winter of forty-eight, Bill felt a pain in his chest, shoveling out the car. He kept going until February. I used to drive around with him on house calls. But it was too much.

WILLIAMS: I had a heart attack. Perhaps it was a good thing. I thought I was God almighty, I guess; in general. But I got over that one.

MRS. WILLIAMS: There wasn't any kind of cerebral trouble until 1950 or so. Bill had given up medicine and we were going down to take the chair of poetry in Washington. But in 1952, when we were up visiting the Abbotts, in New York, Bill had a serious stroke.

WILLIAMS: I tried to play it down. I was conscious, and rational; and I could joke about it. But I was in a strange house, and I needed to get home. I couldn't write—

MRS. WILLIAMS: Then suddenly you could hardly understand him.

WILLIAMS: That was the end. I was through with life.

MRS. WILLIAMS: No, it wasn't the end. You had a lot of life left. You had a whole play running through your mind while you were lying there, *The Cure*. You thought it out and dictated the notes to me. You wrote it when we got home.

INTERVIEWER: That was something of a change in approach.

WILLIAMS: Yes, the novels I just did as I went along, at first; though I tried to think them out as well as I could.

MRS. WILLIAMS: Of course the *White Mule* was about a baby; Bill's favorite subject. But most of the later poems were written after the stroke. Bill used to say things like spelling didn't matter, and he would never correct at all. I think he did much better work after the stroke slowed him down.

WILLIAMS [*perhaps grudgingly*]: The evidence is there.

INTERVIEWER: It was when you were at the Abbotts' that someone read Theocritus to you.

WILLIAMS: Yes, Mrs. Gratwick; I asked her to. Theocritus was always strong in my mind. But I wasn't capable of hearing it in the Greek. I'm in an unfortunate position, because I don't have the original language. For example, I started to take Latin at Horace Mann, but the teacher was withdrawn, to my infinite regret. That was the end of that—all my life, that was the end. And I always regretted too that I didn't know Greek. I don't know, as far as the Theocritus was concerned, whether it came first, or the stroke.

MRS. WILLIAMS: You had talked of doing an adaptation.

INTERVIEWER: Why Theocritus?

WILLIAMS: The pastoral nature of it gave me a chance to spread myself. It was Greek, and it appealed to me; and it was a wonderful chance to record my feeling of respect for the Greek classics.

INTERVIEWER: There was a change in the verse in the fifties. Was this the first time you tried the new measure?

WILLIAMS: "The Descent" was the first. I regard that as an experiment in the variable foot.

INTERVIEWER: You said earlier that you were almost unconscious when you wrote it.

WILLIAMS: Yes, I was. I was very much excited. I wasn't conscious of doing anything unusual but I realized that something had occurred to me, which was a very satisfying conclusion to my poetic process. Something happened to my line that completed it, completed the rhythm, or at least it was satisfying to me. It was still an irregular composition; but not too much so; but I couldn't complete it. I had written that poem to retain the things which *would* have been the completion of the poem. But as for picking the thing up and going on with it, I had to acknowledge I was licked. I didn't dare fool with the poem so that it would have been more rigid; I wouldn't have wanted that.

INTERVIEWER: You felt there was nothing more you could do with it?

WILLIAMS: Nothing more. I felt all that I could do with it had been done, but it was not complete. I returned to it; but the irregularity of that poem could not be repeated by me. It was too . . . I've forgotten.

INTERVIEWER: You feel it wasn't a perfect poem?

WILLIAMS: It was too regular. There were variations of mood which would have led me to make a different poem out of it.

INTERVIEWER: And you don't think anything after "The Descent" goes beyond it?

WILLIAMS: No. I always wanted to do something more with it, but I didn't know why.

MRS. WILLIAMS: There was one written quite a long time before: that was the start of it. Then there was the "Daphne and Virginia"—Virginia, of course, was Paul's wife, and Daphne is Bill's. That poem always makes me sad. "The Orchestra" was written in 1954 or 1955, I think. Bill wrote quite a lot after he had the stroke. It's really amazing what he has done; and he gave readings, too, in Saint Louis, Chicago, Savannah—

WILLIAMS: I couldn't break through.

MRS. WILLIAMS: Harvard, Brandeis, Brown. We took two trips to the coast after that—to U.C.L.A., the University of California, Washington—

WILLIAMS: I've been going down hill rapidly.

INTERVIEWER: And the *Pictures from Brueghel?*

WILLIAMS: Yes, those are late; very late. But they are too regular.

INTERVIEWER: Did you ever grow any fonder of the academic world after your trips around the campuses?

MRS. WILLIAMS: *They* liked *him*, at least. And the girls' colleges all loved him.

WILLIAMS: The high point was the appearance at Wellesley. It was a very successful impromptu appearance; a reading. I always remember the satisfaction I got pleasing the ladies—the kids.

INTERVIEWER: Beginning with the Women's Club in Rutherford.

WILLIAMS: Always. I was always for the ladies.

MRS. WILLIAMS: Bill has always been fond of women, and terribly disappointed not to have had a sister. And he never had a daughter. But women like him; they sensed that he was sympathetic, and they could talk to him.

WILLIAMS: *Very* sympathetic.

INTERVIEWER: Just one or two more questions. Do you think your medical training—your discipline in science—has had any effect on your poetry?

WILLIAMS: The scientist is very important to the poet, because his language is important to him.

INTERVIEWER: To the scientist?

WILLIAMS: Well, and the poet. I don't pretend to go too far. But I have been taught to be accurate in my speech.

INTERVIEWER: But not scholastic. Someone has said you would not make so much of the great American language if you had been judicious about things.

WILLIAMS: It's a point well taken. The writing of English is a great pastime. The only catch to that is when a man adds the specification "English." That is purely accidental and means nothing. Any language could be inserted in its place. But the restrictions that are accepted in the classics of a language enclose it in a corset of mail which becomes its chief distinction.

MRS. WILLIAMS: Bill has always experimented. He was never satisfied to keep doing the same thing. And he has been severely criticized. But I think some of the younger poets are benefiting from it. Like Charles Tomlinson, and Robert Creeley—they've learned a lot from Bill. David Ignatow—any number of them. Allen Ginsberg was a good friend for many years.

WILLIAMS: I am a little concerned about the form. The art of the poem nowadays is something unstable; but at least the construction of the poem should make sense; you should know where you stand. Many questions haven't been answered as yet. Our poets may be wrong; but what can any of us do with his talent but try to develop his vision, so that through frequent failures we may learn better what we have missed in the past.

INTERVIEWER: What do you think you yourself have left of special value to the new poets?

WILLIAMS: The variable foot—the division of the line according to a new method that would be satisfactory to an American. It's all right if you are not intent on being national. But an American is forced to try to give the intonation. Either it *is* important or it is not important. It must have occurred to an American that the question of the line *was* important. The American idiom has much to offer us that the English language has never heard of. As for my own elliptic way of approach, it may be baffling, but it is not unfriendly, and not, I think, entirely empty.

MRS. WILLIAMS: All the young people come out to see Bill. Charles Olsen has been here a lot. Denise Levertov was out last week. Then there is Robert Wallace, Muriel Rukeyser, Charles Bell, Tram Combs. Charles Tomlinson stopped in on his way back to England.

WILLIAMS: Yes. He is writing in my vein. He's even conscious of copying me. I don't think he is too popular with his contemporaries. But it does look suspiciously like the beginning of something in England. I defer to you. But—do you have an example of his poems there?

INTERVIEWER: He seems to be carrying on the new measure. Do you have any comment?

WILLIAMS: The lines are not as I would have done, not loose enough. Not enough freedom. He didn't ignore the rules enough to make it really satisfactory.

INTERVIEWER: But you think he shows your influence in England, finally. That must be a satisfaction.

WILLIAMS: It is.

MRS. WILLIAMS: I think Bill will shortly be published in England.

INTERVIEWER: You would think they might have appreciated the American idiom.

WILLIAMS: Not *my* American idiom.

MRS. WILLIAMS: [*looking about among the books*]: These are some translations of Bill's poems in Italian—the early poems; *Paterson; The Desert Music.*

WILLIAMS: Yes, I was very pleased by those.

MRS. WILLIAMS: Here are some selected poems in German: *Gedichte,* 1962.

WILLIAMS: I'm alive—

MRS. WILLIAMS: There is a selection coming out now in Czechoslovakia. And here is an anthology of "American lyrics" in Norwegian—

WILLIAMS: I'm still alive!

—STANLEY KOEHLER
1964

8. Allen Ginsberg

Allen Ginsberg was born on June 3, 1926, in Paterson, New Jersey, the son of Louis Ginsberg, a poet and schoolteacher. He finished high school in Paterson and was graduated from Columbia in 1948. During the late forties and early fifties he held innumerable jobs: dishwasher in Manhattan, spot-welder in the Brooklyn Navy Yard, night porter with the May Company in Denver, book reviewer for *Newsweek*.

His long, angry, and influential poem "Howl," published in San Francisco in 1956, was seized by U.S. Customs and the local police and was the subject of an obscenity trial. After poets and critics testified in its behalf, the poem was released for distribution. As the acknowledged leader of the Beat Generation poets, Ginsberg traveled widely, reading his poetry and writing. He described his travels in the late fifties: "West coast 3 years. Later Arctic Sea Trip, Tangier, Venice, Amsterdam, Paris, read at Oxford Harvard Columbia Chicago."

Ginsberg has since spent extended periods of time in London, Havana, Calcutta, and Prague, and his appearances have frequently involved him in legal controversies. His work has been translated into many languages: French, Italian, Finnish, Japanese, and Bengali, among others. He has appeared in two films: *Pull My Daisy* (1961) with Jack Kerouac; and Jonas Mekas's *Guns of the Trees* (1962). Ginsberg's published works include *Empty Mirror* (1960), *Kaddish* (1960), *Reality Sandwiches* (1963), and several anthologies: *Planet News 1961–1967* (1968), *Collected Poems 1947–1980* (1980), and *White Shroud: Poems 1980–1985* (1985).

Ginsberg was the recipient of the American Institute of Arts and Letters Award (1969) and won the National Book Award for poetry in 1974 for *The Fall of America: Poems of These States 1965–1971* (1973). He lives in New York City.

Manuscript page by Allen Ginsberg.

From Journals ~~New York 1961~~

January NY 1961

In bed on my green purple red pink
    yellow orange bolivian blanket,
the tick of the clock, my back against the wall
--staring into black circled eyes magician
    man's bearded glance & story
the kitchen spun in a wheel of virtigo,
the eye in the center of the moving
    mandala--the
      eye in the hand
      the eye in the asshole
    The serpent eating or
~~in the black signatted jiteeti the working~~
      vomiting its tail
--the blank air a solid wall revolving
    around my retina--
The wheel of jewels and fire I saw moving
    vaster than my head in Peru
   Band circling in band and a black
    hole of Calcutta thru which
      I stared at my Atman
        without a body--
The Giotto window on Boston & giving
    to a scene in Bibled Palestine
    A golden star
   and the flight from Egypt
      in an instant now
Come true again--the Kabbala sign
    in the vomit on the floor--
On a window in Riverside drive,
    the boat moving slowly
up the flowing river, small autos
crawling up Hudson Drive
    a plash of white snow on
      the Palisades

① Sept 28 1964

E. 2 STREET
HIGH
✳
W/ Harry Smith
✳
OPTICAL
PHENOMENA
✳

REMEMBERING
LEARY'S BEDROOM
  HARVARD
JACK HALLUCINATING
  ✳
OUT ROBT.
LOWELL'S WINDOW

Ginsberg in Cuba, with plane shot down at Bay of Pigs (Photo: Tom Maschler).

Allen Ginsberg

Allen Ginsberg was elected King of the May by Czech students in Prague on May Day 1965. Soon afterward he was expelled by the Czech government. He had been traveling for several months—in Cuba, Russia, and Poland—and from Prague he flew to London to negotiate the English publication of his poems. I didn't know he was in the country, but one night in Bristol before a poetry reading I saw him in a bar. He read that night; I hadn't heard him read before and was struck that evening by the way he seemed to enter each of his poems emotionally while reading them, the performance as much a discovery for him as for his audience.

Ginsberg and I left Bristol the day after the reading, and hitch-hiked to Wells Cathedral and then to Glastonbury, where he picked a flower from King Arthur's grave to send, he said, to Peter Orlovsky. He studied carefully the exhibit of tools and weapons under the huge conical chimney of the ancient Abbot's kitchen, as later in Cambridge he was to study the Fitzwilliam Museum's store of

Blake manuscripts; Ginsberg's idea of a Jerusalemic Britain oc-curring now in the day of long hair and new music meant equally the fulfillment of Blake's predictions of Albion. As we came out of a teashop in Glastonbury (where customers had glanced cau-tiously at the bearded, prophetic—and unfazed—stranger), Allen spoke of Life's simulacrum of a report of his Oxford encounter with Dame Edith Sitwell. ("Dope makes me come out all over in spots," she's supposed to have said.)

Leaving the town, we were caught in a rainstorm, and took a bus to Bath. Then, hitchhiking toward London, we were unsuc-cessful until Ginsberg tried using Buddhist hand signals instead of thumbing; half a minute later a car stopped. Riding through Somerset he talked about notation, *the mode he says he learned from Kerouac and has used in composing his enormous journals; he read from an account he'd made of a recent meeting with the poets Yevtushenko and Vozhneshensky in Moscow, and then, look-ing up at a knot in a withered oak by the road, said, "The tree has cancer of the breast . . . that's what I mean. . . ."*

Two weeks later he was in Cambridge for a reading, and I asked him to submit to this interview. He was still busy with Blake, and roaming and musing around the university and countryside in his spare moments; it took two days to get him to sit still long enough to turn on the tape-recorder. He spoke slowly and thoughtfully, tiring after two hours. We stopped for a meal when guests came— when Ginsberg learned one of them was a biochemist he questioned him about viruses and DNA for an hour—then we returned to record the other half of the tape. The words that follow are his, with little alteration save the omission of repetitive matter in half a dozen places.

INTERVIEWER: I think Diana Trilling, speaking about your read-ing at Columbia, remarked that your poetry, like all poetry in English when dealing with a serious subject, naturally takes on the iambic pentameter rhythm. Do you agree?

GINSBERG: Well, it really isn't an accurate thing, I don't think. I've never actually sat down and made a technical analysis of the rhythms that I write. They're probably more near choriambic—

Greek meters, dithyrambic meters—and tending toward de DA de de DA de de . . . what is that? Tending toward dactylic, probably. Williams once remarked that American speech tends toward dactylic. But it's more complicated than dactyl because dactyl is a three, three units, a foot consisting of three parts, whereas the actual rhythm is probably a rhythm which consists of five, six, or seven, like DA de de DA de de DA de de DA DA. Which is more toward the line of Greek dance rhythms—that's why they call them choriambic. So actually, probably it's not really technically correct, what she said. But—and that applies to certain poems, like certain passages of "Howl" and certain passages of "Kaddish"—there are definite rhythms which could be analyzed as corresponding to classical rhythms, though not necessarily *English* classical rhythms; they might correspond to Greek classical rhythms, or Sanskrit prosody. But probably most of the other poetry, like "Aether" or "Laughing Gas" or a lot of those poems, they simply don't fit into that. I think she felt very comfy, to think that that would be so. I really felt quite hurt about that, because it seemed to me that she ignored the main prosodic technical achievements that I had proffered forth to the academy, and they didn't even recognize it. I mean not that I want to stick her with being the academy.

INTERVIEWER: And in "Howl" and "Kaddish" you were working with a kind of classical unit? Is that an accurate description?

GINSBERG: Yeah, but it doesn't do very much good, because I wasn't really working with a classical unit, I was working with my own neural impulses and writing impulses. See, the difference is between someone sitting down to write a poem *in* a definite preconceived metrical pattern and filling in that pattern, and someone working with his physiological movements and *arriving* at a pattern, and perhaps even arriving at a pattern which might even have a name, or might even have a classical usage, but arriving at it organically rather than synthetically. Nobody's got any objection to even iambic pentameter if it comes from a source deeper than the mind—that is to say, if it comes from the breathing and the belly and the lungs.

INTERVIEWER: American poets have been able to break away

from a kind of English specified rhythm earlier than English poets have been able to do. Do you think this has anything to do with a peculiarity in English spoken tradition?

GINSBERG: No, I don't really think so, because the English don't speak in iambic pentameter either; they don't speak in the recognizable pattern that they write in. The dimness of their speech and the lack of emotional variation is parallel to the kind of dim diction and literary usage in the poetry now. But you can hear all sorts of Liverpudlian or Gordian—that's Newcastle—you can hear all sorts of variants aside from an upper-tone accent, a high-class accent, that don't fit into the tone of poetry being written right now. It's not being used like in America—I think it's just that British poets are more cowardly.

INTERVIEWER: Do you find any exception to this?

GINSBERG: It's pretty general, even the supposedly avant-garde poets. They write, you know, in a very toned-down manner.

INTERVIEWER: How about a poet like Basil Bunting?

GINSBERG: Well, he was working with a whole bunch of wild men from an earlier era, who were all breaking through, I guess. And so he had that experience—also he knew Persian, he knew Persian prosody. He was better educated than most English poets.

INTERVIEWER: The kind of organization you use in "Howl," a recurrent kind of syntax—you don't think this is relevant any longer to what you want to do?

GINSBERG: No, but it was relevant to what I wanted to do then, it wasn't even a conscious decision.

INTERVIEWER: Was this related in any way to a kind of music or jazz that you were interested in at the time?

GINSBERG: Mmm . . . the myth of Lester Young as described by Kerouac, blowing eighty-nine choruses of "Lady Be Good," say, in one night, or my own hearing of Illinois Jacquet's *Jazz at the Philharmonic*, Volume 2; I think "Can't Get Started" was the title.

INTERVIEWER: And you've also mentioned poets like Christopher Smart, for instance, as providing an analogy—is this something you discovered later on?

GINSBERG: When I looked into it, yeah. Actually, I keep reading, or earlier I kept reading, that I was influenced by Kenneth Fearing and Carl Sandburg, whereas actually I was more conscious of Christopher Smart, and Blake's Prophetic Books, and Whitman and some aspects of Biblical rhetoric. And a lot of specific prose things, like Genet, Genet's *Our Lady of the Flowers* and the rhetoric in that, and Céline; Kerouac, most of all, was the biggest influence I think—Kerouac's prose.

INTERVIEWER: When did you come onto Burroughs's work?

GINSBERG: Let's see . . . Well, first thing of Burroughs's I ever read was 1946 . . . which was a skit later published and integrated in some other work of his, called *So Proudly We Hail,* describing the sinking of the *Titanic* and an orchestra playing, a spade orchestra playing "The Star Spangled Banner" while everybody rushed out to the lifeboats and the captain got up in woman's dress and rushed into the purser's office and shot the purser and stole all the money, and a spastic paretic jumped into a lifeboat with a machete and began chopping off people's fingers that were trying to climb into the boat, saying, "Out of the way, you foolth . . . dirty thunthufbithes." That was a thing he had written up at Harvard with a friend named Kells Elvins. Which is really the whole key of all his work, like the sinking of America, and everybody like frightened rats trying to get out, or that was his vision of the time.

Then he and Kerouac later in 1945—forty-five or forty-six— wrote a big detective book together, alternating chapters. I don't know where that book is now—Kerouac has his chapters and Burroughs's are somewhere in his papers. So I think in a sense it was Kerouac that encouraged Burroughs to write really, because Kerouac was so enthusiastic about prose, about writing, about lyricism, about the honor of writing . . . the Thomas Wolfe-ian delights of it. So anyway he turned Burroughs on in a *sense,* because Burroughs found a companion who could write really interestingly, and Burroughs admired Kerouac's perceptions. Kerouac could imitate Dashiell Hammett as well as Bill, which was Bill's natural style: dry, bony, factual. At that time Burroughs was reading John O'Hara, simply for facts, not for any sublime stylistic thing, just because he was a hard-nosed reporter.

Then in Mexico around 1951 he started writing *Junkie*. I've forgotten what relation I had to that—I think I wound up as the agent for it, taking it around New York trying to get it published. I think he sent me portions of it at the time—I've forgotten how it worked out now. This was around 1949 or 1950. He was going through a personal crisis, his wife had died. It was in Mexico or South America . . . but it was a very generous thing of him to do, to start writing all of a sudden. Burroughs was always a very *tender* sort of person, but very dignified and shy and withdrawn, and for him to *commit* himself to a big autobiographical thing like that was . . . at the time, struck me as like a piece of eternity is in love with the . . . what is it, "Eternity is in love with the productions of Time"? So he was making a production of Time then.

Then I started taking that around. I've forgotten who I took that to but I think maybe to Louis Simpson who was then working at Bobbs-Merrill. I'm not sure whether I took it to him—I remember taking it to Jason Epstein who was then working at Doubleday I think. Epstein at the time was not as experienced as he is now. And his reaction to it, I remember when I went back to his office to pick it up, was, well this is all very interesting, but it isn't really interesting, on account of if it were an autobiography of a junkie written by Winston *Churchill* then it'd be interesting, but written by somebody he'd never heard of, well then it's *not* interesting. And anyway I said what about the *prose*, the prose is interesting, and he says, oh, a difference of opinion on that. Finally I wound up taking it to Carl Solomon who was then a reader for A. A. Wynn Company, which was his uncle; and they finally got it through there. But it was finally published as a cheap paperback. With a whole bunch of frightened footnotes; like Burroughs said that marijuana was nonhabit-forming, which is now accepted as a fact, there'd be a footnote by the editor, "Reliable, er, responsible medical opinion does not confirm this." Then they also had a little introduction . . . literally they were afraid of the book being censored or *seized* at the time, is what they said. I've forgotten what the terms of censorship or seizure were that they were worried about. This was about 1952. They *said* that they were afraid to publish it straight for fear there would be a Congressional investigation or something, I don't know what. I think there was some noise about narcotics at the time. Newspaper noise . . . I've forgotten exactly what the arguments were. But anyway they had to write a preface which hedged on the book a lot.

INTERVIEWER: Has there been a time when fear of censorship or similar trouble has made your own expression difficult?

GINSBERG: This is so complicated a matter. The beginning of the fear with me was, you know what would my father say to something that I would write. At the time, writing "Howl"—for instance, like I assumed when writing it that it was something that *could* not be published because I wouldn't want my daddy to see what was in there. About my sex life, being fucked in the ass, imagine your father reading a thing like that, was what I thought. Though that disappeared as soon as the thing was real, or as soon as I manifested my . . . you know, it didn't make that much importance finally. That was sort of a help for writing, because I assumed that it wouldn't be published, therefore I could say anything that I wanted. So literally just for myself or anybody that I knew personally well, writers who would be willing to appreciate it with a breadth of tolerance—in a piece of work like "Howl"—who wouldn't be judging from a moralistic viewpoint but looking for evidences of humanity or secret thought or just actual truthfulness.

Then there's later the problem of publication—we had a lot. The English printer refused at first I think, we were afraid of customs; the first edition we had to print with asterisks on some of the dirty words, and then the *Evergreen Review* in reprinting it used asterisks, and various people reprinting it later always wanted to use the *Evergreen* version rather than the corrected legal City Lights version—like I think there's an anthology of Jewish writers, I forgot who edited that, but a couple of the high-class intellectuals from Columbia. I had written asking them specifically to use the later City Lights version, but they went ahead and printed an asterisked version. I forget what was the name of that—something like *New Generation of Jewish Writing,* Philip Roth, et cetera.

INTERVIEWER: Do you take difficulties like these as social problems, problems of communication simply, or do you feel they also block your own ability to express yourself for yourself?

GINSBERG: The problem is, where it gets to literature, is this. We all talk among ourselves and we have common understandings, and we say anything we want to say, and we talk about our assholes, and we talk about our cocks, and we talk about who we fucked last night, or who we're gonna fuck tomorrow, or what kind love affair we have, or when we got drunk, or when we stuck a broom in our ass in the Hotel Ambassador in Prague—anybody tells one's friends about that. So then—what happens if you make a distinction between what you tell your friends and what you tell your Muse? The problem is to break down that distinction: when you approach the Muse to talk as frankly as you would talk with yourself or with your friends. So I began finding, in conversations with Burroughs and Kerouac and Gregory Corso, in conversations with people whom I knew well, whose souls I respected, that the things we were telling each other for real were totally different from what was already in literature. And that was Kerouac's great discovery in *On the Road.* The kinds of things that he and Neal Cassady were talking about, he finally discovered were *the* subject matter for what he wanted to write down. That meant, at that minute, a complete revision of what literature was supposed to be, in *his* mind, and actually in the minds of the people that first read the book. Certainly in the minds of the critics, who had at first attacked it as not being . . . proper structure, or something. In other words, a gang of friends running around in an automobile. Which obviously is like a great picaresque literary device, and a classical one. And was *not* recognized, at the time, as suitable literary subject matter.

INTERVIEWER: So it's not just a matter of themes—sex, or any other one—

GINSBERG: It's the ability to commit to writing, to *write,* the same way that you . . . are! Anyway! You have many writers who have preconceived ideas about what literature is supposed to be, and their ideas seem to exclude that which makes them most charming in private conversation. Their faggishness, or their campiness, or their neurasthenia, or their solitude, or their goofiness, or their—even—masculinity, at times. Because they think that they're gonna write something that sounds like something else that they've read before, instead of sounds like them. Or comes from their own life. In other words, there's no distinction, there should be no distinction between what we write down, and what we really know, to begin with. As we know it every day, with each other. And the hypocrisy of literature has been—you know like there's supposed to be formal literature, which is supposed to be different from . . . in subject, in diction, and even in organization, from our quotidian inspired lives.

It's also like in Whitman, "I find no fat sweeter than that which sticks to my own bones"—that is to say the self-confidence of someone who knows that he's really alive, and that his existence is just as good as any other subject matter.

INTERVIEWER: Is physiology a part of this too—like the difference between your long breath line, and William Carlos Williams's shorter unit?

GINSBERG: Analytically, ex post facto, it all begins with fucking around and intuition and without any idea of *what* you're doing, I think. Later, I have a tendency to explain it, "Well, I got a longer breath than Williams, or I'm Jewish, or I study yoga, or I sing long lines. . . ." But anyway, what it boils down to is this, it's my *movement*, my feeling is for a big long clanky statement— partly that's something that I share, or maybe that I even got from Kerouac's long prose line; which is really, like he once remarked, an extended poem. Like one long sentence page of his in *Doctor Sax* or *Railroad Earth* or occasionally *On the Road*—if you examine them phrase by phrase they usually have the density of poetry, and the beauty of poetry, but most of all the single elastic rhythm running from beginning to end of the line and ending "mop!"

INTERVIEWER: Have you ever wanted to extend this rhythmic feeling as far as, say, Artaud or now Michael McClure have taken it—to a line that is actually animal noise?

GINSBERG: The rhythm of the long line is also an animal cry.

INTERVIEWER: So you're following that feeling and not a thought or a visual image?

GINSBERG: It's simultaneous. The poetry generally is like a rhythmic articulation of feeling. The feeling is like an impulse that rises within—just like sexual impulses, say; it's almost as definite as that. It's a feeling that begins somewhere in the pit of the stomach and rises up forward in the breast and then comes out through the mouth and ears, and comes forth a croon or a groan or a sigh. Which, if you put words to it by looking around and seeing and trying to describe what's making you sigh—and sigh in words—you simply articulate what you're feeling. As simple as that. Or actually what happens is, at best what happens, is there's a definite body rhythm that has no definite words, or may have one or two words attached to it, one or two key words attached to it. And then, in writing it down, it's simply by a process of association that I find what the rest of the statement is—what can be collected around that word, what that word is connected to. Partly by simple association, the first thing that comes to my mind like "Moloch is" or "Moloch who," and then whatever comes out. But that also goes along with a definite rhythmic impulse, like DA de de DA de de DA de de DA DA. "Moloch whose *eyes* are a *thou*sand blind *windows.*" And before I wrote "Moloch whose eyes are a thousand blind windows," I had the word, "Moloch, Moloch, Moloch," and I also had the feeling DA de de DA de de DA de de DA DA. So it was just a question of looking up and seeing a lot of windows, and saying, Oh, windows, of course, but what kind of windows? But not even that—"Moloch whose eyes." "Moloch whose *eyes*"—which is beautiful in itself—but what about it, Moloch whose eyes are *what*? So Moloch whose eyes—then probably the next thing I thought was "thousands." O.K., and then thousands *what*? "Thousands blind." And I had to finish it somehow. So I hadda say "windows." It looked good *afterward.*

Usually during the composition, step by step, word by word and adjective by adjective, if it's at all spontaneous, I don't know whether it even makes sense sometimes. Sometimes I do know it makes complete sense, and I start crying. Because I realize I'm hitting some area which is absolutely true. And in that sense applicable universally, or understandable universally. In that sense able to survive through time—in that sense to be read by somebody and wept to, maybe, centuries later. In that sense prophecy, because it touches a common key . . . what prophecy actually is is not that you actually know that the bomb will fall in 1942. It's that you know and feel something which somebody knows and feels in a hundred years. And maybe articulate it in a hint—concrete way that they can pick up on in a hundred years.

INTERVIEWER: You once mentioned something you had found in Cézanne—a remark about the reconstitution of the *petites sensations* of experience, in his own painting—and you compared this with the methods of your poetry.

GINSBERG: I got all hung up on Cézanne around 1949 in my last year at Columbia, studying with Meyer Schapiro. I don't know how it led into it—I think it was about the same time that I was having these Blake visions. So. The thing I understood from Blake was that it was possible to transmit a message through time which could reach the enlightened, that poetry had a definite effect, it wasn't just pretty, or just beautiful, as I had understood pretty beauty before—it was something basic to human existence, or it reached something, it reached the bottom of human existence. But anyway the impression I got was that it was like a kind of time machine through which he could transmit, Blake could transmit, his basic consciousness and communicate it to somebody else after he was dead—in other words, build a time machine.

Now just about that time I was looking at Cézanne and I suddenly got a strange shuddering impression looking at his canvases, partly the effect when someone pulls a Venetian blind, reverses the Venetian—there's a sudden shift, a flashing that you see in Cézanne canvases. Partly it's when the canvas opens up into three dimensions and looks like wooden objects, like solid-space objects, in three dimensions rather than flat. Partly it's the enormous spaces which open up in Cézanne's landscapes. And it's partly that mysterious quality around his figures, like of his wife or the cardplayers or the postman or whoever, the local Aix characters. They look like great huge 3-D wooden dolls, sometimes. Very *uncanny* thing, like a very mysterious thing—in other words, there's a strange sensation that one gets, looking at his canvases, which I began to associate with the extraordinary sensation—cosmic sensation, in fact—that I had experienced catalyzed by Blake's "Sun-flower" and "Sick Rose" and a few other poems. So I began studiously investigating Cézanne's intentions and method, and looking at all the canvases of his that I could find in New York, and all the reproductions I could find, and I was writing at the time a paper on him, for Schapiro at Columbia in the fine-arts course.

And the whole thing opened up, two ways: first, I read a book on Cézanne's composition by Earl Loran, who showed photographs, analyses and photographs of the original motifs, side by side with the actual canvases—and years later I actually went to Aix, with all the postcards, and stood in the spots, and tried to find the places where he painted Mont-Sainte-Victoire from, and got in his studio and saw some of the motifs he used, like his big black hat and his cloak. Well, first of all, I began to see that Cézanne had all sorts of literary symbolism in him, on and off. I was preoccupied with Plotinian terminology, of time and eternity, and I saw it in Cézanne paintings, an early painting of a clock on a shelf which I associated with time and eternity, and I began to think he was a big secret mystic. And I saw a photograph of his studio in Loran's book and it was like an alchemist's studio, because he had a skull, and he had a long black coat, and he had this big black hat. So I began thinking of him as, you know, like a magic character. Like the original version I had thought of him was like this austere dullard from Aix. So I began getting really interested in him as a hermetic type, and then I symbolically read into his canvases things that probably weren't there, like there's a painting of a winding road which turns off, and I saw that as the mystical path: it turns off into a village and the end of the path is hidden. Something he painted I guess when he went out painting with Bernard. Then there was an account of a very fantastic conversation that he had had. It's quoted in Loran's book: there's a long long long paragraph where he says, "By means of squares, cubes, triangles, I try to reconstitute the impression that I have from nature: the means that I use to reconstitute the impression of solidity that I think-feel-see when I am looking at a motif like Victoire is to reduce it to some kind of pictorial language, so I use these squares, cubes, and triangles, but I try to build them together so interknit [*and here in the conversation he held his hands together with his fingers interknit*] so that *no light gets through.*" And I was mystified by that, but it seemed to make sense in terms of the grid of paint strokes that he had on his canvas, so that he produced a solid two-dimensional surface which when you looked *into* it, maybe from a slight distance with your eyes either unfocused or your eyelids lowered slightly, you could see a great three-dimensional opening, mysterious, stereoscopic, like going into a stereopticon. And I began discovering in "The Cardplayers" all sorts of sinister symbols, like there's one guy leaning against the wall with a stolid expression on his face, that he doesn't want to get involved; and then there's two guys who are peasants, who are looking as if they've just been dealt *Death* cards; and then the *dealer* you look at and he turns out to be a city slicker with a big blue cloak and almost rouge doll-like cheeks and a fat-faced Kafkian-agent impression about him, like he's a cardsharp, he's a cosmic cardsharp dealing out Fate to all these people. This looks like a great big hermetic Rembrandtian portrait in Aix! That's why it has that funny monumentality—aside from the quote plastic values unquote.

Then, I smoked a lot of marijuana and went to the basement of the Museum of Modern Art in New York and looked at his water colors and that's where I began really turning on to space in Cézanne and the way he built it up. Particularly there's one of rocks, I guess "Rocks at Garonne," and you look at them for a while, and after a while they seem like they're rocks, just the rock parts, you don't know where they are, whether they're on the ground or in the air or on top of a cliff, but then they seem to be floating in space like clouds, and then they seem to be also a bit like they're amorphous, like kneecaps or cockheads or faces without eyes. And it has a very mysterious impression. Well, that may have been the result of the pot. But it's a definite thing that I got from that. Then he did some very odd studies after classical statues, Renaissance statues, and they're great gigantesque herculean figures with little tiny pinheads . . . so that apparently was his comment on them!

And then . . . the things were endless to find in Cézanne. Finally I was reading his letters and I discovered this phrase again, *mes petites sensations*—"I'm an old man and my passions are not, my senses are not coarsened by passions like some *other* old men I know, and I have worked for years trying to," I guess it was the phrase, "*reconstitute* the *petites sensations* that I get from nature, and I could stand on a hill and merely by moving my head half an inch the composition of the landscape was totally changed." So apparently he'd refined his optical perception to such a point where it's a real contemplation of optical phenomena in an almost yogic way, where he's standing there, from a specific point studying the optical field, the depth in the optical field, looking, actually looking at his own eyeballs in a sense. The attempting to reconstitute the sensation in his own eyeballs. And what does he say finally—in a very weird statement which one would not expect of the austere old workman—he said, "And this *petite sensation* is nothing other than *pater omnipotens aeterna deus.*"

So that was, I felt, the key to Cézanne's hermetic method . . . everybody knows his workman-like, artisan-like, pettified-like painting method which is so great, but the really ro*man*ticistic motif behind it is absolutely marvelous, so you realize that he's really a saint! Working on his form of yoga, all that time, in obvious saintly circumstances of retirement in a small village, leading a relatively nonsociable life, going through the motions of going to church or not, but really containing in his skull these supernatural phenomena, and observations . . . you know, and it's very humble actually, because he didn't know if he was crazy or not—that is a flash of the physical, miracle dimensions of existence, trying to reduce that to canvas in two dimensions, and then trying to do it in such a way as it would look—if the observer looked at it long enough—it would look like as much three dimension as the actual *world* of optical phenomena when one looks through one's eyes. Actually he's reconstituted the whole fucking universe in his canvases—it's like a fantastic thing!—or at least the appearance of the universe.

So. I used a lot of this material in the references in the last part of the first section of "Howl": "sensation of Pater Omnipotens Aeterna Deus." The last part of "Howl" was really an homage to art but also in specific terms an homage to Cézanne's method, in a sense I adapted what I could to writing; but that's a very complicated matter to explain. Except, putting it very simply, that just as Cézanne doesn't use perspective lines to create space, but it's a juxtaposition of one color against another color (that's one element of his space), so, I had the idea, perhaps overrefined, that by the unexplainable, unexplained nonperspective line, that is, juxtaposition of one *word* against another, a *gap* between the two words—like the space gap in the canvas—there'd be a gap between the two words which the mind would fill in with the sensation of existence. In other words when I say, oh . . . when Shakespeare says, "In the dread vast and middle of the night," something happens between "dread vast" and "middle." That creates like a whole space of, spaciness of black night. How it gets that is very odd, those words put together. Or in the haiku, you have two distinct images, set side by side without drawing a connection, without drawing a logical connection between them: the *mind* fills in this . . . this space. Like

> O ant
> *crawl up Mount Fujiyama,*
> *but slowly, slowly.*

Now you have the small ant and you have Mount Fujiyama and you have the slowly, slowly, and what happens is that you feel almost like . . . a cock in your mouth! You feel this enormous space-universe, it's almost a tactile thing. Well, anyway, it's a phenomenon-sensation, phenomenon hyphen sensation, that's created by this little haiku of Issa, for instance.

So, I was trying to do similar things with juxtapositions like "hydrogen jukebox." Or . . . "winter midnight smalltown streetlight rain." Instead of cubes and squares and triangles. Cézanne is reconstituting by means of triangles, cubes, and colors—I have to reconstitute by means of words, rhythms of course, and all that—but say it's words, phrasings. So. The problem is then to reach the different parts of the mind, which are existing simultaneously, choosing elements from both, like: jazz, jukebox, and all that, and we have the jukebox from that; politics, hydrogen bomb, and we have the hydrogen of that, you see "hydrogen jukebox." And that actually compresses in one instant like a whole series of things. Or the end of "Sun-flower" with "cunts of wheelbarrows," whatever that all meant, or "rubber dollar bills"—"skin of machinery"; see, and actually in the moment of composition I don't necessarily *know* what it means, but it comes to mean something later, after a year or two, I realize that it meant something clear, unconsciously. Which takes on meaning in time, like a photograph developing slowly. Because we're not really always conscious of the entire depth of our minds—in other words, we just know a lot more than we're able to be aware of, normally—though at moments we're completely aware, I guess.

There's some other element of Cézanne that was interesting . . . oh, his patience, of course. In recording the optical phenomena. Has something to do with Blake: *with* not *through* the eye—"You're led to believe a lie when you see with not through the eye." He's seeing through his eye. One can see *through* his canvas to God, really, is the way it boils down. Or to Pater Omnipotens Aeterna Deus. I could imagine someone not prepared, in a peculiar chemical-physiological state, peculiar mental state, psychic state, someone not prepared who had no experience of eternal ecstasy, passing in front of a Cézanne canvas, distracted and without noticing it, his eye traveling in, to, through the canvas into the space and suddenly stopping with his hair standing on end, dead in his tracks, *seeing* a whole universe. And I think that's what Cézanne really does, to a lot of people.

Where were we now? Yeah, the idea that I had was that gaps in space and time through images juxtaposed, just as in the haiku you get two images which the mind connects in a flash, and so that *flash* is the *petite sensation*; or the *satori*, perhaps, that the Zen haikuists would speak of—if they speak of it like that. So, the poetic experience that Housman talks about, the hair-standing-on-end or the hackles-rising, whatever it is, visceral thing. The interesting thing would be to know if certain combinations of words and rhythms actually had an electrochemical reaction on the body, which could catalyze specific states of consciousness. I think that's what probably happened to me with Blake. I'm *sure* it's what happens on a perhaps lower level with Poe's "Bells" or "Raven," or even Vachel Lindsay's "Congo": that there is a hypnotic rhythm there, which when you introduce it into your nervous system, causes all sorts of electronic changes—permanently alters it. There's a statement by Artaud on that subject, that certain music when introduced into the nervous system changes the molecular composition of the nerve cells or something like that, it permanently alters the being that has experience of this. Well, anyway, this is certainly true. In other words, any experience we have is recorded in the brain and goes through neural patterns and whatnot: so I suppose brain recordings are done by means of shifting around of little electrons—so there is actually an electrochemical effect caused by art.

So . . . the problem is what is the maximum electrochemical effect in the desired direction. That is what I was taking Blake as having done to me. And what I take as one of the optimal possibilities of art. But this is all putting it in a kind of bullshit abstract way. But it's an interesting—toy. To play with. That idea.

INTERVIEWER: In the last five or six months you've been in Cuba, Czechoslovakia, Russia, and Poland. Has this helped to clarify your sense of the current world situation?

GINSBERG: Yeah, I no longer feel—I didn't ever feel that there was any answer in dogmatic Leninism-Marxism—but I feel very definitely now that there's no answer to my desires there. Nor do most of the people in those countries—in Russia or Poland or

Cuba—really feel that either. It's sort of like a religious theory imposed from above and usually used to beat people on the head with. Nobody takes it seriously because it doesn't mean anything, it means different things in different countries anyway. The general idea of revolution against American idiocy is good, it's still sympathetic, and I guess it's a good thing like in Cuba, and obviously Viet Nam. But what's gonna follow—the dogmatism that follows is a big drag. And everybody apologizes for the dogmatism by saying, well, it's an inevitable consequence of the struggle against American repression. And that may be true too.

But there's one thing I feel certain of, and that's that there's no human answer in communism or capitalism as it's practiced outside of the U. S. in any case. In other words, by hindsight, the interior of America is not bad, at least for me, though it might be bad for a spade, but not too bad, creepy, but it's not impossible. But traveling in countries like Cuba and Viet Nam I realize that the people that get the real evil side effects of America are there— in other words, it really is like imperialism, in that sense. People in the United States all got money, they got cars, and everybody else *starves* on account of American foreign policy. Or is being bombed out, torn apart, and bleeding on the street, they get all their teeth bashed in, tear gassed, or hot pokers up their ass, things that would be, you know, considered terrible in the United States. Except for Negroes.

So I don't know. I don't see any particular answer, and *this* month it seemed to me like actually an atomic war was inevitable on account of both sides were so dogmatic and frightened and had nowhere to go and didn't know what to do with themselves anymore except fight. Everybody too intransigent. Everybody too mean. I don't suppose it'll take place, but . . . Somebody has got to sit in the British Museum again like Marx and figure out a new system; a new blueprint. Another century has gone, technology has changed everything completely, so it's time for a new utopian system. Burroughs is almost working on it.

But one thing that's impressive is Blake's idea of Jerusalem, Jerusalemic Britain, which I think is *now* more and more valid. He, I guess, defined it. I'm still confused about Blake, I still haven't read him all through enough to understand what direction he was really pointing to. It seems to be the *naked human form divine*, seems to be Energy, it seems to be sexualization, or sexual liberation, which are the directions we all believe in. He also seems, however, to have some idea of imagination which I don't fully understand yet. That is, it's something outside of the body, with a rejection of the body, and I don't quite understand that. A life after death even. Which I still haven't comprehended. There's a letter in the Fitzwilliam Museum, written several months before he died. He says, "My body is in turmoil and stress and decaying, *but* my ideas, my power of ideas and my imagination, are stronger than ever." And I find it hard to conceive of that. I think if I were lying in bed dying, with my body pained, I would just give up. I mean, you know, because I don't think I could *exist* outside my body. But he apparently was able to. Williams didn't seem to be able to. In other words Williams's universe was tied up with his body. Blake's universe didn't seem to be tied up with his body. Real mysterious, like far other worlds and other seas, so to speak. Been puzzling over that today.

The Jerusalemic world of Blake seems to be Mercy-Pity-Peace. Which has human form. Mercy has a human face. So that's all clear.

INTERVIEWER: How about Blake's statement about the senses being the chief inlets of the soul in this age—I don't know what "this age" means; is there another one?

GINSBERG: What he says is interesting because there's the same thing in Hindu mythology, they speak of This Age as the Kali Yuga, the age of destruction, or an age so sunk in materialism. You'd find a similar formulation in Vico, like what is it, the Age of Gold running on to the Iron and then Stone, again. Well, the Hindus say that *this* is the Kali Age or Kali Yuga or Kali Cycle, and we are also so sunk in matter, the five senses are matter, sense, that they say there is absolutely no way out by intellect, by thought, by discipline, by practice, by sadhana, by jnanayoga, nor karma yoga—that is, doing good works—no way out through our own will or our own effort. The *only* way out that they generally now prescribe, generally in India at the moment, is through bhakti yoga, which is Faith-Hope-Adoration-Worship, or like probably the equivalent of the Christian Sacred Heart, which I find a very lovely doctrine—that is to say, pure delight, the only way you can be saved is to sing. In other words, the only way to drag up, from the depths of this depression, to drag up your soul to its proper bliss, and understanding, is to give yourself, completely, to your heart's desire. The image will be determined by the heart's compass, by the compass of what the heart moves toward and desires. And then you get on your knees or on your lap or on your head and you sing and chant prayers and mantras, till you reach a state of ecstasy and understanding, and the bliss overflows out of your body. They say intellect, like Saint Thomas Aquinas, will never do it, because it's just like me getting all hung up on whether I could remember what happened before I was born—I mean you could get lost there very easily, and it has no relevance *anyway*, to the existent flower. Blake says something similar, like Energy, and Excess . . . leads to the palace of wisdom. The Hindu bhakti is like excess of devotion; you just, you know, give yourself all out to devotion.

Very oddly a lady saint Shri Matakrishnaji in Brindaban, whom I consulted about my spiritual problems, told me to take Blake for my guru. There's all kinds of different gurus, there can be living and nonliving gurus—apparently whoever initiates you, and I apparently was initiated by Blake in terms of at least having an ecstatic experience from him. So that when I got here to Cambridge I had to rush over to the Fitzwilliam Museum to find his misspellings in *Songs of Innocence*.

INTERVIEWER: What was the Blake experience you speak of?

GINSBERG: About 1945 I got interested in Supreme Reality with a capital S and R, and I wrote big long poems about a last voyage looking for Supreme Reality. Which was like a Dostoevskian or Thomas Wolfeian idealization or like Rimbaud—what was Rimbaud's term, new vision, was that it? Or Kerouac was talking about a new vision, verbally, and intuitively out of longing, but also out of a funny kind of tolerance of this universe. In 1948 in East Harlem in the summer I was living—this is like the Ancient Mariner, I've said this so many times: "stoppeth one of three./

'By thy long grey beard . . . ' " Hang an albatross around your neck. . . . The one thing I felt at the time was that it would be a terrible horror, that in one or two decades I would be trying to explain to people that one day something like this happened to me! I even wrote a long poem saying, "I will grow old, a grey and groaning man,/ and with each hour the same thought, and with each thought the same denial./ Will I spend my life in praise of the *idea* of God?/ Time leaves no hope. We creep and wait. We wait and go alone." Psalm II—which I never published. So anyway—there I was in my bed in Harlem . . . jacking off. With my pants open, lying around on a bed by the window sill, looking out into the cornices of Harlem and the sky above. And I had just come. And had perhaps hardly even wiped the come off my thighs, my trousers, or whatever it was. As I often do, I had been jacking off while reading—I think it's probably a common phenomenon to be noticed among adolescents. Though I was a little older than an adolescent at the time. About twenty-two. There's a kind of interesting thing about, you know, distracting your attention while you jack off—that is, you know, reading a book or looking out of a window, or doing something else with the conscious mind which kind of makes it sexier.

So anyway, what I had been doing that week—I'd been in a very lonely solitary state, dark night of the soul sort of, reading Saint John of the Cross, maybe on account of that everybody'd gone away that I knew, Burroughs was in Mexico, Jack was out in Long Island and relatively isolated, we didn't see each other, and I had been very close with them for several years. Huncke I think was in jail, or something. Anyway, there was nobody I knew. Mainly the thing was that I'd been making it with N.C., and finally I think I got a letter from him saying it was all off, no more, we shouldn't consider ourselves lovers any more on account of it just wouldn't work out. But previously we'd had an understanding that we—Neal Cassady, I said "N.C." but I suppose you can use his name—we'd had a big tender lovers' understanding. But I guess it got too much for him, partly because he was three thousand miles away and he had six thousand girl friends on the other side of the continent, who were keeping him busy, and then here was my lone cry of despair from New York. So. I got a letter from him saying, Now, Allen, we gotta move on to *new* territory. So I felt this is like a great mortal blow to all of my tenderest hopes. And I figured I'd never find any sort of psychospiritual sexo-cock jewel fulfillment in my existence! So, I went into . . . like I felt cut off from what I'd idealized romantically. And I was also graduating from school and had nowhere to go and the difficulty of getting a job. So finally there was nothing for me to do except to eat vegetables and live in Harlem. In an apartment I'd rented from someone. Sublet.

So, in that state therefore, of hopelessness, or dead end, change of phase, you know—growing up—and in an equilibrium in any case, a psychic, a mental equilibrium of a kind, like of having no New Vision and no Supreme Reality and nothing but the world in front of me, and of not knowing what to do with *that* . . . there was a funny balance of tension, in every direction. And just after I came, on this occasion, with a Blake book on my lap—I wasn't even reading, my eye was idling over the page of "Ah, Sun-flower," and it suddenly appeared—the poem I'd read a lot of times before, overfamiliar to the point where it didn't make any particular meaning except some sweet thing about flowers—and suddenly I realized that the poem was talking about *me*. "Ah, Sun-flower! weary of time, / Who countest the steps of the sun; / Seeking after that sweet golden clime, / Where the traveller's journey is done." Now, I began understanding it, the poem while looking at it, and suddenly, simultaneously with understanding it, heard a very deep earthen grave voice in the room, which I immediately assumed, I didn't think twice, was Blake's voice; it wasn't any voice that I knew, though I had previously had a conception of a voice of rock, in a poem, some image like that—or maybe that came after this experience.

And my eye on the page, simultaneously the auditory hallucination, or whatever terminology here used, the apparitional voice, in the room, woke me further deep in my understanding of the poem, because the voice was so completely tender and beautifully . . . ancient. Like the voice of the Ancient of Days. But the peculiar quality of the voice was something unforgettable because it was like God had a human voice, with all the infinite tenderness and anciency and mortal gravity of a living Creator speaking to his son. "Where the Youth pined away with desire, / And the pale Virgin shrouded in snow, / Arise from their graves, and aspire / Where my Sun-flower wishes to go." Meaning that there *was* a *place*, there was a sweet golden clime, and the *sweet golden*, what was that . . . and simultaneous to the voice there was also an emotion, risen in my soul in response to the voice, and a sudden *visual* realization of the same awesome phenomena. That is to say, looking out at the window, through the window at the sky, suddenly it seemed that I saw into the depths of the universe, by looking simply into the ancient sky. The sky suddenly seemed very *ancient*. And this was the very ancient place that he was talking about, the sweet golden clime, I suddenly realized that *this* existence was *it*! And, that I was born in order to experience up to this very moment that I was having this experience, to realize what this was all about—in other words that this was the moment that I was born for. This initiation. Or this vision or this consciousness, of being alive unto myself, alive myself unto the Creator. As the son of the Creator—who loved me, I realized, or who responded to my desire, say. It was the same desire both ways.

Anyway, my first thought was this was what I was born for, and second thought, never forget—never forget, never renege, never deny. Never deny the voice—no, never *forget* it, don't get lost mentally wandering in other spirit worlds or American or job worlds or advertising worlds or war worlds or earth worlds. But the spirit of the universe was what I was born to realize. What I was speaking about visually was, immediately, that the cornices in the old tenement building in Harlem across the back-yard court had been carved very finely in 1890 or 1910. And were like the solidification of a great deal of intelligence and care and love also. So that I began noticing in every corner where I looked evidences of a living hand, even in the bricks, in the arrangement of each brick. Some hand placed them there—that some hand had placed the whole universe in front of me. That some hand had placed the sky. No, that's exaggerating—not that some hand had placed the sky but that the sky was the living blue hand itself. Or that God was in front of my eyes—existence itself was God. Well, the formulations are like that—I didn't formulate it in exactly those terms; what I was seeing was a visionary thing, it was a lightness in my body . . . my body suddenly felt *light*, and a sense of cosmic consciousness, vibrations, understanding, awe, and wonder and surprise. And it was a sudden awakening into a totally deeper real universe than I'd been existing in. So, I'm trying to avoid generalizations about that sudden deeper real universe and keep it strictly to observations of phenomenal data, or a voice with a certain sound, the appearance of cornices, the appearance of the sky, say, of the great blue hand, the living hand—to keep to images.

But anyway—the same . . . *petite sensation* recurred several minutes later, with the same voice, while reading the poem "The Sick Rose." This time it was a slightly different sense-depth-mystic impression. Because "The Sick Rose"—you know I can't interpret the poem now, but it had a meaning—I mean I can interpret it on a verbal level, the sick rose is my self, or self, or the living body, sick because the mind, which is the worm "That flies in the night, In the howling storm," or Urizen, reason; Blake's character might be the one that's entered the body and is destroying it, or let us say death, the worm as being death, the natural process of death, some kind of mystical being of its own trying to come in and devour the body, the rose. Blake's drawing for it is complicated, it's a big drooping rose, drooping because it's dying, and there's a worm in it, and the worm is wrapped around a little sprite that's trying to get out of the mouth of the rose.

But anyway, I experienced "The Sick Rose," with the voice of Blake reading it, as something that applied to the whole universe, like hearing the doom of the whole universe, and at the same time the inevitable beauty of doom. I can't remember now, except it was very beautiful and very awesome. But a little of it slightly scary, having to do with the knowledge of death—my death and also the death of being itself, and that was the great pain. So, like a prophecy, not only in human terms but a prophecy as if Blake had penetrated the very secret core of the *entire* universe and had come forth with some little magic formula statement in rhyme and rhythm that, if properly heard in the inner inner ear, would deliver you beyond the universe.

So then, the other poem that brought this on in the same day was "The Little Girl Lost," where there was a repeated refrain,

> 'Do father, mother, weep?
> Where can Lyca sleep?
>
> 'How can Lyca sleep
> If her mother weep?
>
> 'If her heart does ache
> Then let Lyca wake;
> If my mother sleep,
> Lyca shall not weep.'

It's that hypnotic thing—and I suddenly realized that Lyca was me, or Lyca was the self; father, mother seeking Lyca, was God seeking, Father, the Creator; and " 'If her heart does ache / Then let Lyca wake' "—wake to what? *Wake* meaning wake to the same awakeness I was just talking about—of existence in the entire universe. The total consciousness then, of the compete universe. Which is what Blake was talking about. In other words a break-through from ordinary habitual quotidian consciousness into consciousness that was really seeing all of heaven in a flower. Or what was it—eternity in a flower . . . heaven in a grain of sand? As I was seeing heaven in the cornice of the building. By heaven here I mean this imprint or concretization or living form, of an intelligent hand—the work of an intelligent hand, which still had the intelligence molded into it. The gargoyles on the Harlem cornices. What was interesting about the cornice was that there's cornices like that on every building, but I never noticed them before. And I never realized that they meant spiritual labor, to anyone—that somebody had labored to make a curve in a piece to tin—to make a cornucopia out of a piece of industrial tin. Not only that man, the workman, the artisan, but the architect had thought of it, the builder had paid for it, the smelter had *smelt* it, the miner had dug it up out of the earth, the earth had gone through aeons preparing it. So the little molecules had slumbered for . . . for Kalpas. So out of *all* of these Kalpas it all got together in a great succession of impulses, to be frozen finally in that one form of a cornucopia cornice on the building front. And God knows how many people made the moon. Or what spirits labored . . . to set fire to the sun. As Blake says, "When I look in the sun I don't see the rising sun, I see a band of angels singing holy, holy, holy." Well, his perception of the field of the sun is different from that of a man who just sees the sun sun, without any emotional relationship to it.

But then, there was a point later in the week when the intermittent flashes of the same . . . bliss—because the experience was quite blissful—came back. In a sense all this is described in "The Lion for Real" by anecdotes of different experiences—actually it was a very difficult time, which I won't go into here. Because suddenly I thought, also simultaneously, Ooh, I'm going *mad*! That's described in the line in "Howl," "who thought they were *only* mad when Baltimore gleamed in supernatural ecstasy"—"who thought they were *only* mad. . . ." If it were only that easy! In other words it'd be a lot easier if you just were crazy, instead of—then you could chalk it up, "Well, I'm nutty"—but on the other hand what if it's all true and you're *born* into this great cosmic universe in which you're a spirit angel—terrible fucking situation to be confronted with. It's like being woken up one morning by Joseph K's captors. Actually what I think I did was there was a couple of girls living next door and I crawed out on the fire escape and tapped on their window and said, "I've seen God!" and they *banged* the window shut. Oh, what tales I could have told them if they'd let me in! Because I was in a very exalted state of mind and the consciousness was still with me— I remember I immediately rushed to Plato and read some great image in the *Phaedrus* about horses flying through the sky, and rushed over to Saint John and started reading fragments of *con un no saber sabiendo . . . que me quede balbuciendo,* and rushed to the other part of the bookshelf and picked up Plotinus about The Alone—the Plotinus I found more difficult to interpret. But I *immediately* doubled my thinking process, quadrupled, and I was able to read almost any text and see all sorts of divine significance in it. And I think that week or that month I had to take an examination in John Stuart Mill. And instead of writing about his ideas I got completely hung up on his experience of reading—was it Wordsworth? Apparently the thing that got him back was an experience of nature that he received keyed off by reading Wordsworth, on "sense sublime" or something. That's a very good description, that sense sublime of something far more deeply interfused, whose dwelling is the light of setting suns, and the round ocean, and the . . . the *living* air, did he say? The living air—see just that hand again—*and* in the heart of man. So I think this experience is characteristic of all high poetry. I mean that's the way I began seeing poetry as the communication of the particular experience—not just any experience but *this* experience.

INTERVIEWER: Have you had anything like this experience again?

GINSBERG: Yeah. I'm not finished with this period. Then, in my room, I didn't know what to do. But I wanted to bring it up, so I began experimenting with it, without Blake. And I think it was one day in my kitchen—I had an old-fashioned kitchen with a sink with a tub in it with a board over the top—I started moving around and sort of shaking with my body and dancing up and down on the floor and saying, "Dance! dance! dance! dance! spirit! spirit! spirit! dance!" and suddenly I felt like Faust, calling up the devil. And then it started coming over me, this big . . . creepy feeling, cryptozoid or monozoidal, so I got all scared and quit.

Then I was walking around Columbia and I went in the Co-lumbia bookstore and was reading Blake again, leafing over a book of Blake, I think it was "The Human Abstract": "Pity would be no more. . . ." And suddenly it came over me in the bookstore again, and I was in the eternal place *once more*, and I looked around at everybody's faces, and I saw all these wild animals! Because there was a bookstore clerk there who I hadn't paid much attention to, he was just a familiar fixture in the bookstore scene and everybody went in the bookstore every day like me, because downstairs there was a café and upstairs there were all these clerks that we were all familiar with—this guy had a very *long* face, you know some people look like giraffes. So he looked kind of giraffish. He had a kind of a long face with a long nose. I don't know what kind of sex life he had, but he must have had something. But anyway, I looked in his face and I suddenly saw like a great tormented soul—and he had just been somebody whom I'd regarded as perhaps a not particularly beautiful or sexy character, or lovely face, but you know someone familiar, and perhaps a pleading cousin in the universe. But all of a sudden I realized that *he* knew also, just like I knew. And that everybody in the bookstore knew, and that they were all hiding it! They all had the consciousness, it was like a great *un*conscious that was running between all of us that everybody *was* completely conscious, but that the fixed expressions that people have, the habitual expression, the manners, the mode of talk, are all masks hiding this consciousness. Because almost at that moment it seemed that it would be too terrible if we communicated to each other on a level of total consciousness and awareness each of the other— like it would be too terrible, it would be the end of the bookstore, it would be the end of civ— . . . not civilization, but in other words the position that everybody was in was *ridiculous*, everybody running around peddling books to each other. Here in the universe! Passing money over the counter, wrapping books in bags and guarding the door, you know, stealing books, and the people sitting up making accountings on the upper floor there, and people worrying about their exams walking through the bookstore, and all the millions of thoughts the people had—you know, that I'm worrying about—whether they're going to get laid or whether anybody loves them, about their mothers dying of cancer or, you know, the complete death awareness that everybody has continuously with them all the time—all of a sudden revealed to me at once in the faces of the people, and they all looked like horrible grotesque masks, grotesque because *hiding* the knowledge from each other. Having a habitual conduct and forms to prescribe, forms to fulfill. Roles to play. But the main insight I had at that time was that everybody knew. Everybody knew completely everything. Knew completely everything in the terms which I was talking about.

INTERVIEWER: Do you still think they know?

GINSBERG: I'm more sure of it now. Sure. All you have to do is try and make somebody. You realize that they knew all along you were trying to make them. But until that moment you never break through to communication on the subject.

INTERVIEWER: Why not?

GINSBERG: Well, fear of rejection. The twisted faces of all those people, the faces were twisted by rejection. And hatred of self, finally. The internalization of that rejection. And finally disbelief in that shining self. Disbelief in that infinite self. Partly because that particular . . . partly because the *awareness* that we all carry is too often painful, because the experience of rejection and lack-love and cold war—I mean the whole cold war is the imposition of a vast mental barrier on everybody, a vast antinatural psyche. A hardening, a shutting off of the perception of desire and tenderness which everybody *knows* and which is the very structure of . . . the atom! Structure of the human body and organism. That desire built in. Blocked. "Where the Youth pined away with desire, / And the pale Virgin shrouded in snow." Or as Blake says, "On every face I see, I meet / Marks of weakness, marks of woe." So what I was thinking in the bookstore was the marks of weakness, marks of woe. Which you can just look around and look at anybody's face right next to you now always—you can see it in the way the mouth is pursed, you can see it in the way the eyes blink, you can see it in the way the gaze is fixed down at the matches. It's the self-consciousness which is a substitute for communication with the outside. This consciousness pushed back into the self and thinking of how it will hold its face and eyes and hands in order to make a mask to hide the flow that is going on. Which it's aware of, which everybody is aware of really! So let's say, shyness. Fear. Fear of like total feeling, really, total being is what it is.

So the problem then was, having attained realization, how to safely manifest it and communicate it. Of course there was the old Zen thing, when the sixth patriarch handed down the little symbolic oddments and ornaments and books and bowls, stained bowls too . . . when the *fifth* patriarch handed them down to the sixth patriarch he told him to hide them and don't tell anybody you're patriarch because it's dangerous, they'll kill you. So there was that immediate danger. It's taken me all these years to manifest it and work it out in a way that's materially communicable to people. Without scaring them or me. Also movements of history and breaking down the civilization. To break down everybody's masks and roles sufficiently so that everybody has to face the universe *and* the possibility of the sick rose coming true and the atom bomb. So it was an immediate messianic thing. Which seems to be becoming more and more justified. And more and more reasonable in terms of the existence that we're living.

So. Next time it happened was about a week later walking along in the evening on a circular path around what's now I guess the garden or field in the middle of Columbia University, by the library. I started invoking the spirit, consciously trying to get another depth perception of cosmos. And suddenly it began occurring again, like a sort of break-through again, but this time— this was the last time in that period—it was the same depth of consciousness or the same cosmical awareness but suddenly it was not blissful at all but it was *frightening*. Some like real serpent-fear entering the sky. The sky was not a blue hand anymore but like a hand of death coming down on me—some really scary presence, it was almost as if I saw God again except God was the devil. The consciousness itself was so vast, much more vast than any idea of it I'd had or any experience I'd had, that it was not even human any more—and was in a sense a threat, because I was going to die into that inhuman ultimately. I don't know *what* the score was there—I was too cowardly to pursue it. To attend and experience completely the Gates of Wrath—there's a poem of Blake's that deals with that, "To find a Western Path / Right through the Gates of Wrath." But I didn't urge my way there, I shut it all off. And got scared, and thought, I've gone too far.

INTERVIEWER: Was your use of drugs an extension of this experience?

GINSBERG: Well, since I took a vow that this was the area of, that this was my existence that I was placed into, drugs were obviously a technique for experimenting with consciousness, to get different areas and different levels and different similarities and different reverberations of the same vision. Marijuana has some of it in it, that awe, the cosmic awe that you get sometimes on pot. There are certain moments under laughing gas and ether that the consciousness does intersect with something similar—for me—to my Blake visions. The gas drugs were apparently interesting too to the Lake Poets, because there were a lot of experiments done with Sir Humphrey Davy in his Pneumatic Institute. I think Coleridge and Southey and other people used to go, and De Quincy. But serious people. I think there hasn't been very much written about that period. *What went on* in the Humphrey Davy household on Saturday midnight when Coleridge arrived by foot, through the forest, by the lakes? Then, there are certain states you get into with opium, and heroin, of almost disembodied awareness, looking down back at the earth from a place after you're dead. Well, it's not the same, but it's an interesting state, and a useful one. It's a normal state also, I mean it's a holy state of some sort. At times. Then, mainly, of course, with the hallucinogens, you get some states of consciousness which subjectively seem to be cosmic-ecstatic, or cosmic-demonic. Our version of expanded consciousness is as much as *un*conscious information—awareness comes up to the surface. Lysergic acid, peyote, mescaline, sylocidin, Ayahuasca. But I can't stand them any more, because something happened to me with them very similar to the Blake visions. After about thirty times, thirty-five times, I began getting monster vibrations again. So I couldn't go any further. I may later on again, if I feel more reassurance. *

---

* Between occasion of interview with Thomas Clark June '65 and publication May '66 more reassurance came. I tried small doses of LSD twice in secluded tree and ocean cliff haven at Big Sur. No monster vibration, no snake universe hallucinations. Many tiny jeweled violet flowers along the path of a living brook that looked like Blake's illustration for a canal in grassy Eden: huge Pacific watery shore. Orlovsky dancing naked like Shiva

However, I did get a lot out of them, mainly like emotional understanding, understanding the female principle in a way—women, more sense of the softness and more desire for women. Desire for children also.

INTERVIEWER: Anything interesting about the actual experience, say with hallucinogens?

GINSBERG: What I do get is, say if I was in an apartment high on mescaline, I felt as if the apartment and myself were not merely on East Fifth Street but were in the middle of all space time. If I close my eyes on hallucinogens, I get a vision of great scaly dragons in outer space, they're winding slowly and eating their own tails. Sometimes my skin and all the room seem sparkling with scales, and it's all made out of serpent stuff. And as if the whole illusion of life were made of reptile dream.

Mandala also. I use the mandala in an LSD poem. The associations I've had during times that I was high are usually referred to or built in some image or other to one of the other poems written on drugs. Or after drugs—like in "Magic Psalm" on ly-

---

long-haired before giant green waves, titanic cliffs that Wordsworth mentioned in his own Sublime, great yellow sun veiled with mist hanging over the plant's oceanic horizon. No harm. President Johnson that day went into the Valley of Shadow operating room because of his gall bladder & Berkeley's Vietnam Day Committee was preparing anxious manifestoes for our march toward Oakland police and Hell's Angels. Realizing that more vile words from me would send out physical vibrations into the atmosphere that might curse poor Johnson's flesh and further unbalance his soul, I knelt on the sand surrounded by masses of green bulb-headed Kelp vegetable-snake undersea beings washed up by last night's tempest, and prayed for the President's tranquil health. Since there has been so much legislative miscomprehension of the LSD boon I regret that my unedited ambivalence in Thomas Clark's tape transcript interview was published wanting this footnote.

Your obedient servant
Allen Ginsberg, *aetat* 40
June 2, 1966

sergic acid. Or mescaline. There's a long passage about a mandala in the LSD poem. There is a good situation since I was high and I was looking at a mandala—before I got high I asked the doctor that was giving it to me at Stanford to prepare me a set of mandalas to look at, to borrow some from Professor Spiegelberg who was an expert. So we had some Sikkimese elephant mandalas there. I simply describe those in the poem—what they look like while I was high.

So—summing up then—drugs were useful for exploring perception, sense perception, and exploring different possibilities and modes of consciousness, and exploring the different versions of *petites sensations*, and useful then for composing, sometimes, while under the influence. Part II of "Howl" was written under the influence of peyote, composed during peyote vision. In San Francisco—"Moloch." "Kaddish" was written with amphetamine injections. An injection of amphetamine plus a little bit of morphine, plus some Dexedrine later on to keep me going, because it was all in one long sitting. From a Saturday morn to a Sunday night. The amphetamine gives a peculiar metaphysical tinge to things, also. Space-outs. It doesn't interfere too much there because I wasn't habituated to it, I was just taking it that one weekend. It didn't interfere too much with the emotional charge that comes through.

INTERVIEWER: Was there any relation to this in your trip to Asia?

GINSBERG: Well, the Asian experience kind of got me out of the corner. I painted myself in with drugs. That corner being an inhuman corner in the sense that I figured I was expanding my consciousness and I had to go through with it but at the same time I was confronting this serpent monster, so I was getting in a real terrible situation. It finally would get so if I'd take the drugs I'd start vomiting. But I felt that I was duly bound and obliged for the sake of consciousness expansion, and this insight, and breaking down my identity, and seeking more direct contact with primate sensation, nature, to continue. So when I went to India, all the way through India, I was babbling about that to all the holy men I could find. I wanted to find out if they had any suggestions. And they all did, and they were all good ones. First one I saw was Martin Buber, who was interested. In Jerusalem, Peter and I went in to see him—we called him up and made a date and had a long conversation. He had a beautiful white beard and was friendly; his nature was slightly austere but benevolent. Peter asked him what kind of visions he'd had and he described some he'd had in bed when he was younger. But he said he was *not* any longer interested in visions like that. The kind of visions he came up with were more like spiritualistic table rappings. Ghosts coming into the room through his window, rather than big beautiful seraphic Blake angels hitting him on the head. I was thinking like loss of identity and confrontation with non-human universe as the main problem, and in a sense whether or not man had to evolve and change, and perhaps become non-human too. Melt into the universe, let us say—to put it awkwardly and inaccurately. Buber said that he was interested in man-to-man relationships, human-to-human—that he thought it was a human universe that we were destined to inhabit. And so therefore human relationships rather than relations between the human and the nonhuman. Which was what I was thinking that I had to go into. And he said, "Mark my word, young man, in two years you will realize that I was right." He was right—in two years I marked his words. Two years is sixty-three—I saw him in sixty-one. I don't know if he said two years—but he said "in years to come." This was like a real terrific classical wise man's "Mark my words, young man, in several years you will realize that what I said was true!" Exclamation point.

Then there was Swami Shivananda, in Rishikish in India. He said, "Your own heart is your guru." Which I thought was very sweet, and very reassuring. That is the sweetness of it I felt—in my heart. And suddenly realized it was the heart that I was seeking. In other words it wasn't consciousness, it wasn't *petites sensations*, sensation defined as expansion of mental consciousness to include more data—as I was pursuing that line of thought, pursuing Burroughs's cutup thing—the area that I was seeking was heart rather than mind. In other words, in mind, through mind or imagination—this is where I get confused with Blake now—in mind one can construct all sorts of universes, one can construct model universes in dream and imagination, and with the speed of light; and with nitrous oxide you can experience several million universes in rapid succession. You can experience a whole gamut of possibilities of universes, including the final possibility that there is none. And then you go unconscious—which is exactly what happens with gas when you go unconscious. You see that the universe is going to disappear with your consciousness, that it was all dependent on your consciousness.

Anyway, a whole series of India holy men pointed back to the body—getting *in* the body rather than getting out of the human form. But living in and inhabiting the human form. Which then goes back to Blake again, the human form divine. Is this clear? In other words, the psychic problem that I had found myself in was that for various reasons it had seemed to me at one time or another that the best thing to do was to drop dead. Or not be afraid of death but go into death. Go into the nonhuman, go into the cosmic, so to speak; that God was death, and if I wanted to attain God I had to die. Which *may* still be true. So I thought that what I was put up to was to therefore break out of my body, if I wanted to attain complete consciousness.

So now the next step was that the gurus one after another said, Live in the body: this is the form that you're born for. That's too long a narration to go into. Too many holy men and too many different conversations and they all have a little *key* thing going. But it all winds up in the train in Japan, then a year later, the poem "The Change," where all of a sudden I renounce drugs, I don't renounce drugs but I suddenly didn't want to be *dominated* by that nonhuman any more, or even be dominated by the moral obligation to enlarge my consciousness any more. Or do anything any more except *be* my heart—which just desired to be and be alive now. I had a very strange ecstatic experience then and there, once I had sort of gotten that burden off my back, because I was suddenly free to love myself again, and therefore love the people around me, in the form that they already were. And love myself in my own form as I am. And look around at the other people and so it was *again* the same thing like in the bookstore. Except this time I was completely in my body and had no more mysterious obligations. And nothing more to fulfill, except to be willing to die when I am dying, whenever that be. And be willing to live as a human in this form now. So I started weeping, it was such a happy moment. Fortunately I was able to write then, too, "So that I do live I will die"—rather than be cosmic consciousness, immortality, Ancient of Days, perpetual consciousness existing forever.

Then when I got to Vancouver, Olson was saying "I am one with my skin." It *seemed* to me at the time when I got back to Vancouver that everybody had been precipitated back into their bodies at the same time. It seemed that's what Creeley had *been* talking about all along. The *place*—the terminology he used, the *place* we are. Meaning this place, here. And trying to like be real in the real place . . . to be aware of the place where he is. Because I'd always thought that that meant that he was cutting off from divine imagination. But what that meant for him was that this place would be everything that one would refer to as divine, if one were really here. So that Vancouver seems a very odd moment, at least for me—because I came back in a sense completely bankrupt. My energies of the last . . . oh, 1948 to 1963, all completely washed up. On the train in Kyoto having renounced Blake, renounced visions—renounced *Blake!*—too. There was a cycle that began with the Blake vision which ended on the train in Kyoto when I realized that to attain the depth of consciousness that I was seeking when I was talking about the Blake vision, that in order to attain it I had to cut myself off from the Blake vision and renounce it. Otherwise I'd be hung up on a memory of an experience. Which is not the actual awareness of now, now. In order to get back to now, in order to get back to the total awareness of now and contact, sense perception contact with what was going on around me, or direct vision of the moment, now I'd have to give up this continual churning thought process of yearning back to a visionary state. It's all very complicated. And idiotic.

INTERVIEWER: I think you said earlier that "Howl" being a lyric poem, and "Kaddish" basically a narrative, that you now have a sense of wanting to do an epic. Do you have a plan like this?

GINSBERG: Yeah, but it's just . . . ideas, that I've been carrying around for a long time. One thing which I'd like to do sooner or later is write a long poem which is a narrative and description of all the visions I've ever had, sort of like the *Vita Nuova*. And travels, now. And another idea I had was to write a big long poem about everybody I ever fucked or slept with. Like sex . . . a love poem. A long love poem, involving all the innumerable lays of a lifetime. The epic is not that, though. The epic would be a poem including history, as it's defined. So that would be one about present-day politics, using the methods of the Blake *French Revolution*. I got a lot written. Narrative was "Kaddish." Epic— there has to be totally different organization, it might be simple free association on political themes—in fact I think an epic poem including history, at this stage. I've got a lot of it written, but it would have to be Burroughs' sort of epic—in other words, it would have to be *dis*sociated thought stream which includes politics and history. I don't think you could do it in narrative form, I mean what would you be narrating, the history of the Korean War or something?

INTERVIEWER: Something like Pound's epic?

GINSBERG: No, because Pound seems to me to be over a course of years fabricating out of his reading and out of the museum of literature; whereas the thing would be to take all of contemporary history, newspaper headlines and all the pop art of Stalinism and Hitler and Johnson and Kennedy and Viet Nam and Congo and Lumumba and the South and Sacco and Vanzetti—whatever floated into one's personal field of consciousness and contact. And then to compose like a basket—like weave a basket, basket-weaving out of those materials. Since obviously nobody has any idea where it's all going or how it's going to end unless you have some vision to deal with. It would have to be done by a process of association, I guess.

INTERVIEWER: What's happening in poetry now?

GINSBERG: I don't know yet. Despite all confusion to the contrary, now that time's passed, I think the best poet in the United States is Kerouac still. Given twenty years to settle through. The main reason is that he's the most free and the most spontaneous.

Has the greatest range of association and imagery in his poetry. Also in "Mexico City Blues" the sublime as subject matter. And, in other words the greatest facility at what might be called projective verse, if you want to give it a name. I think that he's stupidly underrated by almost everybody except for a few people who are aware how beautiful his composition is—like Snyder or Creeley or people who have a taste for his tongue, for his line. But it takes one to know one.

INTERVIEWER: You don't mean Kerouac's prose?

GINSBERG: No, I'm talking about just a pure poet. The verse poetry, the "Mexico City Blues" and a lot of other manuscripts I've seen. In addition he has the one sign of being a great poet, which is he's the only one in United States who knows how to write haikus. The only one who's written any good haikus. And everybody's been writing haikus. There are all these *dreary* haikus written by people who think for weeks trying to write a haiku, and finally come up with some dull little thing or something. Whereas Kerouac thinks in haikus, every time he writes anything—talks that way and thinks that way. So it's just natural for him. It's something Snyder noticed. Snyder has to labor for years in a Zen monastery to produce one haiku about shitting off a log! And actually does get one or two good ones. Snyder was always astounded by Kerouac's facility . . . at noticing winter flies dying of old age in his medicine chest. Medicine cabinet. "In my medicine cabinet / the winter flies / died of old age." He's never published them actually—he's published them on a record, with Zoot Sims and Al Cohn, it's a very beautiful collection of them. Those are, as far as I can see, the only real American haikus.

So the haiku is the most difficult test. He's the only *master* of the haiku. Aside from a longer style. Of course, the distinctions between prose and poetry are broken down anyway. So much that I was saying like a long page of oceanic Kerouac is sometimes as sublime as epic line. It's there that also I think he went further into the existential thing of writing conceived of as an irreversible action or statement, that's unrevisable and unchangeable once it's made. I remember I was thinking, yesterday in fact, there was

a time that I was absolutely astounded because Kerouac told me
that in the future literature would consist of what people actually
wrote rather than what they tried to decieve other people into
thinking they wrote, when they revised it later on. And I saw
opening up this whole universe where people wouldn't be able
to lie any more! They wouldn't be able to *correct* themselves any
longer. They wouldn't be able to hide what they said. And he
was willing to go all the way into that, the first pilgrim into that
new-found land.

INTERVIEWER: What about other poets?

GINSBERG: I think Corso has a great imaginative genius. And
also amongst the greatest *shrewdness*—like Keats or something. I
like Lamantia's nervous wildness. Almost anything he writes I
find interesting—for one thing he's always registering the forward
march of the soul, in exploration; spiritual exploration is always
there. And also chronologically following his work is always exciting. Whalen and Snyder are both very wise and very reliable.
Whalen I don't *understand* so well. I did, though, earlier—but
I have to sit down and study his work, again. Sometimes he seems
sloppy—but then later on it always seems right.

McClure has tremendous energy, and seems like some sort of
a . . . seraph is not the word . . . not herald either but a
. . . not demon either. Seraph I guess it is. He's always moving—
see when I came around to, say, getting in my skin, there I found
McClure sitting around talking about being a mammal! So I
suddenly realized he was way ahead of me. And Wieners . . . I
always *weep* with him. Luminous, luminous. They're all old
poets, everybody knows about those poets. Burroughs is a poet
too, really. In the sense that a page of his prose is as *dense* with
imagery as anything in St.-John Perse or Rimbaud, now. And it
has also great repeated rhythms. Recurrent, recurrent rhythms,
even rhyme occasionally! What else . . . Creeley's very stable,
solid. I get more and more to like certain poems of his that I
didn't understand at first. Like "The Door," which completely
baffled me because I didn't understand that he was talking about
the same heterosexual problem that I was worried about. Olson,
since he said, "I feel one with my skin." First thing of Olson's

that I liked was "The Death of Europe" and then some of his later Maximus material is nice. And Dorn has a kind of long, *real* spare, manly, political thing—but his great quality inside also is tenderness—"Oh the graves not yet cut." I also like that whole line of what's happening with Ashbery and O'Hara and Koch, the area that they're going for, too. Ashbery—I was listening to him read "The Skaters," and it sounded as inventive and exquisite, in all its parts, as "The Rape of the Lock."

INTERVIEWER: Do you feel you're in command when you're writing?

GINSBERG: Sometimes I feel in command when I'm writing. When I'm in the heat of some truthful tears, yes. Then, complete command. Other times—most of the time not. Just diddling away, woodcarving, getting a pretty shape; like most of my poetry. There's only a few times when I reach a state of complete command. Probably a piece of "Howl," a piece of "Kaddish," and a piece of "The Change." And one or two moments of other poems.

INTERVIEWER: By "command" do you mean a sense of the whole poem as it's going, rather than parts?

GINSBERG: No—a sense of being self-prophetic master of the universe.

—THOMAS CLARK
1966

9. Conrad Aiken

Born in Savannah, Georgia, on August 5, 1889, Conrad Aiken was taken to New Bedford, Massachusetts, in 1900 to be brought up by his great-great-aunt after a violent disagreement between his parents ended with his father killing his mother and then himself.

His first collections of poems were published in 1914 and 1916. Among his early volumes of verse are *The Jig of Forslin: A Symphony* (1916), *Nocturne of Remembered Spring* (1917), *The Charnel Rose* (1918), and *Senlin: A Biography and Other Poems* (1918). His more important volumes include *Preludes for Memnon* (1931); *The Kid* (1947); *Skylight One* (1949); *Collected Poems* (1953), for which he won the 1954 National Book Award; *Selected Poems* (1961); and *Preludes* (1966). He also wrote five novels, including the highly acclaimed *Great Circle* (1933); many short stories, which were gathered together in *Bring! Bring! and Other Stories* (1925), *Costumes by Eros* (1928), *Among the Lost People* (1934), and *Collected Short Stories* (1960); an experimental autobiography, *Ushant: An Essay* (1952); and a great deal of literary criticism, much of which was written at the suggestion of Marianne Moore when she was editor of *The Dial*. Aiken collected the best of his criticism in *A Reviewer's ABC* (1958).

From 1950 to 1952 he held the chair of poetry at the Library of Congress. Among his other honors were the Pulitzer Prize for the best volume of verse in 1929; the Bollingen Prize (1956); a Gold Medal for poetry from the National Institute of Arts and Letters (1958); the Huntington Hartford Foundation Award in Literature (1961); the Brandeis medal for poetry (1967); and membership in the American Academy of Arts and Letters. In 1969 he won the National Medal of Literature.

He lived in his Brewster home until his death on August 17, 1973.

2

M

by these translated
and made an ecstasy.
Thus in our transient and translunar love
translate the love to you and me.
Now that is gone,
and love undone.

He

against   *M*

I invoke, then, a particular day. The clock strikes one.
Now the ~~first~~ snowflake floats ~~upon~~ the stone
curved   and perishes ~~in there~~. Our eyes are filled
with immortal light, clear ~~recognition~~, clear knowledge
of all that's past and to come:
yes, those histories and prophecies you speak of, the secret
tangents of sense thrust against sense
but only to illumine: the I and You,
opposed in a compelled counterpoint
which willy nilly joins them. Of all this
what shall we remember? Simply, the first snowflake falling:
while, from the distance of a breath, for the first time,
I observe the ~~pale and delicate~~ shape of a closed eyelid
and shall   closed on the vulnerable secret of ~~the flower~~
we say.   (yourself the ~~flower~~) _____ *Scent*
and yet inviolable as death.

She

Yes. Remember ~~that.~~
I saw your head   And I too will remember ~~something.~~
bowing against the   When my eyes opened, your hand was holding the umbrella
snow   and the green transparent shadow changed your face.
ow whether   These shall be time and place.
that the green
translucent light
He
shifted across
your submarine   And now, since there's no help, without a kiss we'll part.
faces
She

Each with a separate but remembering heart.

Early draft of the concluding lines of "Love's Grammarians."

Karl Bissinger

Conrad Aiken

The interview took place in two sessions of about an hour each in September 1963, at Mr. Aiken's house in Brewster, Massachusetts. The house, called Forty-one Doors, was a typical old Cape Cod farmhouse dated largely from the eighteenth century; the rooms were small but many, opening in all directions off what must originally have been the most important room, the kitchen. The house was far enough from the center of town to be reasonably quiet even at the height of the summer, and it was close enough to the North Cape shore for easy trips to watch the gulls along the edges of relatively unspoiled inlets.

Mr. Aiken dressed typically in a tweed sports coat, a wool or denim shirt, and a heavy wool tie. A fringe of sparse white hair gave him a curiously friarly appearance, belied by his irreverence and love of bawdy puns.

He answered the questions about his own work seriously and carefully but did not appear to enjoy them; not that he seemed to

find them too pressing or impertinent, rather as if answering them
was simply hard work. He enjoyed far more telling anecdotes about
himself and his friends and chuckled frequently in recalling these
stories.

By the end of each hour Mr. Aiken, who had been seriously ill
the previous winter, was visibly tired; but once the tape recorder
was stilled and the martinis mixed and poured into silver cups—
old sculling or tennis trophies retrieved from some pawn or antique
shop—he quickly revived. He was glad to be interviewed, but more
glad still when it was over.

Later, shortly before the interview went to press, a dozen or so
follow-up questions were sent to him at the Cape; the answers to
these were spliced into the original interview. "You may find you
will need to do a bit of dovetailing here and there," he wrote, "the
old mens isn't quite, may never be, as sana as before, if indeed it
ever was." But there was no real problem; his mind and memory
had remained clear and precise despite the physical frailties that
age had brought.

INTERVIEWER: In *Ushant* you say that you decided to be a poet
when you were very young—about six years old, I think.

AIKEN: Later than that. I think it was around nine.

INTERVIEWER: I was wondering how this resolve to be a poet
grew and strengthened?

AIKEN: Well, I think *Ushant* describes it pretty well, with that
epigraph from *Tom Brown's School Days:* "I'm the poet of White
Horse Vale, Sir, with Liberal notions under my cap." For some
reason those lines stuck in my head, and I've never forgotten
them. This image became something I *had* to be.

INTERVIEWER: While you were at Harvard, were you constantly
aware that you were going to be a poet; training yourself in most
everything you studied and did?

AIKEN: Yes. I compelled myself all through to write an exercise
in verse, in a different form, every day of the year. I turned out
my page everyday, of some sort—I mean I didn't give a damn
about the meaning, I just wanted to master the form—all the
way from free verse, Walt Whitman, to the most elaborate of

villanelles and ballad forms. Very good training. I've always told everybody who has ever come to me that I thought that was the first thing to do. And to study all the vowel effects and all the consonant effects and the variation in vowel sounds. For example, I gave Malcolm Lowry an exercise to do at Cuernavaca, of writing ten lines of blank verse with the caesura changing one step in each line. Going forward, you see, and then reversing on itself.

INTERVIEWER: How did Lowry take to these exercises?

AIKEN: Superbly. I still have a group of them sent to me at his rented house in Cuernavaca, sent to me by hand from the bar with a request for money, and in the form of a letter—and unfortunately not used in his collected letters; very fine, and very funny. As an example of his attention to vowel sounds, one line still haunts me: "Airplane or aeroplane, or just plain plane." Couldn't be better.

INTERVIEWER: What early readings were important to you? I gather that Poe was.

AIKEN: Oh, Poe, yes. I was reading Poe when I was in Savannah, when I was ten, and scaring myself to death. Scaring my brothers and sisters to death, too. So I was already soaked in him, especially the stories.

INTERVIEWER: I see you listed occasionally as a Southern writer. Does this make any sense to you?

AIKEN: Not at all. I'm not in the least Southern; I'm entirely New England. Of course, the Savannah *ambiente* made a profound impression on me. It was a beautiful city and so wholly different from New England that going from South to North every year, as we did in the summers, provided an extraordinary counterpoint of experience, of sensuous adventure. The change was so violent, from Savannah to New Bedford or Savannah to Cambridge, that it was extraordinarily useful. But no, I never was connected with any of the Southern writers.

INTERVIEWER: In what way was the change from Savannah to New England "useful" to you?

AIKEN: Shock treatment, I suppose: the milieu so wholly different, and the social customs, and the mere *transplantation*; as well as having to change one's accent twice a year—all this quite

apart from the astonishing change of landscape. From swamps
and Spanish moss to New England *rocks*.

INTERVIEWER: What else at Harvard was important to your
development as a poet, besides the daily practice you described?

AIKEN: I'm afraid I wasn't much of a student, but my casual
reading was enormous. I did have some admirable courses, especially two years of English 5 with Dean Briggs, who was a great
teacher, I think, and that was the best composition course I ever
had anywhere.

INTERVIEWER: How did Briggs go about teaching writing?

AIKEN: He simply let us write, more or less, what we wanted
to. Then discussion (after his reading aloud of a chosen specimen)
and his own marvelous comments: He had genius, and emanated
it. Then, at the end of class, we had ten minutes in which to
write a short critique of the piece that had been read. This was
so helpful to *me* that I took the course for two years.

INTERVIEWER: Was Copeland still teaching then? What did you
think of him?

AIKEN: Brilliant reader, not a profound teacher. Vain. At the
end of the year he asked me, "Aiken, do you think this course
has benefited you?" I was taken aback and replied, "Well, it has
made me write often." He replied, "Aiken, you're a very *dry*
young man."

INTERVIEWER: Eliot mentioned in an interview with *The Paris
Review* that while he was reading French poetry at Harvard, you
were reading Italian and Spanish poets.

AIKEN: Yes, I had begun to read Spanish poetry, come to think
of it, and Italian, that's true. I'd begun reading Leopardi in 1911,
and the French poets I didn't get around to until senior year at
Harvard when I discovered Symond's *Symbolist Poets* and swallowed that in one gulp.

INTERVIEWER: None of these foreign readings had anything like
the same effect on your work that Eliot's reading of the French
symbolists had on his, did they?

AIKEN: I don't think so.

INTERVIEWER: You kept rather to the English Romantic
tradition—

AIKEN: Yes, and Whitman had a profound influence on me. That was during my sophomore year when I came down with a bad attack of Whitmanitis. But he did me a lot of good, and I think the influence is discoverable.

INTERVIEWER: What was the good he did? Mainly enabling you to get away from Victorian forms?

AIKEN: General loosening up, yes. He was useful to me in the perfection of form, as a sort of compromise between the strict and the free.

INTERVIEWER: Was William James still at Harvard when you were there?

AIKEN: No, he retired the year I got there, or the year before, but was still around, and you felt his presence very much. But Santayana was the real excitement for me at Harvard, especially "Three Philosophical Poets," which he was inventing that year as he went along—so we were getting the thing right off the fire.

INTERVIEWER: Santayana's insistence that philosophical content—the "vision" of philosophy—is one of the things that can give the greatest effect to poetry—this, I gather, impressed you quite highly at the time?

AIKEN: Oh, much. Tremendously. It really fixed my view of what poetry should ultimately be.

INTERVIEWER: That it was greatest if it thought most deeply?

AIKEN: That it really had to begin by *understanding*, or trying to understand.

INTERVIEWER: Did you know Eliot quite well at Harvard?

AIKEN: Eliot and I must have met at the end of my freshman year, when I was elected to the *Harvard Advocate*. We saw a great deal of each other, in spite of the fact that we were a year apart, and remained very close.

INTERVIEWER: Was your conversation largely about poetry, or did you share other interests and activities?

AIKEN: Of course, at the beginning, on the *Advocate*, we talked chiefly about poetry, or literature in general. But as the friendship, or kinship developed—for in a way I became his younger brother—it widened to take in everything. And we met on very, very many quite frivolous occasions. Sports, comics, everything.

We developed a shorthand language of our own which we fell into for the rest of our lives whenever we met, no holds barred—all a matter of past reference, a common language, but basically *affection*, along with humor, and appreciation of each other's minds, and of Krazy Kat. Faced with England, and the New World, and Freud and all, we always managed to *relax*, and go back to the kidding, and bad punning, and drinking, to the end. It really was marvelous.

INTERVIEWER: Did you see Eliot much after the war brought you back to the States?

AIKEN: Only when he paid his infrequent visits here, when we invariably met to get drunk together. There was a splendid occasion when he and I and our wives dined at "The Greeks' " after he'd received a silver bowl from the Signet Society; he was wearing a cowboy hat, and we all got plastered. We went on to the Red Lion Grill, after many drinks at the Silver Dollar Bar, the two toughest and *queerest* joints in Boston. He couldn't walk, for his ankles were crossed, so Valerie *lifted* him into the taxi.

INTERVIEWER: Did Eliot's early work—such as "Prufrock"—help you in developing your own style?

AIKEN: Oh, "Prufrock" had a tremendous influence on me. You can see it all through the verse symphonies.

INTERVIEWER: The use of the interior monologue in particular?

AIKEN: I don't know whether that came from him. In fact, the whole complex of our relationship is a very subtle thing. I think there was a lot of interchange. For example, I did for English 5 in my extra year at Harvard—the fall of 1911—a poem called "The Clerk's Journal," which was about the life of a little stool-sitting clerk in a bank and his mundane affairs, his little love affair, his worry about clothes . . . and telephone wires in the moonlight. This was three years before "Prufrock."

INTERVIEWER: Do you still have this poem?

AIKEN: Yes, I've still got it, with Briggs' comment on the back of it. This was an anticipation. In other words, I was thinking in this direction before "Prufrock," and I have no doubt that Tom saw this poem, "The Clerk's Journal." The juices went both ways.

INTERVIEWER: There's a lot of what we now think of as *"The Waste Land* attitude" in your verse symphonies, isn't there? In *Forslin* and *The House of Dust,* which came well before *The Waste Land?*

AIKEN: Yes, there's a lot in *The Waste Land* that owes something, I think, to *The House of Dust* and *Forslin.*

INTERVIEWER: Did you ever see *The Waste Land* in manuscript?

AIKEN: No, I never did. Not as a whole. But I had seen whole sections which prior to *The Waste Land* existed as separate small poems, I believe not then intended for any other purpose, which were later conglomerated into *The Waste Land.*

INTERVIEWER: How did Pound come across "Prufrock"? Did you take it to him, or did Eliot do that after he came to England himself?

AIKEN: In 1914 I persuaded Tom to let me take "Prufrock" to England; he wasn't at all sure of it. I tried it everywhere—not even Harold Monro of the famous Poetry Bookshop could see it, thought it crazy; many years later he said it was the Kubla Khan of the twentieth century. Then I met Pound, showed it to him, and he was at once bowled over. He sent it to *Poetry.* So, when Tom had to retreat from Germany, when the war started, one of his first moves was to go and see Ezra.

Of course, Tom insisted all his life that I had made him cut a whole page or more out of "Prufrock." I don't remember this, but he claimed it was so—that there was a page or something like that that I thought didn't belong, so he took it out. It may be true, or he may have been confusing it with the major operation that Ezra performed on *The Waste Land.* I'm sorry about it, if so, because there's thirty lines lost!

INTERVIEWER: You knew Maxwell Bodenheim, didn't you? (*A new paperback copy of Bodenheim's* My Life and Loves *in Greenwich Village was on the coffee table.*)

AIKEN: Oh, very well. He was a great friend of mine. He used to catch me now and then, touring the country. I don't know how he managed it, but periodically he'd show up in Boston on his way to or from Chicago or New York. He was quite a fascinating creature. He really was a *dedicated* bum and poet.

INTERVIEWER: Did he have an effect on other poets that we've lost sight of?

AIKEN: Yes, I think so. He was a fascinating talker, in spite of the stammer, and he knew everybody. He was a great friend of Bill Williams. You must have heard the story of his broken arm? He called up Williams at Rutherford and said, "I've broken my arm. Can I come and stay with you till it heals?" Bill said, "Certainly." About a month or two went by, and Max did nothing about having the cast examined or changed, so finally Bill insisted on looking at it and discovered that there had never been any broken arm.

INTERVIEWER: Did you see a good bit of Pound in the early days?

AIKEN: I saw a lot of him for about six weeks in 1914 in London. I had a letter of introduction to him from Herman Hagedorn, who, it turned out, really didn't know Pound at all. But Pound was extraordinarily kind to me and really took pains to take me around and introduce me to people and to publishers, not always with luck.

INTERVIEWER: Was he any help to you in your own work?

AIKEN: Not a bit. We agreed to disagree about that right off, and I felt right off, too, that he was not for me, that he would become the old man of the sea and be on my shoulders in no time—which is exactly the experience that Williams had with him. I remember Williams describing how when he walked with Pound in London, Pound was always one step ahead. This gradually annoyed Williams to death, so he made a point of being right beside Pound. Very typical that—tells a lot, I think.

INTERVIEWER: How about John Gould Fletcher? You worked with him, were very close to him, in Boston and Cambridge, weren't you?

AIKEN: Yes, just after the war began, about 1915, he came back to Boston, and we lived next door to each other for three years. I saw a great deal of him, and we swapped notes and what-not; and agreed to disagree about many things because he was more involved in imagism or "Amy" gism than I proposed to be. But I think he had great talent which didn't quite come off somehow.

INTERVIEWER: He's practically unread now.

AIKEN: I know. He wrote me a tragic letter in 1949, I think it was, saying, "You know, Aiken, we are forgotten. We might as well face it." This was only a year or two before he jumped into the lake.

INTERVIEWER: Did Fletcher's organization of material, the sort of thing he was experimenting with in the color symphonies, bear any relation to the work you were doing with music in your verse symphonies?

AIKEN: I don't know. I don't think we influenced each other, but we were interested in the same sort of thing, in a very different way, of course. He was going for this abstract color business and, I think, with more French influence behind him than I had.

INTERVIEWER: When did you first meet Malcolm Lowry?

AIKEN: In 1929. He came to Cambridge to work with me one summer on *Ultramarine*.

INTERVIEWER: How old was he then?

AIKEN: Barely nineteen, I think. He went back to matriculate at Cambridge that autumn.

INTERVIEWER: Later you moved back to England yourself?

AIKEN: Yes, the next year. Then it was that his father turned him over to me *in loco parentis*.

INTERVIEWER: To keep him out of trouble or to teach him poetry?

AIKEN: To take care of him and to work with him. So he spent all his holidays with us in Rye or went with us if we went abroad. During his years at Cambridge, he was with me constantly.

INTERVIEWER: What was he working on at this time?

AIKEN: He was finishing *Ultramarine*. I've still got about a third of one version of *Ultramarine*. An interesting specimen of his deliberate attempt to absorb me came to light because there was a page recounting the dream of eating the father's skeleton which comes into my own novel, *Great Circle*. He was going to put this in his book and it didn't seem to matter at all that *I'd* had the dream and written it out.

INTERVIEWER: He doesn't put that in the final version?

AIKEN: No. I said, "No, Malcolm, this is carrying it *too* far."

INTERVIEWER: What about *Under the Volcano?* Did you work with him on that also?

AIKEN: No. The first version was already finished when I arrived in Mexico in 1937. He'd been there two or three years. The extraordinary thing is that it was not published for another ten years, during which time he was constantly revising and rewriting. He changed the end, I think entirely, from the version I saw. But the book was already finished and so was another novel called *In Ballast to the White Sea*, which was lost. I think it was in his shack that burnt down at Dollarton, Vancouver.

That was a remarkable thing, too, although very derivative. You could swim from one influence to another as you went from chapter to chapter. Kafka and Dostoevsky and God knows what all. But it was a brilliant thing, had some wonderful stuff in it, including, I remember, a description of a drunken steamboat ride up the Manchester Canal from Liverpool to Manchester.

INTERVIEWER: He lived through a lot that he was able to use very effectively.

AIKEN: Oh, he didn't miss a trick. He was a born observer.

INTERVIEWER: Was Lowry a disciplined writer? His life seems to have been so undisciplined.

AIKEN: Yes, when it came to writing, Malcolm was as obsessed with style as any Flaubert and read enormously to *feed* himself. As I mentioned, he wrote and rewrote *Volcano* for ten years. He once chided me for not taking more pains to "decorate the page."

INTERVIEWER: Do you think writers—fiction writers, particularly—should try deliberately to get out and live through the sort of thing he did? Search for experience? I doubt if he did it quite so consciously, but he lived a very active and varied life.

AIKEN: No, I don't think that was the intention, or not wholly the intention in his case. He really had a yen for the sea. And he came by it naturally; I think his mother's father had something to do with the sea. Of course, that's how we met, through his reading *Blue Voyage*. And he always assumed that in some mystic way the fact I had dedicated *Blue Voyage* to C. M. L. was a dedication to him. Those are his initials. Actually these were the initials of my second wife. But he always thought this was the finger pointing.

The very first night he arrived in Hampton Hall, on Plympton Street where I was living, next door to the Crimson Building, he and I and my youngest brother Robert had a sort of impromptu wrestling match. In the course of this I suggested we use the lid of the w.c. tank and each take hold of one end of it and wrestle for possession of this thing. So I got it all right; I got it away from Malcolm but fell right over backward into the fireplace and went out like a light; and when I came to, all I could see was red. I was stripped to the waist and lying in bed by myself. They'd disappeared, of course—we'd been imbibing a little bit—and I galloped down the hall to the elevator not knowing what to do. I thought I'd better get a doctor because blood was pouring down my face. It turned out I had a fracture of the skull, and I was in bed for the next two or three weeks. Malcolm would sometimes remembering to bring me a bottle of milk, and sometimes not. And during all this we were working on *Ultramarine*. That was the day's work, always.

INTERVIEWER: To turn to your own work—and the prototypical *Paris Review* question: How do you write? You've told me before that you compose on the typewriter.

AIKEN: Yes, ever since the early twenties. I began by doing book reviews on the typewriter and then went over to short stories on the machine, meanwhile sticking to pencil for poetry.

INTERVIEWER: So your verse symphonies were all written in long hand?

AIKEN: They were all written in little exercise books, with pencil.

INTERVIEWER: When did you start writing poetry on the typewriter?

AIKEN: About the middle of the twenties, I think. It was largely in the interests of legibility because my handwriting was extremely small and not very distinct, and the pencil *faded*. And so this was a great advantage and saved me the pains of copying because in many instances the short stories in *Bring! Bring!* were sent out exactly as written. They were composed straight off my head. I didn't change anything. It's a great labor-saving device—with some risks, because if you lost a copy in the mails it was gone!

INTERVIEWER: You didn't make carbons?

AIKEN: I never used a carbon because that made me self-conscious. I can remember discussing the effect of the typewriter on our work with Tom Eliot because he was moving to the typewriter about the same time I was. And I remember our agreeing that it made for a slight change of style in the prose—that you tended to use more periodic sentences, a little shorter, and a rather choppier style—and that one must be careful about that. Because, you see, you couldn't look ahead quite far enough, for you were always thinking about putting your fingers on the bloody keys. But that was a passing phase only. We both soon discovered that we were just as free to let the style throw itself into the air as we had been writing manually.

INTERVIEWER: Did writing on the typewriter have any comparable effect on the style of the poetry?

AIKEN: I think it went along with my tendency to compress the poetry that began about the midtwenties, '23 or '24, thereabouts. But revision was always done manually. I preferred yellow paper because it's not so responsible looking, and I would just let fly and then put the thing away after it was written and not look at it until the next day. Then go to work on it with a pencil—chop and change and then copy that off again on the yellow paper—and this would go on for days sometimes. There are some instances, especially in later work, when there have been something like twenty versions of a poem.

INTERVIEWER: In the verse symphonies, you did less revising?

AIKEN: Much less. It came out like a ribbon and lay flat on the brush.

INTERVIEWER: Did you often work on two or three poems at once? Particularly when you were doing the shorter poems, like the ones in the two series of *Preludes?*

AIKEN: No, not so much. I usually stayed with the individual item until it was satisfactory. Although sometimes I would do two or three preludes in a day, first drafts. And then all three would come in for retooling, so to speak, the next day or the day after.

Those happened very fast, the preludes—especially the *Time in the Rock* ones. They were outpourings as I've only really known during that period. Didn't matter when or where I was. I remember in "Jeake's House" in Rye when carpenters were going through the kitchen and the dining room all the time, which is where I worked at a long refectory table, and I would just go cheerfully on turning out preludes while hammering and sawing and what-not happened about me.

INTERVIEWER: But most of your other poems have come much more slowly?

AIKEN: Yes, much. Things like A *Letter from Li Po* and "The Crystal" were immensely labored over. Months. Very different procedure entirely. I had the idea, but it had to be developed very slowly.

INTERVIEWER: In revising, say, the shorter poems like the *Preludes*, did you usually find it possible to revise so that you were eventually satisfied with the poem, or have you often discarded poems along the way?

AIKEN: Oh, I've discarded a great many. And occasionally I've discarded and then resurrected. I would find a crumpled yellow ball of paper in the wastebasket, in the morning, and open it to see what the hell I'd been up to; and occasionally it was something that needed only a very slight change to be brought off, which I'd missed the day before.

INTERVIEWER: Do you tend now to look on the two series of *Preludes* as your major poetry?

AIKEN: I think those two books are central, along with *Osiris Jones* and *Landscape West of Eden*, but I still don't think the symphonies are to be despised. They've got to be looked at in an entirely different way; and allowances must be made for the diffuseness and the musical structure, which I think I overdid sometimes. Although *Senlin* I think stands up fairly well. And *Festus*, too.

INTERVIEWER: You speak of your "verse symphonies." Where did you get the idea of adapting musical structures to poetry?

AIKEN: For one thing, I always hankered to be a composer—I was mad about music, though I never studied seriously, and can't read a note. But I learned to play the piano and became pretty skillful at improvisation, especially after a drop or two. And from the beginning I'd thought of the two realms as really one: They were saying the same thing but in two voices. Why not marry them? A young composer named Bainbridge Crist, whom I met in London in 1913, introduced me to the tone poems of Strauss, and out of this came an early poem, "Disenchantment," now disavowed (though I still like parts of it). And then the symphonies. They had the tone of the time, and they married the unlikely couple of Freud and music.

INTERVIEWER: What about your new poem, *Thee*? Is it related to some of this earlier work?

AIKEN: No, *Thee* is something else again. This is nearer to some of the *Preludes*—not so much aimed at music (*pace* the title *Preludes*) as at meaning. But this poem, like "Blues for Ruby Matrix," for another example, just came like Topsy. It seized me at lunch, the first section, and I had to leave the table to put it down. Then it finished itself. In a way I had little to do with it. The theme is much like that of the *Preludes*, but the style very different: I think I'd learned a trick or two from my children's book, *Cats and Bats and Things with Wings*. Short lines, no adjectives, and, for its purpose, *very* heavy rhyming. None of which was in the least calculated. Who dunnit?

INTERVIEWER: You stress in *Ushant* that about the time you were writing *Landscape West of Eden* and the *Preludes* you were beginning to formulate a view of poetry, or of a poetic comprehension of the world, as the only religion any longer tenable or viable. Should we be seeing this more clearly in the two series of *Preludes* than we have, or than most critics have?

AIKEN: Yes, it was there, all right. Actually Houston Peterson in *The Melody of Chaos* got a little close to it although he had only seen the first ten or twelve of *Memnon*. But he, I think, detected the novelty of this approach to the world, or something.

INTERVIEWER: What about your later poems—are *Li Po* and "The Crystal," for example, related to the work you did in the thirties?

AIKEN: Yes, I think you can see their roots in the *Preludes*. But again, of course, it's a more expanded thing, as the earlier work was more expansive, in a different way. "The Crystal" and the poem about my grandfather, "Halloween," and *Li Po* and "A Walk in the Garden"—I think you can see how that whole group grew out of the *Preludes*.

INTERVIEWER: You mention "Halloween"—this has an emphasis on the American past, as does *The Kid*, which is quite a bit different from the work you did in England. Is *The Kid*—

AIKEN: That's a sort of *sport* in my career, I would say. And the vaudeville poems are another sort of deliberate divagation.

INTERVIEWER: You mean the ones you were doing very early, in the 1910s?

AIKEN: Yes. Those were based on observation; I was an addict of vaudeville, and Boston was marvelous for it. You had about three levels of vulgarity or refinement, whichever way you want to put it. The refinement being Keiths at the top, of course, and the bottom being Waldron's Casino, and in between Loews Theatre. And Loews was really the best. It was a wonderful mixture of vulgarity and invention, of high spirits and dirty cracks.

INTERVIEWER: When you started writing fiction—I suppose in the early twenties—what made you turn away from poetry, which you'd been doing up until then? Were you looking for a wider public?

AIKEN: No, it was almost wholly financial. Our income wasn't quite sufficient, and I thought maybe if I could turn out some short stories, I could make a little money. But of course that proved to be an illusion because the sort of stories I wrote could only be sold to things like *The Dial* or *The Criterion*, and I didn't make any more than I would have out of poetry. But then I got involved in it and found that it was fun, in its different way, and that in fact the short story is a kind of poem, or for *my* purposes it was. And so on it went, *pari passu* with the poetry.

INTERVIEWER: Some of your stories, like "Mr. Arcularis" and "Silent Snow, Secret Snow," have become classics. Where did you get the ideas for these stories? Dreams? Did reading Freud have anything to do with them?

AIKEN: Of course Freud was in everything I did, from 1912 on.

But there was no special influence on these. "Arcularis" *did* come out of a dream, plus a meeting with a man of that name on a ship. "Silent Snow" was a complete invention; or, let's say, a projection of my own inclination to insanity.

INTERVIEWER: Then you started working with the longer fiction—*Blue Voyage* and *Great Circle?*

AIKEN: Yes, and that was another reason for going into the short stories. Because I actually wrote one chapter of *Blue Voyage* and then stopped dead. I thought no, I really don't know enough about the *structure* of fiction—perhaps I'd better play with the short story for a while and learn something about this. And also make a little money. So it was after *Bring! Bring!* was finished that I went back to *Blue Voyage.*

Blue Voyage was another matter. I really wanted, sort of in midcareer, to make a statement about the predicament of the would-be artist and just what made him tick, and what was wrong with him, and why he went fast or slow. Just as *Ushant* was the other end of that statement. "D." of *Ushant* is Demarest of *Blue Voyage*, grown fatter and balder. That was always planned—that I should, as it were, give myself away, to such extent as I could bear it, as to what made the wheels go round. Feeling that this was one of the responsibilities of a writer—that he should take off the mask.

INTERVIEWER: Show just exactly how his own mind and his own experience go into his work—

AIKEN: Yes, and to what extent accidents helped him, and mistakes even, and failures in character, and so forth.

INTERVIEWER: Did you ever meet Freud? Wasn't H.D. trying for a while to get you to go and work with him?

AIKEN: Freud's influence—*and* along with his, that of Rank, Ferenczi, Adler, and (somewhat less) Jung—was tremendous. And I wrote one letter to Freud, to which he never replied. I was being groomed by H.D. and Bryher to go to Vienna and take over what H.D. had been doing, that is, observer: observing: reciprocal analysis. Freud had read *Great Circle*, and I'm told kept a copy on his office table. But I didn't go, though I started to. Misgivings set in, and so did poverty.

INTERVIEWER: You've spoken a couple of times—in *Ushant* and more guardedly or more subtly in the poetry—of your faith in consciousness. You speak of the "teleology of consciousness" at one point. This sounds almost as if you're looking for a new spiritual attitude toward life, a new religion not based on religious dogma or revelation or a conventional God. Is there anything to this?

AIKEN: Possibly. I don't know whether I'd put it quite like that. Of course I do believe in this evolution of consciousness as the only thing which we can embark on, or in fact, willy-nilly, *are* embarked on; and along with that will go the spiritual discoveries and, I feel, the inexhaustible wonder that one feels, that opens more and more the more you know. It's simply that this increasing knowledge constantly enlarges your kingdom and the capacity for admiring and loving the universe. So in that sense I think what you say is correct. *Ushant* says this.

INTERVIEWER: One statement that's always impressed me is the preface you recreated for *The House of Dust* in 1948 in which you wrote that "implicit in this poem was the theory that was to underlie much of the later work—namely, that in the evolution of man's consciousness, ever widening and deepening and sub-tilizing his awareness, and in his dedication of himself to this supreme task, man possesses all that he could possibly require in the way of a religious credo: when the halfgods go, the gods arrive; he can, if he only will, become divine." Is that too extreme a statement, do you feel, now?

AIKEN: No, I would stand by that. Which is really, in sum, more or less what my Grandfather Potter preached in New Bedford.

INTERVIEWER: When did you first come across your Grandfather Potter's sermons?

AIKEN: I've been carrying the *corpus* of my grandfather—to change the famous saying—with me all my life. I was given very early two volumes of his sermons; and I never go anywhere without them.

INTERVIEWER: What is it in them that's been so important to you?

AIKEN: Well, the complete liberation from dogma; and a determined acceptance of Darwin and all the rest of the scientific fireworks of the nineteenth century.

INTERVIEWER: This was toward the end of the nineteenth century?

AIKEN: Middle of the century. He actually took his parish out of the Unitarian Church. As he put it, "They have defrocked not only me, but my church." For thirty years he and the church, the New Bedford parish, were in the wilderness. Then the Unitarians, about 1890, caught up with him and embraced him. By this time he was president of the Free Religious Association and was lecturing all over the country on the necessity for a religion without dogma.

And this inheritance has been my guiding light; I regard myself simply as a continuance of my grandfather, and primarily, therefore, as a teacher and preacher, and a distributor, in poetic terms, of the *news* of the world, by which I mean new knowledge. This is gone into at some length in *Ushant*. And elsewhere I have said repeatedly that as poetry is the highest speech of man, it can not only accept and contain, but in the end express best everything in the world, or in himself, that he discovers. It will absorb and transmute, as it always has done, and glorify, all that we can know. This has always been, and always will be, poetry's office.

INTERVIEWER: You once wrote, speaking of the great writers of the American nineteenth century—Whitman, Melville, Hawthorne, James, Poe: "We isolate, we exile our great men, whether by ignoring them or praising them stupidly. And perhaps this isolation we offer them is our greatest gift." It seems to me you didn't receive much attention from the time of your Pulitzer Prize in 1930 until, at best, fairly recently—that you were ignored in the way you speak of for almost thirty years. "This isolation we offer" as "our greatest gift"—would this be true of yourself also?

AIKEN: I think so. I think it's very useful to be insulated from your surrounds, and this gives it to you because it gives you your inviolate privacy, without pressures, so that you can just be yourself. I think that what's happening today, with all the young poets rushing from one college to another, lecturing at the drop of a hat and so on, is not too good; I think it might have a bad effect on a great many of the young poets. They—to quote Mark Twain—"swap juices" a little too much, so that they are in danger of losing their own identity and don't give themselves time enough in which to work out what's really of importance to them—they're too busy. I think Wordsworth and Coleridge had the right idea, too—they deliberately sequestered themselves.

INTERVIEWER: What do you think of the state of poetry today? We sometimes think of the period from 1910 to 1940 or so as being the Golden Era of modern American poetry. Do you think there is anything being done now comparable to the work that was done in those years?

AIKEN: No, I don't think there is. I think we've come to a kind of splinter period in poetry. These tiny little bright fragments of observation—and not produced under sufficient pressure—some of it's very skillful, but I don't think there's anywhere a discernible major poet in the process of emerging; or if he is, I ain't seen him. But I think there's an enormous lot of talent around, and somewhere amongst these I'm sure that something will emerge, given time.

INTERVIEWER: In an interview for *The Paris Review* Robert Lowell said: "Poets of my generation and particularly younger ones . . . write a very musical, difficult poem with tremendous skill, perhaps there's never been such skill. Yet the writing seems divorced from culture somehow. It's become too much something specialized that can't handle much experience. It's become a craft, purely a craft, and there must be some breakthrough back into life." He speaks almost as if there's *too* much skill, that it's become something that's holding younger poets back; as if they're concentrating so much on finding the perfect line or the perfect image that they aren't thinking or feeling—

AIKEN: Well, I don't think that's so, and I think possibly there Lowell is really reflecting one of his own defects, because he *is* a little awkward. What really astonished me in that interview with him is his description of his method of writing verse nowadays —writing out a prose statement first and then trying to translate it to metrics without sacrificing the phrases. Well, this is really the damnedest way of writing a poem that I ever heard of, and I don't think it's any wonder that sometimes his things sound so —so prosaic—if I may go so far.

INTERVIEWER: Poets now seem so wrapped up in the short poem and the perfect small statement; this seems to grow out of the early experiments of Pound and Williams, imagism also. Do you think that these tendencies have taken poets' minds away from larger subjects—from really *thinking* about what they're going to write about?

AIKEN: I think quite likely. That's a little apropos of what I called the "splinter" stage of poetry. And I think this does go back to the imagists and Pound, T. E. Hulme, and H.D., primarily. And of course that, as a lot of us were quick to see at the time, did impose limitations and very serious ones. That's why I suppose you could say that Williams, for all his power, never really came out with a *final* thing. In fact, I think one of his completest statements is in one of his earliest poems, "The Wanderer," which is much better than *Paterson* because in that he has a real continuing line which goes from one section to another, and it isn't so fragmented.

INTERVIEWER: What about Pound's later works? Do you think that in the *Cantos* he's found a way to give a larger organization, make a larger statement, from the earlier techniques?

AIKEN: No, I don't think so. I think that's a majestic failure. There, too, it's—he described it himself in one of his own lines: "A broken bundle of mirrors." That's exactly what it is—brilliant fragments here and there, and beautiful—but it doesn't work; there isn't sufficient mind behind it, or organizing theme. He's said this himself—but I take that with a grain of salt.

INTERVIEWER: What do you think about the contemporary poets who talk about "mind expanding" or "consciousness expanding"—Ginsberg and his group? Do you think drugs can expand a writer's awareness or perceptions?

AIKEN: I've tried it long ago, with hashish and peyote. Fascinating, yes, but no good, no. This, as we find in alcohol, is an *escape* from awareness, a cheat, a momentary substitution, and in the end a destruction of it. With luck, someone might have a fragmentary Kubla Khan vision. But with no meaning. And with the steady destruction of the observing and remembering mind.

INTERVIEWER: Do you still waver between the view of the artist as simply supplying vicarious experience and your later view that the artist is the leader in the expansion of man's awareness and consciousness?

AIKEN: I think they can function together. I think they do. It's like two parts of the same machine; they go on simultaneously.

INTERVIEWER: When you speak of the artist as the creator and purveyor of new knowledge, doesn't this, to be effective, demand a fairly wide audience?

AIKEN: To be effective?

INTERVIEWER: Yes, socially effective.

AIKEN: No, not necessarily. I mean that can come serially, with time. A small but brilliant advance made today by someone's awareness may for the moment reach a very small audience, but insofar as it's valid and beautiful, it will make its way and become part of the whole world of consciousness. So in that sense it's all working toward this huge audience, and all working toward a better man.

—ROBERT HUNTER WILBUR

1970

10. Anne Sexton

Born on November 9, 1928, Anne Sexton was brought up in Wellesley, Massachusetts, attended Garland Junior College, and at twenty married a salesman. She became a fashion model in Boston and had two daughters. When her second child was born, she suffered a mental breakdown and twice tried to commit suicide. For a number of years she was in and out of mental hospitals.

At the age of thirty, as a means of recovery, Anne Sexton started writing. With the publication of each book, grants and awards followed. *To Bedlam and Part Way Back* (1960) led to admittance to Radcliffe's Institute for Independent Study. *All My Pretty Ones* (1962) brought her the first traveling fellowship offered by the American Academy of Arts and Letters (1963–64), a Ford Foundation grant in playwriting (1964–65), and the first literary-magazine travel grant from the Congress for Cultural Freedom (1965). In 1965 her *Selected Poems* appeared in England, and she was elected a Fellow of the Royal Society of Literature in London. Her third book, *Live or Die* (1966), won the Pulitzer Prize and the Shelley Award from the Poetry Society of America. Five more books followed: *Love Poems* (1969), *Transformations* (1971), *The Book of Folly* (1972), *The Death Notebooks* (1974), and *An Awful Rowing Towards God* (1975).

In 1972 she served as Cranshaw Professor of Literature at Colgate University and was a Professor of Creative Writing at Boston University from 1970 to 1974. She took her own life on October 4, 1974.

THE ADDICT

Sleep monger / death monger,
with capsules in my palms nightly,
eight ×××××× at a time if you want to know--
Now they say I'm an addict.
Now they ask why.
Why?

Don't you know I promised to die!
The pills are a mother, but better,
every color and as good as sour balls.
I'm on a kind of diet from death.
Oh my!

Why ××××× You know I get just a little
socked in the eye by them, hauled away by
the pink, the orange, the green and the white
goodnights. I'm becoming something of
a chemical mixture.
That's it!

Yes,
I try
to kill myself in small amounts,
an innocuous ××××××. Yes, yes, I admit
that actually I'm hung up on it.
But remember I don't make so much of a noise.
And frankly no one has to carry me out.
So now why do you ask my why?

When ×××××××××××××××will last for years.
×××××××××, for I like them more than I like ×××
Stubborn as hell, they won't let go.
It's a kind of marraige. It's a kind of war
where I plant bombs inside of my ××××××××self
and try
all the time
to
die.

                              Feb 1966

                    the year of ××××××
                              Vietnam

Anne Sexton manuscript page.

Anne Sexton

The interview took place over three days in the middle of August 1968. When asked about dates of publications or other events, Anne Sexton kept saying, "Let me think, I want this to be accurate," and she'd use the births of her children as reference dates to chronicle the event in question. Sometimes her distinctions between real and imagined life blurred, as in scenes from Pirandello. Often, her answers sounded like incantations, repetitious chants that, if pared down, would lose something of their implications, and so, for the most part, they are preserved in their entirety. Even when replying from written notes, she read with all the inflections and intonations of—as she described her readings—"an actress in her own autobiographical play."

INTERVIEWER: You were almost thirty before you began writing poetry. Why?

SEXTON: Until I was twenty-eight I had a kind of buried self who didn't know she could do anything but make white sauce and diaper babies. I didn't know I had any creative depths. I was a victim of the American Dream, the bourgeois, middle-class dream. All I wanted was a little piece of life, to be married, to have children. I thought the nightmares, the visions, the demons would go away if there was enough love to put them down. I was trying my damnedest to lead a conventional life, for that was how I was brought up, and it was what my husband wanted of me. But one can't build little white picket fences to keep nightmares out. The surface cracked when I was about twenty-eight. I had a psychotic break and tried to kill myself.

INTERVIEWER: And you began to write after the nervous breakdown?

SEXTON: It isn't quite as simple as all that. I said to my doctor at the beginning, "I'm no good; I can't do anything; I'm dumb." He suggested I try educating myself by listening to Boston's educational TV station. He said I had a perfectly good mind. As a matter of fact, after he gave me a Rorschach test, he said I had creative talent that I wasn't using. I protested, but I followed his suggestion. One night I saw I. A. Richards on educational television reading a sonnet and explaining its form. I thought to myself, "I could do that, maybe; I could try." So I sat down and wrote a sonnet. The next day I wrote another one, and so forth. My doctor encouraged me to write more. "Don't kill yourself," he said. "Your poems might mean something to someone else someday." That gave me a feeling of purpose, a little cause, something to *do* with my life, no matter how rotten I was.

INTERVIEWER: Hadn't you written limericks before that?

SEXTON: I did write some light verse—for birthdays, for anniversaries, sometimes thank-you notes for weekends. Long before, I wrote some serious stuff in high school; however, I hadn't been exposed to any of the major poets, not even the minor ones. No one taught poetry at that school. I read nothing but Sara Teasdale. I might have read other poets, but my mother said as I graduated from high school that I had plagiarized Sara Teasdale. Something about that statement of hers . . . I had been writing a poem a day for three months, but when she said that, I stopped.

INTERVIEWER: Didn't anyone encourage you?

SEXTON: It wouldn't have mattered. My mother was top billing in our house.

INTERVIEWER: In the beginning, what was the relationship between your poetry and your therapy?

SEXTON: Sometimes, my doctors tell me that I understand something in a poem that I haven't integrated into my life. In fact, I may be concealing it from myself, while I was revealing it to the readers. The poetry is often more advanced, in terms of my unconscious, than I am. Poetry, after all, milks the unconscious. The unconscious is there to feed it little images, little symbols, the answers, the insights I know not of. In therapy, one seeks to hide sometimes. I'll give you a rather intimate example of this. About three or four years ago my analyst asked me what I thought of my parents having intercourse when I was young. I couldn't talk. I knew there was suddenly a poem there, and I selfishly guarded it from him. Two days later, I had a poem, entitled, "In the Beach House," which describes overhearing the primal scene. In it I say, "Inside my prison of pine and bedspring,/over my window sill, under my knob,/it is plain they are at/the royal strapping." The point of this little story is the image, "the royal strapping." My analyst was quite impressed with that image, and so was I, although I don't remember going any further with it then. About three weeks ago, he said to me, "Were you ever beaten as a child?" I told him that I had been when I was about nine. I had torn up a five-dollar bill that my father gave to my sister; my father took me into his bedroom, laid me down on his bed, pulled off my pants, and beat me with a riding crop. As I related this to my doctor, he said, "See, that was quite a royal strapping," thus revealing to me, by way of my own image, the intensity of that moment, the sexuality of that beating, the little masochistic seizure—it's so classic, it's almost corny. Perhaps it's too intimate an example, but then both poetry and therapy are intimate.

INTERVIEWER: Are your poems still closely connected to your therapy as in the past?

SEXTON: No. The subject of therapy was an early theme—the

process itself as in "Said the Poet to the Analyst," the people of my past, admitting what my parents were really like, the whole Gothic New England story. I've had about eight doctors, but only two that count. I've written a poem for each of the two—"You, Doctor Martin" and "Cripples and Other Stories." And that will do. These poems are about the two men as well as the strange process. One can say that my new poems, the love poems, come about as a result of new attitudes, an awareness of the possibly good as well as the possibly rotten. Inherent in the process is a rebirth of a sense of self, each time stripping away a dead self.

INTERVIEWER: Some critics admire your ability to write about the terror of childhood guilts, parental deaths, breakdowns, suicides. Do you feel that writing about the dark parts of the human psyche takes a special act of courage?

SEXTON: Of course, but I'm tired of explaining it. It seems to be self-evident. There are warnings all along the way. "Go—children—slow." "It's dangerous in there." The appalling horror that awaits you in the answer.

INTERVIEWER: People speak of you as a primitive. Was it so natural for you to dig so deeply into the painful experiences of your life?

SEXTON: There was a part of me that was horrified, but the gutsy part of me drove on. Still, part of me was appalled by what I was doing. On the one hand I was digging up shit, with the other hand, I was covering it with sand. Nevertheless, I went on ahead. I didn't know any better. Sometimes, I felt like a reporter researching himself. Yes, it took a certain courage, but as a writer one has to take the chance on being a fool . . . yes, to be a fool, that perhaps requires the greatest courage.

INTERVIEWER: Once you began writing, did you attend any formal classes to bone up on technique?

SEXTON: After I'd been writing about three months, I dared to go into the poetry class at the Boston Center for Adult Education taught by John Holmes. I started in the middle of the term, very shy, writing very bad poems, solemnly handing them in for the eighteen others in the class to hear. The most important aspect of that class was that I felt I belonged somewhere. When I first got sick and became a displaced person, I thought I was quite alone, but when I went into the mental hospital, I found I wasn't, that there were other people like me. It made me feel better— more real, sane. I felt, "These are my people." Well, at the John Holmes class that I attended for two years, I found I belonged to the poets, that I was *real* there, and I had another, "These are my people." I met Maxine Kumin, the poet and novelist, at that class. She is my closest friend. She is part superego, part sister, as well as pal of my desk. It's strange because we're quite different. She is reserved, while I tend to be flamboyant. She is an intel- lectual, and I seem to be a primitive. That is true about our poetry as well.

INTERVIEWER: You once told me, "I call Maxine Kumin every other line." Is that a slight exaggeration?

SEXTON: Yes. But often, I call her draft by draft. However, a lot of poems I did without her. The year I was writing my first book, I didn't know her well enough to call that often. Later, when she didn't approve of such poems as "Flee on Your Don- key"—that one took four years to complete—I was on my own. Yet once, she totally saved a poem, "Cripples and other Stories."

INTERVIEWER: In the early days, how did your relatives react to the jangling of family skeletons?

SEXTON: I tried not to show my relatives any of the poems. I do know that my mother snuck into my desk one time and read "The Double Image" before it was printed. She told me just before she died that she liked the poem, and that saved me from some added guilt. My husband liked that poem, too. Ordinarily, if I show him a poem, something I try not to do, he says, "I don't think that's too hotsy-totsy," which puts me off. I try not to do it too often. My in-laws don't approve of the poems at all. My children do—with a little pain, they do.

INTERVIEWER: In your poems, several family skeletons come out of the camphor balls—your father's alcoholic tendencies, your mother's inability to deal with your suicide attempt, your great- aunt in a straitjacket. Is there any rule you follow as to which skeletons you reveal and which you don't?

SEXTON: I don't reveal skeletons that would hurt anyone. They may hurt the dead, but the dead belong to me. Only once in a while do they talk back. For instance, I don't write about my husband or his family, although there are some amazing stories there.

INTERVIEWER: How about Holmes or the poets in your class, what did they say?

SEXTON: During the years of that class, John Holmes saw me as something evil and warned Maxine to stay away from me. He told me I shouldn't write such personal poems about the madhouse. He said, "That isn't a fit subject for poetry." I knew no one who thought it was; even my doctor clammed up at that time. I was on my own. I tried to mind them. I tried to write the way the others, especially Maxine, wrote, but it didn't work. I always ended up sounding like myself.

INTERVIEWER: You have said, "If anything influenced me, it was W. D. Snodgrass's 'Heart's Needle.' " Would you comment on that?

SEXTON: If he had the courage, then I had the courage. That poem about losing his daughter brought me to face some of the facts about my own life. I had lost a daughter, lost her because I was too sick to keep her. After I read the poem, "Heart's Needle," I ran up to my mother-in-law's house and brought my daughter home. That's what a poem should do—move people to action. True, I didn't keep my daughter at the time—I wasn't ready. But I was beginning to be ready. I wrote a disguised poem about it, "Unknown Girl in the Maternity Ward." The pain of the loss . . .

INTERVIEWER: Did you ever meet Snodgrass?

SEXTON: Yes. I'd read "Heart's Needle" in *The New Poets of England and America.* I'd written about three quarters of *To Bedlam and Part Way Back* at the time, and I made a pilgrimage to Antioch Writer's Conference to meet and to learn from Snodgrass. He was a surprising person, surprisingly humble. He encouraged me, he liked what I was doing. He was the first established poet to like my work, and so I was driven to write harder and to allow myself, to dare myself to tell the whole story. He also suggested that I study with Robert Lowell. So I sent Mr.

Lowell some of my poems and asked if he would take me into the class. By then I'd had poems published in *The New Yorker* and around a bit. At any rate, the poems seemed good enough for Lowell, and I joined the class.

INTERVIEWER: Which poems did you submit to Lowell?

SEXTON: As far as I can remember, the poems about madness— "You, Doctor Martin," "Music Swims Back to Me" . . . about ten or fifteen poems from the book.

INTERVIEWER: Was this before or after Lowell published *Life Studies*?

SEXTON: Before. I sent him the poems in the summer; the following spring *Life Studies* came out. Everyone says I was influenced by Robert Lowell's revelation of madness in that book, but I was writing *To Bedlam and Part Way Back*, the story of my madness, before *Life Studies* was published. I showed my poems to Mr. Lowell as he was working on his book. Perhaps I even influenced him. I never asked him. But stranger things have happened.

INTERVIEWER: And when was your first book, *To Bedlam and Part Way Back*, published?

SEXTON: It was accepted that January; it wasn't published for a year and a half after that, I think.

INTERVIEWER: Where was Lowell teaching then?

SEXTON: The class met at Boston University on Tuesdays from two to four in a dismal room. It consisted of some twenty students. Seventeen graduates, two other housewives who were graduates or something, and a boy who had snuck over from M.I.T. I was the only one in that room who hadn't read *Lord Weary's Castle*.

INTERVIEWER: And Lowell, how did he strike you?

SEXTON: He was formal in a rather awkward New England sense. His voice was soft and slow as he read the students' poems. At first I felt the impatient desire to interrupt his slow, line by line readings. He would read the first line, stop, and then discuss it at length. I wanted to go through the whole poem quickly and then go back. I couldn't see any merit in dragging through it until you almost hated the damned thing, even your own poems, especially your own. At that point, I wrote to Snodgrass about my impatience, and his reply went this way, "Frankly, I used to nod my head at his every statement, and he taught me more than a whole gang of scholars could." So I kept my mouth shut, and Snodgrass was right. Robert Lowell's method of teaching is intuitive and open. After he had read a student's poem, he would read another evoked by it. Comparison was often painful. He worked with a cold chisel, with no more mercy than a dentist. He got out the decay, but if he was never kind to the poem, he was kind to the poet.

INTERVIEWER: Did you consult Robert Lowell on your manuscript of *To Bedlam and Part Way Back* before you submitted it to a publisher?

SEXTON: Yes. I gave him a manuscript to see if he thought it was a book. He was enthusiastic on the whole, but suggested that I throw out about half of it and write another fifteen or so poems that were better. He pointed out the weak ones, and I nodded and took them out. It sounds simple to say that I merely, as he once said, "jumped the hurdles that he had put up," but it makes a difference who puts up the hurdles. He defined the course, and acted as though, good race horse that I was, I would just naturally run it.

INTERVIEWER: Ultimately, what can a teacher give a writer in a creative-writing class?

SEXTON: Courage, of course. That's the most important ingredient. Then, in a rather plain way, Lowell helped me to distrust the easy musical phrase and to look for the frankness of ordinary speech. Lowell is never impressed with a display of images or sounds—those things that a poet is born with anyhow. If you have enough natural imagery, he can show you how to chain it in. He didn't teach me what to put into a poem, but what to leave out. What he taught me was taste—perhaps that's the only thing a poet can be taught.

INTERVIEWER: Sylvia Plath was a member of Lowell's class also, wasn't she?

SEXTON: Yes. She and George Starbuck heard that I was auditing Lowell's class. They kind of joined me there for the second term. After the class, we would pile in the front seat of my old Ford, and I would drive quickly through the traffic to the Ritz. I would always park illegally in a "Loading Only Zone," telling them gaily, "It's O.K., we're only going to get loaded." Off we'd go, each on George's arm, into the Ritz to drink three or four martinis. George even has a line about this in his first book of poems, *Bone Thoughts*. After the Ritz, we would spend our last pennies at the Waldorf Cafeteria—a dinner for seventy cents— George was in no hurry. He was separated from his wife; Sylvia's Ted [Hughes] was busy with his own work, and I had to stay in the city for a seven P.M. appointment with my psychiatrist . . . a funny three.

INTERVIEWER: In Sylvia Plath's last book, written just before her suicide, she was submerged by the theme of death, as you are in your book, *Live or Die*. Did you ever get around to talking about death or your suicides at the Ritz?

SEXTON: Often, very often. Sylvia and I would talk at length about our first suicide, in detail and depth—between the free potato chips. Suicide is, after all, the opposite of the poem. Sylvia and I often talked opposites. We talked death with burned-up intensity, both of us drawn to it like moths to an electric light bulb, sucking on it. She told the story of her first suicide in sweet and loving detail, and her description in *The Bell Jar* is just that same story. It is a wonder we didn't depress George with our egocentricity; instead, I think, we three were stimulated by it— even George—as if death made each of us a little more real at the moment.

INTERVIEWER: In a BBC interview, Sylvia Plath said, "I've been very excited by what I feel is the new breakthrough that came with, say, Robert Lowell's *Life Studies* . . . This intense break-through into very serious, very personal emotional experience, which I feel has been partly taboo . . . I think particularly of the poetess Anne Sexton, who writes also about her experiences as a mother; as a mother who's had a nervous breakdown, as an ex-tremely emotional and feeling young woman. And her poems are wonderfully craftsmanlike poems, and yet they have a kind of emotional psychological depth, which I think is something perhaps quite new and exciting." Do you agree that you influenced her?

SEXTON: Maybe. I did give her a sort of daring, but that's all she should have said. I remember writing to Sylvia in England after her first book, *The Colossus*, came out and saying something like, "If you're not careful, Sylvia, you will out-Roethke Roethke." She replied that I had guessed accurately. But maybe she buried her so-called influences deeper than that, deeper than any one of us would think to look, and if she did, I say, "Good luck to her!" Her poems do their own work. I don't need to sniff them for distant relatives: I'm against it.

INTERVIEWER: Did Sylvia Plath influence your writing?

SEXTON: Her first book didn't interest me at all. I was doing my own thing. But after her death, with the appearance of *Ariel*, I think I was influenced, and I don't mind saying it. In a special sort of way, it was daring again. She had dared to do something quite different. She had dared to write hate poems, the one thing I had never dared to write. I'd always been afraid, even in my life, to express anger. I think the poem, "Cripples and Other Stories," is evidence of a hate poem somehow, though no one could ever write a poem to compare to her "Daddy." There was a kind of insolence in them, saying, "Daddy, you bastard, I'm through." I think the poem, "The Addict," has some of her speech rhythms in it. She had very open speech rhythms, something that I didn't always have.

INTERVIEWER: You have said, "I think the second book lacks some of the impact and honesty of the first, which I wrote when I was so raw that I didn't know any better." Would you describe your development from the second book to the third and from your third to the fourth?

SEXTON: Well, in the first book, I was giving the experience of madness; in the second book, the causes of madness; and in the third book, finally, I find that I was deciding whether to live or to die. In the third I was daring to be a fool again—raw, "uncooked," as Lowell calls it, with a little camouflage. In the fourth book, I not only have lived, come on to the scene, but loved, that sometime miracle.

INTERVIEWER: What would you say about the technical development from book to book?

SEXTON: In *Bedlam*, I used very tight form in most cases, feeling that I could express myself better. I take a kind of pleasure, even now, but more especially in *Bedlam*, in forming a stanza, a verse, making it an entity, and then coming to a little conclusion at the end of it, of a little shock, a little double rhyme shock. In my second book, *All My Pretty Ones*, I loosened up and in the last section didn't use any form at all. I found myself to be surprisingly free without the form which had worked as a kind of superego for me. The third book I used less form. In *Love Poems*, I had one long poem, eighteen sections, that is in form, and I enjoyed doing it in that way. With the exception of that and a few other poems, all of the book is in free verse, and I feel at this point comfortable to use either, depending on what the poem requires.

INTERVIEWER: Is there any particular subject which you'd rather deal with in form than in free verse?

SEXTON: Probably madness. I've noticed that Robert Lowell felt freer to write about madness in free verse, whereas it was the opposite for me. Only after I had set up large structures that were almost impossible to deal with did I think I was free to allow myself to express what had really happened. However in *Live or Die*, I wrote "Flee on Your Donkey" without that form and found that I could do it just as easily in free verse. That's perhaps something to do with my development as a human being and understanding of myself, besides as a poet.

INTERVIEWER: In *Live or Die*, the whole book has a marvelous structured tension—simply by the sequence of the poems which pits the wish to live against the death instinct. Did you plan the book this way? Lois Ames speaks of you as wishing to write more "live" poems because the "die" poems outnumbered them.

SEXTON: I didn't plan the book any way. In January of 1962, I started collecting new poems the way you do when a book is over. I didn't know where they would go or that they would go anywhere, even into a book. Then at some point, as I was collecting these poems, I was rereading *Henderson the Rain King* by Saul Bellow. I had met Saul Bellow at a cocktail party about a year before, and I had been carrying *Henderson the Rain King* around in my suitcase everywhere I traveled. Suddenly there I was meeting Saul Bellow, and I was overenthusiastic. I said, "Oh, oh, you're Saul Bellow, I've wanted to meet you," and he ran from the room. Very afraid. I was quite ashamed of my exuberance, and then sometime, a year later, reading *Henderson the Rain King* over again, at three in the morning, I wrote Saul Bellow a fan letter about Henderson, saying that he was a monster of despair, that I understood his position because Henderson was the one who had ruined life, who had blown up the frogs, made a mess out of everything. I drove to the mail box then and there! The next morning I wrote him a letter of apology.

Saul Bellow wrote me back on the back of a manuscript. He said to me, "Luckily, I have a message to you from the book I am writing [which was *Herzog*]. I have both your letters—the good one which was written that night at three A.M. and then the contrite one, the next day. One's best things are always followed by apoplectic, apologetic seizure. Monster of despair could be *Henderson*'s subtitle." The message that he had encircled went this way, "With one long breath caught and held in his chest, he fought his sadness over his solitary life. Don't cry you idiot, live or die, but don't poison everything." And in circling that and in sending it to me, Saul Bellow had given me a message about my whole life. That I didn't want to poison the world, that I didn't want to be the killer; I wanted to be the one who gave birth, who encouraged things to grow and to flower, not the poisoner. So I stuck that message up over my desk and it was a kind of hidden message. You don't know what these messages mean to you, yet you stick them up over your desk or remember them or write them down and put them in your wallet. One day I was reading a quote from Rimbaud that said, "Anne, Anne, flee on your donkey," and I typed it out because it had my name in it and because I wanted to flee. I put it in my wallet, went to see my doctor, and at that point was committed to a hospital for about the seventh or eighth time. In the hospital, I started to write the poem, "Flee on Your Donkey," as though the message had come to me at just the right moment. Well, this was true with Bellow's quote from his book. I kept it over my desk, and when I went to Europe, I pasted it in the front of my manuscript. I kept it there as a quotation with which to preface my book. It must have just hit me one day that *Live or Die* was a damn good title for the book I was working on. And that's what it was all about, what all those poems were about. You say there's a tension there and a structure, but it was an unconscious tension and an unconscious structure that I didn't know was going on when I was doing it.

INTERVIEWER: Once you knew the title of the book, did you count up the "live" poems and count up the "die" poems and then write any more poems because of an imbalance?

SEXTON: No, no, that's far too rigid. You can't write a poem because of an imbalance. After that I wrote "Little Girl, My Stringbean, My Lovely Woman." Then I wrote a play, then "A Little Uncomplicated Hymn" and other poems. Some were negative, and some were positive. At this time I knew that I was trying to get a book together. I had more than enough for a book, but I knew I hadn't written out the live or die question. I hadn't written the poem "Live." This was bothering me because it wasn't coming to me. Instead of that, "Cripples and Other Stories" and "The Addict" were appearing, and I knew that I wasn't finishing the book, that I hadn't come to the cycle, I hadn't given a reason. There's nothing I could do about this and then suddenly, our dog was pregnant. I was supposed to kill all the puppies when they came; instead, I let them live, and I realized that if I let *them* live, that I could let *me* live, too, that after all I wasn't a killer, that the poison just didn't take.

INTERVIEWER: Although you received a European traveling fellowship from the American Academy of Arts and Letters, there are, to date, very few poems published about your European experience. Why?

SEXTON: First of all poems aren't post cards to send home. Secondly I went to Europe with a purpose as well as with a grant.

My great-aunt, who was really my best childhood friend, had sent letters home from Europe the three years that she lived there. I had written about this in a poem called "Some Foreign Letters." I had her letters with me as I left for Europe, and I was going to walk her walks and go to her places, live her life over again, and write letters back to her. The two poems that I did write about Europe mention the letters. In "Crossing the Atlantic," I mention that I have read my grandmother's letters and my mother's letters. I had swallowed their words like Dickens, thinking of Dickens' journals in America. The second poem, "Walking in Paris," was written about my great-aunt, how she used to walk fourteen or fifteen miles a day in Paris, and I call her Nana. Some critics have thought I meant Zola's Nana, but I didn't any more than I meant the Nana in Peter Pan. However the letters were stolen from my car in Belgium. When I lost the letters in Brussels, that was the end of that kind of poem that I had gone over there to write.

INTERVIEWER: You were to go abroad for a year, but you only stayed two months. Do you want to comment on that?

SEXTON: Two and a half months. I got sick over there; I lost my sense of self. I had, as my psychiatrist said, "a leaky ego" and I had to come home. I was in the hospital for a while, and then I returned to my normal life. I had to come home because I need my husband and my therapist and my children to tell me who I am. I remember, I was talking with Elizabeth Hardwick on the phone and saying, "Oh, I feel so guilty. I couldn't get along without my husband. It's a terrible thing, really, a modern woman should be able to do it." Although I may be misquoting her, I may have remembered it the way I needed to hear it, she said to me, "If I were in Paris without my husband, I'd hide in a hotel room all day." And I said, "Well, think of Mary McCarthy." And Elizabeth Hardwick said, "Mary McCarthy, she's never been without a man for a day in her life."

INTERVIEWER: From 1964 to 1965, you held a Ford Foundation Grant in playwriting and worked at Boston's Charles Street Playhouse. How did you feel writing something that had to be staged?

SEXTON: I felt great! I used to pace up and down the living

room shouting out the lines, and what do they call it . . . for walking around the stage . . . *blocking* out the play as I would go along.

INTERVIEWER: Was the play [*Mercy Street*] ever performed?*

SEXTON: There were little working performances at the Charles Playhouse when we had time. It was pretty busy there. Now and then they would play out a scene for me, and then I would rewite it and send it in to the director special delivery. He would call me up the next morning and say, "It's not right," and then I would work on it again, send it to him that evening, and then the next morning, he'd call, and so on it went. I found that I had one whole character in the play who was unnecessary because, as they acted it, the director had that person be quiet and say nothing. I realized that that dialogue was totally unnecessary, so I cut out that character.

INTERVIEWER: Did you find that the themes in your poetry overlapped into your play? Was your play an extension of your poetry?

SEXTON: Yes. Completely. The play was about a girl shuffling between her psychiatrist and a priest. It was the priest I cut out, realizing that she really wasn't having a dialogue with him at all. The play was about all the subjects that my poems are about— my mother, my great-aunt, my father, and the girl who wants to kill herself. A little bit about her husband, but not much. The play is really a morality play. The second act takes place after death.

INTERVIEWER: Many of your poems are dramatic narratives. Because you're accustomed to handling a plot, was it easy for you to switch from verse to scene writing?

SEXTON: I don't see the difference. In both cases, the character is confronting himself and his destiny. I didn't know I was writing scenes; I thought I was writing about people. In another context— helping Maxine Kumin with her novel—I gave her a bit of advice. I told her, "Fuck structure and grab your characters by the time

* Editor's Note: *Mercy Street* was eventually produced at New York's American Place Theater in 1969.

balls." Each one of us sits in our time; we're born, live and die. She was thinking this and that, and I was telling her to get inside her characters' lives—which she finally did.

INTERVIEWER: What were your feelings when you received the Pulitzer Prize for Poetry for *Live or Die* in 1967?

SEXTON: Of course, I was delighted. It had been a bad time for me. I had a broken hip, and I was just starting to get well, still crippled, but functioning a little bit. After I received the prize, it gave me added incentive to write more. In the months following, I managed to write a poem, "Eighteen Days Without You," in fourteen days—an eighteen-section poem. I was inspired by the recognition that the Pulitzer gave me, even though I was aware that it didn't mean all that much. After all, they have to give a Pulitzer Prize every year, and I was just one in a long line.

INTERVIEWER: Do you write a spate of poems at one time, or are you disciplined by a writing schedule?

SEXTON: Well, I'm very dissatisfied with the amount I write. My first book—although it took three years to complete—was really written in one year. Sometimes ten poems were written in two weeks. When I was going at that rate, I found that I could really work well. Now I tend to become dissatisfied with the fact that I write poems so slowly, that they come to me so slowly. When they come, I write them; when they don't come, I don't. There's certainly no disciplined writing schedule except for the fact that when a poem comes a person must be disciplined and ready, flexing his muscles. That is, they burst forth, and you must put everything else aside. Ideally it doesn't matter what it is unless your husband has double pneumonia, or the child breaks his leg. Otherwise, you don't tear yourself away from the typewriter until you must sleep.

INTERVIEWER: Do the responsibilities of wife and mother interfere with your writing?

SEXTON: Well, when my children were younger, they interfered all the time. It was just my stubbornness that let me get through with it at all, because here were these young children saying, "Momma, Momma," and there I was getting the images, structuring the poem. Now my children are older and creep around the house saying, "Shh, Mother is writing a poem." But then again, as I was writing the poem, "Eighteen Days Without You"—the last poem in *Love Poems*—my husband said to me, "I can't stand it any longer, you haven't been with me for days." That poem originally was "Twenty-one Days Without You" and it became "Eighteen Days" because he had cut into the inspiration; he demanded my presence back again, into his life, and I couldn't take that much from him.

INTERVIEWER: When writing, what part of the poem is the prickliest part?

SEXTON: Punctuation, sometimes. The punctuating can change the whole meaning, and my life is full of little dots and dashes. Therefore, I have to let the editors help me punctuate. And, probably the rhythm. It's the thing I have to work hardest to get in the beginning—the feeling, the voice of the poem, and how it will come across, how it will feel to the reader, how it feels to me as it comes out. Images are probably the most important part of the poem. First of all, you want to tell a story, but images are what are going to shore it up and get to the heart of the matter— but I don't have to work too hard for the images—they have to come—if they're not coming, I'm not even writing a poem, it's pointless. So I work hardest to get the rhythm, because each poem should have its own rhythm, its own structure. Each poem has its own life, each one is different.

INTERVIEWER: How do you decide a length of line? Does it have something to do with the way it looks on a page as well as how many beats there are to a line?

SEXTON: How it looks on a page. I don't give a damn about the beats in a line, unless I want them and need them. These are just tricks that you use when you need them. It's a very simple thing to write with rhyme and rhythmic beat—those things anyone can do nowadays; everyone is quite accomplished at that. The point, the hard thing, is to get the true voice of the poem, to make each poem an individual thing, give it the stamp of your own voice, and at the same time to make it singular.

INTERVIEWER: Do you ever find yourself saying, "Oh, yes, I've explored that in another poem," and discarding a poem?

SEXTON: No, because I might want to explore it in a new way
. . . I might have a new realization, a new truth about it. Recently
I noticed in "Flee on Your Donkey" that I had used some of the
same facts in *To Bedlam and Part Way Back*, but I hadn't realized
them in their total ugliness. I'd hidden from them. This time was
really raw and really ugly and it was all involved with my own
madness. It was all like a great involuted web, and I presented it
the way it really was.

INTERVIEWER: Do you revise a great deal?

SEXTON: Constantly.

INTERVIEWER: Do you have any ritual which gets you set for
writing?

SEXTON: I might, if I felt the poem come on, put on a certain
record, sometimes the "Bachianas Brasileiras" by Villa-Lobos. I
wrote to that for about three or four years. It's my magic tune.

INTERVIEWER: Is there any time of day, any particular mood
that is better for writing?

SEXTON: No. Those moments before a poem comes, when the
heightened awareness comes over you, and you realize a poem
is buried there somewhere, you prepare yourself. I run around,
you know, kind of skipping around the house, marvelous elation.
It's as though I could fly, almost, and I get very tense before I've
told the truth—hard. Then I sit down at the desk and get going
with it.

INTERVIEWER: What is the quality of feeling when you're
writing?

SEXTON: Well, it's a beautiful feeling, even if it's hard work.
When I'm writing, I know I'm doing the thing I was born
to do.

INTERVIEWER: Do you have any standard by which you judge
whether to let an image remain in a poem, or be cut?

SEXTON: It's done with my unconscious. May it do me
no ill.

INTERVIEWER: You've said, "When I'm working away on a
poem, I hunt for the truth . . . It might be a poetic truth, and
not just a factual one." Can you comment on that?

SEXTON: Many of my poems are true, line by line, altering a

few facts to get the story at its heart. In "The Double Image," the poem about my mother's death from cancer and the loss of my daughter, I don't mention that I had another child. Each poem has its own truth. Furthermore, in that poem, I only say that I was hospitalized twice, when in fact, I was hospitalized five times in that span of time. But then, poetic truth is not necessarily autobiographical. It is truth that goes beyond the immediate self, another life. I don't adhere to literal facts all the time; I make them up whenever needed. Concrete examples give a verisimilitude. I want the reader to feel, "Yes, yes, that's the way it is." I want them to feel as if they were touching me. I would alter any word, attitude, image, or persona for the sake of a poem. As Yeats said, "I have lived many lives, I have been a slave and a prince. Many a beloved has sat upon my knee, and I have sat upon the knee of many a beloved. Everything that has been shall be again."

INTERVIEWER: There Yeats is talking about reincarnation.

SEXTON: So am I. It's a little mad, but I believe I am many people. When I am writing a poem, I feel I am the person who should have written it. Many times I assume these guises; I attack it the way a novelist might. Sometimes I become someone else, and when I do, I believe, even in moments when I'm not writing the poem, that I am that person. When I wrote about the farmer's wife, I lived in my mind in Illinois; when I had the illegitimate child, I nursed it—in my mind—and gave it back and traded life. When I gave my lover back to his wife, in my mind, I grieved and saw how ethereal and unnecessary I had been. When I was Christ, I felt like Christ. My arms hurt, I desperately wanted to pull them in off the Cross. When I was taken down off the Cross and buried alive, I sought solutions; I hoped they were Christian solutions.

INTERVIEWER: What prompted you to write "In the Deep Museum," which recounts what Christ could have felt if he were still alive in the tomb? What led you to even deal with such a subject?

SEXTON: I'm not sure. I think it was an unconscious thing. I think I had a kind of feeling Christ was speaking to me and telling me to write that story . . . the story he hadn't written. I thought to myself, this would be the most awful death. The Cross, the Crucifixion, which I so deeply believe in, has almost become trite, and that there was a more humble death that he might have had to seek for love's sake, because his love was the greatest thing about him—not his death.

INTERVIEWER: Are you a believing nonbeliever? Your poems, such as "The Division of Parts" and "With Mercy for the Greedy," suggest you would like to believe, indeed struggle to believe, but can't.

SEXTON: Yes. I fight my own impulse. There is a hard-core part of me that believes, and there's this little critic in me that believes nothing. Some people think I'm a lapsed Catholic.

INTERVIEWER: What was your early religious training?

SEXTON: Half-assed Protestant. My Nana came from a Protestant background with a very stern patriarchal father who had twelve children. He often traveled in Europe, and when he came back and brought nude statues into his house, the minister came to call and said, "You can't come to church if you keep these nude statues." So he said, "All right, I'll never come again." Every Sunday morning he read the Bible to his twelve children for two hours, and they had to sit up straight and perfect. He never went to church again.

INTERVIEWER: Where do you get the "juice" for your religious poetry?

SEXTON: I found, when I was bringing up my children, that I could answer questions about sex easily. But I had a very hard time with the questions about God and death. It isn't resolved in my mind to this day.

INTERVIEWER: Are you saying then that questions from your children are what prompted you to think about these poems—that doesn't sound quite right.

SEXTON: It isn't. I have visions—sometimes ritualized visions—that come to me of God, or of Christ, or of the Saints, and I feel that I can touch them almost . . . that they are part of me. It's the same "Everything that has been shall be again." It's reincarnation, speaking with another voice . . . or else with the Devil.

If you want to know the truth, the leaves talk to me every June.

INTERVIEWER: How long do your visions last? What are they like?

SEXTON: That's impossible to describe. They could last for six months, six minutes, or six hours. I feel very much in touch with things after I've had a vision. It's somewhat like the beginning of writing a poem; the whole world is very sharp and well defined, and I'm intensely alive, like I've been shot full of electric volts.

INTERVIEWER: Do you try to communicate this to other people when you feel it?

SEXTON: Only through the poems, no other way. I refuse to talk about it, which is why I'm having a hard time now.

INTERVIEWER: Is there any real difference between a religious vision and a vision when you're mad?

SEXTON: Sometimes, when you're mad, the vision—I don't call them visions, really—when you're mad, they're silly and out of place, whereas if it's a so-called mystical experience, you've put everything in its proper place. I've never talked about my religious experiences with anyone, not a psychiatrist, not a friend, not a priest, not anyone. I've kept it very much to myself—and I find this very difficult, and I'd just as soon leave it, if you please.

INTERVIEWER: A poem like "The Division of Parts" has direct reference to your mother's dying. Did those excruciating experiences of watching someone close to you disintegrate from cancer force you to confront your own belief in God or religion?

SEXTON: Yes, I think so. The dying are slowly being rocked away from us and wrapped up into death, that eternal place. And one looks for answers and is faced with demons and visions. Then one comes up with God. I don't mean the ritualized Protestant God, who is such a goody-goody . . . but the martyred saints, the crucified man . . .

INTERVIEWER: Are you saying that when confronted with the ultimate question, death, that your comfort comes, even though watered down, from the myths and fables of religion?

SEXTON: No myth or fable ever gave me any solace, but my own inner contact with the heroes of the fables, as you put it, my very closeness to Christ. In one poem about the Virgin Mary,

"For the Year of the Insane," I believed that I was talking to Mary, that her lips were upon my lips; it's almost physical . . . as in many of my poems. I become that person.

INTERVIEWER: But is it the fact in your life of someone you know dying that forces you into a vision?

SEXTON: No, I think it's my own madness.

INTERVIEWER: Are you more lucid, in the sense of understanding life, when you are mad?

SEXTON: Yes.

INTERVIEWER: Why do you think that's so?

SEXTON: Pure gift.

INTERVIEWER: I asked you, are you a believing disbeliever. When something happens like a death, are you pushed over the brink of disbelieving into believing?

SEXTON: For a while, but it can happen without a death. There are little deaths in life, too—in your own life—and at that point, sometimes you are in touch with strange things, otherworldly things.

INTERVIEWER: You have received a great deal of fan mail from Jesuits and other clergy. Do any of them interpret what you write as blasphemy?

SEXTON: No. They find my work very religious, and take my books on retreats, and teach my poems in classes.

INTERVIEWER: Why do you feel that most of your critics ignore this strain of religious experience in your poetry?

SEXTON: I think they tackle the obvious things without delving deeper. They are more shocked by the other, whereas I think in time to come people will be more shocked by my mystical poetry than by my so-called confessional poetry.

INTERVIEWER: Perhaps your critics, in time to come, will associate the suffering in your confessional poetry with the kind of sufferers you take on in your religious poetry.

SEXTON: You've summed it up perfectly. Thank you for saying that. That ragged Christ, that sufferer, performed the greatest act of confession, and I mean with his body. And I try to do that with words.

INTERVIEWER: Many of your poems deal with memories of

suffering. Very few of them deal with memories that are happy ones. Why do you feel driven to write more about pain?

SEXTON: That's not true about my last book, which deals with joy. I think I've dealt with unhappy themes because I've lived them. If I haven't lived them, I've invented them.

INTERVIEWER: But surely there were also happy moments, joyous, euphoric moments in those times as well.

SEXTON: Pain engraves a deeper memory.

INTERVIEWER: Are there any poems you wouldn't read in public?

SEXTON: No. As a matter of fact, I sing "Cripples and Other Stories" with my combo to a Nashville rhythm.

INTERVIEWER: What is your combo?

SEXTON: It's called "Her Kind"—after one of my poems. One of my students started putting my poems to music—he's a guitarist, and then we got an organist, a flutist, and a drummer. We call our music "Chamber Rock." We've been working on it and giving performances for about a year. It opens up my poems in a new way by involving them in the sound of rock music, letting my words open up to sound that can be actually heard, giving a new dimension. And it's quite exciting for me to hear them that way.

INTERVIEWER: Do you enjoy giving a reading?

SEXTON: It takes three weeks out of your life. A week before it happens, the nervousness begins, and it builds up to the night of the reading when the poet in you changes into a performer. Readings take so much out of you because they are a reliving of the experience, that is, they are happening all over again. I am an actress in my own autobiographical play. Then there is the love . . . When there is a coupling of the audience and myself, when they are really with me, and the Muse is with me, I'm not coming alone.

INTERVIEWER: Can you ever imagine America as a place where thousands of fans flock to a stadium to hear a poet, as they do in Russia?

SEXTON: Someday, perhaps. But our poets seem to be losing touch. People flock to Bob Dylan, Janis Joplin, the Beatles—

these are the popular poets of the English-speaking world. But I don't worry about popularity; I'm too busy.

INTERVIEWER: At first your poetry was a therapeutic device. Why do you write now?

SEXTON: I write because I'm driven to—it's my bag. Though after every book, I think there'll never be another one. That's the end of that. Good-by, good-by.

INTERVIEWER: And what advice would you give to a young poet?

SEXTON: Be careful who your critics are. Be specific. Tell almost the whole story. Put your ear close down to your soul and listen hard.

INTERVIEWER: Louis Simpson criticized your poetry, saying, "A poem titled 'Menstruation at Forty' was the straw that broke this camel's back." Is it only male critics who balk at your use of the biological facts of womanhood?

SEXTON: I haven't added up all the critics and put them on different teams. I haven't noticed the gender of the critic especially. I talk of the life-death cycle of the body. Well, women tell time by the body. They are like clocks. They are always fastened to the earth, listening for its small animal noises. Sexuality is one of the most normal parts of life. True, I get a little uptight when Norman Mailer writes that he screws a woman anally. I like Allen Ginsberg very much, and when he writes about the ugly vagina, I feel awful. That kind of thing doesn't appeal to me. So I have my limitations, too. Homosexuality is all right with me. Sappho was beautiful. But when someone hates another person's body and somehow violates it—that's the kind of thing I mind.

INTERVIEWER: What do you feel is the purpose of poetry?

SEXTON: As Kafka said about prose, "A book should serve as the axe for the frozen sea within us." And that's what I want from a poem. A poem should serve as the axe for the frozen sea within us.

INTERVIEWER: How would you apply the Kafka quote to your new book, *Love Poems*?

SEXTON: Well, have you ever seen a sixteen-year-old fall in love? The axe for the frozen sea becomes imbedded in her. Or have you ever seen a woman get to be forty and never have any love in her life? What happens to her when she falls in love? The axe for the frozen sea.

INTERVIEWER: Some people wonder how you can write about yourself, completely ignoring the great issues of the times, like the Vietnam war or the civil-rights crisis.

SEXTON: People have to find out who they are before they can confront national issues. The fact that I seldom write about public issues in no way reflects my personal opinion. I am a pacifist. I sign petitions, etc. However, I am not a polemicist. "The Fire Bombers"—that's a new poem—is about wanton destruction, not about Vietnam, specifically; when Robert Kennedy was killed, I wrote about an assassin. I write about human emotions; I write about interior events, not historical ones. In one of my love poems, I say that my lover is unloading bodies from Vietnam. If that poem is read in a hundred years, people will have to look up the war in Vietnam. They will have mixed it up with the Korean or God knows what else. One hopes it will be history very soon. Of course, I may change. I could use the specifics of the war for a backdrop against which to reveal experience, and it would be just as valid as the details I am known by. As for the civil-rights issue, I mentioned that casually in a poem, but I don't go into it. I think it's a major issue. I think many of my poems about the individual who is dispossessed, who must play slave, who cries "Freedom Now," "Power Now," are about the human experience of being black in this world. A black emotion can be a white emotion. It is a crisis for the individual as well as the nation. I think I've been writing black poems all along, wearing my white mask. I'm always the victim . . . but no longer!

—BARBARA KEVLES

1971

11. W. H. Auden

W. H. Auden was born in York, England, on February 21, 1907, and was educated at Gresaham's School, Holt, and Christ Church, Oxford. In the 1930s he collaborated with Christopher Isherwood, an old school companion, on the plays *The Dog Beneath the Skin* (1935), *The Ascent of F6* (1936), and *On the Frontier* (1938), as well as on *Journey to a War*, a prose record of his 1938 travels in China. Auden's early volumes of poetry include *Poems* (1930), *The Orators* (1932), *Look, Stranger!* (1936), and *On This Island* (1937).

In 1938 Auden left England for America; he became a U. S. citizen in 1946. In addition to teaching at many American universities, he edited the *Oxford Book of Light Verse* (1938) and published more poetry, including *Another Time* (1940); *For the Time Being* (1944); and *The Age of Anxiety* (1947), for which he won the Pulitzer Prize. These were followed by *Nones* (1951); *The Shield of Achilles* (1955), for which he won the National Book Award; *About the House* (1965); *City Without Walls* (1969); *Epistle to a Godson and Other Poems* (1972); and *Thank You, Fog* (1974).

Auden was also the author of occasional prose, including *The Enchafèd Flood* (1950); *Making, Knowing and Judging*, his inaugural lecture as Professor of Poetry at Oxford (1956); and *The Dyer's Hand* (1962). In collaboration with Chester Kallman, Auden wrote libretti for operas by Stravinsky, Hans Werner Henze, and other composers.

Dr. Auden received many honors, among them two Guggenheim Fellowships; the Award of Merit from the American Academy of Arts and Letters (1945), the Bollingen Prize (1954), the Feltrinelli Prize (1957), the Alexander Droutzkoy Memorial Award (1959), the Guinness Poetry Award (1959), and the National Medal for Literature (1967). Dr. Auden died in Vienna on September 28, 1973.

```
Last night, sucked giddy down

The funnel of my dream,

I saw myself within

A buried engine-room.

Dynamos, boilers, lay

In tickling silence, I,

Gripping an oily rail,

Talked feverishly with an  ᵗᵐᵉ

Hare-lipped philosopher,

Who spluttered "Is that all?",

And winked a lecher's eye,

"Puella defututa"

And laughed himself away.
```

Professional listeners
Who splutter feverishly month as how
In ecstasy of pain
I know, I know, I know,
And reached his hand for mine.

W. H. Auden manuscript, *page 2 of* Poem II (*"I chose this lean country"*) *from* Poems 1928. *From the Henry W. and Albert A. Berg Collection,* The New York Public Library, Astor, Lenox and Tilden Foundations.

P. Kureth

W. H. Auden

AUDEN: *What's that again?*

INTERVIEWER: *I wondered which living writer you would say has served as the prime protector of the integrity of our English tongue . . . ?*

AUDEN: *Why me, of course!*

Conversation, Autumn 1972

He was sitting beneath two direct white lights of a plywood portico, drinking a large cup of strong breakfast coffee, chain-smoking cigarettes and doing the crossword puzzle which appears on the daily book review page of The New York Times—*which, as it happened, this day contained, along with his photo, a review of his most recent volume of poetry.*

When he had completed the puzzle, he unfolded the paper, glanced at the obits, and went to make toast.

Asked if he had read the review, Auden replied: "Of course not. Obviously these things are not meant for me . . ."

His singular perspectives, priorities and tastes, were strongly manifest in the décor of his New York apartment, which he used in the winter. Its three large high-ceilinged main rooms were painted dark gray, pale green, and purple. On the wall hung drawings of friends—Elizabeth Bishop, E. M. Forster, Paul Valéry, Chester Kallman—framed simply in gold. There was also an original Blake watercolor, The Act of Creation, *in the dining room, as well as several line drawings of male nudes. On the floor of his bedroom, a portrait of himself, unframed, faced the wall.*

The cavernous front living room, piled high with books, was left dark except during his brief excursions into its many boxes of manuscripts or for consultations with the Oxford English Dictionary.

Auden's kitchen was long and narrow, with many pots and pans hanging on the wall. He preferred such delicacies as tongue, tripe, brains, and Polish sausage, ascribing the eating of beefsteak to the lower orders ("it's madly non-U!"). *He drank Smirnoff martinis, red wine, and cognac, shunned pot, and confessed to having, under a doctor's supervision, tried LSD:* "Nothing much happened, but I did get the distinct impression that some birds were trying to communicate with me."

His conversation was droll, intelligent, and courtly, a sort of humanistic global gossip, disinterested in the machinations of ambition, less interested in concrete poetry, absolutely exclusive of electronic influence.

As he once put it: "I just got back from Canada, where I had a run-in with McLuhan. I won."

INTERVIEWER: You've insisted we do this conversation without a tape recorder. Why?

AUDEN: Because I think if there's anything worth retaining, the reporter ought to be able to remember it. Truman Capote tells the story of the reporter whose machine broke down halfway into an interview. Truman waited while the man tried in vain to fix it and finally asked if he could continue. The reporter said not to bother—he wasn't used to listening to what his subjects said!

INTERVIEWER: I thought your objection might have been to the instrument itself. You have written a new poem condemning the camera as an infernal machine.

AUDEN: Yes, it creates sorrow. Normally, when one passes someone on the street who is in pain, one either tries to help him, or one simply looks the other way. With a photo there's no human decision; you're not there; you can't turn away; you simply gape. It's a form of voyeurism. And I think close-ups are rude.

INTERVIEWER: Was there anything that you were particularly afraid of as a child? The dark, spiders, and so forth.

AUDEN: No, I wasn't very scared. Spiders, certainly—but that's different, a personal phobia which persists through life. Spiders and octopi. I was certainly never afraid of the dark.

INTERVIEWER: Were you a talkative child? I remember your describing somewhere the autistic quality of your private world.

AUDEN: Yes, I was talkative. Of course there were things in my private world that I couldn't share with others. But I always had a few good friends.

INTERVIEWER: When did you start writing poetry?

AUDEN: I think my own case may be rather odd. I was going to be a mining engineer or a geologist. Between the ages of six and twelve, I spent many hours of my time constructing a highly elaborate private world of my own based on, first of all, a land-scape, the limestone moors of the Pennines; and secondly, an industry—lead mining. Now I found in doing this, I had to make certain rules for myself. I could choose between two machines necessary to do a job, but they had to be real ones I could find in catalogues. I could decide between two ways of draining a mine, but I wasn't allowed to use magical means. Then there came a day which later on, looking back, seems very important. I was planning my idea of the concentrating mill—you know, the platonic idea of what it should be. There were two kinds of machinery for separating the slime, one I thought more beautiful than the other, but the other one I knew to be more efficient. I felt myself faced with what I can only call a moral choice—it was my duty to take the second and more efficient one. Later, I

realized, in constructing this world which was only inhabited by
me, I was already beginning to learn how poetry is written. Then,
my final decision, which seemed to be fairly fortuitous at the
time, took place in 1922, in March when I was walking across a
field with a friend of mine from school who later became a painter.
He asked me, "Do you ever write poetry?" and I said, "No"—
I'd never thought of doing so. He said: "Why don't you?"—and
at that point I decided that's what I would do. Looking back, I
conceived how the ground had been prepared.

INTERVIEWER: Do you think of your reading as being an influence in your decision?

AUDEN: Well, up until then the only poetry I had read, as a
child, were certain books of sick jokes—Belloc's *Cautionary
Tales*, *Struwwelpeter* by Hoffmann, and Harry Graham's *Ruthless
Rhymes for Heartless Homes*. I had a favorite, which went like
this:

> *Into the drinking well*
> *The plumber built her*
> *Aunt Maria fell;*
> *We must buy a filter.*

Of course I read a good deal about geology and lead mining.
Sopwith's *A Visit to Alston Moore* was one, *Underground Life*
was another. I can't remember who wrote it. I read all the books
of Beatrix Potter and also Lewis Carroll. Andersen's "The Snow
Queen" I loved, and also Haggard's *King Solomon's Mines*. And
I got my start reading detective stories with Sherlock Holmes.

INTERVIEWER: Did you read much of Housman?

AUDEN: Yes, and later I knew him quite well. He told me a
very funny story about Clarence Darrow. It seems that Darrow
had written him a very laudatory letter, claiming to have saved
several clients from the chair with quotes from Housman's poetry.
Shortly afterwards, Housman had a chance to meet Darrow. They
had a very nice meeting, and Darrow produced the trial transcripts
he had alluded to. "Sure enough," Housman told me, "there
were two of my poems—both misquoted!" These are the minor

headaches a writer must live with. My pet peeve is people who send for autographs but omit putting in stamps.

INTERVIEWER: Did you meet Christopher Isherwood at school?

AUDEN: Yes, I've known him since I was eight and he was ten, because we were both in boarding school together at St. Edmund's School, Hindhead, Surrey. We've known each other ever since. I always remember the first time I ever heard a remark which I decided was witty. I was walking with Mr. Isherwood on a Sunday walk—this was in Surrey—and Christopher said, "I think God must have been tired when He made this country." That's the first time I heard a remark that I thought was witty.

INTERVIEWER: Did you have good teachers?

AUDEN: Except in mathematics, I had the good luck to have excellent teachers, especially in science. When I went up for my *viva*, Julian Huxley showed me a bone and asked me to tell him what it was. "The pelvis of a bird," I said, which happened to be the right answer. He said: "Some people have said it was the skull of an extinct reptile."

INTERVIEWER: Have you ever taught writing?

AUDEN: No, I never have. If I had to "teach poetry," which, thank God, I don't, I would concentrate on prosody, rhetoric, philology, and learning poems by heart. I may be quite wrong, but I don't see what can be learned except purely technical things—what a sonnet is, something about prosody. If you did have a poetic academy, the subjects should be quite different— natural history, history, theology, all kinds of other things. When I've been at colleges, I've always insisted on giving ordinary academic courses—on the eighteenth century, or Romanticism. True, it's wonderful what the colleges have done as patrons of the artists. But the artists should agree not to have anything to do with contemporary literature. If they take academic positions, they should do academic work, and the further they get away from the kind of thing that directly affects what they're writing, the better. They should teach the eighteenth century or something that won't interfere with their work and yet earn them a living. To teach creative writing—I think that's dangerous. The only possibility I can conceive of is an apprentice system like those they had in the Renaissance—where a poet who was very busy got students to finish his poems for him. Then you'd *really* be teaching, and you'd be responsible, of course, since the results would go out under the poet's name.

INTERVIEWER: I noticed that in your early works, there seems to be a fierceness towards England. There's a sense of being at war with where you are—and that this is lacking in poems you've written here in the United States: that you seem more at home.

AUDEN: Yes, quite. I'm sure it's partly a matter of age. You know, everybody changes. It's frightfully important for a writer to be his age, not to be younger or older than he is. One might ask, "What should I write at the age of sixty-four," but never, "What should I write in 1940." It's always a problem, I think.

INTERVIEWER: Is there a certain age when a writer is at the height of his powers?

AUDEN: Some poets, like Wordsworth, peter out fairly early. Some, like Yeats, have done their best work late in life. Nothing is calculable. Aging has its problems, but they must be accepted without fuss.

INTERVIEWER: What made you choose the U.S. as a home?

AUDEN: Well, the difficulty about England is the cultural life —it *was* certainly dim, and I suspect it still is. In a sense it's the same difficulty one faces with some kinds of family life. I love my family very dearly, but I don't want to live with them.

INTERVIEWER: Do you see any demarcation between the language you have used since you came to America, and the language you used in England?

AUDEN: No, not really. Obviously you see little things, particularly when writing prose: very minor things. There are certain rhymes which could not be accepted in England. You would rhyme "clerk" and "work" here, which you can't in England. But these are minor—saying "twenty of" instead of "twenty to" or "aside from" instead of "apart from."

INTERVIEWER: How long have you lived here, and where in America were you before taking this apartment?

AUDEN: I've been here since '52. I came to America in '39. I lived first in Brooklyn Heights, then taught for a while in Ann

Arbor, then at Swarthmore. I did a stint in the army, with the U.S. *Strategic Bombing Survey*. The army didn't like our report at all because we proved that, in spite of all of our bombing of Germany, their weapons production didn't go down until after they had lost the war. It's the same in North Vietnam—the bombing does no good. But you know how army people are. They don't like to hear things that run contrary to what they've thought.

INTERVIEWER: Have you had much contact with men in politics and government?

AUDEN: I have had very little contact with such men. I knew some undergraduates, of course, while I was at Oxford, who eventually made it—Hugh Gaitskell, Crossman, and so forth. I think we should do very well without politicians. Our leaders should be elected by lot. The people could vote their conscience, and the computers could take care of the rest.

INTERVIEWER: How about writers as leaders? Yeats, for instance, held office.

AUDEN: And he was terrible! Writers seldom make good leaders. They're self-employed, for one thing, and they have very little contact with their customers. It's very easy for a writer to be unrealistic. I have not lost my interest in politics, but I have come to realize that, in cases of social or political injustice, only two things are effective: political action and straight journalistic reportage of the facts. The arts can do nothing. The social and political history of Europe would be what it has been if Dante, Shakespeare, Michelangelo, Mozart, et al., had never lived. A poet, *qua* poet, has only one political duty, namely, in his own writing to set an example of the correct use of his mother tongue which is always being corrupted. When words lose their meaning, physical force takes over. By all means, let a poet, if he wants to, write what is now called an *'engagé'* poem, so long as he realizes that it is mainly himself who will benefit from it. It will enhance his literary reputation among those who feel the same as he does.

INTERVIEWER: Does this current deterioration and corruption of language, imprecision of thought, and so forth scare you—or is it just a decadent phase?

AUDEN: It terrifies me. I try by my personal example to fight it; as I say, it's a poet's role to maintain the sacredness of language.

INTERVIEWER: Do you think the present condition of our civilization will be seen by the future, if there is one, as a prewar decadence?

AUDEN: No, I don't think it has anything to do with the fact of another war. But in the old days people knew what the words meant, whatever the range of their vocabulary. Now people hear and repeat a radio and TV vocabulary thirty per cent larger than they know the meaning of. The most outrageous use of words I've ever experienced was once when I was a guest on the David Susskind TV program. During a break he had to do a plug for some sort of investment firm, and he announced that these people were "integrity-ridden!" I could not believe my ears!

INTERVIEWER: You have said bad art is bad in a very contemporary way.

AUDEN: Yes. Of course one can be wrong about what is good or bad. Taste and judgment can differ. But one has to be loyal to oneself and trust one's own taste. I can, for instance, enjoy a good tear-jerking movie, where, oh, an old mother is put away in a home—even though I know it's terrible, the tears will run down my cheeks. I don't think good work ever makes one cry. Housman said he got a curious physical sensation with good poetry—I never got any. If one sees *King Lear*, one doesn't cry. One doesn't have to.

INTERVIEWER: You have said that the story of your patron Saint Wystan was rather Hamlet-like. Are you a Hamlet-poet?

AUDEN: No, I couldn't be less. For myself I find that Shakespeare's greatest influence has been his use of a large vocabulary. One thing that makes English so marvelous for poetry is its great range and the fact that it is an uninflected language. One can turn verbs into nouns and vice versa, as Shakespeare did. One cannot do this with inflected languages such as German, French, Italian.

INTERVIEWER: In the early thirties, did you write for an audience that you wanted to jolt into awareness?

AUDEN: No, I just try to put the thing out and hope somebody will read it. Someone says: "Whom do you write for?" I reply: "Do you read me?" If they say, "Yes," I say, "Do you like it?" If they say, "No," then I say, "I don't write for you."

INTERVIEWER: Well, then, do you think of a particular audience when writing certain poems?

AUDEN: Well, you know it's impossible to tell. If you have someone in mind . . . well, most of them are probably dead. You wonder whether they'll approve or not, and then you hope—that somebody will even read you after you're dead *yourself*.

INTERVIEWER: You have always been a formalist. Today's poets seem to prefer free verse. Do you think that's an aversion to discipline?

AUDEN: Unfortunately that's too often the case. But I can't understand—strictly from a hedonistic point of view—how one can enjoy writing with no form at all. If one plays a game, one needs rules, otherwise there is no fun. The wildest poem has to have a firm basis in common sense, and this, I think, is the advantage of formal verse. Aside from the obvious corrective advantages, formal verse frees one from the fetters of one's ego. Here I like to quote Valéry, who said a person is a poet if his imagination is stimulated by the difficulties inherent in his art and *not* if his imagination is dulled by them. I think very few people can manage free verse—you need an infallible ear, like D. H. Lawrence, to determine where the lines should end.

INTERVIEWER: Are there any poets you've read who have seemed to you to be kindred spirits? I'm thinking of Campion here, with whom you share a great fascination with metrics.

AUDEN: Yes, I do have several pets, and Campion is certainly among them. Also George Herbert and William Barnes, and yes, all shared a certain interest in metrics. These are the poets I should have liked to have had as friends. As great a poet as Dante might have been, I wouldn't have had the slightest wish to have known him personally. He was a terrible prima donna.

INTERVIEWER: Can you say something about the genesis of a poem? What comes first?

AUDEN: At any given time, I have two things on my mind: a

theme that interests me and a problem of verbal form, meter, diction, etc. The theme looks for the right form: the form looks for the right theme. When the two come together, I am able to start writing.

INTERVIEWER: Do you start your poems at the beginning?

AUDEN: Usually, of course, one starts at the beginning and works through to the end. Sometimes, though, one starts with a certain line in mind, perhaps a last line. One starts, I think, with a certain idea of thematic organization, but this usually alters during the process of writing.

INTERVIEWER: Do you have any aids for inspiration?

AUDEN: I never write when I'm drunk. Why should one need aids? The Muse is a high-spirited girl who doesn't like to be brutally or coarsely wooed. And she doesn't like slavish devotion—then she lies.

INTERVIEWER: And comes up with "moon-faced Nonsense, that erudite forger," as you said in one of your "Bucolics."

AUDEN: Quite. Poetry is not self-expression. Each of us, of course, has a unique perspective which we hope to communicate. We hope that someone reading it will say, "Of course, I knew that all the time but never realized it before." On the whole I agree here with Chesterton, who said, "The artistic temperament is a disease that affects amateurs."

INTERVIEWER: Many poets are night workers, manic, irregular in their habits.

AUDEN: Sorry, my dear, one mustn't be bohemian!

INTERVIEWER: Why do you disapprove of the recent publication of Eliot's *Waste Land* drafts?

AUDEN: Because there's not a line he left out which makes one wish he'd kept it. I think this sort of thing encourages amateurs to think, "Oh, look—I could have done as well." I think it shameful that people will spend more for a draft than for a completed poem. Valerie Eliot didn't like having to publish the drafts, but once they were discovered, she knew they would have to come out eventually—so she did it herself to insure that it was done as well as possible.

INTERVIEWER: But isn't there some truth to be had from the

knowledge that a poet does quite literally start in the "foul rag and bone shop of the heart?"

AUDEN: It may be necessary for him to start there, but there is no reason for others to pay it a visit. Here I like the quote of Valéry, which says that when people don't know anything else they take their clothes off.

INTERVIEWER: In your *Commonplace Book* you've written: Behaviorism works—so does torture.

AUDEN: It does work. But I'm sure if I were given Professor B. F. Skinner and supplied with the proper drugs and appliances, I could have him in a week reciting the Athanasian Code—in public. The problem with the behavioralists is that they always manage to exclude themselves from their theories. If all our acts are conditioned behavior, surely our theories are, too.

INTERVIEWER: Do you see any spirituality in all those hippies out on St. Marks Place? You've lived among them for some time now.

AUDEN: I don't know of any of them, so how could I tell? What I do like about them is that they have tried to revive the spirit of "Carnival," something which has been conspicuously lacking in our culture. But I'm afraid that when they renounce work entirely, the fun turns ugly.

INTERVIEWER: Your new poem "Circe" deals with this subject, particularly:

> She does not brutalise her victims (beasts could
> bite or bolt). She simplifies them to flowers,
> sessile fatalists, who don't mind and only
>   can talk to themselves.

Obviously you know that generation better than you admit.

AUDEN: I must say that I do admire the ones who won't compete in the rat race, who renounce money and worldly goods. I couldn't do that, I'm far too worldly.

INTERVIEWER: Do you own any credit cards?

AUDEN: One. I never use it if I can help it. I've used it only once, in Israel, to pay a hotel bill. I was brought up believing that you should not buy anything you cannot pay cash for. The idea of debt appalls me. I suppose our whole economy would collapse if everyone had been brought up like me.

INTERVIEWER: Are you a good businessman—do you drive a hard bargain, and so forth?

AUDEN: No. That's not a subject I care to think about.

INTERVIEWER: But you do get what you can for your poetry. I was surprised the other day to see a poem of yours in *Poetry*— which only pays fifty cents a line.

AUDEN: Of course I get what I can—who wouldn't? I think I got my check from them the other day and used it up before I noticed I'd gotten it.

INTERVIEWER: Are you a gourmet?

AUDEN: I'm very fond of my food. I'm lucky when I'm in Austria because my friend Mr. Kallman is an expert chef, so I'm rather spoiled in the summer. It's different here where I live alone. Sometimes when one is cooking for oneself, one gets a craze for something. Once I had a craze for turnips. But with solitary eating one doesn't like to spend much time and simply gobbles it up fast. Certainly I like good wine, but I don't make a thing of it. There's a red table wine, Valpolicella, which I like to drink both when I'm in Austria and when I'm here. It travels much better than Chianti, which, when you drink it here, always tastes like red ink.

INTERVIEWER: Do you ever miss a meal while in the process of writing?

AUDEN: No. I live by my watch. I wouldn't know to be hungry if I didn't have my watch on!

INTERVIEWER: What are the worst lines you know—preferably by a great poet?

AUDEN: I think they occur in Thomas Hardy's *The Dynasts*, in which Napoleon tries to escape from Elba. There's a quatrain which goes like this:

> *Should the corvette arrive*
> *With the aging Scotch colonel,*
> *Escape would be frustrate,*
> *Retention eternal.*

That's pretty hard to beat!

INTERVIEWER: How about Yeats'

> *Had de Valera eaten Parnell's heart*

or Eliot's

> *Why should the aged eagle stretch its wings?*

AUDEN: Those aren't bad, really, just unintentionally comic. Both would have made wonderful captions for a Thurber cartoon. As an undergraduate at Oxford I came up with one:

> *Isobel with her leaping breasts*
> *Pursued me through a summer . . .*

Think what a marvelous cartoon Thurber could have done to that! Whoops! Whoops! Whoops!

INTERVIEWER: What's your least favorite Auden poem?

AUDEN: "September 1, 1939." And I'm afraid it's gotten into a lot of anthologies.

INTERVIEWER: Of which poem are you proudest?

AUDEN: It occurs in my commentary on Shakespeare's *Tempest*, a poem written in prose, a pastiche of the late Henry James— "Caliban's Speech to the Audience."

INTERVIEWER: Have you ever finished a book you've hated?

AUDEN: No, I've skipped . . . actually I did, once. I read the whole of *Mein Kampf* because it was necessary to know what he thought. But it was not a pleasure.

INTERVIEWER: Have you reviewed a book you've hated?

AUDEN: Vary rarely. Unless one is a regular reviewer, or one is reviewing a book of reference where the facts are wrong—then it's one's duty to inform the public, as one would warn them of watered milk. Writing nasty reviews can be fun, but I don't think the practice is very good for the character.

INTERVIEWER: What's the nicest poetic compliment you've ever received?

AUDEN: It came in a most unusual way. A friend of mine, Dorothy Day, had been put in the women's prison at 6th Avenue and 8th Street for her part in a protest. Well, once a week at this place, on a Saturday, the girls were marched down for a shower. A group were being ushered in when one, a whore, loudly proclaimed:

> *Hundreds have lived without love,*
> *But none without water . . .*

A line from a poem of mine which had just appeared in *The New Yorker*. When I heard this, I knew I hadn't written in vain!

INTERVIEWER: Have you read any books on Women's Lib?

AUDEN: I'm a bit puzzled by it. Certainly they ought to complain about the ad things, like ladies' underwear, and so forth.

INTERVIEWER: Are there any essential differences between male and female poetry?

AUDEN: Men and women have opposite difficulties to contend with. The difficulty for a man is to avoid being an aesthete—to avoid saying things not because they are true, but because they are poetically effective. The difficulty for a woman is in getting sufficient distance from the emotions. No woman is an aesthete. No woman ever wrote nonsense verse. Men are playboys, women realists. If you tell a funny story—only a woman will ever ask: "Did it really happen?" I think if men knew what women said to each other about them, the human race would die out.

INTERVIEWER: Do you think it would be better if women ran the human race?

AUDEN: I think foreign policy should definitely be taken out of men's hands. Men should continue making machines, but women ought to decide which machines ought to be made. Women have far better sense. They would never have introduced the internal combustion engine or any of the evil machines. Most kitchen machines, for example, are good; they don't obliterate other skills. Or other people. With our leaders it is all too often a case of one's little boy saying to another, "My father can lick your father." By now, the toys have gotten far too dangerous.

INTERVIEWER: Have you known any madmen?

AUDEN: Well, of course, I've known people who went off their heads. We all have. People who go into the bin and out again. I've known several people who were manic-depressives. I've often

thought a lot of good could be done for them if they would
organize a manic-depressives anonymous. They could get together and do each other some good.

INTERVIEWER: I don't think it would work.

AUDEN: Well, everybody has their ups and downs!

INTERVIEWER: If you were to go mad, what do you think your
madness would be?

AUDEN: I couldn't imagine going mad. It's simply something
my imagination cannot take. One can be dotty—but that's different! There's a very funny book called *The Three Christs of
Ypsilanti*, about a hospital in which there are three gents, all of
whom believe themselves to be the Lord. Which is common
enough, except in the case of one—who had actually found a
disciple!

INTERVIEWER: What about collaboration? Did you ever go
through your poems with T. S. Eliot?

AUDEN: No, one can't expect other people to do such things.
He was very good to me; he encouraged me. He wasn't jealous
of other writers. I had met him just before I left Oxford. I'd sent
him some poems, and he asked me to come to see him. He
published the first thing of mine that was published—it was "Paid
on Both Sides"—which came out in *The Criterion* in '28 or '29.

INTERVIEWER: Was Isherwood helpful at this time?

AUDEN: Oh, enormously. Of course one depends at that age
on one's friends; one reads one's work, and they criticize it. That's
the same in every generation.

INTERVIEWER: Did you collaborate with him at this point, at
Oxford?

AUDEN: The first time I collaborated with Isherwood must have
been in '33 or '34—*The Dog Beneath the Skin*. I've always enjoyed
collaborating very much. It's exciting. Of course, you can't collaborate on a particular poem. You can collaborate on a translation, or a libretto, or a drama, and I like working that way,
though you can only do it with people whose basic ideas you
share—each can then sort of excite the other. When a collaboration works, the two people concerned become a third person,
who is different from either of them in isolation. I have observed

that when critics attempt to say who wrote what they often get it wrong. Of course, any performed work is bound to be a collaboration, anyway, because you're going to have performers and producers and God knows what.

INTERVIEWER: How do you look back now on the early plays you wrote with Isherwood?

AUDEN: None of them will quite do, I think. I have a private weakness for *Dogskin*, which I think, if properly done, is fun, except that you have to cut all the choruses. There is some quite nice poetry in there, but dramatically it won't do. This was something that was just selfish on my part, wanting to write some poetry which had nothing to do, really, with drama.

INTERVIEWER: Do you feel that the state of the theater today is conducive to poetic drama?

AUDEN: The difficulty, I think, is that the tradition of actors and verse has been so lost. In opera, for example, the whole tradition of singing has never stopped. The trouble with people who write official poetic drama—drama written in verse—is that they can default so easily either by writing something which is so nearly prose that it might just as well *be* prose—or something which is not theatrical. Actually, Mr. Kallman and I had a very interesting experience. We'd done a translation of *The Magic Flute* for NBC television, and we decided to put the spoken interludes into couplets. Nearly everybody in the cast, of course, were singers . . . who had never spoken verse before; there was only one part played by a professional actor. With the singers, we could teach them immediately how to speak verse. The singers, who had never spoken verse before, could get it in ten minutes because they knew what a beat was. But we had awful trouble with the professional actor.

INTERVIEWER: Do you feel that the conventions of acting in the American theater destroy this ability to speak a line even more?

AUDEN: They won't keep still, of course. It's like a football match. Poetry is very unnaturalistic. One of the great things about opera singing is that you cannot pretend it's naturalistic.

INTERVIEWER: Do you feel an opera libretto is limiting—that it requires sacrifices . . . ?

AUDEN: Well, yes. Of course, you have to forget all about what you ordinarily mean by writing poetry when you're writing poetry to be read or spoken or sung. It's a completely different art. Naturally, one's subordinate to the composer. And one's judged, really, by how much one stimulates him. But that's half the fun of it: being limited. Something you think of, which in cold blood would be absolute trash, suddenly, when it is sung, becomes interesting. And vice versa.

INTERVIEWER: Which harks back to Addison's remark about Italian opera in London at the turn of the eighteenth century— that whatever is too stupid to say can be sung.

AUDEN: Well, it's not quite true—particularly these days when composers are much more dependent on the quality of the libretto than they were. It has been true ever since Strauss and Hofmannsthal that the librettist isn't a pure flunky.

INTERVIEWER: How did the collaboration of *The Rake's Progress* proceed?

AUDEN: Mr. Kallman and I prepared the libretto beforehand, though I talked to Mr. Stravinsky first, and we got some idea of the kind of thing he wanted to do. What had excited him was an idea that he felt would be an interesting subject for an opera. It was the last Hogarth scene in Bedlam where there was a blond man with a sort of broken fiddle. Now, actually Stravinsky never used this, but intuitively he thought, "Now this is an interesting idea." In the end it wasn't used at all.

INTERVIEWER: Could you characterize your working relationship with Stravinsky.

AUDEN: He was always completely professional. He took what I sent to him and set it to music. He always took enormous trouble to find out what the rhythmic values were, which must have been difficult for him, since prior to my working with him he had never set in English.

INTERVIEWER: Did you correspond as did Strauss and Hofmannsthal?

AUDEN: No. The funny thing about their correspondence—which we're very fortunate to have—was that they chose to work through the mails because they couldn't stand one another!

INTERVIEWER: Did you and Stravinsky discuss the work over the phone?

AUDEN: No, I don't like the phone very much and never stay on long if I can help it. You get some people who simply will not get off the line! I remember the story of the man who answered the phone and was kept prisoner for what seemed an age. The lady talked and talked. Finally, in desperation, he told her, "Really, I must go. I hear the phone ringing!"

INTERVIEWER: What is your Hans Werner Henze opera about?

AUDEN: It's about the early twentieth-century sort of artist-genius who, in order to get his work done, must exploit other people. A sort of real monster. A poet. It is set in an Austrian mountain inn in the year 1910. There was an amusing mix-up about its title, *Elegy for Young Lovers*, which appeared on a lawyer's power-of-attorney document as *Allergy for Young Lovers*.

INTERVIEWER: Did you involve yourself in its production?

AUDEN: Naturally. As much as I was allowed to, which with modern stage directors is not always easy.

INTERVIEWER: Do you enjoy all the ruckus?

AUDEN: Yes, I do. I'm terribly short-tempered.

INTERVIEWER: Does poetry contain music?

AUDEN: One can speak verbal "music" so long as one remembers that the sound of words is inseparable from their meaning. The notes in music do not denote anything.

INTERVIEWER: What is the difference in your aims when you write a piece of verse which is to be set to music? Is there a difference in your method?

AUDEN: In writing words to be set to music, one has to remember that, probably, only one word in three will be heard. So, one must avoid complicated imagery. Suitable are verbs of motion, interjections, lists, and nouns like Moon, Sea, Love, Death.

INTERVIEWER: You wrote the U.N. anthem to be set by Casals. What were your aims and methods there?

AUDEN: The problem in writing the U.N. theme, in which one

must not offend anybody's conception of Man, Nature, the world, was how to avoid the most dreary clichés. I decided that the only thing to do was to make all the imagery musical, for music, unlike language, is international. Casals and I corresponded, and he was extremely generous about altering his music if, as once or twice, I felt he had accented syllables wrongly.

INTERVIEWER: Where did you pick up your interest in the Icelandic Sagas?

AUDEN: My father brought me up on them. His family originated in an area which once served as headquarters for the Viking army. The name *Auden* is common in the Sagas, usually spelled *Audun*. But we have no family trees or anything like that. My mother came from Normandy—which means that she was half Nordic, as the Normans were. I had an ancestor named Birch, who married Constable. The family, I understand, was furious that she had married a painter. I've seen some of his portraits of her—she must have been quite beautiful. I've another relative who's married to a Hindu. This goes along better, I think, with the family line, which says that either one marries an Englishman—or one marries a Brahmin!

INTERVIEWER: And your father was a doctor?

AUDEN: Yes, he was. But at the time my mother married him, medicine was not considered one of the respectable professions. One of her aunts told her shortly before the wedding, "Well, marry him if you must, but no one will call on you!"

INTERVIEWER: You believe in class distinctions, then, social forms and formats?

AUDEN: To a degree, yes; one talks to people one has something to say to—it keeps things running a bit more smoothly. And I think the first prerequisite to civilization is an ability to make polite conversation.

AUDEN: Many artists and writer either join the media or use its techniques in composing or editing their work.

AUDEN: It certainly has never tempted me. I suppose with some people like Norman Mailer it works out all right. Personally, I don't see how any civilized person can watch TV, far less own a set. I prefer detective stories, especially Father Brown. I also don't particularly care for science fiction. I read some Jules Verne in my youth, but I'm not very interested in other planets. I like them where they are, in the sky.

INTERVIEWER: Are there any media which to you are strictly taboo?

AUDEN: Yes: TV, all movies except the comic ones—Charlie Chaplin and the Marx Brothers were quite funny—and rock and roll all are taboo for me.

INTERVIEWER: Newspapers?

AUDEN: They're painful, but one has to read them to know whatever is happening. I try to get through them as soon as possible. It's never very pleasant in the morning to open *The New York Times*.

INTERVIEWER: Have you read, or tried to read, *Finnegans Wake?*

AUDEN: I'm not very good on Joyce. Obviously he's a very great genius—but his work is simply too long. Joyce said himself that he wanted people to spend their life on his work. For me life is too short, and too precious. I feel the same way about *Ulysses*. Also, *Finnegans Wake* can't be read the way one reads ordinarily. You can dip in, but I don't think anyone could read it straight through and remember what happened. It's different in small doses. I remember when *Anna Livia Plurabelle* came out, published separately, I was able to get through it and enjoy it. On the whole I like novels to be short, and funny. There are a few exceptions, of course; one knows with Proust, for instance, that it couldn't have been any shorter. I suppose my favorite modern novelists are Ronald Firbank and P. G. Wodehouse—because both deal with Eden.

INTERVIEWER: Are you aware, by the way, that you are mentioned on page 279 of *Finnegans Wake?*

AUDEN: That I know. I could not have given you the page number—but I have seen the footnote.

INTERVIEWER: Would you care to comment on Yeats?

AUDEN: I find it very difficult to be fair to Yeats because he had a bad influence on me. He tempted me into a rhetoric which was, for me, oversimplified. Needless to say, the fault was mine, not his. He was, of course, a very great poet. But he and Rilke had a bad effect on me, so it's difficult for me to judge either fairly.

INTERVIEWER: What about Eliot's influence?

AUDEN: Eliot can have very little direct stylistic influence on other poets, actually. What I mean is that it is very rare that one comes across a poem and can say, "Ah, he's been reading Eliot." One can with Yeats or Rilke, but not with Eliot. He's a very idiosyncratic poet and not imitatable. My work is much easier to use as a stylistic model. And I don't say this about Eliot in any pejorative sense at all. It's the same with Gerard Manley Hopkins—both are extremely idiosyncratic and cannot readily be adapted to one's own sensibility. When it's attempted, what you end up with is simply Hopkins-and-water.

INTERVIEWER: Do you think "Gerontion" is Eliot's greatest poem?

AUDEN: Again, this idea of choosing. Why should one? Obviously, one wants a lot of them.

INTERVIEWER: Well, then, do you think "Gerontion" is a very mystical poem?

AUDEN: I'm not sure if "mystical" is quite the right word. Certainly a part of his work is based on a rather peculiar vision he's had. That's part of why he's so idiosyncratic. Proabably something in his early youth. Here I think a comment he made about Dante's Beatrice is very revealing. Although Dante claimed to have been nine when he met her, Eliot was sure they must have met at a still earlier age. I think that's very revealing about Eliot. And all those images of children swinging from apple trees . . . must refer to some very powerful early vision. But he wasn't a confessional poet, so we don't know who it was.

INTERVIEWER: Eliot was purportedly influenced in that direction by the poetry of St. John of the Cross, which we can safely say is mystical. Do you read him much?

AUDEN: His poetry is very remarkable, but not exactly my cup of tea. Essentially because I don't think the mystical experience can be verbalized. When the ego disappears, so does power over language. I must say that he was extremely daring—he uses the most daring metaphors for orgasm. This probably had to do with the fact that in both cases, orgasm and mystical union, the ego is forgotten.

INTERVIEWER: Do you spend much time on affairs of the Church?

AUDEN: No—apart from going on Sundays.

INTERVIEWER: But do you have a reputation in theological circles; you've had some doings with The Guild of Episcopal Scholars.

AUDEN: Oh, that just had to do with some advice they wanted on the revision of the Psalms. Actually, I'm passionately antiliturgical-reform, and would have The Book of Common Prayer kept in Latin. Rite is the link between the dead and the unborn and needs a timeless language, which in practice means a dead language. I'm curious to know what problems they are having in Isreal, where they speak what was long an unspoken language.

INTERVIEWER: Do you speak Hebrew?

AUDEN: No, I wish I knew it. Obviously it's a marvelous language. Something else I wish we had in my Church is the Seder. I've been to one or two and was enormously impressed. We don't have anything like that. The Last Supper is a communal thing, but not a family thing.

INTERVIEWER: What about the rites of marriage?

AUDEN: Well, I'm perfectly congenial to the idea of weddings, but what I think ruins so many marriages, though, is this romantic idea of falling in love. It happens, of course, I suppose to some people who are possessed of unusually fertile imaginations. Undoubtedly it is a mystical experience which occurs. But with most people who think they are in love I think the situation can be described far more simply, and, I'm afraid, brutally. The trouble with all this love business is one or the other partner ends up feeling bad or guilty because they don't have it the way they've read it. I'm afraid things went off a lot more happily when marriages were arranged by parents. I do think it is absolutely essential that both partners share a sense of humor and an outlook on life. And, with Goethe, I think marriages should be celebrated more quietly and humbly, because they are the beginning of something. Loud celebrations should be saved for successful conclusions.

INTERVIEWER: What is that big book over there?

AUDEN: It's Goethe's autobiography. It's amazing. If I were asked to do an autobiography of my first twenty-six years, I don't think I could fill up sixty pages. And her Goethe fills up eight hundred! Personally I'm interested in history, but not in the past. I'm interested in the present and in the next twenty-four hours.

INTERVIEWER: What's the name of your cat?

AUDEN: I haven't got any now.

INTERVIEWER: What about Mosé?

AUDEN: Mosé was a dog.

INTERVIEWER: Who was Rolfi Strobl?

AUDEN: Our housekeeper's dog, an Alsatian. There must have been a bitch in the neighborhood because the poor thing ran out on the Autobahn one day and was run over. We had a very funny experience with Mosé one time. We had gone to Venice for the opening of *The Rake's Progress*, which was being broadcast over the radio. Mosé was staying with some friends at the time, who were listening in. The minute my voice came over the airwaves, Mosé's ears perked up, and he ran over to the speaker—just like His Master's Voice!

INTERVIEWER: What happened to your cats?

AUDEN: They had to be put away because our housekeeper died. They, too, were named from opera, Rudimace and Leonora. Cats can be very funny, too, and have the oddest ways of showing they're glad to see you. Rudimace always peed in our shoes.

INTERVIEWER: And then there's your new poem, "Talking to Mice." Have you any favorite mythological mice?

AUDEN: Mythological! What on earth could you be referring to? Are there any, aside from Mickey Mouse? You must mean fictional mice!

INTERVIEWER: I must.

AUDEN: Oh yes, there's the mice of Beatrix Potter, of which I'm quite fond.

INTERVIEWER: How about Mickey?

AUDEN: He's all right.

INTERVIEWER: Do you believe in the Devil?

AUDEN: Yes.

INTERVIEWER: In Austria you live on Audenstrasse. Do your neighbors know who you are?

AUDEN: My neighbors there know I'm a poet. The village I live in was the home of a famous Austrian poet, Joseph Weinheber, so they're used to having a poet around the place. He committed suicide in '45.

INTERVIEWER: How about your neighbors here?

AUDEN: I don't know. My stock went up last year, I know. There was a feature on me in the *Daily News*—which everyone here seems to read. After that they figured I must be somebody. It was very nice to get all that attention.

INTERVIEWER: Do you think writers receive more respect abroad than here?

AUDEN: I wouldn't say so. I've told people I'm a medieval historian when asked what I do. It freezes conversation. If one tells them one's a poet, one gets these odd looks which seem to say, "Well, what's he living off?" In the old days a man was proud to have in his passport, Occupation: Gentleman. Lord Antrim's passport simply said, Occupation: Peer—which I felt was correct. I've had a lucky life. I had a happy home, and my parents provided me with a good education. And my father was both a physician and a scholar, so I never got the idea that art and science were opposing cultures—both were entertained equally in my home. I cannot complain. I've never had to do anything I really disliked. Certainly I've had to do various jobs I would not have taken on if I'd had the money; but I've always considered myself a worker, not a laborer. So many people have jobs they don't like at all. I haven't, and I'm grateful for that.

—MICHAEL NEWMAN
1973

12. Archibald MacLeish

Archibald MacLeish was, at different times, a soldier, lawyer, staff writer on *Fortune* magazine, librarian of Congress (1939–44), assistant secretary of state (1944–45), cofounder of UNESCO, and Boylston Professor of Rhetoric and Oratory at Harvard University. For him all this had one meaning—the practice of poetry.

He was born in Glencoe, Illinois, on May 7, 1892, and was educated at Yale and the Harvard Law School. His collegiate career at Yale was a varied one: he was editor of the literary magazine and a member of both the football and swimming teams. In 1916, at the end of his first year at the Harvard Law School, he married Ada Hitchcock and at the end of his second year he went off to France and the First World War.

After the war and his graduation from law school in 1919, MacLeish briefly taught constitutional law at Harvard College but moved to France in 1923 to pursue his writing career. One year later his first book of poems, *The Happy Marriage*, was published. Through the rest of the decade he concentrated on writing poetry while his wife began an illustrious career as a singer.

His many works include *The Pot of Earth* (1925), *The Hamlet of A. MacLeish* (1928), and *Conquistador* (1932), winner of that year's Pulitzer Prize in poetry. For his *Collected Poems 1917–1952* MacLeish was awarded a second Pulitzer Prize as well as the Bollingen Prize and the National Book Award in 1953, and *J. B.*, a verse play, won both the Pulitzer Prize in drama and the Antoinette Perry Award for best play in 1959. His last book of verse, *New and Collected Poems 1917 to 1976*, appeared in 1976, and a prose collection, *Riders on the Earth*, was published in 1978.

MacLeish was a passionate civil libertarian, his life marked by distinguished public service. He lived with his wife in Conway, Massachusetts, until his death in 1982.

Whistler in the Dark

George Barker, British poet,
writes a eulogy of Dylan Thomas,
calls him whistler in the dark
and great because the dark is getting darker.

Is it? Was the dark not always darker?
Have we not always had these silver whistlers?
Listen! ...
      That's Chaucer like a bobolink.

I think it's not the darkness, Mr Barker
makes for whistling well. I think
perhaps it's knowing how to whistle.
Listen! ...
      That's Dylan trilling like a lark

Archie

Dear George,

Will this do as a manuscript? It doesn't show corrections but it shows me up as a pencil man and, worse still, a slave to the eraser. (Black Wing pencils have erasers which eradicate clean as time.)

As for the lines themselves—they went into a notebook and never came out again because Dylan's death was too great a loss and George Barker's piece was too deeply felt to fool with in a tone like this one.

But that's all in the past now. People die too absolutely these days—disappear like pencil marks to an eraser—black wing.

Yours ever,
Archie

Sketch by Dolbin, courtesy The Bettmann Archive

Archibald MacLeish

Archibald MacLeish wintered in Antigua, but the bearable portion of the year found him at Uphill Farm, a country place in Conway, Massachusetts, bought in the twenties on the MacLeishes' return from Europe. The region had meaning for him because his Connecticut Yankee mother's family, the Hillards, "knew these hills well." His Hillard grandfather was a Congregational minister who worked his way north up the Connecticut River in the years of the Civil War, fighting with his deacons—many of whom were copperheads—and finally ending his journey in the 1880s when he crossed the Massachusetts state line and eventually settled in Conway itself.

The poet greeted his guests in countryman clothes—fine confident head, a manner of kindly command—and led the way to the pool. The impression everywhere—sharpest in MacLeish's style of talk, but no less evident in the domestic arrangements—was of a world well managed. MacLeish was a short man with bearing—

powerful shoulders gave good drive to his crawl in the pool. There were drinks outside, soufflé, salad, and Riesling in a dining room with a mountain view, and some jokes with Mrs. MacLeish, whose voice Joyce praised, about certain of her husband's poems making her out to be U.S. Champion Homemaker and Breadbaker while omitting she sings Poulenc. MacLeish laughed hardest at himself and his wife took back her complaint charmingly: "I never minded at all." Thereafter a descent down stone stairs to the music room— past a wall of framed honorary degrees, pictures of treasured friends (Felix Frankfurter, for one), a huge photo of the moon. The poet spoke graciously of his hope that someday there would be a conversation, not just a tape, and then it was time to work.

INTERVIEWER: Can we start outside the gates and work in? You're seen as a writer with unusual experience of the public world—perhaps as a "public man." Is A. MacLeish as a public man recognizable to you?

MACLEISH: No, but I've had him pointed out to me. I suppose all writers have that experience sooner or later—the double personality—the "other" you're supposed to be and can't remember ever having met. Except that in this case the problem is complicated by the fact that those who see me as a "public man" don't always mean it kindly. There are those on the fringes of the art who think that poetry and the public world should be mutually exclusive—as though poets were the internists of the profession and should stick to their bowels. I've been hearing from them for some time. After my tour of public duty during the Second World War, I published a poem called "Actfive," which was a kind of report on the look and feel of things "out there." Random House published it, and before it appeared Bob Linscott, then an editor at Random House, warned me that I was to be disciplined as a renegade. I didn't believe him, but so it turned out. There were no reviews. There were even letters to the *Times about* there being no reviews.

INTERVIEWER: The silence meant somebody thought the "public man" thing had violated the poet?

MACLEISH: Something like that. Though the poem itself, if they had read it, wouldn't have given them much comfort. I suppose it is now the most frequently reprinted—quoted from—of my books. No, it was the usual ideological nonsense: the usual nonsense to which ideology leads unthinking men—even unthinking critics. I don't know how it was with Terence, to whom nothing human was indifferent, but I do know how it is with the practice of the art of poetry. You can't cut off a part of human life by critical fiat and expect your poets to be whole. Poetry is the art of understanding what it is to be alive and a poet isn't alive by quarter-acres or front-feet. He's alive as a man. With a world to live in. No poet down to very recent times—not even the privatest, the most confessional—ever doubted that. And the greatest of recent poets is the most convincing proof that the old poets were right. It was when Yeats broke through the fences around the Lake Isle of Innisfree and took to ranging the public world of Ireland that he became what he became. Discovering his time he discovered himself. And what was true for Yeats in 1914 is even truer for us in the angry and bewildered world we live in. Take away a poet's public life by critical edict in a time like ours and what do you leave him? Not, certainly, himself.

INTERVIEWER: But staying in touch with the whole self is tough work, isn't it, if you're trying to make reasonable words in the media about Apollo Eight or the Pentagon Papers? You don't feel squeezed?

MACLEISH: Tougher, you mean, than keeping in touch with the *whole* self when you're writing about a private part of your experience? It isn't the subject that betrays a writer, but the way he takes the subject. Rhetoric, in the bad sense of that abused word, is just as bad in confessional writing as it is out in the open air. What matters in either case is the truth of the feeling—the feel of the truth. If you can break through the confusion of words about a political crisis like the Pentagon Papers to the human fact—such as the human reality of an attorney general's behavior—you have *written* the experience. And the fact that the writing appears in *The New York Times* won't change that fact for better or worse. Journalism also has its uses—and to poets as well as to journalists. You spoke of the Apollo flight—the first circumnavigation of the moon—the one that produced that now familiar, but still miraculous, photograph of the earth seen off beyond the threshold of the moon . . . "small and blue and beautiful in that eternal silence where it floats." This was one of the great revolutionary moments of the human consciousness, but the moment was not explicit in the photograph nor in the newspaper accounts of the voyage. Only the imagination could recognize it—make imaginative sense of it. Are we seriously to be told that the imagination has no role to play here because the event is in the newspapers? Or is it the publication in the newspapers of the imaginative labor which offends?

INTERVIEWER: The way the writer "takes the subject"—that depends a lot on what the writer knows about it, right? How far around and in he's been? Can I ask about the uses of public range, social reference, all that? Is there a way of getting beyond the cliché about "the value of the experience," saying something true about how general knowledge ought to sit in a writer?

MacLEISH: I don't know that anything as essential as experience can ever be a cliché, even when parroted in the way you mean. You have to live to write in more senses than one, and no one can ever live enough—there will always be cracks in the knowledge and they will always show. But we have been talking about this rather factitious distinction between the public world and the private world, and that does raise the question of knowledge of the public world. Well, there is one thing you can say about that, because poetry has said it over and over from the first beginnings. One of the dimensions of great poetry—one of the dimensions by which poetry becomes great—is precisely the public dimension: that vast landscape off beyond—the human background, total human background—what we call "the world." It is there in Shakespeare: even in *Hamlet*, the most inward of the great plays, Denmark is behind the scene—beyond the garden where the king is murdered. And so too, obviously, of Dante: Dante's Hell is under Italy—actual Italy, historic Italy. As Homer's Troy, Homer's Aegean, contains the poems. So Tu Fu's China. So the Thebes of *Oedipus*. *Oedipus Rex* is, I suppose, by common agreement one of the keys to the secret human heart, but what would the play be without Thebes?

The Greeks regarded what we call "public" experience as part of *human* experience. That's what a man was: he was a member of his city. And if he was a poet he was a *poet* who was a member of his city. This is what gives such ground and scope and humanity to Greek poetry at its greatest. The Greek poets knew what a city was *to them*—what a war was, a people. They *knew*. Compare them with Pound. I have great admiration for Pound: he is aware of the city, of the well-ordered state, of the long tradition—the enduring ethic. But he doesn't *know*. He hasn't been there. And it shows. Carl Sandburg was one of the few contemporary poets who was able to take the state in his stride. Perhaps he took it in too easy a stride: Edmund Wilson thought so—you remember his contemptuous dismissal. But Carl will have the last word there. This is perhaps one way of answering the question: that a man who excludes, who really—not perhaps willfully or explicitly but by subconscious habit, by conforming unthinkingly to the current fashion—*excludes* the public part of his experience is apt to end up finding himself excluded. We talk about the play within the play: there is also a play *without* the play—which contains everything.

INTERVIEWER: What about the question of work-life and art-life—say in Stevens? Poetry here, business there. Aren't we headed into a time when there's a demand that a writer get himself wholly together—*mean* it across the board? He'll be hung for fraud if he finds a condition of marginality acceptable for poetry?

MACLEISH: Wallace Stevens "meant it": the fact that he had a living to earn affected that no more than it affected Shakespeare. Stevens was the head, as I understood it, of the whole trial operation of the Hartford Accident, with lawyers all over the country trying cases for him. He tried very few cases himself, but he oversaw the trying of cases and was helpful and very intelligent, a good lawyer and useful and a well-paid officer of the Hartford Accident. I think very well paid. In other words, his life, his professional life, what you called his work-life, was successful.

His poetry was something else. The trying of cases, the defending of who ran over a child and so forth, never, *as such*, enters his poetry. It might have if he had had a little streak of Masters in him. It might have, but it didn't. HIs metaphysical mind escaped—and escaped is the right word—escaped out of Hartford Accident into those deeper and deeper examinations of the metaphysical universe. So that the question with Stevens isn't really a question of public against private because his business life was private also. I don't think he was ever interested in a political question in his life. I never heard him mention one. But he is a perfect example—perhaps the most successful and admirable example—of a man who made a go of poetry *and* business. Your word is the right one. Poetry and business in the modern world. I never made a go of it. I tried everything from the law through journalism and government service to teaching at Harvard, and for each one I had to pay a price. Stevens made the art and the work go together. He fitted them together. He had, as you say, carefully planned work habits. Does this have anything to do with the "marginality" of poetry in contemporary life? I don't think so. I think it has to do with the "marginality" of poetry in *Stevens's* life. In terms of the hours of his life, poetry was necessarily pushed to the margin. But in the margin it *was* his life. And it was superb poetry. Not in a relative sense: superb *as* poetry. Nothing else matters. Nothing matters with any man but the work. The rest is biography.

INTERVIEWER: Everyman his own margin maker, is that it? I mean, every poet . . .

MACLEISH: We look back at Mr. W. S. and we say to ourselves, well, we don't know much about him. We know he was an actor. Anyway, he supported himself somehow or other in the theater. Shall we say the theater makes poetry marginal except when Mr. W. S. practices it? Shall we make a distinction between a poet supported by patrons (or, in the contemporary world, by poetry audiences) and a poet who supports himself? Is the second "marginal" whereas the first isn't? Because the first is free to devote all his time to writing? But is he? He usually has to please his patron and that can be fairly time-consuming. The truth is that neither you nor I have ever known a poet who wasn't more or less in that situation—who wasn't with the left hand trying to store up enough birdseed so he could go on with the right hand and write some poetry.

INTERVIEWER: Marginal or not, the theater is a cooperative enterprise. It forces the writer into a public situation. How do you feel about losing control? Is that a special hell?

MACLEISH: It could be, I suppose. I have had two very different approaches to Broadway production. In the first I had no intention of a Broadway production whatever. I wrote *J. B.* because I had a theme that wouldn't leave me alone. I knew that it had to be a verse play and that was about all I knew to begin with. So I wrote it as a verse play and published the first part of it in the *Saturday Review* and the finished poem with my publishers, Houghton Mifflin. I thought that was the end of it. It never occurred to me that anybody would want to produce it. Then Curt Canfield, who was Dean of the Yale Drama School, said he wanted to produce it at Yale. I said, "Fine, great." No changes of any kind except some cuts for length. Don Oenschlager designed the set—very handsome—and Curt directed with student actors and we opened. Brooks Atkinson came up to see it and reviewed it in the *Times,* and the next morning nine producers were on the telephone. Alfred deLiagre, with more courage, I thought, than sound sense, took it on and he interested Gadge Kazan, who was the great director of the generation. Gadge came up here during the summer and he and I spent weeks in this room going over and over the play. Still very little rewriting—almost none. Things for purposes of stage continuity. The real problems occurred during tryout in Washington. In other words, I was deep in a Broadway production before I rightly realized that I was headed for Broadway. It was in Washington we discovered that we had no "end"—that the end of the play had to be reconceived. But even then I did not "lose control" of the play. By this time Gadge and I were closer than brothers—communicated almost without words. We both knew the end was wrong, but what to do about it was my problem. So I rewrote the end of the play and rewrote it and rewrote it, and was very unhappy about it. And then we opened in New York. The publicity people were in a terrible situation. They had a verse play on a Biblical theme on their hands. And as if that wasn't enough, the newspapers were struck, so that everything was against us. Well, what happened was that we ran on Broadway for a year.

INTERVIEWER: And weren't ground up in a machine.

MACLEISH: Nor was I in the second Broadway play, *Scratch*, though *Scratch* was a Broadway project from the start. By which I mean that it began not with a play but with a producer. Stuart Ostrow wanted to make a musical out of Steve Benet's short story, "The Devil and Daniel Webster," with Bob Dylan and me as the concocters. I had little interest in that, and less and less the more I heard of it, but eventually I became excited about a straight play based on Steve's story, or what lay behind it, and Ostrow, when he read the first draft, gave up the idea of the musical. *Scratch*, in other words, was written not only *for* the Broadway stage, but practically *on* the Broadway stage. And yet, even so, I never felt I had lost control. It was a joint undertaking certainly—producer, director, actors, playwright—but the theme was mine from the start and the words were always mine—the play.

But if I were to generalize about this, I think I'd say *J. B.* was right and *Scratch* was wrong—wrong I mean *for me*. For a man who is primarily not a playwright, not a theater hand, to start out on Broadway is probably a mistake, Broadway being what it has become in the last ten years. If I were ever to write a play again—which I won't—I'd start with a play as I did in *J.B.*, get it produced, if I could, in one of the fine repertory theaters outside New York, and keep it outside until it was ready for the buzzards.

INTERVIEWER: That implies self-restraint. Where do you buy it in a culture that teaches writers they "personally" matter? Can you say anything about that?

MACLEISH: I don't know if there is anything I can say about it, but by God something ought to be said. Let me begin with two people whom I knew, one very well and one quite well: Ernest Hemingway and Scott Fitzgerald. The tragedy—and it is a tragedy—of Hemingway's fame is that his life and his dramatization of himself have been built up, not by him, or let me say, not altogether by him, to such a point that the myth of the man is more important than the achievement—the work. And the same thing is true of Scott, Scott having done less about dramatizing himself, but having had more done for him. In each case, the *literary figure*—capital "L", capital "F"—has been so blown up, so exaggerated, that the work has been diminished. You would know better than I how permanently, but in any case damage has been done. And the same thing is true of Robert Frost. Robert was himself the villain there, because, as anybody who knew him knows, he worked very hard at his own reputation even when he had no need to—when his greatness was acknowledged. This was damaging only to him. But the real question is what you do about this sort of thing. I don't know that pontificating about it does any good. My own conviction is that the literary person as such just doesn't count—doesn't matter. Some are interesting and some are dull. The only thing that matters is the work. And the amplification of the amplifying device, which is the man himself, is not good for the art of writing, is not good for the writer, is not good. Ernest used to love to come up and go to the nightclubs in New York. Why? To be recognized? But, for God's sake, he had been recognized in better ways before. I am not throwing off on Ernest. He is still the great prose stylist of the century. But if ever there was a cult of personality . . . ! Well, the one thing a young writer ought to swear to on his sword never to do is never to dramatize himself, whatever he may want to do about his work.

INTERVIEWER: What are the other dangers a writer might be wise to look out for?

MACLEISH: Innumerable, of course, like all the ills humanity is heir to, but self-dramatization will stand for a lot of them. The essential is not to think of one's self as a writer and to do nothing which will put one's self in that popinjay attitude. You don't write as a writer, you write as a man—a man with a certain hard-earned skill in the use of words, a particular, and particularly naked, consciousness of human life, of the human tragedy and triumph—a man who is moved by human life, who cannot take it for granted. Donne was speaking of all this when he told his congregation not to ask for whom the bell tolls. His learned listeners thought he was speaking as a divine—as a stoic. He was speaking from his poet's heart: he meant that when *he* heard the bell *he* died. It's all in Keats's letters—that writer's bible which every young man or woman with this most dangerous of lives before him should be set to read. Keats is already a poet in these letters—he is certain, in spite of the reviewers, that he will be among the English poets at his death. But they are not the letters of a poet. They are the letters of a boy, a young man, who will write great poems. Who never postures. Who laughs at himself and who, when he holds his dying brother in his arms, thinks of his dying brother, not the pathos of the scene. You can put it down, I think, as gospel that a self-advertising writer is always a self-extinguished writer. Why do anonymous writers speak to us most directly? Why are the old, old writers—the old Chinese and the vanished Greeks—most truly ours?

INTERVIEWER: What about the company a writer *does* keep. Does it matter?

MACLEISH: I don't suppose anything matters more. The subject of art is life. You learn life by living it. And you don't live it alone—even on Walden Pond—as *Walden* proves on every page. You live it with and by people—yourself in your relation with people, with and by living things, yourself in your relation to living things. The mistake is Scott Fitzgerald's mistake, for example—to lump all this as something called "experience" and to put yourself outside it looking in like a kind of glorified journalist of the ultimate reality. Scott dancing around the dance floor beside a couple of pederasts, asking them intimate questions, as though the answers would be answers. Ernest's urgent feeling that he had to know all sorts and kinds, as though he were still a reporter for the Kansas City *Star*. What you really have to know is one: yourself. And the only way you can know that one is in the mirror of the others. And the only way you can see into the mirror of the others is by love or its opposite—by profound emotion. Certainly not by curiosity—by dancing around asking, looking, making notes. You have to *live* relationships to *know*. Which is why a lifetime marriage with a woman you love is a great gift, and five marriages in a raddled row is a disaster to everyone,

including the marrier. The great luck—the immeasurable luck—
for a man trying to write the poem of his life is to have known
good men and women and to have loved them well enough to
learn the differences from himself. It won't guarantee the poem
will get written but it is immeasurable luck. A Jim Agee. A B.
Hand. A Mark Van Doren. Felix Frankfurter. Jack Bate. Mac
Bundy. Carl Sandburg. Dean Acheson . . . my wife.

INTERVIEWER: What about writers as friends? Easy friends, I
mean. Can the relation be other than competitive? I remember
your story about traveling out to Montana when Hemingway had
that car accident.

MACLEISH: You mean Hemingway's remark that I had come out
to watch him die? You can't generalize from Hemingway. He
knew I'd come at considerable cost and inconvenience (travel on
Northwest Airlines in those days was anything but a pleasure),
and it embarrassed him. Also, he had grown his first beard—the
first I saw, anyway—and looked like anything but a dying man;
Pauline had to fight the nurses out of the room. But to answer
your question . . . my own observation had been that writers can
be "easy friends" and often are—but not as writers. Mark Van
Doren and I are the easiest of friends. Hemingway and I were
friends—close friends, I won't lean on the "easy"—from '24 or
'25 until along in the thirties. Dos was a close friend always. So
was John Peale Bishop. But these were—are—human friendships,
friendships between men, not literary friendships. Reading Scott
Fitzgerald's letters to Ernest is illuminating in this connection:
you see at once what was wrong with that friendship. Scott writes
as a writer. And in friendship, in human relations, in life, there
is no such thing as a writer: there is merely a *man* who sometimes
writes. I can't imagine anything shallower than a friendship based
on a common interest in the production of literature. *Look* at
those letters of Scott's! They throw light on Scott's novels, sure,
but on the relation of two remarkable men . . . ?

INTERVIEWER: What are the prices? What are the necessary
disciplines of writing?

MACLEISH: The first discipline is the realization that there *is* a
discipline—that all art begins and ends with discipline, that any

art is first and foremost a craft. We have gone far enough on the road to self-indulgence now to know that. The man who announces to the world that he is going to "do his thing" is like the amateur on the high-diving platform who flings himself into the void shouting at the judges that he is going to do whatever comes naturally. He will land on his ass. Naturally. You'd think, to listen to the loudspeakers which surround us, that no man had ever tried to "do his thing" before. Every poet worth reading has, but those really worth reading have understood that to do your thing you have to learn first what your thing is and second how to go about doing it. The first is learned by the difficult labor of living, the second by the endless discipline of writing and rewriting and rerewriting. There are no shortcuts. Young writers a while back, misreading Bill Williams, decided to ignore the fact that poems are made of words as sounds as well as of words as signs— decided not to learn the art of words as sounds, not to be bothered with it. They were not interested in poems. They were interested in doing their thing. They did—and that was that.

INTERVIEWER: Who do you read now? Who counts?

MACLEISH: Read for pleasure or read from necessity? I suppose I read for pleasure as everyone else does—what comes along. What's "new," as Ezra used to say. (Not much *is* what it says it is but one always hopes.) But necessity is something else. You *have* to read in order to write, no matter what you pretend to yourself. Art is a seamless web, and we all latch into it where we find a loose end. But the problem is to find the connection. And hence the necessities haven't changed over fifty years. You would think they'd have to in a time like this, but they don't. Robert Frost is out of fashion—or so they tell me—but fashion is irrelevant: Robert is still what he always was, and still necessary to me. So, even more, is Yeats. So is Perse. So is Pound. Eliot. That particular, unique, and irreplaceable tone—timbre—of Carl Sandburg. And back of the men of my own time the necessity leads by the same curious—oh, it is curious enough—path: Hopkins, Rilke, Rimbaud, Emily, Emerson, Keats, Milton, Donne, and so to the great inland ocean of Shakespeare and back of that to Chaucer and Dante and the Greeks and off around the world to Li Po and Tu Fu. No pattern I or anyone else can see, but all of it somehow making a whole—all of it *necessary*. Necessary as bread. More than bread—water. Still. Fifty years later.

INTERVIEWER: Fifty years ago means the twenties. You have reason to remember the twenties; why does everyone else want to? Why all this nagging of that time?

MACLEISH: No idea. From any point of view, the decade of the twenties was a terrible decade: it was self-indulgent, it was fat, it was rich, it was full of the most loathsome kinds of open and flagrant money-making. All the worst aspects of the French came out as the franc dropped. And yet that decade in Paris was perfect. I suppose it was the right period for *us*. Because of the war, I was a lot older than I should have been to do what I was doing— trying to learn an art. But I was trying to do it alone, which is the best way to try to do it, and I was living in a city where you could *be* alone without ever being lonely, and I had Ada with me. She—I don't need to tell *you*—was a singer. A lovely singer with a beautiful, clear, high voice, and a superb musician. She was going great guns singing new songs from Stravinsky and Poulenc and Copland. So we were right in the middle of the most exciting period in almost a century of music. Also, the people who drifted along—Ernest, Dos, Scott, Gerald Murphy, above all, the Murphys—were the people of extraordinary interest who were also—or became, most of them—close friends. I can see why this still interests *me*—I love to go back to it in my mind— but why anybody else forty, fifty, sixty years younger should be interested in it, I just don't understand.

INTERVIEWER: What was the special pull of the Murphys? Why did they give up that mode of life? Did Gerald Murphy's friends try to persuade him to stick to the arts?

MACLEISH: Three questions. The last two are tragically easy to answer. Gerald gave up painting when his youngest child, Patrick, who had had turberculosis and, he thought, recovered, became ill again. Gerald wasn't Irish for nothing. He bore the stigmata— including the deep Puritan wound which afflicts Irish Catholicism and distinguishes the Gaels of Eire from the Gaels of the Scottish islands in the Hebrides. Gerald took that second (and fatal) illness as a judgment on himself. He hadn't "earned" the right to art. When, after the agony was over, the Murphys settled in New York, Gerald threw everything out of his room but the bed and a chair—white plaster walls, a white bed and chair. Did his friends try to dissuade him? How could they? And yet I remember an ambiguous scene. A Paris concert hall. An "occasion" of some kind: the Murphys are in a box and Ada and I with them. Picasso appears in front of the box looking at Gerald—smiling at him. Gerald stares over his head. Picasso turns away. But I am not answering your questions. Why did they give up "that mode of life"? It was the other way around. Their older son, Baoth, who had always been well, happy, a golden child, died suddenly, brutally, at sixteen. Then Patrick—an extraordinary human being, "un monsieur," as Picasso said, "qui est par hazard un enfant"—died after years of dying, also at sixteen. Then there were the consequences of all that doctoring and hospitalization— years in Montana-Vermala, in the Adirondacks, Depression income. Their money was all gone. They had never been "rich" by American standards, but they had always spent money as though they were, having a blithe contempt for money as such— a healthy conviction that money should be used for the purposes of life, the living of life, the defeat of illness and death. One has to pay for a faith like that, and Gerald and Sara paid without a whimper. He went back to Mark Cross, the business his father had founded. I never heard him complain of anything except the boredom. But he put up with that, supported his wife and daughter, saved his sister's holdings, and made Mark Cross, for a few, vivid years, a creative enterprise . . . not necessarily profitable, but real. "Merchant prince" he used to call himself in those days, mocking his life. But when he was dying (of cancer) René d'Harnoncourt, then the head of the Museum of Modern Art, told me I might tell him the museum had accepted his *Pear and Wasp* for its permanent collection. I feel sure he died thinking of himself as a painter. He should have. He was a painter. And a man. A man who loved life and learned how to live it. And how to die— something not all men learned even in that generation.

That or something like it would be the answer to your first

question—the "special pull," I think you said. No one has ever been able quite to define it. Scott tried in *Tender Is the Night*. Dos tried in more direct terms. Ernest tried by not trying. I wrote a "Sketch for a Portrait of Mme. G——M——," a longish poem. They escaped us all. There was a shine to life wherever they were: not a decorative *added* value, but a kind of revelation of inherent loveliness, as though custom and habit had been wiped away and the thing itself was, for an instant, *seen*. Don't ask me how.

INTERVIEWER: Did the Americans in Paris in the twenties know who they were? Was there any sense among them that what they were doing would have overwhelming impact before they were through?

MACLEISH: I can only answer for myself—what I saw and heard. Everyone was aware, I think, that work was being produced in Paris which was magnificent by any standard. This was true of all the arts—the arts generally—the arts as practiced by artists of many nationalities: French, Spanish, Russian, Irish, German, Greek, Austrian. We knew we belonged to a great, a greatly creative, generation—that we lived in a generative time. Everything seemed possible—*was* possible. To be young in a time like that was incredible luck—to be young and in Paris. That much is certain: The witnesses are innumerable. But when you narrow the circle to the American the answers are not so easy. American letters at the turn of the century had reached something which looked to my generation like rock bottom, and the achievements of Eliot and Pound during and after the First World War, though they had raised our hearts, had not wholly persuaded us that *we* belonged in this great resurgence of all the arts which was evident in Paris—this world resurgence of great art. So our excitement, real enough, was a little hesitant, a little tentative. Hemingway's *In Our Time* was the first solid American proof to appear on the Seine—proof that a master of English prose had established himself and that this master was indubitably American, American not only by blood but by eye and ear. But *In Our Time* was a collection of short stories. Would there be a great novel? A great *American* novel? We didn't know in Paris in the twenties. We only knew anything was possible.

INTERVIEWER: In that twenties community, how much exchange of ideas went on . . . reading of each other's manuscripts, advice sought and given . . . ?

MACLEISH: None. None so far as I was concerned. I met Hemingway a year or so after we got to Paris and Gerald Murphy about the same time . . . Dos, Estlin Cummings, Bishop, Scott . . . but there was no "community" in the sense in which you, I think, are using the word. No Americans-in-Paris community. That notion is a myth concocted after the event by critics with fish to fry. There was the literary-tourist world of the Dôme and the Rotonde but no work came out of that. The real "community" was, of course, Paris—the Paris of Valéry and Fargue and Larbaud—the world center of art which had drawn Picasso from abroad, and Juan Gris and Stravinsky and all the rest of that great international generation including, first and foremost, Joyce. The world center of poetry which held Alexis Léger down at the Quai d'Orsay in his anonymity as St.-J. Perse. That community—real community—drew and sustained the young Americans who lived in Paris in those years, but they didn't belong to it nor did they communicate with it, except to watch and wonder like the rest of the world. I knew Fargue and Larbaud, and Jules Romains through Adrienne Monnier. Alexis Léger became a close friend many years afterward, when all this was gone and Paris was a Nazi slum. I knew Joyce and marveled at him. But I was not part of *that* Paris nor were any Americans I knew, with the possible exceptions of Tom Eliot and Ezra Pound, who sometimes appeared. In a touching letter toward the end of his life, Scott speaks of "the last American season" in Paris. If there ever was an "American season" in Paris in the twenties, Paris was not aware of it. Nor, I think, was anyone else.

INTERVIEWER: Can I try instant analysis about why we're so interested in that time, that romance? Part of what the period means, part of the reason people come back to it, is that the glamour is forgivable in a way that glamour isn't forgivable now. People could live as they lived without the sense that all around was an active enmity to their values, their standards, their way of perceiving. In a sense going back to the twenties—you called

it that "self-indulgent" time—is trying to find a release from the pressure of justifiable hostility. Possible?

MACLEISH: I'm not sure I'd use the word "glamour"—not, certainly, of *our* life, Ada's and mine. But there was a certain relaxation. We were all of us out of that "worst of wars." Ernest had been shot up. Scott had not really been involved in it, but that was tragedy too. I had had a year of it in France. My brother had been killed. Almost everybody that we saw—certainly all the French, and all the English in Paris at that time—had lived through it. So the whole city gave off a sense that you had something coming to you—just what, you never asked . . . or learned.

INTERVIEWER: You were talking at lunch about people perceiving themselves as images of themselves rather than as genuine functions in the world and so on. Do you think that being a writer now is essentially a different kind of act from what it once was, a different kind of performance?

MACLEISH: Not "essentially"—essentially there is only one life a writer can live. But different—yes. Because the world is different. The economic "reality" is different. The Republic doesn't have the self-generated surge forward that it seemed to have a generation ago. We've come in out of the dream, and we have to think about the world we see around us, do something about it, at least be sensitive to it. Which means be sensitive to it *as* poets. And yet all the time and in spite of the changes in the world—the rapid and incoherent changes—the question at the center, the poet's question, remains the same: Who am I? The figures out on the lawn playing croquet have changed. They are not playing croquet anymore. They aren't dressed as they once were, and there's somebody with a gun back of the bush. But the question remains. So that the problem is to answer the old question in a new scene, a new setting, with other angles of light, refractions of sound, shadows moving—but still, somehow, to answer it.

INTERVIEWER: So writing now is different. But more difficult?

MACLEISH: Well, I have just had the experience, as I've said, of writing a play—*Scratch*—the whole purpose of which was to

try to find out what has become of the Republic in this new world we've been talking about. I found the critic of the *Times*, who exercises the power of life and death in the New York theater, totally impenetrable by this idea, buttoned up, occluded. He was an Englishman at that period—an Englishman and an authority on the dance—and he simply didn't understand what was being said on the stage twenty feet in front of him. Which suggests to me that the problem of writing about the public world may have become more difficult than it was forty years ago. Or perhaps it is only the problem of getting through that particular infarct to the live audience behind him.

INTERVIEWER: I remember when you were teaching you were strong for "alive" and "living" as "critical terms." What are the referents, anyway? What gives the edge?

MACLEISH: To start negatively, "alive" is what is not "literary." Or, in positive terms, what has a speaker—a voice. No writing is alive which is merely *written*. Donne, for example. Why is Donne so *present*? Why is Hopkins so much Hopkins? Or Cummings? Or Mark Van Doren? Or Agee? Cal Lowell? Wilbur? Not because they write well but because they *speak*. Each with his own voice. There's a man there, a woman—Emily. The lawyers have a useful word—"fungible." Wheat is fungible: substitute one bushel for another. Poets can't be substituted. Each has his own let's call it breath, except that it goes on and on with the words— doesn't end with the man. So that the words remain *his*. And alive.

INTERVIEWER: Breath?

MACLEISH: Well, the use of the language. The *way* a man *uses* it. You don't choose a word if you're a writer as a golf pro chooses a club with the *shot* in mind. You choose it with *yourself* in mind—*your* needs, *your* passions, feelings. It has to carry the green, yes, but it must also carry *you*. Not only your "meaning," but you yourself meaning it. You're quite right—this does seem to me the fundamental criterion in the use of language as material for art. You *create* your words in choosing them. You make them yours—spoken with your breath. Youngsters tend to think the trick is to break down the syntax—be careless—write the way they

think they talk. Nothing could be farther from the truth. To make a word your own is a year's labor—maybe a life's.

INTERVIEWER: The MacLeish poems I like best give this sense that metaphors are racing and expending energy fiercely—the edge of a moment. "Cook County," "You, Andrew Marvell," "The Genius," for example. Did they come in a rush?

MACLEISH: Those are golden words; I shouldn't let myself think about them. Because even at my age a man shouldn't let himself believe what he most wants to believe. You delight me by saying some of my poems sound as though they had come in a rush, but none of them have with the exception of "You, Andrew Marvell," which was there at the end of a morning and finished by night. I am sure—I mean I am not sure at all but I believe—the master poets must come at their poems as a hawk on a pigeon in one dive. I can't. I chip away like a stonemason who has got it into his head that there is a pigeon in that block of marble. But there's a delight in the chipping. At least there's a delight in it when your hunch that the pigeon in there is stronger than you are carries you along. There is no straining then nor *are* you strained—all assurance and confidence. Oh, you can be fooled, of course—there may be nothing there but a stone. But until you are . . .

I said something a minute ago about a long breath that sustains itself. If you find anything like that in any poem, then the impulse which drove the poem at the start is still alive in the poem printed on the page. So that the length of that poem is not the length (endless) of the work but the length of the impulse: exhausted—and achieved—in a breath.

I used to run into students who thought impulse meant idea: you got an idea and somehow you made a poem of it. A poem made out of an idea could run on forever. No single breath there. Impulse as one finds it in this art—maybe in all art—is a glimpse. Of a relationship, a possible relationship—Baudelaire's *analogie universelle*. The impulse, the urge, the emotion, begins in that cloudy glimpse, and the whole labor of art is to create the form which will contain the relationship—turn glimpse into image. But in such a way that the poem—if you are lucky, if there *is* a poem at the end—will carry *not only* the image but the impulse which produced it, that single breath—its own.

INTERVIEWER: If I understand it, then really it's all in the end of "Reason for Music"—"meaning the movement of the sea." Can you say that in any other way? Can you translate?

MACLEISH:

> *Why do we labor at the poem?*
> *Out of the turbulence of the sea,*
> *Flower by brittle flower, rises*
> *The coral reef that calms the water*
>
> *Generations of the dying*
> *Fix the sea's dissolving salts*
> *In stone, still trees, their branches immovable,*
> *Meaning,*
> > *the movement of the sea.*

Translate? Well, I am not one of those who believe that poems can't be translated; it would be an impoverished world if they couldn't. But not, I think, *out* of their images. Suppose you say that poets, like those tiny coral insects—generations of the dying— fix the sea's dissolving salts in stone, still trees, their branches immovable, which means—what? The movement of the sea. What have you gained? It's obvious what you have lost: the rhythms which suspend the words in a relationship of their own without which the world of the poem—of any poem—collapses. (A fact of art which one of my admired contemporaries, Bill Williams, tried to forget, misleading a whole generation of the dying as a result.) But still what *have* you gained? Why do we labor at the poem? To hold the evanescent *still* in its evanescence. I think the poem says it better—but perhaps I should not attempt to judge.

INTERVIEWER: There's a struggle going on in the stillness, though. I'm thinking about "The Captivity of a Fly" . . . "My heart against the hard-rib bone beat like a fly." What is the theme exactly—"a prisoner of the open wall"? It comes back in Job, too, as though it were a "personal remark" in some way. "It had gone free, my heart, it might have gone free, but the shining world so shone."

MACLEISH: The image, of course, is the commonest of all images—the fly against the windowpane that "flings itself in flightless flight." "So it loves light." And the refraction of the image is as obvious. We are all "prisoners of the open wall." What else is "the burden of the mystery" which so weighed on John Keats? Easy enough to turn away from the glass and go free—but not if you're a fly. Easy enough to put off the burden of the mystery—but not if you're human. You spoke of Job. Of course. Easy enough for Job to get down from his dung heap and walk off—if he could stop being Job, the man with a passion for justice and therefore the need to confront God. Job is the opposite of the existentialist as he is the opposite of the "good Catholic." His world *has* to mean, because God made it. It is because he loves God that he is certain there are meanings—not the other way around. What satisfies Sartre won't satisfy Job. Nor what satisfies Job's friends. He sees the light and so is prisoner of the glass.

INTERVIEWER: Are you ever completely satisfied with a finished work?

MACLEISH: Not at first. Not while the thing is still malleable. It's like the homicide experts in the movies who judge by the stiffening of the corpse: you can tell—God knows how—when a poem has settled into itself. After that you touch it at your peril: the whole thing may disintegrate if you change a word. It's for that reason I formed the habit long ago of putting new poems into a desk drawer and letting them lie there to ripen (or the opposite) like apples. I suppose everyone else does the same thing. I learned early and by sad experience never to publish a green poem. Who in hell wrote *that?* Instead, I pull them out after a few weeks or months and say, "Well . . . possibly . . ." and start all over. Or consign the whole thing to the wood fire and hope the seed, whatever it was, will sow itself again. I doubt if it does. It's sick of me by that time.

INTERVIEWER: Could we talk for a minute about "reputation"? Can a good writer make his way without cultivating his own reputation? Interviews, luncheons, appearance, backscratching, all that crap. A lot of people still feel there is an Establishment to be cracked or supplanted before they can start to breathe.

MACLEISH: That word, "Establishment," has a lot to answer for. If it is intended to refer to anything more than the distinction between the old men *now* established and the young men who *want* to be—if, that is to say, it is intended to imply a kind of conspiracy by a few established characters to suppress *les autres*—it is a fraud, or worse, a kind of escape mechanism . . . an excuse. The real question is the one you put first: how to "arrive" in the world (if it is one) of the arts in our time, a world on which all those monsters you name—television and luncheons and appearances and the rest—batten and feed. Do you have to "arrive"? Not really, but it's convenient if you want to eat regularly. But suppose you do want to eat regularly, do you have to submit to all that nonsense? Because most of it, though there are some intelligent interviewers, *is* nonsense. I don't think so. The fact is that nothing matters ultimately in any art but the *work* of art— *the* poem, *the* fiction. *That* comes first and it is *that* which remains at the last. Cal Lowell began with a poem. So did Dick Wilbur. Frost began with a book of poems. To go at it the other way around is to invite disaster: straw without bricks. Believe in the work. Believe in your own work. No poem was ever suppressed— if it *was* a poem. Belayed, yes. Muffled. Ignored for a generation or a century. But not suppressed.

INTERVIEWER: You wrestled once with the problem of reputation in the arts—in "Poetical Remains." You talked about leaving behind an "anthological rubble," "mind mingled with mind," "odd and even coupled." What is the state of feeling behind the words?

MACLEISH: I suppose you start out (I can only suppose, because it must be a very private experience for each man) with that lust for fame to which Keats confessed and to which, I guess, we should all confess—all of us who practice an art, certainly. That lust for fame is a lust for personal fame. You want to be distinguished from the others who are remembered—if anybody indeed is going to be remembered. And then, as time goes by and you begin to get a little hindsight, you look back. What really does happen to poets? Most of them leave a few fragments which go into the rubble heap, where the next generation can feed on them. They don't intend to but they do. Well, eventually, thinking about all this, you get to the point where you realize that personal fame is not at all what you're concerned with really— that old Robert was right when he said he hoped to leave half a dozen poems which would be hard to get rid of. Wonderful way of saying it. You begin to see that what is really going to happen is not that half a dozen but two, three, four poems, or maybe lines of poems, or fragments—some things may get shelved, shored up, or left behind. But left behind not alone but in a conjunction. So that you begin to think of yourself in terms of the others who were with you in this place—your contemporaries. "Oh living men, Remember me, Receive me among you." And you realize that's how you are really going to end up. You're going to be part of that, of them. And finally you begin to think, that's the way it ought to be. You ought to make the world fruitful that way. Rot! Leaving those fragments—those few poems that will be hard to get rid of.

Obviously, these are very subjective emotions. But I think, even so, even if they are subjective, one can make some generalizations about them. How to go about it? Let me try this way. I think, as you move along . . . now, this may simply be a result of the blessed accident that befell me when I found myself, far too old, teaching at Harvard. I began to understand then, by teaching a course in which I tried to find out for myself, what poetry is, what it *really* is. I began to understand that it is a part of a process which extends beyond poetry but which is most apparent *in* poetry, of trying to *see* human experience, trying to *see* "the world." "The world" being what a man feels *about* the world. Now if you realize this—what the purpose of your art is— you come to see that you are laboring at your art not only to make works of art but to make sense of your life—those dark and bewildering moments of experience. And to make sense of it not only for yourself. In other words, those poems are not works to be published for the glory of A. MacLeish—so that A. MacLeish may be spoken of. Not at all. They are steps in an attempt to stop time in terms of time so that it may be *seen*. To stop time, but to stop it on its own terms. Let men see it. Make it *visible* to men. Therefore, whatever you leave behind you exists in terms of those others who have read it, who were aware of it, who were moved by it. And the consequence is that you *do* have a totally different attitude toward fame. It isn't that you want to be admired any the less. Of course you want to be admired. Any poet wants to be admired—to be a great poet. But who is a great poet? Maybe a handful in the world's history. So that's irrelevant. What's really going to come out of your work is something else. If you have succeeded at all you have become part—however small a part— of the consciousness of your time. Which is enough. No?

—BENJAMIN DeMOTT
1974

13. James Dickey

James Dickey, the son of a suburban Atlanta attorney, was born on February 2, 1923. He joined the air force after his freshman year at Clemson University, flying over one hundred combat missions during the Second World War, and he later described this experience as a kind of seasoning: "I look on existence from the standpoint of a survivor." He has also attributed his initial interest in writing to the war and the long hours between missions.

After the war Dickey returned to school and subsequently received an M.A. in English from Vanderbilt University. While teaching English at Rice University, Dickey began publishing his poetry in the *Sewanee Review*, the *Atlantic, Partisan Review*, and *Harper's*. Another tour of duty during the Korean War, a year-long European sabbatical, additional teaching posts, and six years in the advertising business preceded the publication of his first poetry collection, *Into the Stone and Other Poems* (1960), which gave his literary career its decisive push forward. In 1965 his volume of poetry *Buckdancer's Choice* won both the Melville Cane Award and the National Book Award. The following year he was appointed to succeed Stephen Spender as consultant in poetry to the Library of Congress. Dickey's other books of poetry include *Drowning with Others* (1962), *Helmets* (1964), the prose poem *Jericho* (1974), *The Zodiac* (1976), *God's Images* (1977), and *The Strength of Fields* (1979), the title poem of which he delivered at the inauguration of President Jimmy Carter in 1976. He is also the author of a volume of poetry criticism, *Babel to Byzantium* (1968), as well as of the novel *Deliverance*, which he later adapted for the popular motion picture.

Poet-in-Residence and professor of English at the University of South Carolina, Columbia, since 1969, Dickey lives with his second wife, Deborah Dobson. He has two sons and a grandson.

Falling

Transcontinental   low moon   the states are dark   each successively
as dark as the last. There is some leak of air somewhere in the cabin
And someone is disturbed. In her blue uniform, there near the galley
with racks of trays, she gets a blanket, and begins to pin it up
over the faint ear-whistle of air coming in from the darkness.
Then she is in total dark and cold. The door blew out   and she found
Herself with her arms and legs in the killing dark and her cry   one
Long way turning to wind. Can this be me / here in this place turning
To nothing myself   feeling around me the flutter   of garments in this
Cold of God   and yet I am spaced some way or other   on air   I can
Flare my hands and feet in it   death is still three or four miles
Down   it is not so cold as it was   but cold. I have tried to look
At everything in the dark. There are lights   a highway   towns
And there the glitter of water   the moon racing slowly through
The curves of a river   a lake opens its eye   the darks change
Throughout the enormous air. I can spread my legs   and my skirt
Catches on the air   I can circle until there is little there is no
Sense of falling   but flight (delicately) maintained   the air whistles
faintly but I am suspended between earth and heaven   the plane I was
on is probably landing in Chicago   I have been falling for hours
It is warmer   I can see the shape of the continent   lose its
Shape   If I fell into water I might live   so let me begin
To plane across the air in my jacket and skirt   moving like an owl
Across the space of midnight   toward the glitter of water   It is
a journey through the uncreated   through chaos   where nothing
Holds   Here is a usual young woman flying upon the dark like a goddess
Heading for the slowly opening eye   of water   cross-country
Cross-country through the country of the air   possessing for an
Instant the continent as a diess would possess it   travelling above the
Heads of sleepers on farms   the hawmows sharpening as I pass over
Them   the boys' penises rising   the farm girls feeling the goddess
In them brooding on the four posts of the beds   dreaming of fire
Of comets and javelins fireworks   a great woman scrawled in stars
Overhead in the calm night   and will wake to see a woman   struggling
The stars struggling to become a woman. Water is nearer and now I am
Over but cannot fall into it   I am streaking like a jet in my jet
Stewardess's uniform And the ground is closer   the dark
Of fields a total dark and I have just time to fling off my one
Shoe   to pull off my stockings   It is abnormally easy to undress
Tumbling   I can assume any position the air has to offer   take off
The sad rings of my jacket   the bat's guiding leather of my skirt
The intimate flying-garment   The inner flying garment of my slip
The long airstreams of my stockings   my breassiere letting my breasts
Warm on the air   and my girdle   and all of us float down almost
Together   but myself gradually leaving them   finally fighting away
From my head my shoe, the last thing   and will descend now in this
State into the warm fields   trying as I can to land   on my back.
Whoever finds me will find me as I am   and will not understand
My shut will, more deeply. It will all be broken this kind of thing
Is what one does when there is nothing to be done   makes a gesture
Understood by nothing or by no one   in the dark   and will lie

In the fields   life broken out   but with one breath   believing I could
Have made it back to water I overpassed   when in the goddess state
Having flown too close to *[handwritten]*   *[handwritten]*   Ah, but
[handwritten]   the   goddess state to *[illegible]*

Page one of "Falling," courtesy of Washington University at St. Louis.

James Dickey

In 1960, when he was thirty-eight—an age at which most men have abandoned pretenses at having creative gifts—James Dickey published his first book of poetry, Into the Stone, a Scribner's Poets of Today volume that he shared with two other unknown poets, Paris Leary and Jon Swan. In the years since, Dickey has become one of the most powerful voices in American poetry.

But, ironically, it was fiction, not poetry, that made Dickey's name a household word. After toying with Deliverance for nearly ten years, he finished it in a great thrust of energy in 1969. Those who knew Dickey closely, however, were aware that Deliverance, while a publishing phenomenon, was not the center of his creative objective. He once remarked to a student, "The Eye-Beaters is worth a hundred Deliverances."

This interview took place in Dickey's Lake Katherine home in Columbia, South Carolina. It was recorded in three sessions (two in May 1972 and one in May 1974) in his huge den with an *inch-thick gray carpet and an appropriate wall of books. Dickey, a large, bearish man, has a voice to match. Throughout the tapings he poised on his chair's edge, sucking air through his teeth in anger at incompetent poets, and often shaking with laughter at good one-liners. On the first day he wore a pink shirt with French cuffs; the next sessions found him garbed in jackets and pants of leather or suede. After each day's taping, Dickey played the guitar, took his interviewer canoeing, or demonstrated his skill with the bow and arrow. He is adroit with all three, perhaps excelling on the six-string. He has contributed numerous guitar tapes to the Library of Congress in addition to providing some of the music for* Deliverance.

INTERVIEWER: You have said you got where you are today, an established poet and novelist, "the hardest way possible, unsolicited manuscripts." Can you tell us about it?

DICKEY: It was very difficult to do; I didn't have any precedent; I didn't know any writers, editors, publishers, or agents. They might have been in the outer part of the solar system as far as I was concerned. I just knew that I liked to write and I had some ideas that I thought might work out as poems. So I wrote them, then sent them around. As they say, I could have papered my bedroom wall with the rejections.

I began to send stuff out when I was at Vanderbilt, and the only way that I knew where to send anything was to go into the stacks of the library and get a magazine out that I admired, like the *Sewanee Review*, and get the address off the masthead and send the poem to the guy who was the editor at that address. I sent poems in and I kept getting back these form rejections. In 1948 or 1949 I remember with what wonder I saw a true human handwriting on the rejection slip. It said, "Not bad."

INTERVIEWER: What made you decide to commit yourself to writing?

DICKEY: Like most American writers I kind of backed into it. I liked poetry; I liked to read it. I'm the kind of person who can't be interested in a thing without wanting to see if I can't get out there and do a little of it myself. If I see somebody shooting arrows, I want to get a bow and see if I can shoot some myself.

INTERVIEWER: Did the legendary Vanderbilt crowd have much effect on you?

DICKEY: There is no sense in which it could be said that I was a latter-day Fugitive or Agrarian. But Donald Davidson was my teacher, and he's the single best teacher that I've ever had with the possible exception of Monroe Spears. He made poetry and intellectual life important; all you had to do was walk into his classroom and you knew you were in the presence of some important spirit. I got interested in anthropology, astronomy, the kind of thing that Donald Davidson stood for. But the whole Vanderbilt ethos and Agrarianism and cultural pluralism were just academic subjects to me. I'm much more interested in them now than when I was in the milieu that produced them.

INTERVIEWER: What did you do when you graduated?

DICKEY: I took an M.A. in 1950 and became an instructor in technical English and report writing at what was then called Rice Institute in Houston, Texas, but almost immediately after my appointment I went off to the Korean War.

INTERVIEWER: When did you get into the advertising business?

DICKEY: A few years after the war—1956, and I stayed in it until 1962. I worked with three different agencies—first I was with McCann-Erickson, on the Coca-Cola account, where I was known not as Jungle Jim, but as Jingle Jim. I then moved to Atlanta and worked with an agency called Liller Neal and Battle, where I worked on fertilizer accounts, mainly. Also banks and Pimento products. I then took a position as creative director and vice-president of an Atlanta agency called Burke Dowling Adams, where I engineered the advertising campaign dealing with the awarding of the transcontinental run by Delta to the West Coast. Now, in connection with my film work, I fly that airline all the time.

INTERVIEWER: How important was your work to you? Do you regret leaving it?

DICKEY: No. I'm glad I left it. But if I had four or five different lives, or the proverbial nine lives, I would like to spend one of them in business. It's a fascinating and exciting way to live. It's very frustrating; it's got its hang-ups; it's a man-killing pace; and it's tremendously difficult. But I love business people and I met some really terrific people whom otherwise I wouldn't have known. I wouldn't have had any relationship to them unless *that* were the relationship: making deals, working with them on their problems, and selling their products. I enjoyed it. There's something about the nine-to-five existence and the five-thirty cocktails after work on Friday afternoons and talking over the problems of the week with your buddies who are working on the same problems that's really kind of nice. I remember it with affection and with a certain amount of gratitude. Nevertheless, I don't have that many lives. I have only one, so when it was time for me to leave, I left.

INTERVIEWER: What were you writing during your business period?

DICKEY: I wrote my whole first book, *Into the Stone*, on company time. I had a typewriter and I had a bunch of ads stacked up in those famous brown envelopes with work orders on them. When I had a minute or two, I'd throw a poem into the typewriter and try to work out a line or get a transition from one stanza to the next. But the business world gives you almost no time to do anything but business. You are selling your soul to the devil all day and trying to buy it back at night. This can work out fine for a while, but after that the tensions and the difficulties begin to mount up and you see that you are going to have to make a choice. This took place with me after about five and a half or six years.

INTERVIEWER: What made you decide to make your final commitment to writing, to say, "This is it, I am leaving"?

DICKEY: Age. I knew I couldn't have it both ways much longer, and as they say in the pro football games or basketball games on Sunday afternoons, "The clock is running." I didn't have that much time. I needed a lot more time to do my work and not *their* work. And there is also the feeling of spending your substance, your vital substance, on something that is really not that important—of giving the best of yourself, every day, to selling soda pop. You just don't want to let yourself go that easily. You can't. Or I couldn't, anyway.

INTERVIEWER: Do you think in some ways it is a commitment to a kind of artificial moral order?

DICKEY: Well, if you work for the Coca-Cola Company, the first thing you're told is how many people's jobs and lives depend on the drink and how old and venerable and honorable the company is, that the pension plans are good, the medical plans are good, and so on. But after all, it's only soda pop, and you're quite sure in the end that you don't want to spend your vital substance on something that's not any more important than a soft drink. If you go with the Coca-Cola Company, Pepsi-Cola, R.C., or any of them, you enlist yourself in a war that was going on before you were born, and will go on after you die. It's a little bit—I hate to drag this in—like Vietnam. You fight limited engagements in limited areas and nobody ever wins.

INTERVIEWER: After *Into the Stone* came out, did you think that you were going to succeed as a poet?

DICKEY: I didn't know then, and I still don't know. The Guggenheim people wrote to me and asked me if I would like to stand for a fellowship and to send in whatever I had to offer. I was in one of those Scribner three-decker, large economy-size packages of young poets with Paris Leary and Jon Swan, and I sent them that, and presto, lo and behold, they gave me some money—several thousand dollars. I said to Maxine, "This is our escape hatch. Let's sell the house and go and live in Italy. Why the hell not? When are we ever going to get another chance?" I swore I was going to go back to Europe before I was forty. I made it at the age of thirty-nine.

INTERVIEWER: What sort of effect did Europe have on you and your writing?

DICKEY: Italy was especially good. First of all, there was what Davidson used to talk about all the time, cultural pluralism: different wines, different dishes, different paintings, different lifestyles, all kinds of different things which give such richness and variety to life. What we'll end up with if the world gets increasingly

Americanized is life in a gigantic Rexall's. Of course, you can
go into Rexall's and get a lot of things you need. You can also
get a lot of things you don't need, but might be interested in
having. There are a lot of diversified products in Rexall's. But
Rexall's is Rexall's. It's not the same as going to a bullfight or
going to a folk dance in Sicily or going into the Uffizi Museum
in Florence.

When an American goes to Europe, he doesn't go there to get
just another version of America. He wants *difference*. You see
fields of tulips in Holland. You never saw anything like that in
your life. You see cliffs down on the Amalfi Drive, you see people
in an Italian village. The guys having a drink together: why, by
God, they fall into each other's arms—and they just *saw* each
other last night; they were probably drunk together last night.
You don't see Americans do that. Americans are pushing each
other away all the time, even the men and women.

INTERVIEWER: Would you advise a young writer to abroad for
a while?

DICKEY: Yes. I believe that a broad scan of experience can be
nothing but beneficial to a young writer. It may be confusing at
the beginning, but the increment of his personal memory bank
can be only for the best. To cite but one example, look at Hemingway's experience of Paris. Take others: Henry James's experience of London, J. B. Priestley's sojourn in Arizona, and
Stephen Crane's in Cuba. You name it.

INTERVIEWER: What other advice would you give?

DICKEY: I don't know. The talent game is a tough game. Luck
plays an enormous part in it. It's not like business, though luck
has a very strong place in business too. You can write one good
poem by luck or hazard that's going to make people want your
work. Whether or not you can produce anything good later on
is not the important thing. It's that you struck it right then. It's
the same with a novel—I wrote *Deliverance*. The movies bought
it; it was serialized, written into a dozen languages; it's the best
novel I can write, but there's also an enormous element of luck
in it. I wrote the right book at the right time. People were caught
up in a savage fable of decent men fighting for their lives and

killing and getting away with it. My next novel could be a failure.

INTERVIEWER: How can a young poet know if his work is really worthwhile?

DICKEY: You never know that. I don't know it; Robert Lowell doesn't know it; John Berryman didn't know it; and Shakespeare probably didn't know it. There's never any final certainty about what you do. Your opinion of your own work fluctuates wildly. Under the right circumstances you can pick up something that you've written and approve of it; you'll think it's good and that nobody could have done exactly the same thing. Under different circumstances, you'll look at exactly the same poem and say, "My Lord, isn't that *boring*." The most important thing is to be excited about what you are doing and to be working on something that you think will be the greatest thing that ever was. One of the difficulties in writing poetry is to maintain your sense of excitement and discovery about what you write. American literature is full of people who started off excited about poetry and their own contribution to it and their own relationship to poetry and have had, say, a modicum of success and have just gone on writing poetry as a kind of tic, a sort of reflex, when they've lost all their original excitement and enthusiasm for what they do. They do it because they have learned to do it, and that's what they *do*. You have to find private stratagems to keep up your original enthusiasm, no matter what it takes. As you get older, that's tougher and tougher to do. You want to try to avoid, if you possibly can, the feeling of doing it simply because you *can* do it.

INTERVIEWER: What are some of these private stratagems?

DICKEY: A very great deal of exercise, to keep the body moving, because when the body moves the mind is inclined to move with it. At times, a certain amount of alcohol helps. The point is to get to a certain *level* at which the creative flow can best take place. Any means to effect this end is to the good.

INTERVIEWER: How do ideas for poems come to you?

DICKEY: Well, I can give you one example, of course there are many. But, I remember when I was in Okinawa and the war was over and we went out to one of the invasion beaches near Buckner Bay, me and my cofliers, and we went swimming and there was an old amtrack there in ten feet of water that the Japanese had stove in—big holes in the sides of it—and I swam down and sat in the driver's seat. That image stayed with me and years later, twenty or twenty-five years later, I wrote "The Driver."

INTERVIEWER: You also write about things that an ordinary person would pass by, like the jump of a fish, or the movement of trees, or light.

DICKEY: That could almost be cited as the definition of a poet: someone who notices and is enormously taken by things that somebody else would walk by. The major thing for a writer to do is develop some means of selecting the *best* of his memories and ideas and images and to build on them and reluctantly let the others go.

INTERVIEWER: Can you describe the genesis and working out of a poem based on an image that most people would pass by? "Dust," for example?

DICKEY: "Dust" was a collusion between or among two or three different kinds of elements. I wanted to try to utilize a stanza form with a short first line, evolving into longer lines, and at the end coming back to a short line. This is purely a technical problem. The second element was literary: I wanted to work with the Biblical statement, "But dust thou art, to dust returneth." The third element that was important was the sense of lying about half drunk in a California afternoon and looking up through the sunlight shining through the window and really noticing—as one will do when one is about half drunk—these strange little things in the air. They are always spiral shaped and it seemed to me that this might have something to do with venereal disease, with the spirochete and so on. So that was the fourth element. I tried to get all of them together in one poem.

INTERVIEWER: You speak of technical elements. How do you feel about free verse?

DICKEY: I go back and forth. Sometimes I like to write in very strictly measured forms. I think there are tremendous advantages accruing to that. But then I also want to try to open out the poem and make what I have recently been calling the "balanced poem," and make gaps within the lines and write in bursts of words. You shouldn't restrict yourself . . . what Ivor Winters did, and say that it's got to be this way or it's no good at all. You should experiment. You should wander around a bit; you should risk being wrong. Actually, free verse is not a term that I myself care much for. I would call it unrhymed, irregular verse, because I remember what Mr. Eliot said, "No verse is free for the poet that wants to do a good job," and it really *isn't* free. What you are talking about is that you are not writing a rhyming or a regular verse, but more of an open, organic form.

INTERVIEWER: Does form ever control your subject matter?

DICKEY: I used to be much interested in inventing forms; for example, the form in "The Hill below the Lighthouse" dictated the subject matter. What I did was to work out a refrain scheme— I call it a returning rhyme—so that each stanza had an end line which was italicized. And the end stanza of the poem—the sixth or seventh, I forget which—was made up of the refrained lines themselves.

INTERVIEWER: Do you show your poems in a working stage to anyone else?

DICKEY: It depends. There are some things that I show to certain selected people if I think the words have reached the stage where their future development might prove good. But generally I keep the successive drafts of a poem to myself, because I conceive the poetic process as quite a private matter between the poet, his hand, and the blazing white island of paper which he is trying to populate or eliminate.

INTERVIEWER: How many drafts do you usually do?

DICKEY: It depends on the poem. With a longer one like "The Firebombing," I'd say certainly one hundred and fifty to one hundred and seventy-five, because you are searching all the time for some kind of order—some constitution to order whatever it is you are trying to say. Then, you are also trying to render it unforgettable. We poets are shameless people. We try to give whoever reads our poems something that they simply cannot shake. And if you try to do this in a long poem, you have to have some kind of executive order that makes the parts contribute to the whole, so that the audience will remember both the whole and the parts that contributed to it.

INTERVIEWER: What about a shorter poem like "Remnant Water"?

DICKEY: Oh, there are over thirty drafts of that. It's a kind of Vermeer, a still-life piece; this is relatively unusual for me. Most of my things depend on violence and length. But "Remnant Water" is a short piece, and so the whole revolves around the placement of each single word and not the presentation of an action, as it does in "The Firebombing." I worked on that an awful long time. It might point a new direction, I don't know. But it is necessary that one experiment; that a poet should work out different kinds of direction.

INTERVIEWER: Do you ever have the temptation to change a poem after it's published?

DICKEY: I have a paranoid thing about making absolutely sure before I let anything go out under my name that it is as good as I can do at that particular time. I might have second thoughts about it later, but I'm willing to stand on it when I turn it loose; therefore, it gets very hard for me to turn one loose.

INTERVIEWER: When you think about *Poems: 1957–1967*, what poem are you least enchanted with yourself?

DICKEY: Well, I don't know. The title poem "Drowning with Others" is one that I would like to make into a much longer poem—much, much longer. It's anthologized all over the damn place—but I can see possibilities in it now that I didn't see then.

INTERVIEWER: It's always ironic that the more successful a person gets, the more under attack he comes. I've noticed that there is an increasing amount of bitterness by a great number of people toward your work. Do you have any sort of response to their criticism?

DICKEY: Most of the time I don't even know what it is. It seems to me that a lot of it is politically oriented. For some reason or other I've had the right-wing monkey put on my back. But I'm not right wing; I'm not left wing; I'm not any wing.

INTERVIEWER: After all, you did work for Eugene McCarthy at one time as a speech writer.

DICKEY: Yes, I did. He was my closest friend in Washington. That doesn't concern people. The fact that William Buckley is also a very close friend *does* concern people because that gives them an automatic put-down. I just don't worry about it. I've got too much work to do. It seems to be an invariable rule that people who don't have a strong creative drive, but find themselves in the creative competitive market, are eventually and inevitably going to put other writers down by means of politics.

INTERVIEWER: Some of your detractors have mentioned the fact that they felt that you should use your influence, your place in the world, for the "betterment of man."

DICKEY: If I knew what it was, I might do that. But I don't know. There's this tendency in American life to assume that because someone is good or maybe just notorious or publicized in one realm that he's a universal authority on everything. So, Frank Sinatra or John Wayne can tell you how to vote. What competence do *they* have in politics? Or that a poet can tell you about ecology or something of that sort. A poet is only a professional sensibility. His opinion in politics is no better than anyone else's ninety-nine percent of the time. But they're always being interviewed and always being asked their political opinion: what should we do with the military, what should we do with the economy, with government spending, etcetera. Poets don't know anything about that. If they did, they wouldn't be poets. This is not to say that they are precluded from knowing anything about it at *all*; it is to say, however, that just because they are poets their opinions should not be paid any more attention to than anybody else's. It does not give them any privilege or any insight or any clairvoyance as to the political and economic and military future of America.

INTERVIEWER: You don't feel, then, that since a poet has a highly developed sensitivity about our universe and about our place in the world and our society, he should make public pronouncements about the direction our society is taking?

DICKEY: I think in that way lies madness. No; all he's got is his own sensibility and his own opinions as a private citizen. But he has no privilege. Insight, yes. Maybe a poet could come along who could solve all our problems, but I haven't seen him yet. The history of poets pronouncing on public issues is notoriously dismal.

INTERVIEWER: I remember you quoted Auden talking about poetry: "for poetry makes nothing happen." Do you believe that?

DICKEY: I think that if it does make anything happen, it's deep in the individual's sensibilities; it's not in the public arena. As John Peale Bishop says, when the poet, or the critic, mounts the soapbox, the garbage remains in the streets.

INTERVIEWER: Did your job as poetry consultant to the Library of Congress involve you in the political world? One thinks of Archibald MacLeish trying to get Pound out of prison.

DICKEY: Well, Archie was the *librarian* of Congress, and his name is engraved in gold just inside the entrance way of the Library. The consultancy is quite a different thing. I did try to get several of the incarcerated Russian poets out of prison without success. My position was not such as that which Archie occupied. My name is not engraved in gold letters, and I would not have had the capacity to occupy the position which Archie had, nor would I have accepted it if offered. My position was that of being the only equivalent that the United States has of poet laureate. Frost was in the chair, Robert Lowell was in the chair, and Robert Penn Warren was in the chair. The job is as the incumbent conceives it: he can do as much or as little with it as he likes. He can lecture, he can initiate programs that the Library will implement, he can arrange for lectures in the Coolidge auditorium, he can travel for the State Department, or he can do nothing at all except accept the position as a sinecure. I chose to be a working consultant. I set up an arrangement with the local ETV station to film the readings that I proposed, so that the Library would have the nucleus of a filmed archive of writers, novelists, and poets that would eventually be the equivalent of the spoken archives that the Library is famous for. Videotape made this possible. Universities and students may now go to the Library of Congress to see and hear, for example, John Updike reading from his works. Also John Cheever, William Stafford, Josephine Miles, and many another.

It is also part of the tradition of the consultancy that the consultant take at least one extended trip. Frost, for example, went to Russia. I went to New Zealand, Australia, Japan, and Alaska. I made the job hard, and now that it is over, I am glad that I did.

INTERVIEWER: You got into what you call your *one* political foray when Yevtushenko was here, in this country. Why?

DICKEY: Well, he's a close friend. I like him very much, but I profoundly disapprove of the kind of thing he does. He uses poetry as a pretext for making bohemian speeches. He's a great deal better poet than Allen Ginsberg, but he does the same *sort* of thing. I don't think poetry is well served by that. Poetry *can* speak on topical things eloquently. Look at Yeats on the riots of 1916, for example. But we should not be led into the corner of assuming that poetry is no good which does not speak on news items. If a man wants to write about the circle that's made in the water when a fish jumps, he should be able to write about that and should not be charged off as irrelevant because he's not writing about the Vietnam riots. You should have the whole gamut: political action, the jump of the fish, or the space program. You should have anything you want.

INTERVIEWER: It seems Allen Ginsberg is the diametrical opposite of you.

DICKEY: I certainly hope so. I think Ginsberg has done more harm to the craft that I honor and live by than anybody else by reducing it to a kind of mean that enables the most dubious practitioners to claim they are poets because they think, If the kind of thing Ginsberg does is poetry, I can do *that*. They damn themselves to a life of inconsequentiality when they could have been doing something more useful. They could have been garbage collectors, or grocery store managers. Poetry is, as Yeats has said, "a high and lonely profession." It is very easy, too easy, to pick up on the latest thing in the newspapers and write a poem. That's all Ginsberg does. He just doesn't have any talent. I'll do a Ginsbergian poem or a Robert Bly poem for you right now.

INTERVIEWER: Do you consider them in the same school?

DICKEY: Well, not exactly the same, but they take off from the same . . . launching pad. Their poem goes:

> It is the hour when the Americans in Vietnam are
>   examining their hands.
> The dead are lying below the tangles of jungle brush.
> All over Minnesota snow is beginning to fall over the
>   missile silos.

INTERVIEWER: A southern writer said, "James Dickey first came to my attention as a reviewer and I thought he was one of the roughest around." You've been pretty rough on some of your contemporaries. For what reason?

DICKEY: Well, I'm not all that rough. I have a very naïve feeling as a reviewer. I don't believe that a reviewer or a critic can really criticize well unless he can praise well. I always liked that about Randall Jarrell. He praised well. James Agee praises well. You've got to be able to like the right things to be enabled to dislike the wrong things. People misconstrue John Simon. He *does* praise well. He doesn't find much to praise, but he praises well. John Simon hates so much so vehemently because he likes so little so strongly.

INTERVIEWER: Let's talk about someone that you do like strongly. What attracts you so much to William Stafford?

DICKEY: It's because he has the ability to say amazing things without seeming to raise his voice. He's kind of *murmuring*. I've never encountered a poet like that. He's not doing a lot of vast, tearing, rhetorical stuff like Lowell does, or a lot of kinky, tacky self-derogation like John Berryman. He's talking like an American midwestern farmer who just has this capacity to say startling, quiet stuff.

INTERVIEWER: Do you feel that Stafford is making a more significant contribution to American letters than Lowell is?

DICKEY: Yes, I do. I think Stafford will mean more to people over a longer period. Maybe not to the makers of textbooks or anthologies, but he's a people's poet of the finest kind; he's instantly understandable, and he gives you an enormous amount to think about without hollering at you, or without beating you down. Roethke was like that. Stafford, in a completely different way, has that same quality. He doesn't have the crazy, apocalyptic kind of a feel that Roethke has, but he's got an easy going, quiet, authoritative, human, imaginative voice.

INTERVIEWER: Did you know Roethke?

DICKEY: Yes, I did indeed. I knew him quite well during the last two years of his life. He was a strange, terrifying, and terrified man. He seemed to have no confidence in himself. He was constantly afraid of being fired from the University of Washington because of his drunkenness and his periodic insanity. He feared becoming destitute, though he had a fine house on John Street overlooking the sea, a devoted wife, and friends who would have gone to the gallows for him. None of this seemed to do him any good. He read, it seemed, every scrap of paper on his work that appeared in print, and conceived endless literary enmities toward this, that, and the other literary critic or rival poet. Despite the fact that he was a little hard to live with, he was on the whole a lovable man, and it is still difficult for me to believe that he is gone from us.

INTERVIEWER: You had an article in the *Atlantic*, "The Greatest American Poet: Theodore Roethke." Why is he the greatest?

DICKEY: I don't see anyone else that has the kind of deep, gut vitality that Roethke's got. Whitman was a great poet, but he's no competition for Roethke. Lowell is a fine poet. He's a narrow, tragic, personal, confessional kind of writer. He's very good. But you can be interested in his hang-ups, his family, for just so long. In order to read Lowell and to like Lowell or Anne Sexton or any of the people that follow after Lowell, what is presupposed is that their life and their situation is going to be eternally fascinating to you. And it isn't. I *am* interested in Roethke's relationship to the ocean, because that gets me *into* it. I can participate. I can't enter Lowell's family. Of course, Lowell is an enormously powerful writer. The measure of his ability is that he can *make* you interested in his family; whereas Sylvia Plath, writing poems like "Daddy," is ridiculously bad; it's embarrassing. Lowell is a big writer, and he *compels* you to be interested. People like Sylvia Plath or Anne Sexton just embarrass you.

INTERVIEWER: How do you respond to the emergence of Sylvia Plath as a celebrated figure?

DICKEY: She's not very good. She's just someone who killed herself out of literary desperation—out of desperation to be literarily notable. Someone ought to write an article called "The Suicide Certification," which assumes that if you're a poet and you kill yourself, then you have *got* to be good. No way.

INTERVIEWER: One time you called it "suicide chic."

DICKEY: Well, of course, if you're taking your own life, that's a horrible situation. Al Alvarez seems to think, in his recent book on suicide, that she was just doing it as a gesture and she hoped it wouldn't come off. So she killed herself by mistake. She's the Judy Garland of American poetry. If you want to kill yourself, you don't make an *attempt*; you do it. You make sure that the thing comes off. Suicide *attempts*, and then writing *poems* about your suicide attempts, is just pure bullshit! Sylvia Plath is of a certain talent, a very modest talent. Anne Sexton is better than she is, and I don't care much for her, either.

INTERVIEWER: What is your opinion of the famous southern women writers—Eudora Welty, Carson McCullers, Katherine Anne Porter, and Flannery O'Connor?

DICKEY: The women of the South have brought into American literature a unique mixture of domesticity and grotesquery. There have been two routes open to the southern woman writer. She could research a historic subject—such as Elizabeth Madox Roberts did in *The Great Meadow*, which deals with the opening up of Kentucky—couple this with domestic images from her own life, and write her fiction out of these two considerations; or she could deal with eccentric village types, such as Carson McCullers and Eudora Welty frequently do and Flannery O'Connor does to an extreme. The southern women writers of the two generations which produced our great ones were singularly immobile, but then so was Emily Brontë. They had little breadth of experience, but much penetration into a specific and still milieu. They are remarkable writers. But their scope is limited to the local and domestic with, in some cases, an admixture of the grotesque. I like it all. This is the way my women see things, and it is an interesting way that sheds light.

INTERVIEWER: Is there something about the South that is peculiarly advantageous for the writing of poetry and fiction?

DICKEY: Yes, I think there is. Due to their past, their history, their rural background, Southerners are lonely people. They very seldom have anyone to talk to. The result of this has been that when a Southerner encounters another human being he talks his head off. Add to this the very strong folklore and the legendary quality of local stories, anecdotes, and jokes, and you have the basis for southern poetry and also for southern fiction. Out of this situation, plus a certain superficial literariness (as in the case of Faulkner), came a great literature. But there are certain obvious defects. One of these is the eternal sameness of southern fiction, which almost always deals with a family either in a single generation or covering several generations. One cannot reasonably assume that a wide reading public is going to be interested in yet another novel dealing with the Lutrell family in Ellijay, Georgia, with its criminally inclined son and its seduceable daughter. With poetry it is quite different. A mystical element enters. It enters into the landscape, the rivers, and the animals. Our greatest poetry has been written out of southern landscape, and not out of southern people. This is to the good, I think.

INTERVIEWER: Has the poetry of Robert Frost, particularly the country poems, been of interest or impact?

DICKEY: I don't care much for Robert Frost, and have never been able to understand his reputation. He says a good thing now and then, but with a strange way of averting his eyes while saying it which may be profound and may be poppycock. If it were thought that anything I wrote was influenced by Robert Frost, I would take that particular work of mine, shred it, and flush it down the toilet, hoping not to clog the pipes.

INTERVIEWER: Did you know him?

DICKEY: Yes, I knew him slightly, and spent a couple of afternoons with him when I was teaching at the University of Florida in 1955, and a more sententious, holding-forth old bore who expected every hero-worshiping adenoidal little twerp of a student-poet to hang on his every word I never saw.

INTERVIEWER: One of the things I think that you do enjoy is an audience. Can that be the death of a poet, if he enjoys performing?

DICKEY: It sure killed off poor Dylan Thomas. He didn't write even *one* poem in the last six years of his life. Everybody adored him, paid him a lot of money; why should he write another book of *poems*, and maybe give the critics a shot at him that would lower his reading fee? Everybody *loved* him; he was screwing all the coeds in America, drinking all the whiskey, and he'd get up there and read his poems, and then he'd go on and read them somewhere else. He got a lot of dough for it. I mean, what incentive for him to write *was* there? To survive, a poet has to find some way of maintaining his original enthusiasm for *poetry*, not for the by-products of poetry, not for the fringe benefits of poetry, but for *it*.

INTERVIEWER: One time you were answering some irate poet and you said, "It's ironic to me that so many poets go about defending themselves in the wrong way; the real test lies in the poem."

DICKEY: Listen, a poet's pages are filled up with what he's done, that he can live on and trade on; but he has *got* to find some way to love that white empty page, those words he hasn't said yet.

INTERVIEWER: I think some people thought that you came out with *Deliverance* as a kind of afterthought, but I know from talking to you earlier that you had thought about *Deliverance* a long time. Why did you decide to finally go ahead and do it?

DICKEY: Well, I did think about it a long time. I started it about ten years ago and finished it about two years ago. It is misleading to leave it at that, because it would cause people to believe that I did nothing but work on *Deliverance* all that time—year after year. I wrote seven or eight other books during that time. *Deliverance* was really not high on the priority list at all. As Thomas Lovell Beddoes said of his own involvement with his lifelong work, never finished, called *Death's Jest Book*, "I just gave it another kick whenever I got around to it." But by damn, when it began to look like *Deliverance* was really capable of being finished, then I started leaning on it and pushing, and working on it until it finally *did* get finished. Nobody was more surprised than I was, because this novel was just something lying around in a drawer. I liked the story, and I got to where I was interested in the characters, and so on. I didn't know anything about writing novels—I still don't know much about it.

INTERVIEWER: What sort of process did you go through in writing the novel—shifting from poems to a fictional work?

DICKEY: The main problem for me, as I recall, was finding out ways to do without the poetic line, because I had really relied heavily on the line, and the way the human eye moves across the page, what happens when you read a line of verse and the way it goes into the next line. I had to learn a whole new set of conventions, to work with the sentence and the paragraph, which I didn't know very much about.

Deliverance was originally written in a very heavily charged prose, somewhat reminiscent of James Agee. But it was too juicy. It detracted from the narrative thrust, which is the main thing that the story has going for it. So I spent two or three drafts taking that quality out. I wanted a kind of unobtrusively remarkable observation that wouldn't call attention to itself. That's why I made the narrator an art director. He's a guy who *would* see things like this; a writer would perform all kinds of cakewalks to be brilliant stylistically, which would have interfered with the narrative drive of the story.

INTERVIEWER: You have so many interesting set pieces in there. One that struck me was that section beginning "there is always something wrong with people in the country" which you ended "and I saw that the only way out was by water from the country of the nine-fingered people." Did you ever feel like putting something like that into a poem?

DICKEY: No, it was the other way around, because some of the same events which are depicted in *Deliverance* have been in poems—such as the boat going by the effluent pipe where the chicken heads and the feathers are. I wrote it into poetry first. Then I pulled it out of the poem and used it in the novel.

INTERVIEWER: Did you feel as if you were reducing it, changing it to prose?

DICKEY: It really wasn't a question of changing over from one thing to the other. It was a question of reconceiving it in terms of another medium. The poems that I wrote were as a kind of three-part sequence, as I remember, called "On the Coosawattee." The same events and circumstances and physical situation over twenty years ago in north Georgia were what I was trying to reconceive in terms of the novel.

INTERVIEWER: What do you feel *Deliverance* is going to say later on?

DICKEY: I don't know. It has been variously reviewed. I don't really read very many reviews of anything I write. If somebody comes up to me and says, "Jim, there's a fabulous review in the *Atlantic* and you must read it; he's crazy about the book," then I'll read it. If the guy says it's a horrible review and that I'm the anti-Christ himself, then I don't read it, because I don't want to go around filled with resentment against some stranger. That bleeds off your energies; you take them out in useless hatred. I need the energy for other things. I've known writers who are absolutely destroyed by adverse opinion, and I think this is a lot of shit. You shouldn't allow that to happen to yourself, and if you do, then it's *your* fault. My course is set; I know what I'm going to do. As Stephen Dedalus says, in *A Portrait of the Artist as a Young Man*, "I'm ready to make a lifelong mistake." I believe in making a lifelong mistake, but I don't believe in being guided by people who write about me. Why, there's not anything that could ever be said about a person either good or bad that hasn't been said about me. But it doesn't matter. I'm going to write my way, and if that doesn't agree with people's sensibilities or even their digestions, it doesn't make any difference to me. If it's a lifelong mistake, it won't be the first one that's been made.

INTERVIEWER: What sort of contribution do you, yourself, feel that *Deliverance* will make?

DICKEY: I'll tell you what I really tried to do in *Deliverance*.

My story is simple: there are bad people, there are monsters among us. *Deliverance* is really a novel about how decent men kill, and the fact that they get away with it raises a lot of questions about staying within the law—whether decent people have the right to go outside the law when they're encountering human monsters. I wrote *Deliverance* as a story where under the conditions of extreme violence people find out things about themselves that they would have no other means of knowing. The late John Berryman, who was a dear friend of mine, said that it bothered him more than anything else that a man could live in this culture all his life without knowing whether he's a coward or not. I think it's necessary to know.

INTERVIEWER: You don't feel, then, as some critics have said, that this particular work can be viewed as an exercise in violence?

DICKEY: No. At least not in the sense that Peckinpah's *Straw Dogs* is an exercise in violence. What I don't like about Sam's work is that it has that obvious element of contrivance in it. *Deliverance* is something that could happen. You run up against bad men who would just as soon shoot you as look at you. In fact, some of them would rather. So what do you do? This is a story about what you *do*.

INTERVIEWER: Do you feel that it is in the tradition of the grand male fraternity that dominates Hemingway's fiction?

DICKEY: Hemingway's people are bullfighters and boxers. Their *business* is violence. My men are decent guys. Lewis is a survival freak who is a nut on special disciplines, such as archery, canoeing, and so on. Suburban people, especially these fellows, are supposed to get out there and look at nature a little bit . . . have fun before it all disappears. Lewis might be a little obsessive about it. But the other guys—Ed Gentry, the narrator, for example, is just a decent guy with the job of providing for his family who happens to be fascinated with Lewis. Ed Gentry is not a bullfighter, a boxer, a tournament archer, or a racing canoeist. He's a guy who has a tangential relationship with these things that his obsessed buddy insists on talking about and doing. Drew is another decent guy, and is untroubled. He's America's own man. He's what the culture develops and the culture hopes for

. . . a decent family man, he tends to his business, he does his job, and he has a couple of mild hobbies, like playing the guitar. Bobby, the other fellow, is a fat, lecherous, country-club guy who never should have been up in the woods to begin with. We get those men together and we have them beset by the blind fury of two disgusting human beings; and we see what the decent guys do.

INTERVIEWER: Is this kind of a warning to us?

DICKEY: I don't know whether it is or not.

INTERVIEWER: Some people felt like it might have been a kind of social commentary, thinly disguised.

DICKEY: I don't know. My interest was in just simply writing the story, and letting the symbolism fall where it may. Hemingway was right about that. You don't try to build in, self-consciously, a bunch of preconceived symbols. If we make a real river, and real canoes, and real men, the real monsters, and real arrows, and real shotguns, and real woods, and real rapids and white water, then all the other stuff will take care of itself.

INTERVIEWER: What of your writing now? What's it like being a post-*Deliverance* writer?

DICKEY: It's not so bad. My preoccupation is with poetry, and everything else is a spin-off from that—novels, literary criticism, screenplays, whatever. If I lose poetry, which is the center of my creative wheel, I lose everything. I don't propose to let that happen. I want to write another book of poems, and then maybe have a big collection in a few years. Then I want to turn away from everything I've ever done in poetry and strike out in a completely new direction, if I can find what it is.

INTERVIEWER: Do you have any ideas?

DICKEY: The main thing in poetry is the discovery of an idiom and the exploitation of it over an area of thought for a long period of time. It is discovering an idom such as Christopher Marlowe did—he really discovered blank verse—that's important. He didn't do it all himself. He found it too early. But Shakespeare *did* do it. I want to get at a kind of new way of using the English language which would not be mannered in such a way as, say, John Berryman is mannered, and would not be so lax as, say, Randall

Jarrell is lax. I don't mean to make them into two possible poles, but we could use them as a starting place. There are some possibilities of the English language which have never even been hinted at. I don't know whether I can get at them or not. It may be a little like the blind man in the blacked-out room looking for the black cat that ain't there. That's very much the feeling I have, and yet I believe I can touch him every now and then. One of these days, I'm going to grab him.

INTERVIEWER: Who do you go back to and want to read again?

DICKEY: My writing really couldn't be assessed by what my tastes are, because I love to read and I'll read anything. I love to read good-bad poets, like Roy Campbell and Vachel Lindsay. If I want to turn my critical apparatus on and write an article, then I can turn my critical apparatus on and write an article. Nothing is easier. But I also like the thrill of a wide reading net, and a lot of the bad poets appeal to me just as much as the good ones do. This may be unfortunate.

INTERVIEWER: If you had to have a frank conversation with Berryman or Vachel Lindsay, what would you say to them?

DICKEY: I'll tell you what I would talk about with Berryman, if I could get him back. Of course, his body lies shattered on the ice of the midwinter Mississippi River. But Berryman was a man of intense friendships. His friendships meant more to him than his love affairs—more than anything else. His experience was very narrow. Sitting around drinking with Delmore Schwartz, or with Randall, or Lowell, was about as intense as John ever got. There was a poem of his in his posthumous book that was based on a phone call that I made to him when I was drunk and he was drunk, and it was a very moving thing for me to open up Berryman's posthumous book and to come upon a poem titled "Damn You, Jim D., You Woke Me Up." His friendships were all-important to him, and *that's* what I would talk to John Berryman about.

INTERVIEWER: How about Lindsay?

DICKEY: It would have to do with the relation of the poet to the public by means of the public reading, communicating with hundreds of strangers. Lindsay was the first great proponent and

probably the greatest practitioner of this form of human communication. The next great one was Dylan Thomas, who could
read, in his rich South Welsh voice, the telephone book and
make it sound like Scripture. People are very deeply moved by
the sound of the human voice that says—that seems to say—deep
rhythmical things. In my own time a whole generation of poets
has been sustained by public appearances and by the deep need
of people to be moved by true, imaginative words.

INTERVIEWER: You've known a great many poets personally.
Do you find some common characteristic—in their madness,
their vision, their discipline?

DICKEY: I would have to put the answer in the form of a paradox.
Most of them are what the world would call weak men and
women. They are wayward, licentious, heavy drinkers, irrespon-
sible, unable to maintain a household properly, and subject to
unpredictable vagaries of conduct. But, turning the coin to its
other side, the best of them are incredibly strong people who will
drive headfirst through a steel wall to get their work done. This
is the type of person I admire most. I admire the type as I do, I
suspect, because I am one of them.

INTERVIEWER: Do you keep in touch with fellow poets?

DICKEY: I am almost completely out of touch with them. They
often write to me, but because of my heavy schedule I almost
never have the time to answer. My correspondence deals with
current and future projects which I am embarked upon. I would
like nothing better than to engage in lengthy literary correspondence about time, life and its meaning, love, death, sex, and art
with poets such as Robert Lowell or James Wright, but I do not
have the time. I suspect that they don't either, but I like to think
that they would welcome such a correspondence, could it be
done. But it can't. My letters should never be collected, for most
of them concern business, which is a very dull subject, for me
no less than for anyone else who might be so underprivileged as
to read them.

INTERVIEWER: We've talked a good deal about American poets,
but English poets are always on the scene; some critics contend
that the best contemporary English poet is Philip Larkin.

DICKEY: Oh, my Lord. Philip Larkin is a small kind of *vers de société* writer. He's one of these Englishmen of the welfare state who write self-effacing poems about how much he hates his record collection. That's not what we need. We need something that will affirm the basic possibility. This self-effacing stuff is so god-damned easy, it's tiresome.

INTERVIEWER: Is this the same poetic attitude you were dis-cussing when, in reviewing James Merrill, you said, "his char-acters are always coming across each other in museums"?

DICKEY: That's right. But I don't have anything against Philip Larkin, or Ted Hughes—who's different. He's a guy who has a kind of ersatz violence that's equally easy to do. Hughes writes the kind of stuff I throw away. Larkin's all right; he's pleasant and kind of low-key—but that's all. No, no, the only really good guy over there and the only one who has any originality or interest in me is W. S. Graham, the Scottish poet. He's the real stuff.

INTERVIEWER: Why do you like Graham?

DICKEY: He has an original language. He can say amazing things. Larkin can't say anything amazing. Ted Hughes gives you the effect of a weight lifter who can't get the weight up.

INTERVIEWER: If there is a direction now in America, what do you think it is?

DICKEY: It could be toward some new and strange simplicity. Stafford has made a run at it.

INTERVIEWER: Is the country more a part of it than the city?

DICKEY: You have to keep to your sources as a writer. There are good writers who have the urban consciousness. John Hol-lander is one of them. He's a very fine writer. Auden is another one. He's always a little bit embarrassed by landscapes, or moun-tains or rivers, or any of the big natural forms.

INTERVIEWER: Except Iceland.

DICKEY: Yes, except Iceland. I don't know what he *did* in Iceland, or what he saw up there, but he was always a little bit embarrassed by nature, and he'd rather write about the city and the glass and chromium kind of culture we have. He didn't like it, but he was *used* to it and he knew it. I think the really good poets of now, and the ones who are going to be good, are going to be poets of dying nature. They're going to be like Lewis in *Deliverance*: people who are paranoid about getting out and seeing a bit of this world before it disappears. I think the great poet, who is going to come, is going to be the poet who can see in a single grass blade—a single surviving grass blade—heaven and earth, or the lost paradise. There are not going to be that many more grass blades. The animals are going, the trees are going, the flowers are going, everything is going. So the poet who is going to be the great poet of the future is going to be that poet who can tell us what that last grass blade, popping up through the cement, means—*really*.

INTERVIEWER: In *This Is My Best*, in which you are collected, you said that you considered "The May Day Sermon" to be your best poem. Do you still?

DICKEY: Yes I do. Certainly. It's the best I can do—my big effort.

INTERVIEWER: Why does it work for you?

DICKEY: I think because it's got that kind of poetical wildness that I seek for. "Falling" has some of it also.

INTERVIEWER: What do you mean by "wildness"?

DICKEY: Something that no one could imagine if he hadn't felt it. It's really a kind of madness I feel when I'm writing. It's not an induced madness from alcohol or other things of that nature. I don't know what it is, but it lets me achieve the kind of thing I did in "Falling," and especially in "The May Day Sermon."

INTERVIEWER: You've talked about age being the great enemy, and here you are fifty years old.

DICKEY: Well, for me it can go two ways. One of them is that I'm at the end, right now, and I've already said my thing and there's no more for me to do. The other side of the coin is that I'm at the beginning, that I have finally arrived at the beginning and it's all to do yet, and what I've done up to this time is nothing at all compared to what might be possible. I think it's necessary for a writer to have this sense of possibility and also to have the sense of being finished, because you don't know which it is.

INTERVIEWER: What are you working on now?

DICKEY: A poem called "The Zodiac." It's about twenty-five

pages long, and it's far better than "The May Day Sermon"
. . . if I can just last. It is the best I can do. . . . But boy, I'll
tell you, the thing that is exciting to me is that I have spent fifty
years crawling up the hill of Parnassus on my hands and knees,
and now I want to see if I can fly.

—FRANKLIN ASHLEY
1976

14. Elizabeth Bishop

Elizabeth Bishop's father died eight months after her birth in April, 1911, and her mother spent long periods in mental institutions during Elizabeth's childhood. She was essentially juggled from relative to relative until her boarding-school years, a history which may explain the importance of travel to both her life and poetry. At Vassar College, from which she graduated in 1934, she met Marianne Moore, with whom she formed a lifelong friendship. Though she majored in music composition and intended to become a composer, Bishop continued to write extensively; she published her first poems long before she earned her degree. Her first collection, *North & South*, which was published in 1946, won the Houghton Mifflin Poetry Award; the following year she was awarded a Guggenheim Fellowship, the first of two she was to be granted. In 1956 she won the Pulitzer Prize for her second volume, *Poems*, and in 1969 she won the National Book Award for *The Complete Poems*, a collection titled with characteristic irony. The recipient of many grants and fellowships, she became the first woman—in fact, the first American—to win the prestigious Books Abroad/Neustadt International Prize for Literature. *Geography III* was her last book before her sudden death in 1979.

Bishop's ties to South America were strong, and she translated much Brazilian literature, including *The Diary of "Helena Morley."* She served as consultant in poetry to the Library of Congress (1949–50) before accepting teaching posts at Harvard, New York University, and The Massachusetts Institute of Technology.

An indefatigable traveler, Elizabeth Bishop lived in New York, Boston, and Key West, although from 1952 until 1971 she considered her home Rio de Janeiro.

A manuscript page from Elizabeth Bishop's "Sonnet," published in 1979.

Elizabeth Bishop

The interview took place at Lewis Wharf, Boston, on the afternoon of June 28, 1978, three days before Miss Bishop and two friends were to leave for North Haven, a Maine island in Penobscot Bay where she summered. Her living room, on the fourth floor of Lewis Wharf, had a spectacular view of Boston Harbor; when I arrived, she immediately took me out on the balcony to point out such Boston landmarks as Old North Church in the distance, mentioning that "Old Ironsides" was moored nearby.

Her living room was spacious and attractive, with wide-planked polished floors, a beamed ceiling, two old brick walls, and one wall of books. Besides some comfortable modern furniture, the room included a jacaranda rocker and other old pieces from Brazil, two paintings by Loren MacIver, a giant horse conch from Key West, and a Franklin stove with firewood in a donkey pannier, also from Brazil. The most conspicuous piece was a large carved figurehead of an unknown beast, open-mouthed, with horns and blue eyes, which hung on one wall below the ceiling.

Her study, a smaller room down the hall, was in a state of disorder. Literary magazines, books, and papers were piled everywhere. Photographs of Marianne Moore, Robert Lowell, and other friends hung on the walls; one of Dom Pedro, the last emperor of Brazil, she especially liked to show to her Brazilian visitors. "Most have no idea who he is," she said. "This is after he abdicated and shortly before he died—he looked very sad." Her desk was tucked in a far corner by the only window, also with a north view of the harbor.

At sixty-seven, Miss Bishop was easily and accurately described by the word "striking," her short, swept-back white hair setting off an unforgettably noble face. She was wearing a black tunic shirt, gold watch and earrings, gray slacks, and flat brown Japanese sandals which made her appear shorter than her actual height: five feet, four inches. Although she looked well and was in high spirits, she complained of having had a recent hay fever attack and declined to have her photograph taken with the wry comment, "Photographers, insurance salesmen, and funeral directors are the worst forms of life."

Seven or eight months later, after reading a profile I had written for The Vassar Quarterly *(which had been based on this interview) and worrying that she sounded like "the soul of frivolity," she wrote me: "I once admired an interview with Fred Astaire in which he refused to discuss 'the dance,' his partners, or his 'career' and stuck determinedly to golf—so I hope that some readers will realize I do think about ART once in a while even if babbling along like a very shallow brook . . ."*

Note: Though Miss Bishop did have the opportunity of correcting those portions of this interview incorporated in the Vassar Quarterly *article, she never saw it in this form.*

INTERVIEWER: Your living room seems to be a wonderful combination of the old and new. Is there a story behind any of the pieces, especially that figurehead? It's quite imposing.

BISHOP: I lived in an extremely modern house in Brazil. It was very beautiful and when I finally moved I brought back things I liked best. So it's just a kind of mixture. I really like modern things but while I was there I acquired so many other things I couldn't bear to give them up. This figurehead is from the São Francisco River. Some are more beautiful; this is a very ugly one.

INTERVIEWER: Is it supposed to ward off evil spirits?

BISHOP: Yes, I think so. They were used for about fifty years on one section, two or three hundred miles, of the river. It's nothing compared to the Amazon but it's the next biggest river in Brazil. This figurehead is primitive folk art. I think I even know who made it. There was a black man who carved twenty or thirty, and it's exactly his style. Some of them are made of much more beautiful wood. There's a famous one called "The Red Horse" made of jacaranda. It's beautiful, a great thing like this one, a horse with its mouth open, but for some reason they all just disappeared. I made a week-long trip on that river in 1967 and didn't see one. The riverboat, a sternwheeler, had been built in 1880—something for the Mississippi, and you can't believe how tiny it was. We splashed along slowly for days and days . . . a very funny trip.

INTERVIEWER: Did you spend so much of your life traveling because you were looking for a perfect place?

BISHOP: No, I don't think so. I really haven't traveled that much. It just happened that although I wasn't rich I had a very small income from my father, who died when I was eight months old, and it was enough when I got out of college to go places on. And I traveled extremely cheaply. I could get along in Brazil for some years but now I couldn't possibly live on it. But the biographical sketch in the first anthology I was in said, "Oh, she's been to Morocco, Spain, etc." and this has been repeated for years even though I haven't been back to any of these places. But I never traveled the way students travel now. Compared to my students, who seem to go to Nepal every Easter vacation, I haven't been anywhere at all.

INTERVIEWER: Well, it always sounds as if you're very adventurous.

BISHOP: I want to do the Upper Amazon. Maybe I will. You start from Peru and go down—

INTERVIEWER: Do you write when you're actually traveling?

BISHOP: Yes, sometimes. It depends. I usually take notes but not always. And I keep a kind of diary. The two trips I've made that I liked best were the Amazon trip and one to the Galapagos Islands three or four years ago . . . I'd like very much to go back to Italy again because I haven't seen nearly enough of it. And Sicily. Venice is wonderful. Florence is rather strenuous, I think. I was last there in '64 with my Brazilian friend. We rented a car and did northern Italy for five or six weeks. We didn't go to Rome. I *must* go back. There are so many things I haven't seen yet. I like painting probably better than I like poetry. And I haven't been back to Paris for years. I don't like the prices!

INTERVIEWER: You mentioned earlier that you're leaving for North Haven in several days. Will this be a "working vacation"?

BISHOP: This summer I want to do a lot of work because I really haven't done anything for ages and there are a couple of things I'd like to finish before I die. Two or three poems and two long stories. Maybe three. I sometimes feel that I shouldn't keep going back to this place that I found just by chance through an ad in the Harvard *Crimson*. I should probably go to see some more art, cathedrals, and so on. But I'm so crazy about it that I keep going back. You can see the water, a great expanse of water and fields from the house. Islands are beautiful. Some of them come right up, granite, and then dark firs. North Haven isn't like that exactly, but it's very beautiful. The island is sparsely inhabited and a lot of the people who have homes there are fearfully rich. Probably if it weren't for these people the island would be deserted the way a great many Maine islands are, because the village is very tiny. But the inhabitants almost all work—they're lobstermen but they work as caretakers. . . . The electricity there is rather sketchy. Two summers ago it was one hour on, one hour off. There I was with *two* electric typewriters and I couldn't keep working. There was a cartoon in the grocery store—it's eighteen miles from the mainland—a man in a hardware store saying, "I want an extension cord eighteen miles long!" Last year they did plug into the main-land—they put in cables. But once in a while the power still goes off.

INTERVIEWER: So you compose on the typewriter?

BISHOP: I can write prose on a typewriter. Not poetry. Nobody can read my writing so I write letters on it. And I've finally trained myself so I can write prose on it and then correct a great deal. But for poetry I use a pen. About halfway through sometimes I'll type out a few lines to see how they look.

William Carlos Williams wrote entirely on the typewriter. Robert Lowell printed—he never learned to write. He printed everything.

INTERVIEWER: You've never been as prolific as many of your contemporaries. Do you start a lot of poems and finish very few?

BISHOP: Yes. Alas, yes. I begin lots of things and then I give up on them. The last few years I haven't written as much because of teaching. I'm hoping that now that I'm free and have a Guggenheim I'll do a lot more.

INTERVIEWER: How long did it take you to finish "The Moose"?

BISHOP: That was funny. I started that *years* ago—twenty years ago, at least—I had a stack of notes, the first two or three stanzas, and the last.

INTERVIEWER: It's such a dreamy poem. It seems to move the way a bus moves.

BISHOP: It was all true. The bus trip took place before I went to Brazil. I went up to visit my aunt. Actually, I was on the wrong bus. I went to the right place but it wasn't the express I was supposed to get. It went roundabout and it was all exactly the way I described it, except that I say "seven relatives." Well, they weren't really relatives, they were various stepsons and so on, but that's the only thing that isn't quite true. I wanted to finish it because I liked it, but I could never seem to get the middle part, to get from one place to the other. And then when I was still living in Cambridge I was asked to give the Phi Beta Kappa poem at Harvard. I was rather pleased and I remembered that I had another unfinished poem. It's about whales and it was written a long time ago, too. I'm afraid I'll never publish it because it looks as if I were just trying to be up-to-date now that whales are a "cause."

INTERVIEWER: But it's finished now?

BISHOP: I think I could finish it very easily. I'm going to take it to Maine with me. I think I'll date it or nobody will believe I started it so long ago. At the time, though, I couldn't find the one about whales—this was in '73 or '74, I think—so I dug out "The Moose" and thought, "Maybe I can finish it," and I did. The day of the ceremony for Phi Beta Kappa (which I'd never made in college) we were all sitting on the platform at Sanders Theater. And the man who had asked me to give the poem leaned across the president and said to me whispering, "What is the name of your poem?" I said, " 'The Moose,' M-o-o-s-e," and he got up and introduced me and said, "Miss Bishop will now read a poem called, 'The *Moos*.' " Well, I choked and my hat was too big. And later the newspaper account read, "Miss Bishop read a poem called 'The Moose' and the tassle of her mortarboard swung back and forth over her face like a windshield wiper"!

The Glee Club was behind us and they sang rather badly, I thought, everybody thought. A friend of mine who couldn't come to this occasion but worked in one of the Harvard houses and knew some of the boys in the Glee Club asked one of them when they came back in their red jackets, "Well, how was it?" He said, "Oh, it was all right but we didn't sing well"—which was true— and then he said, "A woman read a poem." My friend said, "How was it?" And he said, "Well, as poems go, it wasn't bad"!

INTERVIEWER: Have you ever had any poems that were gifts? Poems that seemed to write themselves?

BISHOP: Oh yes. Once in a while it happens. I wanted to write a villanelle all my life but I never could. I'd start them but for some reason I never could finish them. And one day I couldn't believe it—it was like writing a letter.* There was one rhyme I couldn't get that ended in e-n-t and a friend of mine, the poet Frank Bidart, came to see me and I said, "Frank, give me a

---

* The poem is "One Art," in *Geography III*.

rhyme." He gave me a word offhand and I put it in. But neither he nor I can remember which word it was. But that kind of thing doesn't happen very often. Maybe some poets always write that way. I don't know.

INTERVIEWER: Didn't you used to give Marianne Moore rhymes?

BISHOP: Yes, when she was doing the LaFontaine translations. She'd call me up and read me something when I was in New York—I was in Brazil most of that time—and say she needed a rhyme. She said that she admired rhymes and meters very much. It was hard to tell whether she was pulling your leg or not sometimes. She was Celtic enough to be somewhat mysterious about these things.

INTERVIEWER: Critics often talk about your more recent poems being less formal, more "open," so to speak. They point out that *Geography III* has more of "you" in it, a wider emotional range. Do you agree with these perceptions?

BISHOP: This is what critics say. I've never written the things I'd like to write that I've admired all my life. Maybe one never does. Critics say the most incredible things!

INTERVIEWER: I've been reading a critical book about you that Anne Stevenson wrote. She said that in your poems nature was neutral.

BISHOP: Yes, I remember the word "neutral." I wasn't quite sure what she meant by that.

INTERVIEWER: I thought she might have meant that if nature is neutral there isn't any guiding spirit or force.

BISHOP: Somebody famous—I can't think who it was—somebody extremely famous was asked if he had one question to ask the Sphinx and get an answer, what would it be? And he said, "Is nature for us or against us?" Well, I've never really thought about it one way or the other. I like the country, the seashore especially, and if I could drive, I'd probably be living in the country. Unfortunately, I've never learned to drive. I bought two cars. At least. I had a MG I adored for some years in Brazil. We lived on top of a mountain peak, and it took an hour to get somewhere where I could practice. And nobody really had time to take an afternoon off and give me driving lessons. So I never got my license. And I *never* would have driven in Rio, anyway. But if you can't drive, you can't live in the country.

INTERVIEWER: Do you have the painting here that your uncle did? The one "about the size of an old-style dollar bill" that you wrote about in "Poem"?

BISHOP: Oh, sure. Do you want to see it? It's not good enough to hang. Actually, he was my great-uncle. I never met him.

INTERVIEWER: The cows in this really are just one or two brushstrokes!

BISHOP: I exaggerated a little bit. There's a detail in the poem that isn't in the painting. I can't remember what it is now. My uncle did another painting when he was fourteen or fifteen years old that I wrote about in an early poem ["Large Bad Picture"]. An aunt who lived in Montreal had both of these and they used to hang in her front hall. I was dying to get them and I went there once and tried to buy them, but she wouldn't sell them to me. She was rather stingy. She died some years ago. I don't know who has the large one now.

INTERVIEWER: When you were showing me your study, I noticed a shadow-box hanging in the hall. Is it by Joseph Cornell?

BISHOP: No, I did that one. That's one of my little works. It's about infant mortality in Brazil. It's called *anjinhos*, which means "little angels." That's what they call the babies and small children who die.

INTERVIEWER: What's the significance of the various objects?

BISHOP: I found the child's sandal on a beach wading east of Rio one Christmas and I finally decided to do something with it. The pacifier was bright red rubber. They sell them in big bottles and jars in drugstores in Brazil. I decided it couldn't be red, so I dyed it black with India ink. A nephew of my Brazilian friend, a very smart young man, came to call while I was doing this. He brought two American rock-and-roll musicians and we talked and talked and talked, and I never thought to explain in all the time they were there what I was doing. When they left, I thought, "My God, they must think I'm a witch or something!"

INTERVIEWER: What about the little bowls and skillets filled with rice?

BISHOP: Oh, they're just things children would be playing with. And of course rice and black beans are what Brazilians eat every day.

Cornell is superb. I first saw the *Medici Slot Machine* when I was in college. Oh, I loved it. To think one could have *bought* some of those things then. He was very strange. He got crushes on opera singers and ballet dancers. When I looked at his show in New York two years ago I nearly fainted, because one of my favorite books is a book he liked and used. It's a little book by an English scientist who wrote for children about soap bubbles [*Soap Bubbles; their colours and the forces which mold them,* by Sir C. V. Boys, 1889].

His sister began writing me after she read Octavio Paz's poem for Cornell that I translated. (She doesn't read Spanish.) She sent me a German-French grammar that apparently he meant to do something with and never did. A lot of the pages were folded over and they're all made into star patterns with red ink around them. . . . He lived in what was called Elysian Park. That's an awfully strange address to have.

INTERVIEWER: Until recently, you were one of the few American poets who didn't make their living teaching or giving readings. What made you decide to start doing both?

BISHOP: I never wanted to teach in my life. I finally did because I wanted to leave Brazil and I needed the money. Since 1970 I've just been *swamped* with people sending me poems. They start to when they know you're in the country. I used to get them in Brazil, but not so much. They got lost in the mail quite often. I don't believe in teaching poetry at all, but that's what they want one to do. You see so many poems every week, you just lose all sense of judgment.

As for readings, I gave a reading in 1947 at Wellesley College two months after my first book appeared. And I was *sick* for days ahead of time. Oh, it was absurd. And then I did one in Washington in '49 and I was sick again and nobody could hear me.

And then I didn't give any for twenty-six years. I don't mind reading now. I've gotten over my shyness a little bit. I think teaching helps. I've noticed that teachers aren't shy. They're rather aggressive. They get to be, finally.

INTERVIEWER: Did you ever take a writing course as a student?

BISHOP: When I went to Vassar I took sixteenth-century, seventeenth-century, and eighteenth-century literature, and then a course in the novel. The kind of courses where you have to do a lot of reading. I don't think I believe in writing courses at all. There weren't any when I was there. There was a poetry-writing course in the evening, but not for credit. A couple of my friends went to it, but I never did.

The word "creative" drives me crazy. I don't like to regard it as therapy. I was in the hospital several years ago and somebody gave me Kenneth Koch's book, *Rose, Where Did You Get That Red?* And it's true, children sometimes write wonderful things, paint wonderful pictures, but I think they should be *dis*couraged. From everything I've read and heard, the number of students in English departments taking literature courses has been falling off enormously. But at the same time the number of people who want to get in the writing classes seems to get bigger and bigger. There are usually two or three being given at Harvard every year. I'd get forty applicants for ten or twelve places. Fifty. It got bigger and bigger. I don't know if they do this to offset practical concerns, or what.

INTERVIEWER: I think people want to be able to say they do something creative like throw pots or write poems.

BISHOP: I just came back in March from reading in North Carolina and Arkansas, and I swear if I see any more handcrafts I'll go mad! I think we should go right straight back to the machine. You can only use so many leather belts, after all. I'm sorry. Maybe you do some of these things.

INTERVIEWER: Do many strangers send you poems?

BISHOP: Yes. It's very hard to know what to do. Sometimes I answer. I had a fan letter the other day, and it was adorable. It was in this childish handwriting. His name was Jimmy Sparks and he was in the sixth grade. He said his class was putting together a booklet of poems and he liked my poems very much—he mentioned three—because they rhymed and because they were about nature. His letter was so cute I did send him a postcard. I think he was supposed to ask me to send a handwritten poem or photograph—schools do this all the time—but he didn't say anything like that, and I'm sure he forgot his mission.

INTERVIEWER: What three poems did he like? "The Sandpiper"?

BISHOP: Yes, and the one about the mirror and the moon, "Insomnia," which Marianne Moore said was a cheap love poem.

INTERVIEWER: The one that ends, ". . . and you love me"?

BISHOP: Yes. I never liked that. I almost left it out. But last year it was put to music by Elliott Carter along with five other poems of mine* and it sounded much better as a song. Yes, Marianne was very opposed to that one.

INTERVIEWER: Maybe she didn't like the last line.

BISHOP: I don't think she ever believed in talking about the emotions much.

INTERVIEWER: Getting back to teaching, did you devise formal assignments when you taught at Harvard? For example, to write a villanelle?

BISHOP: Yes, I made out a whole list of weekly assignments that I gave the class; but every two or three weeks was a free assignment and they could hand in what they wanted. Some classes were so prolific that I'd declare a moratorium. I'd say, "Please, nobody write a poem for two weeks!"

INTERVIEWER: Do you think you can generalize that beginning writers write better in forms than not?

BISHOP: I don't know. We did a sestina—we started one in class by drawing words out of a hat—and I wish I'd never suggested it because it seemed to have *swept* Harvard. Later, in the applications for my class, I'd get dozens of sestinas. The students seemed to think it was my favorite form—which it isn't.

INTERVIEWER: I once tried a sestina about a woman who watches soap operas all day.

* "Anaphora," "The Sandpiper," "Argument," "O Breath," and "View of the Capitol from The Library of Congress."

BISHOP: Did you watch them in college?

INTERVIEWER: No.

BISHOP: Well, it seemed to be a fad at Harvard. Two or three years ago I taught a course in prose and discovered my students were watching the soap operas every morning and afternoon. I don't know when they studied. So I watched two or three just to see what was going on. They were *boring*. And the advertising! One student wrote a story about an old man who was getting ready to have an old lady to dinner (except she was really a ghost), and he polished a plate till he could see his face in it. It was quite well done, so I read some of it aloud, and said, "But look, this is impossible. You can never see your face in a plate." The whole class, in unison, said, "Joy!" I said, "What? What are you talking about?" Well, it seems there's an ad for Joy soap liquid in which a woman holds up a plate and sees—you know the one? Even so, you can't! I found this very disturbing. TV was *real* and no one had observed that it wasn't. Like when Aristotle was right and no one pointed out, for centuries, that women *don't* have fewer teeth than men.

I had a friend bring me a small TV, black and white, when I was living in Brazil. We gave it to the maid almost immediately because we only watched it when there were things like political speeches, or a revolution coming on. But she loved it. She slept with it in her bed! I think it meant so much to her because she couldn't read. There was a soap opera that year called "The Right to Life." It changed the whole schedule of Rio society's hours because it was on from eight to nine. The usual dinner hour's eight, so either you had to eat dinner before so that the maid could watch "The Right to Life" or eat much later, when it was over. We ate dinner about ten o'clock finally so that Joanna could watch this thing. I finally decided I had to see it, too. It became a chic thing to do and everybody was talking about it. It was absolutely ghastly! They got the programs from Mexico and dubbed them in Portuguese. They were very corny and always very lurid. Corpses lying in coffins, miracles, nuns, even incest.

I had friends in Belo Horizonte and the mother and their cook and a grandchild would watch the soap operas, the *novellas*, they're called, every night. The cook would get so excited she'd talk to the screen: "No! No! Don't do that! You know he's a bad man, Doña So-and-so!" They'd get so excited, they'd cry. And I knew of two old ladies, sisters, who got a TV. They'd knit and knit and watch it and cry and one of them would get up and say, "Excuse me, I have to go to the bathroom," to the television!

INTERVIEWER: You were living in Brazil, weren't you, when you won the Pulitzer Prize in 1956?

BISHOP: Yes, it was pretty funny. We lived on top of a mountain peak—really way up in the air. I was alone in the house with Maria, the cook. A friend had gone to market. The telephone rang. It was a newsman from the American Embassy and he asked me who it was in English, and of course it was very rare to hear someone speak in English. He said, "Do you know you've won the Pulitzer Prize?" Well, I thought it was a joke. I said, "Oh, come on." And he said, "Don't you hear me?" The telephone connection was very bad and he was shrieking. And I said, "Oh, it can't be." But he said it wasn't a joke. I couldn't make an impression on Maria with this news, but I felt I had to share it, so I hurried down the mountain a half mile or so to the next house, but no one was at home. I thought I should do something to celebrate, have a glass of wine or something. But all I could find in that house, a friend's, were some cookies from America, some awful chocolate cookies—Oreos, I think—so I ended up eating two of those. And that's how I celebrated winning the Pulitzer Prize.

The next day there was a picture in the afternoon paper—they take such things very seriously in Brazil—and the day after that my Brazilian friend went to market again. There was a big covered market with stalls for every kind of comestible, and there was one vegetable man we always went to. He said, "Wasn't that Doña Elizabetchy's picture in the paper yesterday?" She said, "Yes, it was. She won a prize." And he said, "You know, it's amazing! Last week Señora (Somebody) took a chance on a bicycle and *she* won! My customers are so lucky!" Isn't that marvelous?!

INTERVIEWER: I'd like to talk a little bit about your stories, especially "In the Village," which I've always admired. Do you see any connection, other than the obvious one of shared subject matter, between your stories and poems? In "method of attack," for example?

BISHOP: They're very closely related. I suspect that some of the stories I've written are actually prose poems and not very good stories. I have four about Nova Scotia. One came out last year in the *Southern Review.* I'm working on a long one now that I hope to finish this summer. . . . "In the Village" was funny. I had made notes for various bits of it and was given too much cortisone—I have very bad asthma from time to time—and you don't need any sleep. You feel wonderful while it's going on, but to get off it is awful. So I couldn't sleep much and I sat up all night in the tropical heat. The story came from a combination of cortisone, I think, and the gin and tonic I drank in the middle of the night. I wrote it in two nights.

INTERVIEWER: That's incredible! It's a long, long story.

BISHOP: Extraordinary. I wish I could do it again but I'll never take cortisone again, if I can possibly avoid it.

INTERVIEWER: I'm always interested in how different poets go about writing about their childhood.

BISHOP: Everybody does. You can't help it, I suppose. You are fearfully observant then. You notice all kinds of things, but there's no way of putting them all together. My memories of some of those days are so much clearer than things that happened in 1950, say. I don't think one should make a cult of writing about childhood, however. I've always tried to avoid it. I find I have written some, I must say. I went to an analyst for a couple of years off and on in the forties, a very nice woman who was especially interested in writers, writers and blacks. She said it was amazing that I would remember things that happened to me when I was two. It's very rare, but apparently writers often do.

INTERVIEWER: Do you know what your earliest memory is?

BISHOP: I think I remember learning to walk. My mother was away and my grandmother was trying to encourage me to walk. It was in Canada and she had lots of plants in the window the way all ladies do there. I can remember this blur of plants and my grandmother holding out her arms. I must have toddled. It seems to me it's a memory. It's very hazy. I told my grandmother years and years later and she said, "Yes, you did learn to walk while your mother was visiting someone." But you walk when you're one, don't you?

I remember my mother taking me for a ride on the swan boats here in Boston. I think I was three then. It was before we went back to Canada. Mother was dressed all in black—widows were in those days. She had a box of mixed peanuts and raisins. There were real swans floating around. I don't think they have them anymore. A swan came up and she fed it and it bit her finger. Maybe she just told me this, but I believed it because she showed me her black kid glove and said, "See." The finger was split. Well, I was thrilled to death! Robert Lowell put those swan boats in two or three of the *Lord Weary's Castle* poems.

INTERVIEWER: Your childhood was difficult, and yet in many of your stories and poems about that time there's a tremendously lyrical quality as well as a great sense of loss and tragedy.

BISHOP: My father died, my mother went crazy when I was four or five years old. My relatives, I think they all felt so sorry for this child that they tried to do their very best. And I think they did. I lived with my grandparents in Nova Scotia. Then I lived with the ones in Worcester, Massachusetts, very briefly, and got terribly sick. This was when I was six and seven. Then I lived with my mother's older sister in Boston. I used to go to Nova Scotia for the summer. When I was twelve or thirteen I was improved enough to go to summer camp at Wellfleet until I went away to school when I was fifteen or sixteen. My aunt was devoted to me and she was awfully nice. She was married and had no children. But my relationship with my relatives—I was always a sort of a guest, and I think I've always felt like that.

INTERVIEWER: Was your adolescence a calmer time?

BISHOP: I was very romantic. I once walked from Nauset Light— I don't think it exists anymore—which is the beginning of the elbow [of Cape Cod], to the tip, Provincetown, all alone. It took me a night and a day. I went swimming from time to time but at that time the beach was absolutely deserted. There wasn't anything on the back shore, no buildings.

INTERVIEWER: How old would you have been?

BISHOP: Seventeen or eighteen. That's why I'd never go back—because I can't bear to think of the way it is now. . . . I haven't been to Nantucket since, well, I hate to say. My senior year at college I went there for Christmas with my then boyfriend. Nobody knew we were there. It was this wonderful, romantic trip. We went the day after Christmas and stayed for about a week. It was terribly cold but beautiful. We took long walks on the moors. We stayed at a very nice inn and we thought that probably the landlady would throw us out (we were very young and this kind of thing wasn't so common then). We had a bottle of sherry or something innocent like that. On New Year's Eve about ten o'clock there was a knock on the door. It was our landlady with a tray of hot grogs! She came in and we had the loveliest time. She knew the people who ran the museum and they opened it for us. There are a couple of wonderful museums there.

INTERVIEWER: I heard a story that you once spent a night in a tree at Vassar outside Cushing dormitory. Is it true?

BISHOP: Yes, it was me, me and a friend whose name I can't remember. We really were crazy and those trees were wonderful to climb. I used to be a great tree climber. Oh, we probably gave up about three in the morning. How did that ever get around? I can't imagine! We stopped being friends afterwards. Well, actually she had invited two boys from West Point for the weekend and I found myself *stuck* with this youth all in—[her hands draw an imagined cape and uniform in the air]—the dullest boy! I didn't know what to say! I nearly went mad. I think I sort of dropped the friend at that point. . . . I lived in a great big corner room on the top floor of Cushing and I apparently had registered a little late because I had a roommate whom I had never wanted to have. A strange girl named Constance. I remember her entire side of the room was furnished in Scotty dogs—pillows, pictures, engravings, and photographs. And mine was rather bare. Except that I probably wasn't a good roommate either, because I had a theory at that time that one should write down all one's dreams. That that was the way to write poetry. So I kept a notebook of my dreams and thought if you ate a lot of awful cheese at bedtime you'd have interesting dreams. I went to Vassar with a pot about this big—it did have a cover!—of Roquefort cheese that I kept in the bottom of my bookcase. . . . I think everyone's given to eccentricities at that age. I've heard that at Oxford Auden slept with a revolver under his pillow.

INTERVIEWER: As a young woman, did you have a sense of yourself as a writer?

BISHOP: No, it all just happens without your thinking about it. I never meant to go to Brazil. I never meant doing any of these things. I'm afraid in my life everything has just *happened*.

INTERVIEWER: You like to think there are reasons—

BISHOP: Yes, that people plan ahead, but I'm afraid I really didn't.

INTERVIEWER: But you'd always been interested in writing?

BISHOP: I'd written since I was a child but when I went to Vassar I was going to be a composer. I'd studied music at Walnut Hill and had a rather good teacher. I'd had a year of counterpoint and I also played the piano. At Vassar you had to perform in public once a month. Well, this terrified me. I really was sick. So I played once and then I gave up the piano because I couldn't bear it. I don't think I'd mind now, but I can't play the piano anymore. Then the next year I switched to English.

It was a very literary class. Mary McCarthy was a year ahead of me. Eleanor Clark was in my class. And Muriel Rukeyser, for freshman year. We started a magazine you may have heard of, *Con Spirito*. I think I was a junior then. There were six or seven of us—Mary, Eleanor Clark and her older sister, my friends Margaret Miller and Frani Blough, and a couple of others. It was during Prohibition and we used to go downtown to a speakeasy and drink wine out of teacups. That was our big vice. Ghastly stuff! Most of us had submitted things to the *Vassar Review* and they'd been turned down. It was very old-fashioned then. We were all rather put out because *we* thought we were good. So we thought, Well, we'll start our own magazine. We thought it would be nice to have it anonymous, which it was. After its third issue the *Vassar Review* came around and a couple of our editors became editors on it and then they published things by us. But we had a wonderful time doing it while it lasted.

INTERVIEWER: I read in another interview you gave that you had enrolled or were ready to enroll after college in Cornell Medical School.

BISHOP: I think I had all the forms. This was the year after I had graduated from Vassar. But then I discovered I would have to take German and I'd already given up on German once, I thought it was so difficult. And I would have had to take another year of chemistry. I'd already published a few things and I think Marianne [Moore] discouraged me, and I didn't go. I just went off to Europe instead.

INTERVIEWER: Did the Depression have much reality for college students in the thirties?

BISHOP: Everybody was frantic trying to get jobs. All the intellectuals were Communist except me. I'm always very perverse so I went in for T. S. Eliot and Anglo-Catholicism. But the spirit was pretty radical. It's funny. The girl who was the biggest radical—she was a year ahead of me—has been married for years and years to one of the heads of Time-Life. I've forgotten his name. He's very famous and couldn't be more conservative. He writes shocking editorials. I can still see her standing outside the library with a tambourine collecting money for this cause and that cause.

INTERVIEWER: Wanting to be a composer, a doctor, or a writer—how do you account for it?

BISHOP: Oh, I was interested in all those things. I'd like to be a painter most, I think. I never really sat down and said to myself, "I'm going to be a poet." Never in my life. I'm still surprised that people think I am. . . . I started publishing things in my senior year, I think, and I remember my first check for thirty-five dollars and that was rather an exciting moment. It was from something called *The Magazine*, published in California. They took a poem, they took a story—oh, I wish those poems had never been published! They're terrible! I did show the check to my roommate.

I was on the newspaper, *The Miscellany*—and I really was, I don't know, mysterious. On the newspaper board they used to sit around and talk about how they could get published and so on and so on. I'd just hold my tongue. I was embarrassed by it. And still am. There's nothing more embarrassing than being a poet, really.

INTERVIEWER: It's especially difficult to tell people you're meeting for the first time that that's what you do.

BISHOP: Just last week a friend and I went to visit a wonderful lady I know in Quebec. She's seventy-four or seventy-five. And she didn't say this to me but she said to my friend, Alice, "I'd like to ask my neighbor who has the big house next door to dinner, and she's so nice, but she'd be bound to ask Elizabeth what she does and if Elizabeth said she wrote poetry, the poor woman wouldn't say another word all evening!" This is awful, you know, and I think no matter how modest you think you feel or how minor you think you are, there must be an awful core of ego somewhere for you to set yourself up to write poetry. I've never *felt* it, but it must be there.

INTERVIEWER: In your letter to me, you sounded rather wary of interviewers. Do you feel you've been misrepresented in interviews? For example, that your refusal to appear in all-women poetry anthologies has been misunderstood as a kind of disapproval of the feminist movement.

BISHOP: I've always considered myself a strong feminist. Recently I was interviewed by a reporter from *The Chicago Tribune*. After I talked to the girl for a few minutes, I realized that she wanted to play me off as an "old-fashioned" against Erica Jong, and Adrienne [Rich], whom I like, and other violently feminist people. Which isn't true at all. I finally asked her if she'd ever read any of my poems. Well, it seemed she'd read *one* poem. I didn't see how she could interview me if she didn't know anything about me at all, and I told her so. She was nice enough to print a separate piece in *The Chicago Tribune* apart from the longer article on the others. I had said that I didn't believe in propaganda in poetry. That it rarely worked. What she had me saying was, "Miss Bishop does not believe that poetry should convey the poet's personal philosophy." Which made me sound like a complete dumbbell! Where she got that, I don't know. This is why one gets nervous about interviews.

INTERVIEWER: Do you generally agree with anthologists' choices? Do you have any poems that are personal favorites? Ones you'd like to see anthologized that aren't?

BISHOP: I'd rather have—well, anything except "The Fish"! I've declared a moratorium on that. Anthologists repeat each other so finally a few years ago I said nobody could reprint "The Fish" unless they reprinted three others because I got so sick of it.

INTERVIEWER: One or two more questions. You went to Yaddo several times early in your career. Did you find the atmosphere at an artist's colony helpful to your writing?

BISHOP: I went to Yaddo twice, once in the summer for two weeks, and for several months the winter before I went to Brazil. Mrs. Ames was very much in evidence then. I didn't like it in the summer because of the incessant coming and going, but the winter was rather different. There were only six of us and just by luck we all liked each other and had a very good time. I wrote one poem, I think, in that whole stretch. The first time I liked the horse races, I'm afraid. In the summer—I think this still goes on—you can walk through the Whitney estate to the tracks. A friend and I used to walk there early in the morning and sit at the track and have coffee and blueberry muffins while they exercised the horses. I loved that. We went to a sale of yearlings in August and that was beautiful. The sale was in a big tent. The grooms had brass dustpans and brooms with brass handles and they'd go around after the little colts and sweep up the manure. That's what I remember best about Yaddo.

INTERVIEWER: It was around the time that you went to Yaddo, wasn't it, that you were consultant in poetry to the Library of Congress? Was that year in Washington more productive than your Yaddo experience?

BISHOP: I've suffered because I've been so shy all my life. A few years later I might have enjoyed it more but at the time I didn't like it much. I hated Washington. There were so many government buildings that looked like Moscow. There was a very nice secretary, Phyllis Armstrong, who got me through. I think she did most of the work. I'd write something and she'd say, "Oh, no, that isn't official," so then she'd take it and rewrite it in gobbledegook. We used to bet on the horses—Phyllis always bet the daily double. She and I would sit there reading the *Racing Form* and poets would come to call and Phyllis and I would be talking about our bets!

All the "survivors" of that job—a lot of them are dead—were invited to read there recently. There were thirteen of us, unfortunately.

INTERVIEWER: A friend of mine tried to get into that reading and she said it was jammed.

BISHOP: *It was mobbed!* And I don't know why. It couldn't have been a duller, more awful occasion. I think we were supposedly limited to ten minutes. I *stuck* to it. But there's no stopping somebody like James Dickey. Stafford was good. I'd never heard him and never met him. He read one very short poem that really brought tears to my eyes, he read it so beautifully.

I'm not very fond of poetry readings. I'd much rather read the book. I know I'm wrong. I've only been to a few poetry readings I could *bear*. Of course, you're too young to have gone through the Dylan Thomas craze. . . .

When it was somebody like Cal Lowell or Marianne Moore, it's as if they were my children. I'd get terribly upset. I went to hear Marianne several times and finally I just couldn't go because I'd sit there with tears running down my face. I don't know, it's sort of embarrassing. You're so afraid they'll do something wrong.

Cal thought that the most important thing about readings was the remarks poets made in between the poems. The first time I heard him read was years ago at the New School for Social Research in a small, gray auditorium. It was with Allen Tate and Louise Bogan. Cal was very much younger than anybody else and had published just two books. He read a long, endless poem—I've forgotten its title*—about a Canadian nun in New Brunswick. I've forgotten what the point of the poem is, but it's very, very

* "Mother Marie Therese" in *The Mills of the Kavanaughs*.

long and it's quite beautiful, particularly in the beginning. Well, he started, and he read very badly. He kind of droned and everybody was trying to get it. He had gotten about two-thirds of the way through when somebody yelled, "Fire!" There was a small fire in the lobby, nothing much, that was put out in about five minutes and everybody went back to their seats. Poor Cal said, "I think I'd better begin over again," so he read the whole thing all over again! But his reading got much, much better in later years.

INTERVIEWER: He couldn't have done any better than the record the Poetry Center recently put out. It's wonderful. And very funny.

BISHOP: I haven't the courage to hear it.

—ELIZABETH SPIRES
1978

15. John Ashbery

Born in Rochester, New York, on July 28, 1927, John Ashbery grew up on a farm near Sodus, New York. He attended Deerfield and Harvard, and later did graduate work in English at Columbia and in French at New York University. From 1955 until 1965, he lived in France, first as a Fulbright Fellow and later as art critic for the *Paris Herald Tribune*. His first book of poems, *Some Trees*, was chosen by W. H. Auden for the Yale Series of Younger Poets Award in 1956. Since 1965 he has lived in New York, working first as executive editor of *ARTnews*, then as professor of writing at Brooklyn College, and most recently as art critic for *Newsweek*.

In 1976 Ashbery was awarded the Pulitzer Prize, the National Book Award, and the National Book Critics Circle Award for his collection *Self-Portrait in a Convex Mirror*. In addition to a novel, *A Nest of Ninnies* (1969), written in collaboration with James Schuyler, and a collection, *Three Plays* (1978), he is the author of twelve books of poetry, the most recent of which is *April Galleons* (1987). The publication of a collection of his essays on art, entitled *Reported Sightings*, is forthcoming. Twice named a Guggenheim Fellow, John Ashbery was awarded the annual Fellowship of the Academy of American Poets in 1982 and was named cowinner of the Bollingen Prize in Poetry for 1985. He received a MacArthur Award in 1985, and the Commonwealth Award in Literature from the Modern Language Association in 1986.

Forties Flick

The shadows of the venetian blinds on the ~~opposite~~ painted wall,
Shadows of the cacti, of the china animals
Focus the tragic melancholy of the bright stare
Into nowhere, a hole like the black holes in space.
In bra and panties she sidles to the window:
Zip! Up with the blind. A fragile street scene offers itself
With wafer-thin pedetstrians who know where they are going.
The blind comes down slowly, the slats are slowly tilted up.

Why must it always ~~come to~~ end like this?
A dais with woman reading, with the eddies of her hair   to her,
And all that is unsaid about her sucking us back with her
Into the silence that night alone doesn't explain?
Silence of the library, of the telephone with its pad
But we didn't have to reinvent these either:
They had gone away into construction of a plot,
The "art" part; ~~or so it seemed~~: knowing what details to leave out
And ~~about the development of character~~: things too real
To be of much concern, hence artificial, yet now all over the page
The indoors with the outside becoming part of you
As you ~~realize~~ you had never left off laughing at death,
The "background," dark vine at edge of porch.

Larry and Herman, Herman and Larry, lumber
Greasers, companions, rivals at the ~~XXXXXXXX~~ compnay
Purposely ~~ignorant~~ of so much that is being said
Yet conspirators too in your ambiguity:
What is it like up on the screen?
Do the faces so adroit at the end of their batons of light
Curl up once "The End" has come ~~XXXXXXXXXXXXXXXXXXXXXXX~~
Or do you figure that by keeping up a front
You will be saved from your own gift of gab
As it becomes time to unravel these old motions
And whatever meant something recedes into the past?

the way character is developed

A *manuscript page from* John Ashbery's Self-Portrait in a Convex Mirror.

John Ashbery

The interview was conducted at John Ashbery's apartment in the section of Manhattan known as Chelsea. When I arrived, Ashbery was away, and the doorman asked me to wait outside. Soon the poet arrived and we went up by elevator to a spacious well-lighted apartment in which a secretary was hard at work. We sat in easy chairs in the living room, Ashbery with his back to the large windows. The predominant decor was blue and white, and books lined the whole of one wall.

We talked for more than three hours with only one short break for refreshment—soda, tea, water, nothing stronger. Ashbery's answers to my questions required little editing. He did, however, throughout the conversation give the impression of distraction, as though he wasn't quite sure just what was going on or what his role in the proceedings might be. The interviewer attempted valiantly to extract humorous material, but—as is often the case for readers of Ashbery's poetry—wasn't sure when he succeeded. Since that afternoon a few additional questions were asked and answered, and these have been incorporated into the whole.

INTERVIEWER: I would like to start at the very beginning. When and why did you first decide on a career as a poet?

ASHBERY: I don't think I ever decided on a career as a poet. I began by writing a few little verses, but I never thought any of them would be published or that I would go on to publish books. I was in high school at the time and hadn't read any modern poetry. Then in a contest I won a prize in which you could choose different books; the only one which seemed appealing was Untermeyer's anthology, which cost five dollars, a great deal of money. That's how I began reading modern poetry, which wasn't taught in the schools then, especially in rural schools like the one I attended. I didn't understand much of it at first. There were people like Elinor Wylie whom I found appealing—wonderful craftsmanship—but I couldn't get very far with Auden and Eliot and Stevens. Later I went back to them and started getting their books out of the library. I guess it was just a desire to emulate that started me writing poetry. I can't think of any other reason. I am often asked why I write, and I don't know really—I just want to.

INTERVIEWER: When did you get more serious about it, thinking about publishing and that sort of thing?

ASHBERY: For my last two years of high school, I went to Deerfield Academy, and the first time I saw my work in print was in the school paper there. I had tried painting earlier, but I found that poetry was easier than painting. I must have been fifteen at the time. I remember reading *Scholastic* magazine and thinking I could write better poems than the ones they had in there, but I was never able to get one accepted. Then a student at Deerfield sent in some of my poems under his name to *Poetry* magazine, and when I sent them the same poems a few months later the editors there naturally assumed that I was the plagiarist. Very discouraging. *Poetry* was the most illustrious magazine to be published in at that time, and for a long time after they shunned my work. Then I went on to Harvard and in my second year I met

Kenneth Koch. I was trying to get on the *Harvard Advocate*, and he was already one of the editors. He saw my poetry and liked it, and we started reading each other's work. He was really the first poet that I ever knew, so that was rather an important meeting. Of course I published in the *Advocate*, and then in 1949 I had a poem published in *Furioso*. That was a major event in my life because, even though it was a relatively small magazine, it did take me beyond the confines of the college. But it was hard to follow that up with other publications, and it really wasn't until my late twenties that I could submit things with some hope of them getting accepted.

INTERVIEWER: Was there ever a time when you thought you would have to make a choice between art criticism and poetry, or have the two just always worked out well together?

ASHBERY: I was never interested in doing art criticism at all— I'm not sure that I am even now. Back in the fifties, Thomas Hess, the editor of *ARTnews*, had a lot of poets writing for the magazine. One reason was that they paid almost nothing and poets are always penurious. Trained art historians would not write reviews for five dollars, which is what they were paying when I began. I needed some bread at the time—this was in 1957 when I was thirty—and my friends who were already writing for *ART-news* suggested that I do it too. So I wrote a review of Bradley Tomlin, an Abstract Expressionist painter who had a posthumous show at the Whitney. After that I reviewed on a monthly basis for a while until I returned to France. Then in 1960 it happened that I knew the woman who was writing art criticism for the *Herald Tribune*. She was going back to live in America and asked if I knew anybody who would like to take over her job. It didn't pay very much, but it enabled me to get jobs doing art criticism, which I didn't want to do very much, but as so often when you exhibit reluctance to do something, people think you must be very good at it. If I had set out to be an art critic, I might never have succeeded.

INTERVIEWER: Are there any aspects of your childhood that you think might have contributed to making you the poet you are?

ASHBERY: I don't know what the poet that I am is, very much.

I was rather an outsider as a child—I didn't have many friends. We lived out in the country on a farm. I had a younger brother whom I didn't get along with—we were always fighting the way kids do—and he died at the age of nine. I felt guilty because I had been so nasty to him, so that was a terrible shock. These are experiences which have been important to me. I don't know quite how they may have fed into my poetry. My ambition was to be a painter, so I took weekly classes at the art museum in Rochester from the age of about eleven until fifteen or sixteen. I fell deeply in love with a girl who was in the class but who wouldn't have anything to do with me. So I went to this weekly class knowing that I would see this girl, and somehow this being involved with art may have something to do with my poetry. Also, my grand-father was a professor at the University of Rochester, and I lived with them as a small child and went to kindergarten and first grade in the city. I always loved his house; there were lots of kids around, and I missed all this terribly when I went back to live with my parents. Then going back there each week for art class was a returning to things I had thought were lost, and gave me a curious combination of satisfaction and dissatisfaction.

INTERVIEWER: These are all rather traumatic things. I think of how most critics seem to see your poetry as rather lighthearted. One critic, however, has spoken of your "rare startlements into happiness." Is happiness so rare in your work?

ASHBERY: Some people wouldn't agree that my poetry is light-hearted. Frank O'Hara once said, "I don't see why Kenneth likes John's work so much because he thinks everything should be funny and John's poetry is about as funny as a wrecked train." In my life I am reasonably happy now. There are days when I think I am not, but I think there are probably more days when I think I am. I was impressed by an Ingmar Bergman movie I saw years ago—I can't remember the name of it—in which a woman tells the story of her life, which has been full of tragic experiences. She's telling the story in the dressing room of a theater where she is about to go on and perform in a ballet. At the end of it she says, "But I am happy." Then it says, "The End."

INTERVIEWER: Do you like to tease or play games with the reader?

ASHBERY: Funny you should ask—I just blew up at a critic who asked me the same question, though I shouldn't have, in a list of questions for a book she is compiling of poets' statements. I guess it depends on what you mean by "tease." It's all right if it's done affectionately, though how can this be with someone you don't know? I would like to please the reader, and I think that surprise has to be an element of this, and that may necessitate a certain amount of teasing. To shock the reader is something else again. That has to be handled with great care if you're not going to alienate and hurt him, and I'm firmly against that, just as I disapprove of people who dress with that in mind—dye their hair blue and stick safety pins through their noses and so on. The message here seems to be merely aggression—"hey, you can't be part of my strangeness" sort of thing. At the same time I try to dress in a way that is just slightly off, so the spectator, if he notices, will feel slightly bemused but not excluded, remembering his own imperfect mode of dress.

INTERVIEWER: But you would not be above inflicting a trick or a gag on your readers?

ASHBERY: A gag that's probably gone unnoticed turns up in the last sentence of the novel I wrote with James Schuyler. Actually it's my sentence. It reads: "So it was that the cliff dwellers, after bidding their cousins good night, moved off towards the parking area, while the latter bent their steps toward the partially rebuilt shopping plaza in the teeth of the freshening foehn." *Foehn* is a kind of warm wind that blows in Bavaria that produces a fog. I would doubt that many people know that. I liked the idea that people, if they bothered to, would have to open the dictionary to find out what the last word in the novel meant. They'd be closing one book and opening another.

INTERVIEWER: Were there older living poets whom you visited, learned from, or studied with as a young writer?

ASHBERY: I particularly admired Auden, whom I would say was the first big influence on my work, more so than Stevens. I wrote an honors thesis on his poetry and got a chance to meet him at

Harvard. When I was at Harvard also I studied with Theodore Spencer, a poet who is no longer very well known. He actually taught a poetry-writing workshop, which was very rare in those days—especially at Harvard, where they still are rare. It wasn't that I was particularly fond of Spencer's poetry, but he was a "genuine" poet, a real-live poet, and the feedback I got from him in class was very valuable to me. I also read Elizabeth Bishop quite early and met her once. I wrote her a letter about one of her poems that I had liked and she wrote back, and then after I moved to New York I met her. But I was rather shy about putting myself forward, so there weren't very many known poets then that I did have any contact with. I wish I could have visited older poets! But things were different then—young poets simply didn't send their poems to older ones with requests for advice and criticism and "suggestions for publication." At least I don't think they did—none of the ones I knew did. Everyone is bolder now. This leads to a sad situation (and I've often discussed this with poets of my generation like Kinnell and Merwin) of having a tremendous pile of unanswered correspondence about poetry—Kinnell calls it his "guilt pile"—from poets who want help and should receive it; only in this busy world of doing things to make a living and trying to find some time for oneself to write poetry, it isn't usually possible to summon the time and energy it would require to deal seriously with so many requests; at least for me it isn't. But I feel sad because I would like to help; you remember how valuable it would have been for you; and it's an honor to get these requests. People think they have gotten to know you through your poetry and can address you familiarly (I get lots of "Dear John" letters from strangers) and that in itself is a tremendous reward, a satisfaction—if only we could attend to everybody! Actually the one poet I really wanted to know when I was young was Auden. I met him briefly twice after he gave readings at Harvard, and later on in New York saw a bit of him through Chester Kallman who was a great friend of Jimmy Schuyler's, but it was very hard to talk to him since he already knew everything. I once said to Kenneth Koch, "What are you supposed to say to Auden?" And he said that about the only thing there was to say was "I'm glad you're alive."

INTERVIEWER: Why is it always Auden?

ASHBERY: It's odd to be asked today what I saw in Auden. Forty years ago when I first began to read modern poetry no one would have asked—he was *the* modern poet. Stevens was a curiosity, Pound probably a monstrosity, William Carlos Williams—who hadn't yet published his best poetry—an "imagist." Eliot and Yeats were too hallowed and anointed to count. I read him at the suggestion of Kathryn Koller, a professor of English at the University of Rochester who was a neighbor of my parents. She had been kind enough to look at my early scribblings and, probably shaking her head over them, suggested Auden as perhaps a kind of antidote. What immediately struck me was his use of colloquial speech—I didn't think you were supposed to do that in poetry. That, and his startling way of making abstractions concrete and alive—remember: "Abruptly mounting her ramshackle wheel/Fortune has pedaled furiously away./The sobbing mess is on our hands today," which seem to crystallize the thirties into a few battered and quirky images. And again a kind of romantic tone which took abandoned mines and factory chimneys into account. There is perhaps a note of both childishness and sophistication which struck an answering chord in me. I cannot agree, though, with the current view that his late work is equal to if not better than the early stuff. Except for "The Sea and the Mirror" there is little that enchants me in the poetry he wrote after coming to America. There are felicities, of course, but on the whole it's *too* chatty and too self-congratulatory at not being "poetry with a capital P," as he put it. Auden was of two minds about my own work. He once said he never understood a line of it. On the other hand he published *Some Trees* in the Yale Younger Poets Series. You'll remember, though, that he once said in later life that one of his early works, *The Orators*, must have been written by a madman.

INTERVIEWER: Tell me about the New York School—were there regular meetings, perhaps classes or seminars? Did you plot to take over the literary world?

ASHBERY: No. This label was foisted upon us by a man named John Bernard Meyers, who ran the Tibor de Nagy Gallery and published some pamphlets of our poems. I found out recently from one of my students that Meyers coined the term in 1961 in an article he wrote for a little magazine in California called *Nomad*. I think the idea was that, since everybody was talking about the New York School of painting, if he created a New York School of poets then they would automatically be considered important because of the sound of the name. But by that time I was living in France, and wasn't part of what was happening in New York. I don't think we ever were a school. There are vast differences between my poetry and Koch's and O'Hara's and Schuyler's and Guest's. We were a bunch of poets who happened to know each other; we would get together and read our poems to each other and sometimes we would write collaborations. It never occurred to us that it would be possible to take over the literary world, so that was not part of the plan. Somebody wrote an article about the New York School a few years ago in the *Times Book Review*, and a woman wrote in to find out how she could enroll.

INTERVIEWER: What was your relation to Paris at the time when you were there—you used to drink Coca-Colas . . .

ASHBERY: That question probably requires a book-length essay. I did at one point in Paris develop an addiction to Coca-Cola which I've never had before or since, but I don't know whether that was due to nostalgia for America or the fact that the French like it so much. Paris is "the city," isn't it, and I am a lover of cities. It can be experienced much more pleasantly and conveniently than any other city I know. It's so easy to get around on the metro, and so interesting when you get there—each *arrondissement* is like a separate province, with its own capital and customs and even costumes. I used to pick a different section to explore and set out on a miniexpedition, often with a movie theater in mind where they were showing some movie I wanted to see, often an old Laurel and Hardy film since I love them, especially when dubbed into French with comic American accents. And then there is always a principal café in the neighborhood where you can sample some nice wine and look at the people. You get to know a lot of life this way. Sometimes I would do a Proustian excursion, looking at buildings he or his characters had lived in. Like his childhood home in the Boulevard Malesherbes or Odette's house in the rue La Pérouse.

I didn't have many friends the first years I was there—they were mainly the American writers Harry Mathews and Elliott Stein, and Pierre Martory, a French writer with whom I lived for the last nine of the ten years I spent in France, and who has remained a very close friend. He once published a novel but never anything after that, though the novel was well received and he continues to write voluminously—poems, novels, and stories which he produces constantly but never tries to publish or show to anybody, even me—the only writer of that kind I've ever met. I've translated a few of his poems but they haven't appeared in France, where they don't fit in with the cliques that prevail there. Some were published in *Locus Solus*, a small magazine Harry Mathews and I edited—the title is taken from a novel by Raymond Roussel, whom we both loved and on whom I was once going to do a dissertation. A little later I met Anne and Rodrigo Moynihan, English painters who live mostly in France, who sponsored a review called *Art and Literature*, which I helped to edit. They too have remained close friends whom I see often. I return to Pierre—most of my knowledge of France and things French comes from him. He is a sort of walking encyclopedia of French culture but at the same time views it all from a perspective that is somewhat American. He once spent six months in New York working for *Paris Match*, for which he still works, and we sailed back to France together on the S.S. *France*. When he set foot on French soil at Le Havre he said, "It is so wonderful to be back in France! *But I hate ze French!*"

INTERVIEWER: What early reading did you do, say in high school or college, that has stayed with you?

ASHBERY: Like many young people, I was attracted by long novels. My grandfather had several sets of Victorian writers in his house. The first long novel I read was *Vanity Fair*, and I liked it so much that I decided to read *Gone With the Wind*, which I liked too. I read Dickens and George Eliot then, but not very much poetry. I didn't really get a feeling for the poetry of the past until I had discovered modern poetry. Then I began to see how nineteenth-century poetry wasn't just something lifeless in an ancient museum but must have grown out of the lives of the people who wrote it. In college I majored in English and read the usual curriculum. I guess I was particularly attracted to the Metaphysical poets and to Keats, and I had a Chaucer course, which I enjoyed very much. I also had a modern poetry course from F. O. Matthiessen, which is where I really began to read Wallace Stevens. I wrote a paper, I recall, on "Chocurua to Its Neighbor." Mostly I wasn't a very good student and just sort of got by—laziness. I read Proust for a course with Harry Levin, and that was a major shock.

INTERVIEWER: Why?

ASHBERY: I don't know. I started reading it when I was twenty (before I took Levin's course) and it took me almost a year. I read very slowly anyway, but particularly in the case of a writer whom I wanted to read every word of. It's just that I think one ends up feeling sadder and wiser in equal proportions when one is finished reading him—I can no longer look at the world in quite the same way.

INTERVIEWER: Were you attracted by the intimate, meditative voice of his work?

ASHBERY: Yes, and the way somehow everything could be included in this vast, open form that he created for himself—particularly certain almost surreal passages. There's one part where a philologist or specialist on place names goes on at great length concerning place names in Normandy. I don't know why it is so gripping, but it seizes the way life sometimes seems to have of droning on in a sort of dreamlike space. I also identified, on account of the girl in my art class, with the narrator, who had a totally impractical passion which somehow both enveloped the beloved like a cocoon and didn't have much to do with her.

INTERVIEWER: You said a minute ago that reading modern poetry enabled you to see the vitality present in older poetry? In your mind, is there a close connection between life and poetry?

ASHBERY: In my case I would say there is a very close but oblique connection. I have always been averse to talking about myself, and so I don't write about my life the way the confessional poets do. I don't want to bore people with experiences of mine that are simply versions of what everybody goes through. For me, poetry starts after that point. I write with experiences in mind, but I don't write about them, I write out of them. I know that I have exactly the opposite reputation, that I am totally self-involved, but that's not the way I see it.

INTERVIEWER: You have often been characterized as a solipsist, and I wonder if this isn't related to your reputation for obscurity. The way the details of a poem will be so clear, but the context, the surrounding situation, unclear. Perhaps this is more a matter of perspective than any desire to befuddle.

ASHBERY: This is the way that life appears to me, the way that experience happens. I can concentrate on the things in this room and our talking together, but what the context is is mysterious to me. And it's not that I want to make it more mysterious in my poems—really, I just want to make it more photographic. I often wonder if I am suffering from some mental dysfunction because of how weird and baffling my poetry seems to so many people and sometimes to me too. Let me read you a comment which appeared in a review of my most recent book, from some newspaper in Virginia. It says: "John Ashbery is emerging as a very important poet, if not by unanimous critical consent then certainly by the admiration and awe he inspires in younger poets. Oddly, no one understands Ashbery." That is a simplification, but in a sense it is true, and I wonder how things happened that way. I'm not the person who knows. When I originally started writing, I expected that probably very few people would read my poetry because in those days people didn't read poetry much anyway. But I also felt that my work was not beyond understanding. It seemed to me rather derivative of or at least in touch with contemporary poetry of the time, and I was quite surprised that nobody seemed to see this. So I live with this paradox: on the one hand, I am an important poet, read by younger writers, and on the other hand, nobody understands me. I am often asked to account for this state of affairs, but I can't.

INTERVIEWER: When you say that sometimes you think your poetry is weird, what do you mean exactly?

ASHBERY: Every once in a while I will pick up a page and it has something, but what is it? It seems so unlike what poetry "as we know it" is. But at other moments I feel very much at home with it. It's a question of a sudden feeling of unsureness at what I am doing, wondering why I am writing the way I am, and also not feeling the urge to write in another way.

INTERVIEWER: Is the issue of meaning or message something that is uppermost in your mind when you write?

ASHBERY: Meaning yes, but message no. I think my poems mean what they say, and whatever might be implicit within a particular passage, but there is no message, nothing I want to tell the world particularly except what I am thinking when I am writing. Many critics tend to want to see an allegorical meaning in every concrete statement, and if we just choose a line at random, I think we will find this isn't the way it works. . . . I can't seem to find anything that's an example of what I mean. Well, let's take this . . . no. Everything I look at does seem to mean something other than what is being said, all of a sudden. Ah, here—the beginning of "Daffy Duck in Hollywood," for instance, where all these strange objects avalanche into the poem. I meant them to be there for themselves, and not for some hidden meaning. Rumford's Baking Powder (by the way, it's actually Rumford and not Rumford's Baking Powder. I knew that, but preferred the sound of my version—I don't usually do that), a celluloid earring, Speedy Gonzales—they are just the things that I selected to be exhibited in the poem at that point. In fact, there is a line here, "The allegory comes unsnarled too soon," that might be my observation of poetry and my poetry in particular. The allegory coming unsnarled meaning that the various things that make it up are dissolving into a poetic statement, and that is something I feel is both happening and I don't want to happen. And, as so often, two opposing forces are working to cancel each other out. "Coming unsnarled" is probably a good thing, but "too soon" isn't.

INTERVIEWER: So for you a poem is an object in and of itself rather than a clue to some abstraction, to something other than itself?

ASHBERY: Yes, I would like it to be what Stevens calls a completely new set of objects. My intention is to present the reader with a pleasant surprise, not an unpleasant one, not a nonsurprise. I think this is the way pleasure happens when you are reading poetry. Years ago Kenneth Koch and I did an interview with each other, and something I said then, in 1964, is pertinent to what we are talking about. "It's rather hard to be a good artist and also be able to explain intelligently what your art is about. In fact, the worse your art is, the easier it is to talk about, at least I would like to think so. Ambiguity seems to be the same thing as happiness or pleasant surprise. I am assuming that from the moment life cannot be one continual orgasm, real happiness is impossible, and pleasant surprise is promoted to the front rank of the emotions. The idea of relief from pain has something to do with ambiguity. Ambiguity supposes eventual resolution of itself whereas certitude implies further ambiguity. I guess that is why so much 'depressing' modern art makes me feel cheerful."

INTERVIEWER: Could you explain the paradox concerning ambiguity and certitude?

ASHBERY: Things are in a continual state of motion and evolution, and if we come to a point where we say, with certitude, right here, this is end of the universe, then of course we must deal with everything that goes on after that, whereas ambiguity seems to take further developments into account. We might realize that the present moment may be one of an eternal or sempiternal series of moments, all of which will resemble it because, in some ways, they are the present, and won't in other ways, because the present will be the past by that time.

INTERVIEWER: Is it bothersome that critics seem to have considerable trouble saying exactly what your poems are about?

ASHBERY: You have probably read David Bromwich's review of *As We Know* in the *Times*. He decided that the entire book deals with living in a silver age rather than a golden age. This is an idea that occurs only briefly, along with a great many other things, in "Litany." By making this arbitrary decision he was able to deal with the poetry. I intended, in "Litany," to write something so utterly discursive that it would be beyond criticism—not because I wanted to punish critics, but because this would somehow exemplify the fullness, or, if you wish, the emptiness, of life, or, at any rate, its dimensionless quality. And I think that any true work of art does defuse criticism; if it left anything important to be said, it wouldn't be doing its job. (This is not an idea I expect critics to sympathize with, especially at a time when criticism has set itself up as a separate branch of the arts, and, perhaps by implication, the most important one.) The poem is of an immense length, and there is a lack of coherence between the parts. Given all this, I don't really see how one could deal critically with the poem, so I suppose it is necessary for the critic to draw up certain guidelines before beginning. It was a very sympathetic review, and I admire Bromwich, but it seemed to leave a great deal out of account. I guess I am pleased that my method has given every critic something to hate or like. For me, my poems have their own form, which is the one that I want, even though other people might not agree that it is there. I feel that there is always a resolution in my poems.

INTERVIEWER: Did you see the controversy that erupted in *The New York Review* about how "Litany" should be read? Whether one should read all of voice A, then all of voice B, or intermingle them in some way . . .

ASHBERY: I don't think there is any particular way. I seem to have opened up a can of worms with my instruction, which the publisher asked me to put in, that the parts should be read simultaneously. I don't think people ever read things the way they are supposed to. I myself will skip ahead several chapters, or read a little bit of this page and a little bit of that page, and I assume that is what everybody does. I just wanted the whole thing to be, as I have said, presentable; it's not a form that has a cohesive structure, so it could be read just as one pleases. I think I consider the poem as a sort of environment, and one is not obliged to take aspect of one's environment—one can't, in fact. came out the way it did.

ER: One's environment at a single moment?

ASHBERY: No, it is a succession of moments. I am always impressed by how difficult and yet how easy it is to get from one moment to the next of one's life—particularly while traveling, as I just was in Poland. There is a problem every few minutes— one doesn't know whether one is going to get on the plane, or will they confiscate one's luggage. Somehow I did all this and got back, but I was aware of so much difficulty, and at the same time of the pleasure, the novelty of it all. Susan Sontag was at this writers' conference also—there were just four of us—and one night in Warsaw we were provided with tickets to a ballet. I said, "Do you think we should go? It doesn't sound like it will be too interesting." And she said "Sure, we should go. If it is boring that will be interesting too"—which turned out to be the case.

INTERVIEWER: Given what you said about "Litany," it seems that in a way you are leaving it up to each reader to make his or her own poem out of the raw materials you have given. Do you visualize an ideal reader when you write, or do you conceive of a multitude of different apprehending sensibilities?

ASHBERY: Every writer faces the problem of the person that he is writing for, and I think nobody has ever been able to imagine satisfactorily who this *"homme moyen sensuel"* will be. I try to aim at as wide an audience as I can so that as many people as possible will read my poetry. Therefore I depersonalize it, but in the same way personalize it, so that a person who is going to be different from me but is also going to resemble me just because he is different from me, since we are all different from each other, can see something in it. You know—I shot an arrow into the air but I could only aim it. Often after I have given a poetry reading, people will say, "I never really got anything out of your work before, but now that I have heard you read it, I can see something in it." I guess something about my voice and my projection of myself meshes with the poems. That is nice, but it is also rather saddening because I can't sit down with every potential reader and read aloud to him.

INTERVIEWER: Your poems often have a spoken quality, as though they are monologues or dialogues. Do you try to create characters who then speak in your poems, or is this all your own voice? In the dialogues perhaps it is two aspects of your own voice that are speaking.

ASHBERY: It doesn't seem to me like my voice. I have had many arguments about this with my analyst, who is actually a South American concert pianist, more interested in playing the piano than in being a therapist. He says, "Yes, I know, you always think that these poems come from somewhere else. You refuse to realize that it is really you that is writing the poems and not having them dictated by some spirit somewhere." It is hard for me to realize that because I have such an imprecise impression of what kind of a person I am. I know I appear differently to other people because I behave differently on different occasions. Some people think that I am very laid-back and charming and some people think I am egotistical and disagreeable. Or as Edward Lear put it in his great poem "How Pleasant to Know Mr. Lear": "Some think him ill-tempered and queer, but a few find him pleasant enough." Any of the above, I suppose. Of course, my reason tells me that my poems are not dictated, that I am not a voyant. I suppose they come from a part of me that I am not in touch with very much except when I am actually writing. The rest of the time I guess I want to give this other person a rest, this other one of my selves that does the talking in my poems, so that he won't get tired and stop.

INTERVIEWER: So you have a sense of several selves?

ASHBERY: No, no more than the average person, I shouldn't think. I mean, we are all different depending on who we happen to be with and what we are doing at a particular moment, but I wouldn't say that it goes any further than that.

INTERVIEWER: Some people have thought that you set up characters who converse in several poems. One could say that in "Litany" you have character A and character B, who are very similar to one another. It is possible at times to see them as lovers on the point of separating, while at other times they look like two aspects of one personality.

ASHBERY: I think I am trying to reproduce the polyphony that goes on inside me, which I don't think is radically different from that of other people. After all, one is constantly changing one's mind and thereby becoming something slightly different. But what was I doing? Perhaps the two columns are like two people whom I am in love with simultaneously. A student of mine who likes this poem says that when you read one column you start to "miss" the other one, as you would miss one beloved when you spend time with the other. I once half-jokingly said that my object was to direct the reader's attention to the white space between the columns. Maybe that's part of it. Reading is a pleasure, but to finish reading, to come to the blank space at the end, is also a pleasure.

INTERVIEWER: This notion of your poems being dictated makes me wonder whether for you composition involves something like inspiration, the poems just springing out already finished, rather than a laborious process of writing and revision.

ASHBERY: That is the way it has happened to me in more recent times. In fact, since I don't have very much free time (poets seldom do, since they must somehow make a living), I've conditioned myself to write at almost any time. Sometimes it doesn't work, but on the whole I feel that poetry is going on all the time inside, an underground stream. One can let down one's bucket and bring the poem back up. (This is very well put in a passage that occurs early on in Heimito von Doderer's novel *The Demons*, which I haven't to hand at the moment.) It will be not dissimilar to what I have produced before because it is coming from the same source, but it will be dissimilar because of the different circumstances of the particular moment.

INTERVIEWER: Many poets have spoken of poetry coming from the subconscious mind rather than the conscious mind. Would you agree with that?

ASHBERY: I think that is where it probably starts out, but I think that in my case it passes through the conscious mind on its way out and is monitored by it. I don't believe in automatic writing as the Surrealists were supposed to have practiced it, simply because it is not a reflection of the whole mind, which is partly logical and reasonable, and that part should have its say too.

INTERVIEWER: Do you compose on the typewriter or in longhand?

ASHBERY: I write on the typewriter. I didn't use to, but when I was writing "The Skaters," the lines became unmanageably long. I would forget the end of the line before I could get to it. It occurred to me that perhaps I should do this at the typewriter, because I can type faster than I can write. So I did, and that is mostly the way I have written ever since. Occasionally I write a poem in longhand to see whether I can still do it. I don't want to be forever bound to this machine.

INTERVIEWER: Do you have rituals?

ASHBERY: Well, one of them is to use this very old, circa 1930 I would say, Royal typewriter I mentioned. I hate to think what will happen when it finally gives out, though you can still find them sometimes in those used office furniture stores on West 23rd Street, which are themselves an endangered species. And then I procrastinate like everybody else, though surely more than most. On days when I want to write I will usually waste the morning and go for an afternoon walk to Greenwich Village. (I live nearby in Chelsea, which is a pleasant place to walk from though maybe not to.) Sometimes this takes too long and my preferred late afternoon moment will pass. I can't really work at night. Nor in the morning, very much, when I have more ideas but am less critical of them, it seems. I never can use the time I waste doing this for some other purpose like answering letters. It's no good for anything but wasting. I've never tried Schiller's rotten apples, but I do drink tea while I write, and that is about the only time I do drink tea. On the whole, I believe I have fewer hang-ups and rituals than I used to. I feel blocked much less often, though it still happens. It's important to try to write when you are in the wrong mood or the weather is wrong. Even if you don't succeed you'll be developing a muscle that may do it later on. And I think writing does get easier as you get older. It's a question of practice and also of realizing you don't have the oceans of time to waste you had when you were young.

INTERVIEWER: Do you revise your poems heavily?

ASHBERY: Not anymore. I used to labor over them a great deal, but because of my strong desire to avoid all unnecessary work, I have somehow trained myself not to write something that I will either have to discard or be forced to work a great deal over. In fact, just last night a friend mentioned that she has a manuscript copy of one of my early poems, "Le livre est sur la table," with a lot of corrections in it. I remember that poem as one that gave me an immense amount of difficulty—I worked over it for a week or so and never did feel really happy with it. When she mentioned that, I realized how much my way of writing has changed over the last thirty years. But, although there are poems even today that I don't find satisfactory once I have finished them, most of the corrections I make are pretty minor. I like the idea of being as close to the original thought or voice as possible and not to falsify it by editing. Here is something I just read by Max Jacob, quoted by André Salmon in the notes to Jacob's book *La Défense de Tartufe*. He talks about composing novels or stories in a notebook while taking long walks through Paris. I'll translate: "The ideas I found in this way seemed sacred to me and I didn't change a comma. I believe that prose which comes directly from meditation is a prose which has the form of the brain and which it is forbidden to touch."

INTERVIEWER: What determines a line break for you? Is there some metrical consideration, or would you say you are writing free verse?

ASHBERY: I don't know. I just know when I feel the line should break. I used to say that my criterion for a line of poetry was that it should have at least two interesting things in it. But this is not the case in a lot of my recent poetry. In "Litany" there are lines that are a single word long. As I was writing that poem—well, actually it began with the long poem before that, the "Nut-Brown Maid"—I became almost intoxicated by the idea of the line break. It seemed as if I were writing just to get to this point, this decision. But, although the line break is very important to me, I don't really understand how I know when it is supposed to happen. I have felt very uncomfortable with iambic pentameter ever since I discovered, when I first began writing poetry, that it was not impossible to write acceptable blank verse. It somehow seems to falsify poetry for me. It has an order of its own that is foreign to nature. When I was in college, I used to write a kind of four-beat line, which seemed much more real, genuine, to me. Now I guess it is free verse, whatever that is.

INTERVIEWER: What gets you started in writing a poem? Is it an idea, an image, a rhythm, a situation or event, a phrase, something else?

ASHBERY: Again, all of the above. An idea might occur to me, something very banal—for example, isn't it strange that it is possible to both talk and think at the same time? That might be an idea for a poem. Or certain words or phrases might have come to my attention with a meaning I wasn't aware of before. Also, I often put in things that I have overheard people say, on the street for instance. Suddenly something fixes itself in the flow that is going on around one and seems to have a significance. In fact, there is an example of that in this poem, "What Is Poetry?" In a bookstore I overheard a boy saying to a girl this last line: "It might give us—what?—some flowers soon?" I have no idea what the context was, but it suddenly seemed the way to end my poem. I am a believer in fortuitous accidents. The ending of my poem "Clepsydra," the last two lines, came from a notebook that I kept a number of years before, during my first trip to Italy. I actually wrote some poems while I was traveling, which I don't usually do, but I was very excited by my first visit there. So years later, when I was trying to end "Clepsydra" and getting very nervous, I happened to open that notebook and found these two lines that I had completely forgotten about: "while morning is still and before the body / Is changed by the faces of evening." They were just what I needed at that time. But it doesn't really matter so much what the individual thing is. Many times I will jot down ideas and phrases, and then when I am ready to write I can't find them. But it doesn't make any difference, because whatever comes along at that time will have the same quality. Whatever was there is replaceable. In fact, often in revising I will remove the idea that was the original stimulus. I think I am more interested in the movement among ideas than in the ideas themselves, the way one goes from one point to another rather than the destination or the origin.

INTERVIEWER: *Three Poems* is largely prose, prose poetry, rather than verse. Some readers would object rather strenuously to calling it poetry. Within this kind of form, I am wondering where, for you, the poetry specifically is to be found? What is the indispensable element that makes poetry?

ASHBERY: That is one of those good but unanswerable questions. For a long time a very prosaic language, a language of ordinary speech, has been in my poetry. It seems to me that we are most ourselves when we are talking, and we talk in a very irregular and antiliterary way. In *Three Poems*, I wanted to see how poetic the most prosaic language could be. And I don't mean just the journalese, but also the inflated rhetoric that is trying very hard to sound poetic but not making it. One of my aims has been to put together as many different kinds of language and tone as possible, and to shift them abruptly, to overlap them all. There is a very naive, romantic tone at times, all kinds of clichés, as well as a more deliberate poetic voice. I also was in a way reacting to the minimalism of some of the poems in *The Tennis Court Oath*, such as "Europe," which is sometimes just a few scattered words. I suppose I eventually thought of covering page after page with words, with not even any break for paragraphs in many cases—could I do this and still feel that I was getting the satisfaction that poetry gives me? I don't quite understand why some people are so against prose poetry, which is certainly a respectable and pedigreed form of poetry. In fact, too much so for my taste. I had written almost none before *Three Poems* because there always seemed to be a kind of rhetorical falseness in much that had been done in the past—Baudelaire's, for instance. I wanted to see if prose poetry could be written without that self-conscious drama that seems so much a part of it. So if it is poetic, it is probably because it tries to stay close to the way we talk and think without expecting what we say to be recorded or remembered. The pathos and liveliness of ordinary human communication is poetry to me.

INTERVIEWER: You were talking once about reading younger poets and being aware that you have influenced their work. You said one of the primary benefits for you in seeing this is that it alerts you to watch out for "Ashberyisms" in your own work. What do you mean by Ashberyisms?

ASHBERY: Well, there are certain stock words that I have found myself using a great deal. When I become aware of them, it is an alarm signal meaning I was falling back on something that had served in the past—it is a sign of not thinking at the present moment, not that there is anything intrinsically bad about certain words or phrases. The word "climate" occurs in my poetry a great deal, for instance. So I try to censor it, unless I feel that there is no alternative. I also seem to be very fond of words involving a kind of osmosis, like "absorb" and "leach," as something leaching into the soil. I don't know why these particular words attract me, unless it's because they are indicative of the slow but kinetic quality of existence and experience. Also there is a typical kind of tone, the chatty quality that my poetry tends to have, the idea behind it being that there are things more important than "all this fiddle," perhaps, and sometimes I correct this.

INTERVIEWER: I suppose there are many things we might expect from a poet who has so strong an interest in painting as you do. Various critics have suggested that you are a Mannerist in words, or an Abstract Expressionist. Are you conscious of anything like that—or perhaps of performing a Cubist experiment with words?

ASHBERY: I suppose the "Self-Portrait in a Convex Mirror" is a Mannerist work in what I hope is the good sense of the word. Later on, Mannerism became mannered, but at first it was a pure novelty—Parmigianino was an early Mannerist, coming right on the heels of Michelangelo. I have probably been influenced, more or less unconsciously I suppose, by the modern art that I have looked at. Certainly the simultaneity of Cubism is something that has rubbed off on me, as well as the Abstract Expressionist idea that the work is a sort of record of its own coming-into-existence; it has an "anti-referential sensuousness," but it is nothing like flinging a bucket of words on the page, as Pollock did with paint. It is more indirect than that. When I was fresh out of college, Abstract Expressionism was the most exciting thing in the arts. Th—— s also experimental music and film, but poetry seemed ventional in comparison. I guess it still is, in a way. accept a Picasso woman with two noses, but an equiv- mpt in poetry baffles the same audience.

INTERVIEWER: Though it has its admirers, *The Tennis Court Oath* seems to have been a widely disliked book—for its difficulty, its obscurity, and so on. How do you feel about that volume from the perspective of today?

ASHBERY: There are a lot of poems in that book that don't interest me as much as those that came before or since. I didn't expect to have a second book published, ever. The opportunity came about very suddenly, and when it did I simply sent what I had been doing. But I never expected these poems to see the light of day. I felt at that time that I needed a change in the way I was writing, so I was kind of fooling around and trying to do something I hadn't done before. I was conscious that often what I hadn't done before was inferior to what I had done. But I like a number of the poems in the book. I hadn't realized this until recently, but there was a period, after I had begun living in Paris and decided that I wanted to write in a different way, when I achieved a kind of intermediate style, say between the poems in *Some Trees* and the poem "Europe." For instance, the poem "They Dream Only of America" or "Our Youth" or "How Much Longer Will I Be Able to Inhabit the Divine Sepulcher. . . ." Those are the earlier poems in *The Tennis Court Oath*. I don't know quite why I stopped writing that way, but I feel that those are valid poems in a new way that I might well have gone on pursuing, but didn't. In the last two or three years, I have gone back and reread some of the poems which I hadn't liked before and decided that they did have something that I could work on again. I think I did this somewhat in "Litany." There are certainly things in that poem that are as outrageous as the poems that outraged the critics of *The Tennis Court Oath*.

INTERVIEWER: How do you feel about the general critical reception of your work?

ASHBERY: I am very pleased that my poems seem to have found readers. I don't know quite how this came about. But it is disappointing to me that my poetry has become a kind of shibboleth, that people feel they have to join one side or the other. It seems to me that the poetry gets lost in all the controversy that surrounds it. I feel often that people on both sides are much more familiar with the myth that has grown up about my work than they are with the work itself. I am either an inspired seer or a charlatan who is trying to torment readers. My work has become a sort of political football and has the quality of a red flag for some people before they have even begun to pay any attention to it. I suppose that is the way reputations, some of them anyway, are created, but I hate to see people intimidated before they even have begun to read me by their preconceived notion of what my poetry is. I think it has something to offer, that it was not written not to be read.

INTERVIEWER: Have you found that your students ever taught you anything about writing?

ASHBERY: I try to avoid the well-known cliché that you learn from your students. Neither do I believe that there's something ennobling for a writer to teach, that it's narcissistic to spend time wallowing in your writing when you could be out helping in the world's work. Writers should write, and poets especially spend altogether too much time at other tasks such as teaching. However, since so many of us have to do it, there are certain things to be said for it. You are forced to bring a critical attention into play when you are reading students' work that you would not use otherwise, and that can help when you return to your own writing. And being immersed in a group of young unproven writers who are fiercely serious about what they are doing can have a chastening effect sometimes on us blasé oldsters. Besides, they may be writing great poetry, only nobody knows it because nobody has seen it yet. I sometimes think that the "greatness" my friends and I used to see in each other's poetry when we were very young had a lot to do with the fact that it was unknown. It could turn out to be anything; the possibilities were limitless, more so than when we were at last discovered and identified and pinned down in our books.

—PETER STITT
1980

16. Robert Fitzgerald

Robert Fitzgerald was born in 1910 and grew up in Springfield, Illinois. He attended the Choate School and then Harvard College, from which he graduated in 1933. Fitzgerald is best known for his translations of Homer's *Iliad* (1974) and *Odyssey* (1961), and more recently Virgil's *Aeneid* (1983). His early translations, carried out in collaboration with Dudley Fitts, include Euripides' *Alcestis* (1936) and Sophocles' *Antigone* (1939) and *Oedipus Rex* (1949). In addition, he translated works by Valery, St.-John Perse, and Borges. Fitzgerald was also the author of three books of poems, collected in *Spring Shade: Poems, 1931–1970* (New Directions, 1971).

While an undergraduate at Harvard, Fitzgerald made the acquaintance of James Agee, and the two worked together at *Time* magazine in the forties. After Agee's death in 1955, Fitzgerald edited his collected poems and short prose. Fitzgerald was also the literary executor of Flannery O'Connor's estate and the co-editor of her posthumously published occasional prose, *Mystery and Manners* (1969).

In the late forties, Fitzgerald was an instructor in literature at Sarah Lawrence College and poetry reviewer for *The New Republic*. Later, he held visiting professorships at Notre Dame (1957), the University of Washington in Seattle (1961), and Mount Holyoke College (1964). From 1965 to 1981, he was Boylston Professor of Rhetoric and Oratory at Harvard. Fitzgerald died at his home in Hamden, Connecticut, in January of 1985.

ΙΛΙΑΔΟΣ Γ

αὐτὰρ ἐπεὶ κόσμηθεν ἅμ' ἡγεμόνεσσιν ἕκαστοι,

Τρῶες μὲν κλαγγῇ τ' ἐνοπῇ τ' ἴσαν ὄρνιθες ὥς,

ἠΰτε περ κλαγγὴ γεράνων πέλει οὐρανόθι πρό,

αἵ τ' ἐπεὶ οὖν χειμῶνα φύγον καὶ ἀθέσφατον ὄμβρον,

κλαγγῇ ταί γε πέτονται ἐπ' ὠκεανοῖο ῥοάων

ἀνδράσι Πυγμαίοισι φόνον καὶ κῆρα φέρουσαι·

ἠέριαι δ' ἄρα ταί γε κακὴν ἔριδα προφέρονται.

οἱ δ' ἄρ' ἴσαν σιγῇ μένεα πνείοντες Ἀχαιοὶ

ἐν θυμῷ μεμαῶτες ἀλεξέμεν ἀλλήλοισιν.

Robert Fitzgerald's worksheet for his translation of the opening of the Third Book of the Iliad.

Robert Fitzgerald

*Robert Fitzgerald met us in his office in Harvard's Pusey Library
one morning in August, 1983. The day was muggy; Fitzgerald
was wearing a blue seersucker suit and a sport shirt. He carried
a worn bookbag over his shoulder, announcing, "I've brought some
exhibits!"*

*Pusey Library is a new building and Fitzgerald's office was a
small, durably-carpeted room, somewhat longer than it was wide.
A bookshelf hung over a desk. In the room there was just enough
space for an easy chair and a straight chair. Standing at the door,
we could see out a narrow window at the opposite end of the room
onto a courtyard, where grass and a few thin trees were trying to
grow. Fitzgerald shook an old, pocket-sized copy of Virgil out of
his bag onto his desk. We sat down, and the interview began.*

*Fitzgerald spoke slowly and very deliberately. When he found
a quotation or phrase or word that seemed particularly telling, he*

marked the occasion with a small click of the tongue. We talked for about an hour and a half, and then went to lunch.

INTERVIEWER: First, we thought we'd ask you what made you want to be a writer?

ROBERT FITZGERALD: I don't think it comes on that way . . . wanting to be a writer. You find yourself at a certain point making something in writing, and this seems to be great fun. I guess in high school—this was in Springfield, Illinois—I discovered that I could put words together and the results were pleasing to me. After I had discovered the charms of verse, I wrote verse all the time. Then when I was a senior, a great, kinetic teacher named Elizabeth Graham conducted something called the Scribbler's Club for a few seniors. It was a class, but it called itself a club, and was engaged in writing throughout the year. They put out a little magazine. I guess that was when the whole thing came to a head. I wrote a lot of verse and prose. So it wasn't so much wanting to be a writer as having a knack or fondness for putting things into verse.

INTERVIEWER: Were there any writers whose work you particularly admired at that time?

FITZGERALD: Well, I was greatly taken by a story called "Fifty Grand" in *Scribner's Magazine*, which came into the Scribbler's Club. I thought it was really wonderful. That was Ernest Hemingway's story about the boxer who's offered $50,000 to throw a fight and, though double-crossed and fouled, still goes on to throw it. It's a faultless story. I was also greatly taken at that time by Willa Cather's *Death Comes for the Archbishop*. And in verse, well, you know, you come across the work of William Butler Yeats at a certain point and your head endures fraction.

INTERVIEWER: Where did you go when you left Springfield?

FITZGERALD: I went to the Choate School in Wallingford, Connecticut. When I got out of high school in Springfield, Illinois in 1928, I had applied for and had been admitted to Yale. My family felt that since I was only seventeen, it would be a little premature to put me in college. So, I went to Choate for a year. While at Choate, I met Dudley Fitts, who was one of the masters there. He had been at Harvard, and I got the idea that where Fitts had gone to college was the place for me to go.

INTERVIEWER: What sort of influence did Fitts have on you?

FITZGERALD: He encouraged me to learn Greek. I would never have gone in for it unless he had dropped the word that it was nice to know a little Greek. So when I got to Harvard, I enrolled in a beginning course. And Fitts was up on Pound and Eliot and Joyce. He read me *The Waste Land*, which changed my life.

INTERVIEWER: Your early poems are full of dislocated, unidentified speakers, images of night and darkness, glinting lights. What drew you to such imagery?

FITZGERALD: I think that the life of the undergraduate, now and certainly in those days, was nocturnal, quite a lot of it.

INTERVIEWER: Do you still feel close to those poems?

FITZGERALD: I recognize them as my own and I don't disown them or feel silly about them. I think some of them are still pretty good, for what they are. I wouldn't have put them in my collection [*Spring Shade*] unless I thought they were worth including.

INTERVIEWER: One of your poems, "Portraits," is a portrait of John Wheelwright. How did you get to know him?

FITZGERALD: It must have been Fitts who introduced me to Wheelwright, and also to Sherry Mangan, a very spectacular literary figure. Both of these gents were socialists and political thinkers. Eventually, Sherry Mangan, whose early poetry was highly stylized and affected, settled into a life of dedication to the Trotskyite cause: socialism without the horrors of Stalinism. Wheelwright, too, was of this persuasion. Well, you probably know something of Wheelwright's place among the eccentrics of Boston of his time. He was always in his great big raccoon-skin coat and he belonged to the best Boston society of the time. Yet after an evening with friends, wherever the Brahmins of the time congregated, he would go out and do a soapbox turn on the Common, lecturing the cause of socialism in his tux and so on. He was also a devout Anglo-Catholic. These figures, along with B. F. Skinner, who was the white-haired boy of psychology around here at that time, and a physicist named Cuthbert Daniel, were all intellectuals of considerable—what?—presence and audacity and interest. None of them had any money and at that time—this was '32, '33—this country had already felt the very cold grip of the Depression. The mystery of what in the world was going on to deprive people of jobs and prospects, and of what was the matter with American society, occupied these guys constantly. I remember that my senior year I went in to see my tutor and I found this man, a tutor in English, reading *Das Kapital*. When I noticed it, he said, "Yes. I don't intend to spend my life taking care of a sick cat"—by which he meant capitalist society.

INTERVIEWER: Were you sympathetic to revolutionary causes too?

FITZGERALD: Not very, although I had to realize that something was going on. It had been taken for granted in my family that I would go to law school after college. It turned out that the wherewithal to go to law school had vanished, so I had to go to work. I went to work on a New York newspaper, the *Herald Tribune*. But I could never get passionate about revolution, at that time or later—it was a passion that was denied me.

INTERVIEWER: So that when, in the poem about Wheelwright, you speak of "the class machine" . . .

FITZGERALD: I've forgotten.

INTERVIEWER: It goes:

But [he] saw the heads of death that rode
Within each scoundrel's limousine,
Grinning at hunger on the road
To incorporate the class machine:

FITZGERALD: Those were images drawn from Wheelwright's own work and his way of looking at things.

INTERVIEWER: Do you admire his work?

FITZGERALD: Well, up to a point. I think it extremely peculiar and difficult and always did. The fantasy can be wonderful, figuring "some unworldly sense." Lately, there's been a little fashion of taking it up. John Ashbery, for example, thinks highly of it. A lot of it simply baffles me and I'd rather not get into it.

INTERVIEWER: Another early poem of yours, "Counselors," is about someone who considers resorting to various professionals for advice, experts in this and that, but decides that on the whole it wouldn't be worth his while. Did you think of Vachel Lindsay, or T. S. Eliot, or Yvor Winters, perhaps, as true counselors?

FITZGERALD: I thought that Vachel was a really great fellow, *molto simpatico*, and very good to me. I wrote about him, by the way, in a recent issue of *Poetry*. And later, Winters always seemed to me, crotchety as he was, to have applied himself with great independence and great purity to the literary business. When I was working at *Time*, in New York, I suppose I held him as an exemplar of serious application to the problems of poetry and literature. I remember in June, 1940, I was sitting in my office when the office boy came in with the afternoon paper, which was the old *World-Telegram*, and threw it down on the desk. The front page consisted of nothing but one large photograph of the Arc de Triomphe, with German troops marching through it down the Champs Elysées. The headline was *Ici Repose un Soldat Français Mort pour la Patrie*. That was all. Think of a New York newspaper doing that! That's when I knew that in a year or so we'd be in that affair. There was no question. So, I walked into the managing editor's office and said, "I resign." I'd saved up enough money to live on for a year and I thought I'd do what I could with my own writing until I got swept up in what I knew was coming. They very kindly turned my resignation into a year's leave of absence. I thought, "Now's the time to see Winters." I went to Palo Alto, got a room in a hotel, and called on him. Winters was very kind. He suggested I go to Santa Fe if I were going to make my effort. So, eventually, I'd say in September or October, I found myself, and my then-wife, in Santa Fe, working at poery, working at Greek—I translated *Oedipus at Colonus*—and spending the year as best I could.

INTERVIEWER: What was your experience of the war?

FITZGERALD: It was very mild. I was in the Navy, and I worked at a shore station in New York. Late in '44, I was assigned to CINCPAC—the Commander-in-Chief Pacific Ocean—at Pearl Harbor, and when that command moved to the Marianas, to Guam, I went along on staff, to do various menial jobs. From, say, February to October of that year, I had nothing to do when

I was off-duty but to read. I took three books in my footlocker. One was the Oxford text of the works of Virgil, one was the *Vulgate New Testament*, and the other was a Latin dictionary. I went through Virgil from stem to stern. That's when I first really read the *Aeneid*. I never took a course on Virgil in college or anything like that. I think that's of some interest . . . that with reference to my eventually doing the translation, my first real exposure to the *Aeneid* was hand to hand, with nothing but a dictionary—no instructor, no scholarship, nothing but the text itself, and the choice, evening after evening, of doing that or going to the Officers' Club and getting smashed.

INTERVIEWER: In your memoir of James Agee [which appears as the introduction to Agee's collected short prose], you speak of how difficult it was to write during the thirties and forties; you seem to mean that it was not only financially difficult to get by as a writer, but also that it was hard to know what to write. Was that so?

FITZGERALD: Well, let's take my first job on the *Herald Tribune*. There was no newspaper guild, no union. It was a six-day work week. For a good part of that year and a half I was coming in, as everybody did, at one-thirty, two o'clock in the afternoon, to pick up assignments—you'd get two or three. Then off you'd go on the subway, up and down the town. From two to six you'd gather the dope. You'd come in around six and knock off, if you could, two or three of these stories. These would be small stories and the result would be a couple of paragraphs each, if anything. Then you'd go to the automat, let's say, and eat something, and then you'd come back and get more assignments. You'd be through, with luck, around midnight. It would be a ten-hour day, and you'd have six of these in a row. I can promise you that on your seventh day, what you did, if you could manage it, was to stay in bed. I can remember literally not being able to move with sheer fatigue. How then were you going to arrange to turn out three hundred Spenserian stanzas per year? What added to the difficulty, for me, was that I do not and never could write fast. God knows how I got through it. I really don't. There was the same problem at *Time*, with the additional element that you had to be pretty clever. A *Time* story had to have a good deal of finish, in its way.

INTERVIEWER: Agee and you once planned a magazine. What was it to be like?

INTERVIEWER: I have his letters but I didn't keep copies of mine, so I don't know what I was proposing. Anyway, it was to be the perfect magazine.

INTERVIEWER: How did you meet T. S. Eliot?

FITZGERALD: I got to know him earlier, when I was in England in '31–'32. Vachel had written to him, and he wrote me at Cambridge to invite me, saying, "Do drop in." You know, at Faber and Faber. I did. I went to see him and we talked about Cambridge, where I was working in philosophy. He was familiar with the people at Cambridge who were then my teachers or lecturers, C. D. Broad and G. E. Moore. This, of course, was a continuing interest in his life. He had, after all, done his dissertation on Bradley. Had he gone on in that direction, he was going to be a philosopher in the philosophy department here at Harvard. I think on the second or third of my visits I had the courage to hand him a poem. He looked at the poem for a long time. Great silence. He studied it, then he looked up and said, "Is this the best you can do?" *Whoo!* Quite a thing to say! I didn't realize then what I realized later—that it was an editor's question: "Shall I publish this or shall I wait until he does something that shows more confidence?" What I thought at the time, and there was also this about it, was that it was fraternal. Just talking to me as one craftsman to another. A compliment, really.

INTERVIEWER: You've said that *The Waste Land* shook your foundations, and that *Ash Wednesday* always seemed to you something that was beyond literature. How so? Particularly *Ash Wednesday*.

FITZGERALD: Well, the music is unearthly—some of it. It seemed that way to me then, and it still does. And the audacity! "Lady, three white leopards sat under a juniper-tree." *Whoo!* Who is the lady? Whose is the' juniper tree? What are the leopards doing there? All these questions were completely subordinate to the audacity of the image—and in what would be called a very religious poem. It needs to be said of Eliot that although in the end the whole corpus has settled in people's minds as a work that comes to its climax with the *Four Quartets*, and is definitely religious (Pound in his kidding way referred to him as the "Reverend" Eliot), that the genius was *a fury, a real fury!* Only a fury could have broken the molds of English poetry in those ways at that time. That's what excited us all. *The Waste Land* was a dramatic experience too. It's very hard, in a few words, to get across the particular kind of excitement, but people ought to realize that at its height this gift was the gift of a Fury—capital *F*.

INTERVIEWER: What led you to translate Homer?

FITZGERALD: Now we come to, say, 1950, '51, '52. We were living in Connecticut and having a baby every year, and I was frantically teaching wherever I could, whatever I could, in order to keep everything going. It occurred to me one day—I was teaching at Sarah Lawrence at the time—driving from Ridgefield, Connecticut to Bronxville, that the best place to get help with the household and the children was overseas. And how could I manage to get abroad? Well, at this time, in the colleges and universities, humanities courses were being developed, and everyone agreed that a good verse translation of the *Odyssey* was something they would love to have. There weren't any. Lattimore had done the *Iliad*, published, I think, in '51. I had reviewed it, admiring it very much. I wrote to Lattimore and I said, "Do you plan to do an *Odyssey* or not?" And he wrote back and said he did not. He had other things he wanted to do. So I thought, "Why don't I try for a Guggenheim with the project of translating this poem?" I felt quite confident I could do something with Homer. Then I went to a publisher, to see if I couldn't set up a contract to do this, maybe entailing advance of a royalty. There was a very bright young man named Jason Epstein, just out of Columbia, who had invented the quality paperback (Anchor Books) at Doubleday, and had made a great killing with these things. So I ended up in the Doubleday office talking to him and, by God, he gave me a contract for an *Odyssey*. This was extraordinary at the time, gambling on me with this contract which assured me of three thousand dollars a year for five years while I was doing the translation. *And* I got the Guggenheim. So, Guggenheim, advance—off we went, to a part of the world where domestic help could be obtained. That's how that worked out. Just a number of favoring circumstances, a concatenation of things, combining to assure me of support, or enough support. We lived very frugally in Italy for several years—no car, no refrigerator, no radio, no telephone—everything was very simple. And so the work began and got done. It was the hand of Providence, something like that, working through these circumstances.

INTERVIEWER: You've said in the past that you came to translate Homer as a kind of amateur or free-lancer, without a full-blown academic background in classics. How did that affect your work?

FITZGERALD: It may have had some ill effects; it wouldn't have done me any harm to have been a better scholar. It wouldn't have done me any harm to have known German. During the whole nineteenth century, you know, German scholars were *it* in Homeric studies. That was a disadvantage.

INTERVIEWER: But don't you think that laboring under that disadvantage perhaps contributed to the immediacy and continuity of your contact with the text?

FITZGERALD: Right. Weighing one thing against the other, I'd rather have had that immediacy than the scholarship. A direct and constant relationship between me and the Greek—that was indispensable. Having the Greek before me and the job of matching the Greek, if I could, from day to day, hour to hour—that was what kept it alive.

INTERVIEWER: Did you set to work with any inviolable principles of translation?

FITZGERALD: Yes, one or two. One was that it didn't matter how long it took. I'd stay with it until I got it right. The other was, roughly, that whoever had composed this poem had imagined people in action and people feeling and saying things out of what they felt; that work of imagining had to be redone. I had to reimagine it, so that it would be alive from start to finish. What had kept it fresh for so many centuries was the sensation you had, when reading it, that *this* was alive.

INTERVIEWER: What considerations went into finding an English equivalent for Homeric Greek?

FITZGERALD: Diction. One wanted the English to be, as I've already said, fully alive. That this should be so, the colloquial register of the language had to enter into it. How far should you go with colloquialism? Would slang be useful? Answer: practically never. One would avoid what was transient in speech. The test of a given phrase would be: Is it worthy to be immortal? To "make a beeline" for something. That's worthy of being immortal and is immortal in English idiom. "I guess I'll split" is not going to be immortal and is excludable, therefore excluded.

INTERVIEWER: Were there any modern English poets who gave you some insight into what kind of line to take in doing the translation?

FITZGERALD: There was, of course, Ezra Pound and his fondness for the *Odyssey*. He had helped W. H. D. Rouse. Rouse was trying to do a prose version and there was a correspondence between them. I always felt that Pound was really dissatisfied and disappointed in the end with what Rouse did. Before I went to Europe, I went to see Pound at St. Elizabeth's. I wanted to tell him what I was going to try to do. I told him what I felt at the time—which was that there was no point in trying to do every line. I would do what I could. I'd hit the high spots. He said, "Oh no, don't do that. Let him say everything he wanted to say." So I had to rethink it and eventually I did let Homer say everything he wanted to say. I sent Pound the first draft of the first book when I got that done in Italy that fall. I got a postcard back, a wonderful postcard, saying, "Too much iambic will kill any subject matter." After that, I was very careful about getting singsong again. Keep the verse alive, that was the main thing. That's what he meant. And then, at a certain point I came across the *Anathemata*, by David Jones, which I thought was beautiful, like a silvery piece of driftwood that you could carry around with you. I carried it around just because of the texture of parts of it, a wonderful texture. I really couldn't pinpoint or put my finger on anything in my work that was directly attributable to David Jones. It was a kind of talisman that I kept with me.

INTERVIEWER: Did you find your trip to Greece and Ithaca to be useful?

FITZGERALD: That was wonderful. It corroborated my sense of the place. There, for example, was the wine-dark sea.

INTERVIEWER: How did you work on the translations?

FITZGERALD: I had this whole routine worked out while doing the Homer. I wrote out every line of Greek in my own hand, book by book, a big notebook for each book. One line to two blank lines. As I went through the Greek and copied it out in my own hand, I would face the difficulties—any crux that turned up, questions of interpretation—and try to work them out. I accumulated editions with notes and so on as I went along. So before I was through, I had acquired some of the scholarship that was relevant to my problems. But always, in the end, it was simply the Greek facing me, in my own hand, in my own notebook.

INTERVIEWER: How different is it when you compose your own verse?

FITZGERALD: You don't have any lines of Greek. And you're not riding the ground swell of another imagination as you are in translating. You have your own imagination.

INTERVIEWER: Would you revise as you went along, book by book, or did you wait until it was over with?

FITZGERALD: Both. It was heavily revised before I got the typescript more or less as I wanted it. Then the routine was for me to send in to the publisher what I had done during that year and at the same time send revisions for what had been submitted the year before. Then at the end, I spent a summer going through the whole damn thing from start to finish. Revising was interminable.

INTERVIEWER: How long did it take altogether?

FITZGERALD: Seven years of elapsed time. I'd say six full *working* years went into this poem.

INTERVIEWER: What were the peculiar satisfactions of translation?

FITZGERALD: Well, this is exaggerating a little bit, but one could say that I eventually felt that I had him, the composer, looking over my shoulder, and that I could refer everything to him. After all, it was being done for his sake, and one could raise the question with him, "Will this do or won't it?" Often the answer would be no. But, when the answer was yes, when you *felt* that it was yes—that is the great satisfaction in writing. It's very precious. Writing is very difficult. It's pure hell, in fact, quite often. But when it does really click, then your little boon is at hand. So that happened sometimes.

INTERVIEWER: Your own poems seem to have fallen off since you began translating Homer.

FITZGERALD: I wonder if they did. I don't know. I think that what roughly happened with my own poems was that, indeed, I had taken on a very large job. The magnitude of that job did rather put in the shade the adventure of making a wonderful page, which is, as I would put it, the pleasure and satisfaction of making a poem: to make which really has about it something wonderful, as a good lyric poem has. On the scale of what I was trying to do, that rather faded away, and I guess I would no longer feel the complete satisfaction that in the old days had come of making a poem. I must have begun to feel that there was a slightness in comparison with the big thing. That's one way of looking at it. And then I think that when I got to Harvard and began teaching, and putting a lot into the teaching, that also took care of a certain amount of what had been taken care of in the old days by making a poem. Instead of making a poem, I was helping other people make poems, and on quite a steady basis too. I was handing it out to other people instead of keeping it. Maybe, anyway. That's possible.

INTERVIEWER: After you finished the *Iliad*, you said that you weren't going to do any more translations. What led you to take up Virgil?

FITZGERALD: Well, the circumstances are really very clear. My first teaching job after the war, at Sarah Lawrence, was to give a course in poetry. I could do anything I liked, so I devised a little course called "Virgil and Dante." Each year I would take a small group of students through the *Aeneid* and through *The Divine Comedy*, using the original languages. When I moved to Harvard after the long interval with Homer, I devised a little course called

"Studies in Homer, Virgil and Dante." That kept the Virgil, so to speak, abreast of the Homer. Kept it alive in my mind. So, in 1978, four years after the completion of the *Iliad*, I was sitting in Boston's South Station waiting to get a train, and going over in my mind the Latin of certain lines at the beginning of Book Two of the *Aeneid*. I found these Latin lines taking English shape in my mind. Aeneas is beginning his remarks to Dido, the queen: a little story of the fall of Troy: So, he says:

> Infandum, regina, iubes renovare dolorem,
> Troianas ut opes et lamentabile regnum
> Eruerint Danai . . .

And he goes on:

> Et iam nox humida caelo
> Praecipitat suadentque cadentia sidera somnos.

"The humid night is going down the sky . . . and the sloping stars are persuading slumber"—a literal translation, the sort of translation that a kid would make in class. So, I found myself uttering *this* sort of thing:

> Now, too, the night is well along, with dewfall
> Out of heaven, and setting stars weigh down
> Our heads toward sleep.

Well, I said to myself, "My God, I've got that!" *Now, too: dewfall*—the end of the line is symmetrical with the beginning of the line. *Out of heaven, and setting stars weigh down: Out* at the beginning of the line; *down* at the end. The secrets of music in this business are very subtle and strange; I did not see these sound patterns at the time, but eventually I realized that what I had had that kind of quality to it. Having done that, I said to myself, "Hmm, if I can do a few lines with this pleasure, why don't I do the whole thing?" And so I did.

INTERVIEWER: Translating Homer, you avoided Latinisms as much as possible and made words of Anglo-Saxon origin the backbone of your language. But in the Virgil you seem to have employed a more Latinate vocabulary. Is the effect of Latin words in Latin really akin to that of Latin-derived words in English, where they've developed new connotations?

FITZGERALD: It's absolutely true that I avoided Latinisms in doing Homer; the Latin forms of the names of people and places were avoided in favor of the Greek. I wanted the *Greekness* of the thing to come across, and a lot of Latinate phrases would irresistibly have taken you back to the neoclassical, which I wanted utterly to skip . . . I wanted to skip Pope and Chapman because they all came to Greek so much through Latin. Their trots were in Latin, and kids in school, of course, learned Latin so thoroughly. Greek was always second for educated people in the seventeenth and eighteenth centuries. I wanted to skip all that and, if possible, to make it a transaction between Homer, 700 B.C., and Fitzgerald, 19-whatever. Between that language at that time and our language at this time. I don't think that these criteria were very much altered in doing the Virgil. A living English in our time had better be careful about Latinisms. Latinisms are so associated with mandarin English, with the English of Englishmen, not of Americans.

INTERVIEWER: In your introduction to Dryden's translation of the *Aeneid*, you speak of Dryden's clear perception of the difficulties any translator of Virgil faces. In Latin words there are, on the whole, as many vowels as consonants, whereas English words are cluttered with the latter. Latin is inflected, English is not, so that Virgil could rearrange word order at will for musical effect. Virgil exploits a nearly endless stock of figurative terms. How did you grapple with these problems?

FITZGERALD: Well, Dryden's despair, you know. I wouldn't say that I was overthrown very often by it, though it is true, toward the end of the poem, that more and more of what Dryden calls "figurative, elegant, and sounding words" keep coming in. The vocabulary is freshened. One copes with that. One keeps on doing the best one can with the problem of the moment, whether it be in speeches or in narrative, always, first of all, making sure that it's idiomatic English . . . that it's not muscle-bound or stiff.

INTERVIEWER: Arnold said that the distinguishing feature of

Homer's verse is its rapidity. What quality of the *Aeneid* did you consistently try to bring over into English?

FITZGERALD: Well, I ventured to put as an epigraph to the book the line "*Aeternum dictis da diva leporem,*" from *De Rerum Natura* of Lucretius. This is a plea that the goddess (whom we may understand as Venus in Lucretiuis' case, or indeed as the Muse) should give eternal charm. Charm to the work. That the product should have an incantatory quality, as a charm, pronounced in the enchanter's way. Insofar as one can make a conscious effort to achieve this kind of thing, I suppose that here and there I've made it. "And setting stars weigh down / Our heads toward sleep" is an example.

INTERVIEWER: When you speak of the music of poetry, what exactly do you mean?

FITZGERALD: Well, take from *Ash Wednesday*:

A pasture scene
And the broadbacked figure drest in blue and green
Enchanted the Maytime with an antique flute . . .

That's music. And one notices in the sounds, "Enchanted the Maytime with an antique flute"—*ant, ant, flute.* What comes into the Maytime thing, the colors blue and green, what the air is like on a day in mid-May, under the magnolias, the lilacs. The little echoing in the line—that's a kind of music, it seems to me. "*Formosam resonare doces Amaryllida silvas.*" This is from the First Eclogue, *Ryllida, silvas*—again an echoing, like a note in the bass on the piano, although in fact the right hand is carrying another melody, so you have this repetition in the left hand which insists on doing a second melody there. What the line is saying is one melody. What in counterpoint these little repetitions of sound are doing is another. The music is enriched as the music in a fugue is enriched by two things going on at once.

INTERVIEWER: In translating, do you try to mimic the music of the original?

FITZGERALD: That, or make an equivalent. It's what I meant when I said in the afterword to the *Odyssey* that translating the

Greek of Homer into English is no more possible than translating
rhododendron into dogwood. On the other hand, suppose you
make dogwood?

INTERVIEWER: But wouldn't you want some relation?

FITZGERALD: You would like to convey as exactly as possible
what is being conveyed in the Latin narrative. You want what is
happening to be exactly what's happening in Homer's imagination, if you can, and then you want an English equivalent of the
Latin music. The Latin music is very elaborate. Listen to this:

> Vertitur interea coelum, et ruit oceano nox.
> Involvens umbra magna terramque polumque
> Myrmidonumque dolos.

That's the full orchestra, really, the full orchestra. Let's see what
the Latin turns out to be in English.

> As heaven turned, Night from the Ocean stream
> Came on, profound in gloom on earth and sky
> And Myrmidons in hiding.

There is at least the matching of the series of long vowels—*night,
ocean, stream, came, profound, gloom, sky, hiding*—long open
vowels that by their succession and echoing give something like
the effect of the Latin. But it's English, it's carrying the story on.
You don't have to listen to this music. If what you want to hear
is the story, read the story.

INTERVIEWER: Robert Lowell wrote a little piece on epics in
which he said, "Homer is blinding Greek sunlight. Virgil is dark,
narrow, morbid, mysterious, and artistic. He fades in translation."
What do you think of those adjectives Lowell racks up?

FITZGERALD: Well, too much has been made of texture. One
of the things that I tried to bring out more fully, as I went along,
was the pure narrative interest of this thing as a story. It's Aeneas's
story, some of which he tells himself, and most of which he
doesn't. The narrative, if it's properly rendered, is extremely interesting and exciting. What happened to Virgil (partly because
of the curse of his being a text in the fourth year of secondary
school, and also because of his having supplied so many tags for

speakers in the House of Lords) is that the poem has been fragmented. The arc, the really quite magnificient arc of the original
narrative, has been rather lost to view. Nobody ever reads the
entire *Aeneid*. They read in school, if they read anything, Books
Two, Four, Six, *maybe*, if they're lucky. That's it. Nobody ever
reads the last six books. Yet in the last six books the whole thing
happens, really. That's the man at war. That's the *arma* and the
virum. I would love to think that the whole story will be restored
to view. People can read it, and will read it, because it turns out
to be readable.

INTERVIEWER: It certainly seems that in the first half, Aeneas
is an oddly stunned sort of hero, while in the second half he is
commanding, even horrifyingly so.

FITZGERALD: Exactly. The tragic import of all this is what happens to a man wielding power, especially in hostilities of that
kind. He goes as berserk as anybody. The point is very abundantly
made that the Roman state was founded on war, on their being
very good at war. I happened to reread Caesar, *The Battle for
Gaul*, during the composition of the last six books, to see what,
in fact, war was like in the generation preceding Virgil. Virgil
certainly knew, as every Roman did, what it cost, and the exertion
that was made to defeat these hordes of extremely hard-fighting
Germans and Gauls. No doubt about the carnage, the incredible
carnage: field after field left absolutely soaked in blood, with
dismembered individuals for miles. The scene was one of great
terror and desolation, all of this in order that Julius should become
first consul and have his career. One does sense throughout the
Aeneid the tragic import of Roman power, of what they were
proudest of: their ability to defeat the tribes that came against
them and then to create some kind of civil order in the provinces
they conquered. But the cost of that, and the dreadful effects of
these encounters of armed men, is very vividly brought out, along
with the *pro forma* praises of the Roman heroes. A Roman *gladius*,
or short sword, honed on both edges, was like a cleaver! A two-
edged cleaver! Just imagine turning twenty thousand men with
two-edged cleavers loose on the opposition!

INTERVIEWER: You once said that English poetry "hungers for

Poets at Work

a sound metaphysic," but that its history is largely a record of a failure of supply. What did you mean?

FITZGERALD: English poetry "hungers for a sound metaphysic"? I was, I think, at the time, interested in the superior precision of Aristotle's *De Anima* as contrasted with Coleridge. I was thinking in particular of the difference between the Aristotelian and the Coleridgean views of what happens in creative work of the mind. I made my remarks, that's it. I never went out to argue.

INTERVIEWER: In the Agee memoir you speak of your brotherhood in the arts with him. Did you have a similar relationship with Lowell or Berryman or Auden? Did you consult them when you were working on your translations?

FITZGERALD: I certainly did. Not W. H. Auden, though, because we met so rarely. John Berryman saw what I was working on at the time and made a suggestion or two on word order which I adopted. Randall Jarrell also saw what I was working on one summer. He had an excellent notion. His notion, to put it briefly, was that if you're going to be colloquial, you can achieve the colloquial thing by gradation. You depart from the formality a little bit and then a little bit more, and then you're colloquial, and then you modulate away from it—modulate toward and modulate away from it. Such a beautiful idea! I don't know whether I really obeyed this or not. And Cal Lowell just said, "You've got it! This is a bullseye!" There is, after all, a brotherhood among people who are working at the same craft, who show each other what they're doing from time to time. The result's likely to be more helpful if your pal simply runs his hand down the page, stops, and does not say a word. Just stops. You see something's wrong where the finger's pointing, and that's enough.

INTERVIEWER: How did you get to know Lowell?

FITZGERALD: I met him through Randall Jarrell. Jarrell was teaching at Sarah Lawrence the first year I taught there, and we therefore saw one another every week and got to be friends. He brought Lowell along some evening or other and we had the evening together.

INTERVIEWER: Nowadays people tend to praise Jarrell's criticism and downplay his poetry. Do you think that's fair to his work?

FITZGERALD: No, I don't. I think quite a few of his poems are very good indeed. No one ever did anything remotely like what he did for the Air Force, for the carrier pilots, and all the rest of that.

INTERVIEWER: You've often said that you think poetry should be "chiefly hair-raising." At the same time, however, you've spoken of the desirability of a strong bond between the poet and the community he lives in—a bond that you seem to believe has been broken in modern times. Do you see any contradiction or tension between such social concern and the requirement that poetry be, above all, hair-raising?

FITZGERALD: Well, don't we have Emily Dickinson, the wondrous lady of Amherst, as an authority for that: "It's a poem if it makes you feel as though your head were taken off"? And A. E. Houseman: "If while I am shaving a line of poetry strays into my mind, my beard bristles so that I can't cut it"? This is an extreme, and this kind of poetry is part of the extreme literary experience—extreme both for the maker and for the reader. That's at one end of the spectrum. At the other end there is Dryden, sitting in his coffeehouse, turning out couplets to insult someone whom he feels like insulting. So, one has the gamut between what is essentially a private, we might say a metaphysical experience, and the other which is simply a refinement of prose—verse devoted to wit, or to the quotidian purpose of making something clear or making somebody ashamed, of exposing somebody, of putting into a witty form someone's foibles . . . which can be read with amusement and without a touch of the other extreme, which is private and rare and precious. I don't see why we can't live with a decent consciousness of these two poles of poetic experience. I once said, too, that poetry is at least an elegance and at most a revelation. That says it pretty well—"is at least an elegance"—something that is well-formed, readable, and then again something that takes you *up*.

INTERVIEWER: How close is the revelation of poetry to the religious experience of revelation?

FITZGERALD: Very close, I think. Very close indeed.

INTERVIEWER: You've spoken of a "third kind of knowledge"

that came out of moments of vision you had as a young man. How important were they?

FITZGERALD: Terribly important. I don't think that anything could be more important than to be reminded that, as Flannery O'Connor used to say, "The church is custodian of the sense of life as a mystery." We get so used to it that we lose the sense. To have the sense restored to us—which the religious experience does and which the poetic experience at its extreme does as well—is a great boon.

INTERVIEWER: You say that you came back to the Church with a "terrific bump." What brought you back?

FITZGERALD: Well, a number of things that I really don't think I can satisfactorily speak of in this context.

INTERVIEWER: Do you think that the integration of poetry and the university since World War II has been harmful?

FITZGERALD: Maybe. At Harvard in my time there was Robert Hillyer's course in versification, and beyond that, very little indeed in the way of writing courses. An exceptional teacher at that time would be *au courant* with what was living and exciting about writing. Hillyer was exceptionally the other way. He was deliberately blind, deaf and dumb to what was going on in the avant-garde. I think one felt, in general, one wasn't going to get much attention from the faculty. If you wanted to put things in the undergraduate literary magazine, *The Advocate*, okay. *The Advocate* was . . . *The Advocate*. I don't think that people on the faculty paid much attention to these half-baked manifestations of literary ambition on the part of the undergraduates.

INTERVIEWER: Can we ask you about Flannery O'Connor and how you came to know her?

FITZGERALD: Flannery O'Connor came with Cal Lowell. Lowell and she and Elizabeth Hardwick turned up in New York together. They'd been at Yaddo and there was a dustup at Yaddo in which I'm afraid Lowell had begun to go off his trolley. At that point nobody really understood that this was the case, but we all understood it before it was over, very thoroughly. It was one of Lowell's very early, maybe his earliest breakdown. We met

Flannery in the course of that, really, and then, of course, we went on independently of Lowell.

INTERVIEWER: You seem to have been something of a counselor to her. She would send her work to you, seeking your comments.

FITZGERALD: I wouldn't want to build myself up. No, no, she knew what she was about. Owed nothing, I don't think, to me so far as the essence of these things were concerned. I supplied her with one title, "The Life You Save May Be Your Own." I'd been driving through the South, and it just happened this was something one saw on the road signs. And I supplied her with some reasons for undertaking a revision of her novel, *The Violent Bear It Away*, which she did. I think she was better pleased with it after she'd done the revision. Those would be practically the only instances in which I had any effect on what she did. She was a good friend. One liked to see what she was working on. That was always great fun to see.

INTERVIEWER: Are there any younger poets whose work strikes you as outstanding?

FITZGERALD: I think that Robert Shaw has done quite beautiful work. He's a good critic and a good poet. He was here ten years ago; he was in my classes and performed very well in them. He went on to teach here and at Yale. Now he's at Mount Holyoke. He's very good. Who else? Brad Leithauser. He was in my writing class and turned out some amazingly good poems. His wife, Mary Jo Salter—she's also very good. And Katha Pollitt. James Atlas went on to do that good biography of Delmore Schwartz. I risk forgetting others who are just as interesting.

INTERVIEWER: So you think the world of poetry prospers apace?

FITZGERALD: That reminds me of Eugenio Montale's great piece on the encouragement of poetry, particularly by the state—National Endowments and things like that. He was very skeptical about the utility of encouraging poetry on a grand scale. Is encouragement what the poet needs? Open question. Maybe he needs discouragement. In fact, quite a few of them need more discouragement, the most discouragement possible.

INTERVIEWER: Has your career so far differed from your early expectations of it? Or didn't you have any expectations?

FITZGERALD: I don't know that I had any. I just hoped to keep on. I suppose I'd have been amazed when I was twenty to hear that before I was through, I would have translated Homer and the *Aeneid*. The notion that I should go in for these gigantic labors would have been completely out of this world. As I remember, when I was signing Elizabeth Bishop's *Iliad* for her, her only remark was, *"My*, all that *work!"*

—EDWIN FRANK
ANDREW McCORD
1983

Notes on the Contributors

FRANKLIN ASHLEY (*interview with James Dickey*) teaches at the college of General Studies at the University of South Carolina in Columbia.

THOMAS CLARK (*interview with Allen Ginsberg*) lives in Berkeley, California. His most recent volumes of poetry include *Disordered Ideas* (1987) and *Easter Sunday* (1987). He is also the author of a novel, *The Exile of Celine* (1986), and has written several biographies of authors, including Damon Runyon and Jack Kerouac. He is currently at work on a biography of Charles Olson.

BENJAMIN DeMOTT (*interview with Archibald MacLeish*) is the Mellon Professor of English at Amherst College, where he has taught since 1951. He is the author of several books, including *Supergrow* (1969), *Surviving the Seventies* (1971), and *America in Literature* (1977).

RALPH ELLISON (*interview with Robert Penn Warren*) is the author of *Invisible Man*, a first novel that won him the Prix de Rome and the National Book Award in 1953, and *Shadow and Act*.

EDWIN FRANK (*interview with Robert Fitzgerald*) is a poet who lives in San Francisco. His work has appeared in *The New York Review of Books* and *Sequoia*.

DONALD HALL (*interviews with T. S. Eliot, Marianne Moore, and Ezra Pound*) was for nine years poetry editor of *The Paris Review*. His most recent work includes *The One Day*, a book-length poem, and a collection of short stories, *The Ideal Bakery* (1987). He reflects on the circumstances of his interviews with Eliot and Pound in his book *Remembering Poets*.

BARBARA KEVLES (*interview with Anne Sexton*) is a charter Contributing Editor to *Working Woman* and a past Contributing Editor to *American Health*, and has written for leading national publications including *The Atlantic, Esquire, New York, The New York Times, Mademoiselle, Glamour, Cosmopolitan, Good Housekeeping, Redbook, Ladies' Home Journal, People, Harper's Bazaar*, and *The Village Voice*. Barbara Kevles authored the Book-of-the-Month Club and Quality Paperback Book Club choice *Basic Magazine Writing* (WDB, '86) and the introduction, "Occupation: Writer," for the 1981 *Writer's Market*. She has taught at New York University/SCE as an Assistant Adjunct Professor of Creative Writing and at The New School (New York City) and held the rank of Adjunct in Writing and Criticism at Empire State College, S.U.N.Y. She co-edited an essay collection on traditional curricular theories and practices, *In Opposition to Core Curriculum* (Greenwood Press, '82).

STANLEY KOEHLER (*interview with William Carlos Williams*) teaches English at the University of Massachusetts. He has been a poetry editor of the *Massachusetts Review* and was formerly a director of the Writers' Workshop at Chautauqua Institution. He has published several collections of poetry, including *The Fact of Fall* (1969).

ANDREW McCORD (*interview with Robert Fitzgerald*) is a reporter for the weekly newspaper *India Abroad*. He lives in New York.

MICHAEL NEWMAN (*interview with W. H. Auden*) studied poetry with Mr. Auden until the poet's death in 1973. His poems and essays have been published in *The New York Times* and *The New York Times Book Review, Poetry*, the *Poetry Anthology, New York Quarterly*, and elsewhere. He is the author and publisher of The Poetry Processor software package and several computer games that teach biology, and his column "Cloned Poems" appeared in *The Sciences*.

RICHARD POIRIER (*interview with Robert Frost*), professor of English at Rutgers University, is the editor of *Raritan Quarterly*. A founder and director of the Library of America, he is the author of several books of criticism, including *Robert Frost: The Work of Knowing*.

FREDERICK SEIDEL (*interview with Robert Lowell*) won the Academy of American Poets' Lamont Prize and the National Book Critics Circle Award for his book *Sunrise*. His most recent book, *Men and Women: New and Selected Poems*, was published by Chatto and Windus in England and a new book of poems, *Untitled*, is forthcoming.

ELIZABETH SPIRES (*interview with Elizabeth Bishop*) recently spent a year in England on an Amy Lowell Traveling Poetry Scholarship working on a new book of poems. She is the author of *Globe* (Wesleyan, 1981), *Swan's Island* (Holt, Rinehart & Winston, 1985), and *Annonciade* (Viking, 1989).

PETER STITT (*interview with John Ashbery*) is the editor of the *Gettysburg Review* and the biographer of James Wright. His book *The World's Hieroglyphic Beauty: Essays on and Interviews with Six Contemporary Poets* was named an Outstanding Academic Book in 1986 by *Choice* magazine.

EUGENE WALTER (*interview with Robert Penn Warren*) has received the Lippincott Prize for his first novel, *The Untidy Pilgrims*, an O. Henry citation for his story "Troubador," which appeared in the first issue of *The Paris Review*, a Sewanee-Rockefeller Fellowship for his *Monkey Poems*, and a Prix Guilloux for his translations of French poetry. His new novel, *Adam's Housecat*, and his book of stories, *The Byzantine Riddle*, will appear shortly, as will a special issue of *Negative Capability* called "The Polyfarious

Eugene Walter," containing much of his new work. He is an advisory editor of *The Paris Review*.

ROBERT HUNTER WILBUR (*interview with Conrad Aiken*) was a speech writer and adviser at the U.S. Mission to the United Nations.

FOR THE BEST IN PAPERBACKS, LOOK FOR THE

In every corner of the world, on every subject under the sun, Penguin represents quality and variety—the very best in publishing today.

For complete information about books available from Penguin—including Pelicans, Puffins, Peregrines, and Penguin Classics—and how to order them, write to us at the appropriate address below. Please note that for copyright reasons the selection of books varies from country to country.

In the United Kingdom: For a complete list of books available from Penguin in the U.K., please write to *Dept E.P., Penguin Books Ltd, Harmondsworth, Middlesex, UB7 0DA.*

In the United States: For a complete list of books available from Penguin in the U.S., please write to *Dept BA, Penguin*, Box 120, Bergenfield, New Jersey 07621-0120.

In Canada: For a complete list of books available from Penguin in Canada, please write to *Penguin Books Ltd, 2801 John Street, Markham, Ontario L3R 1B4.*

In Australia: For a complete list of books available from Penguin in Australia, please write to the *Marketing Department, Penguin Books Ltd, P.O. Box 257, Ringwood, Victoria 3134.*

In New Zealand: For a complete list of books available from Penguin in New Zealand, please write to the *Marketing Department, Penguin Books (NZ) Ltd, Private Bag, Takapuna, Auckland 9.*

In India: For a complete list of books available from Penguin, please write to *Penguin Overseas Ltd, 706 Eros Apartments, 56 Nehru Place, New Delhi, 110019.*

In Holland: For a complete list of books available from Penguin in Holland, please write to *Penguin Books Nederland B.V., Postbus 195, NL-1380AD Weesp, Netherlands.*

In Germany: For a complete list of books available from Penguin, please write to *Penguin Books Ltd, Friedrichstrasse 10-12, D-6000 Frankfurt Main I, Federal Republic of Germany.*

In Spain: For a complete list of books available from Penguin in Spain, please write to *Longman, Penguin España, Calle San Nicolas 15, E-28013 Madrid, Spain.*

In Japan: For a complete list of books available from Penguin in Japan, please write to *Longman Penguin Japan Co Ltd, Yamaguchi Building, 2-12-9 Kanda Jimbocho, Chiyoda-Ku, Tokyo 101, Japan.*